PN
6281
.C59
2002

CANADA COLLEGE LIBRARY
D0197807

PENGUIN BOOKS

The Penguin Dictionary of Epigrams

M. J. Cohen first worked on quotation-collecting as a student with his father, the translator, editor and author J. M. Cohen. Together they were responsible for successive editions of *The Penguin Dictionary of Modern Quotations* until J. M. Cohen's death in 1989. The most recent updates of their two complementary books are *The New Penguin Dictionary of Quotations* and *The Penguin Dictionary of Twentieth-Century Quotations*. When not pursuing the quotable, Mark Cohen was for many years an educational publisher. Now a publishing consultant and editor, he and his artist wife live in north London. They have three daughters.

The Penguin Dictionary of **Epigrams**

M. J. Cohen

PENGUIN BOOKS

LIBRARY - CAÑADA COLLEGE

6/05

PENGUIN BOOKS

Published by the Penguin Group
Penguin Books Ltd, 80 Strand, London WC2R 0RL, England
Penguin Putnam Inc., 375 Hudson Street, New York, New York 10014, USA
Penguin Books Australia Ltd, 250 Camberwell Road, Camberwell, Victoria 3124, Australia
Penguin Books Canada Ltd, 10 Alcorn Avenue, Toronto, Ontario, Canada M4V 3B2
Penguin Books India (P) Ltd, 11, Community Centre, Panchsheel Park, New Delhi – 110 017, India
Penguin Books (NZ) Ltd, Cnr Rosedale and Airborne Roads, Albany, Auckland, New Zealand
Penguin Books (South Africa) (Pty) Ltd, 24 Sturdee Avenue, Rosebank 2196, South Africa

Penguin Books Ltd, Registered Offices: 80 Strand, London WC2R 0RL, England

www.penguin.com

First published as a Penguin hardback 2001
Published in paperback in Penguin Books 2002
5

Copyright © M. J. Cohen, 2001
All rights reserved

The moral right of the author has been asserted

Printed in England by Clays Ltd, St Ives plc

Except in the United States of America, this book is sold subject
to the condition that it shall not, by way of trade or otherwise, be lent,
re-sold, hired out, or otherwise circulated without the publisher's
prior consent in any form of binding or cover other than that in
which it is published and without a similar condition including this
condition being imposed on the subsequent purchaser

LIBRARY - CAÑADA COLLEGE

To Lana

Contents

Acknowledgements

Charmian Brinson for translations of Arthur Schnitzler's aphorisms, Professor Hugh Brogan, Professor D. J. Enright, Ingrid von Essen, Professor Kaiser Haq, Professor Fred Halliday, John Hawkins, Julian Hogg, Nicholas Jacobs, Milein Cosman Keller, Khalid Kishtany, Annie Lee, Ahmad Lutfi, Anthony Wood for translations of Pushkin, John Wynne-Tyson, and the staffs of the British Library, the London Library and the American Embassy Information Resource Center.

What is an Epigram?

The New Penguin English Dictionary defines an epigram as 'a concise, witty and often paradoxical remark or saying' derived from the Greek to 'write on or inscribe'. And Ambrose Bierce – a formidable epigrammatist himself – in his *Devil's Dictionary* suggests:

> **Epigram**, n. A short, sharp saying in prose or verse, frequently characterized by acidity or acerbity and sometimes by wisdom.

We often associate the form with Oscar Wilde, for as Dorothy Parker grumbles:

> If, with the literate, I am
> Impelled to try an epigram,
> I never seek to take the credit;
> We all assume that Oscar said it.

This Wildean monopoly is reinforced by the famous exchange between Wilde and James McNeill Whistler:

> WILDE: I wish I had said that.
> WHISTLER: You will, Oscar, you will.

Wilde remains the emperor of the epigram and is, of course, well represented in this dictionary. The British journalist Julie Burchill is surely right in her recent tribute: 'Wilde's words still have the diamond-sharp power to make you gasp and laugh a hundred years after they were written.'

But just as they were sparkling epigrammatists before Wilde, the century since his death has been blessed by a wonderful variety of descendants. From Woody Allen to Tom Stoppard, from G. K. Chesterton to Quentin Crisp, the epigram is alive and well.

When is an epigram not an epigram?

If, however, the epigram is pithy and witty, there are quite as many memorable lines which are concise and wise. These cousins of the epigram have gone under different names at different times: but whether they come under the label of **aphorism** or **apothegm**, **adage**, **maxim**, **gnome**, **saying**, **sentence**, or **sage saw**, does not matter. They share the epigram's brevity but can be more serious. The one-liner does not have to be throw-away.

Indeed this family of wit and wisdom has a very impressive pedigree, stretching back to the Greeks and the Romans, to the Bible and Confucius, to Taoism, Hinduism and Islam.

The wisest minds throughout the world have always expressed their truths pithily, from the Roman emperor and philosopher Marcus Aurelius to Dr Samuel Johnson, lexicographer and wit; from Plato to Einstein, from the polymathic Goethe to the economist J. K. Galbraith.

The philosopher Friedrich Nietzsche was a great practitioner:

> *In praise of the maxim.* – a good maxim is too hard for the teeth of time and whole millennia cannot consume it, even though it serves to nourish every age: it is thus the great paradox of literature, the imperishable in the midst of change, the food that is always in season, like salt – though, unlike salt, it never loses its savour. (*Human, All Too Human*: 'Assorted Opinions and Maxims')

The commonplace book was a commonplace in many centuries. Francis Bacon tells us that Julius Caesar set great store by his. And as Jonathan Swift ironically put it, though he can't have been referring to Caesar:

> What though his head be empty, provided his commonplace book be full. (*A Tale of a Tub*, Sect. VII)

Ralph Waldo Emerson and H. D. Thoreau in nineteenth-century America kept voluminous journals in which they recorded not only sharp insights of their own but striking quotations from the scientists, philosophers and essayists they read; they preserved lines not only from British and American authors but from Eastern and European sources. Coiners of epigrams and aphorisms have invariably been collectors of others' lines and the trade has been international. As the Bulgarian-born writer and aphorist Elias Canetti puts it in *The Human Province*: 'The great writers of aphorisms read as if they had all known each other very well.' Canetti, in company with many, including the poet W. H. Auden and the novelist E. M. Forster, kept a note of the epigrams and aphorisms that caught his attention.

What is not an epigram or one of its relations?

There are short and snappy lines in all languages and cultures which are properly **proverbs**, and these are the subject of *The Penguin Dictionary of Proverbs*, so this book can be forgiven for excluding them. What, then, is the distinction? It is a delicate one. Where the proverb is totally anonymous, the Wisdom of Solomon is ascribable to an author, even if it was not Solomon himself. This dictionary has also, for similar reasons of space, had to neglect the poetic epigram. These short satirical poems, often squibs in the vein of the first-century Roman poet Martial, have a very different tradition and a literature of their own.

Most anthologists and collectors of bons mots *are like people who eat cherries or oysters, picking the best first and ending up eating the lot.* **Nicholas-Sébastien Chamfort** *Maxims and Considerations*, 1

What is an epigram? A dwarfish whole,
It's body brevity, and wit its soul.
Samuel Taylor Coleridge *On Epigram*

You may cram a truth into an epigram; the truth, never. **Norman Douglas** *An Almanac 1945*

An aphorism is the last link in a long chain of thought. **Maria von Ebner-Eschenbach** *Aphorisms*, epigraph

Windbags can be right. Aphorists can be wrong. It's a tough world. **James Fenton** in *The Times*, 21 February 1985

A collection of anecdotes and maxims is the greatest treasure for a man of the world – as long as he knows how to introduce the former at a strategic place in his conversation and to remember the latter at the right moment. **Johann Wolfgang von Goethe** *Maxims and Reflections* from *Art and Antiquity*, 190

Aphorisms are something like jewels; rarity increases their value, and they are enjoyable only in small doses. **Hermann Hesse** *Reflections*, epigraph

epigram: *A dash of wit and a jigger of wisdom, flavoured with surprise.* **Elbert Hubbard** *The Roycroft Dictionary*

An aphorism never coincides with the truth: it is either a half-truth or one-and-a-half truths. **Karl Kraus** *Half-Truths and One-and-a-Half Truths*: 'Riddles'

An aphorism
should be
like a burr;
sting,
stick,
and leave
a little soreness
afterwards.
Irving Layton *The Whole Bloody Bird*: 'aphs'

Why do I write these short aphorisms? Because words fail me! **Stanislaw Lec** *Unkempt Thoughts*

An epigram is only a wisecrack that's played at Carnegie Hall. **Oscar Levant** *Coronet* magazine, September 1968

The art of newspaper paragraphing is
to stroke a platitude until it purrs like an epigram.
Don Marquis in the *New York Sun*: 'The Sun Dial'

Anyone can tell the truth, but only very few of us can make epigrams. **Somerset Maugham** *A Writer's Notebook*, 1896

A virtue of aphorisms: they're too short to bore. **Joseph Prescott** *Aphorisms and Other Observations, Third Series*: 'Literature'

An aphorism ought to be entirely isolated from the surrounding world like a little work of art and complete in itself like a hedgehog. **Friedrich von Schlegel** *Dialogue on Poetry and Literary Aphorisms*, 206

If one shakes an aphorism, a lie will fall out and a banality remain. **Arthur Schnitzler** *Aphorismen und Betrachtungen*, p. 132

He would stab his best friend for the sake of writing an epigram on his tombstone. **Oscar Wilde** *Vera, or the Nihilists*, Act 2

How to Use the Dictionary

If you want to browse this book the **Theme Finder** will lead you to a topic, and, once there, the authors are quoted in alphabetical order, so wit and wisdom may alternate, Aristotle and Woody Allen cohabit.

At the end of each such section there are suggestions of complementary topics, so that if you have exhausted Truth you can switch to Lies (which surprisingly has only half as many entries); abandon the Past and flip to the Future; desert Poetry for Fiction.

If you want to enter through an author, the index will point you to what she or he said about any one of the topics, from Actions to Youth and Age.

Sometimes it is not quite clear who got there first – as Dorothy Parker felt about Wilde always getting the credit! Or, as Thomas Sheridan, the father of the dramatist Robert Brinsley, delicately put it:

> A thought goes walking about the world, and lodges in several people's heads in such quick succession, that they are sure to quarrel in the end as to who gave it house room at first.

Perhaps, in its turn, close to the complaint of Robert Merton, the American social scientist:

> Anticipatory plagiarism occurs when someone steals your original idea and publishes it a hundred years before you were born.

To help you find a line in the original book, a chapter or section number is given where possible. Where the author does not subdivide a work in this way, a page number indicates the Penguin edition, or, in the absence of a Penguin, the standard edition.

A small point on lines from Shakespeare

The line references are to the single-volume Oxford University edition by W. J. Craig. If a scene contains prose, however, the line reference is in brackets. Your own edition may not coincide exactly.

Theme Finder

R

S

T

U

Actions

1 A conference is a gathering of important people who singly can do nothing, but together can decide that nothing can be done.
Fred Allen in Jonathon Green, *Cassell Dictionary of Cynical Quotations*: 'Committees'

2 All that we do is done with an eye to something else. **Aristotle** *Ethics*

3 And you will give yourself relief, if you approach each action as though it were your last. **Marcus Aurelius** *Meditations*, Bk 2, 5

4 But men must know, that in this theatre of man's life it is reserved only for God and angels to be lookers on.
Francis Bacon *The Advancement of Learning*, Bk 2, xx, 8

5 Appeasers succeed in putting off a necessary operation till it is too late to perform it successfully. **Bernard Berenson** *Notebooks*, probably 1938

6 By their fruits ye shall know them. **Bible, NT** Matthew 7:20

7 Where there's a will there's a won't. **Ambrose Bierce** *The Devil's Dictionary*

8 The world can only be grasped by action, not by contemplation. The hand is more important than the eye . . . The hand is the cutting edge of the mind. **J. Bronowski** *The Ascent of Man*, Ch. 3

9 Every man is the Child of his own works.
Miguel Cervantes *Don Quixote*, Pt 1, 4

10 The contemplative life is often miserable. You should do more, think less and not watch yourself living.
Nicholas-Sébastien Chamfort *Maxims and Considerations*

11 Whatever is worth doing at all is worth doing well and nothing can be well done without attention.

Earl of Chesterfield *Letters to His Son*, 10 March 1746, extending a proverb

See also Chesterton

12 Whoever is in a hurry, shows that the thing he is doing is too big for him. **Earl of Chesterfield** *Letters to His Son*, 30 August 1749

13 If a thing is worth doing it is worth doing badly.

G. K. Chesterton *What's Wrong with the World*: 'Folly and Female Education'

See also Chesterfield

14 Something inherently mean in action! Even the creation of the universe disturbs my idea of the Almighty's greatness.

Samuel Taylor Coleridge *Anima Poetae*, p. 27

15 It was a favourite remark of the late Mr Whitbread's that no man does anything from a single motive.

Samuel Taylor Coleridge *Biographia Literaria*, Ch. 11

16 It's like breaking a few back windows in his house; whereas if you really want to make him sit up you must try at least to raise his roof.

Joseph Conrad *The Secret Agent*

17 To get something done a committee should consist of no more than three men, two of whom are absent.

Robert Copeland in *The Penguin Dictionary of Modern Humorous Quotations*, comp. Fred Metcalf

18 Nothing is ever done until everyone is convinced that it ought to be done, and has been convinced for so long that it is now time to do something else. **F. M. Cornford** *Microcosmographia Academica*, 1

19 Distance doesn't matter; it is only the first step that is difficult.

Marquise du Deffand letter to d'Alembert, 7 July 1763; on the legend that St Denis walked six miles, carrying his head in his hand

20 Man is a marvellously sophisticated and effective agent. It is as a principal that his performance is so erratic. **Michael Frayn** *Constructions*, 93

21 The Day that you do a good thing, there will be seven new Moons.

Dr Thomas Fuller *Gnomologia*, 4468

22 Meetings are indispensable when you don't want to do anything.

J. K. Galbraith *Ambassador's Journal*, Ch. 5

23 Every healthy effort is directed from the inner to the outer world.

Johann Wolfgang von Goethe *Conversations with Eckerman*, in *A Susan Sontag Reader*, ed. Elizabeth Hardwick: 'Debriefing'

24 In the works of mankind, as in those of nature, it is the motive which is chiefly worth attention.

Johann Wolfgang von Goethe *Maxims and Reflections*: 'Life and Character', 10

25 Mankind can do everything, but can only do one thing.

Edmond and Jules de Goncourt *Journal*, 21 May 1866

26 It is much harder to turn word into deed than deed into word.

Maxim Gorky in *USSR in Construction*, April 1937: 'On Plays'

27 Those who have done nothing, fancy themselves capable of everything: while those who have exerted themselves to the utmost only feel the limitation of their powers.

William Hazlitt *Characteristics*, 69

28 We never do anything well till we *cease to think about the manner of doing it.*

William Hazlitt *Essays* in *The Atlas*: 'On Prejudice'

29 Never confuse movement with action.

Ernest Hemingway in A. E. Hochner, *Papa Hemingway*, Pt 1, Ch. 1

30 When we do not do the one thing we ought to do, we have no time for anything else – we are the busiest people in the world.

Eric Hoffer *Between the Devil and the Dragon*, Pt 1: Introduction

31 Honour is flashed off exploit, so we say.

Gerard Manley Hopkins *St Alphonsus Rodriguez*

32 The man who does too much for others leaves himself underdone.

Elbert Hubbard *The Note Book of Elbert Hubbard*, p. 159

33 That action is best which procures the greatest happiness for the greatest numbers.

Francis Hutcheson *Inquiry into the Original of Our Ideas of Beauty and Virtue*, 2, iii

34 People may come do anything almost, by talking of it.

Dr Samuel Johnson in James Boswell, *Life of Johnson*, Vol. 5

35 People spend most of their time and psychological energy on not doing something; the really busy ones are capable of not doing two or three things at the same time. If they only knew that if they reversed that policy, they could live two or three lives instead of none.

Hans Keller *Maxims and Reflections*, 37

36 The greatest pleasure I know is to do a good action by stealth, and to have it found out by accident.

Charles Lamb in *The Athenaeum*: 'Table Talk by the Late Elia', 4 January 1834

37 Most things get done by not being done.

paraphrase of Lao-Tzu *Tao Te Ching* Book 1, iii, 10

38 If you must go nowhere, step out.

Percy Wyndham Lewis *The Human Age*, Bk 1: *The Childermass*, closing words

39 When someone likes doing something very much he almost always has some interest in the thing that is greater than the thing itself.

Georg Christoph Lichtenberg *Aphorisms*, Notebook C, 52

40 Nothing is done while anything remains to be done.

Napoleon Bonaparte *Maxims*

41 One seldom commits only one rash act. In the first rash act one always does too much. For just that reason one usually commits a second – and then one does too little.

Friedrich Nietzsche *Twilight of the Idols*: 'Maxims and Arrows', 30

42 We are used to the actions of human beings, not to their stillness.

V. S. Pritchett *The Living Novel*: 'The Hypocrite'

43 When two people do the same thing, it is not the same thing after all. **Publilius Syrus** *Moral Sayings*, 338

44 It is accordingly easy to define human rights: *everyone has the right to do anything that does not injure another*.

Arthur Schopenhauer *Essays and Aphorisms*: 'On Law and Politics', 1

45 Nothing is ever done in this world until men are prepared to kill one another if it is not done. **George Bernard Shaw** *Major Barbara*, Act 3

46 Extreme *busyness*, whether at school or college, kirk or market, is a symptom of deficient vitality.

Robert Louis Stevenson *Virginibus Puerisque*: 'An Apology for Idlers'

47 Great events do not necessarily have great causes.

A. J. P. Taylor quoted in his obituary in the *Independent*, 8 September 1990

48 The hand which executes a measure should belong to the head which propounds it. **Sir Henry Taylor** *The Statesman*, Ch. 13

49 At the Day of Judgement, we shall not be asked what we have read, but what we have done. **Thomas à Kempis** *The Imitation of Christ*, Bk 1, Ch. 3

50 To affect the quality of the day that is the highest of arts.

H. D. Thoreau *Journal*, after 18 April 1846

51 The chief difference between words and deeds is that words are always intended for men for their approbation, but deeds can be done only for God. **Leo Tolstoy** letter to Percy Redfern, 23 February 1903

52 The one person who has more illusions than the dreamer is the man of action. **Oscar Wilde** *The Critic as Artist*, 1

Advice

1 A woman seldom asks advice before she has bought her wedding clothes.
Joseph Addison *The Spectator*, 475

2 Do not remove a fly from your friend's forehead with a hatchet.
Anon. Chinese

3 When you fall flat,
At least grab a handful of sand.
Anon. *Chinese Couplets, Aphorisms and Apothegms*, ed. W. Dolby, 106

4 Where no counsel is, the people fall: but in the multitude of counsellors there is safety.
Bible, OT Proverbs 11:14

5 **Advice, n.** The smallest current coin.
Ambrose Bierce *The Enlarged Devil's Dictionary*

6 It iz a safer thing enny time, to follow a man's advice, than hiz example.
Josh Billings *Wit and Humor*, Affurisms: 'Ramrods'

7 Advice is seldom welcome; and those who want it the most always want it the least.
Earl of Chesterfield *Letters to His Son*, 29 January 1748

8 Never claim as a right what you can ask as a favour.
John Churton Collins in the *English Review*, April 1914, p. 98

9 The surest way of knowing whether someone has done something is to advise him to do it. He is bound to boast of having already done it.
Comtesse Diane *Les Glanes de la vie*, p. 125

10 Beware of bathroom walls that've not been written on.
Bob Dylan song: *Advice for Geraldine on Her Miscellaneous Birthday*

11 Advice is what we ask for when we already know the answer but wish we didn't.
Erica Jong *How to Save Your Own Life*: 'A day in the life . . .', epigraph

12 Old people are fond of giving good advice: it consoles them for no longer being capable of setting a bad example.
Duc de La Rochefoucauld *Maxims*, 93

13 Better sleep with a sober cannibal than a drunken Christian.
Herman Melville *Moby Dick*, Ch. 3

14 It is better to live with Liberty than with Riches,
With Virtue than with Beauty,
With Love than with Riches,
With Health than with Power,
With Wit than with Company,

With Peace than with Fame,
With Beasts than with Fools.

Margaret, Duchess of Newcastle in *The Cavalier and his Lady*: Aphorisms, 18

15 Never invest in anything that eats while you sleep.

Francis Player fatherly advice to Gary Player and his brother in the *Observer*, 24 February 1991

16 I hope, for his own sake, that he has younger people than me at his disposal if he wishes to ask for bad advice, especially if he means to follow it. **Marcel Proust** *Remembrance of Things Past: Cities of the Plain*, Pt 2, Ch. 1

17 We are so happy to advise others that occasionally we even do it in their interests. **Jules Renard** *Journal 1887–1910*

18 Never trust a husband too far, nor a bachelor too near.

Helen Rowland *A Guide to Men*: 'Third Interlude'

19 Never try to lick ice-cream off a hot sidewalk.

Charles M. Schulz in 'Peanuts' strip cartoon

20 No one wants advice – only corroboration.

John Steinbeck *The Winter of Our Discontent*

21 It is much safer to obey than to rule.

Thomas à Kempis *The Imitation of Christ*, 9

22 You might as well fall flat on your face as lean over too far backward.

James Thurber *Fables for Our Time*: 'The Bear Who Let It Alone'

23 Everybody who tells you how to act has whisky on their breath.

John Updike *Rabbit, Run p. 25*

24 The advice of the elderly may be bright but it gives no heat, like the winter sun. **Marquis de Vauvenargues** *Reflections and Maxims*, 159

25 To advise is to provide someone with a motive for an action of which he is ignorant. **Marquis de Vauvenargues** *Reflections and Maxims*, 473

26 I always pass on good advice. It is the only thing to do with it. It is never any use to oneself. **Oscar Wilde** *An Ideal Husband*, Act 1

Agreement and Disagreement

1 Nowadays most people kick *with* the pricks.

Theodor Adorno *Minima Memoralia*, Pt 2, 72

See also Bible, NT, Acts of the Apostles

2 You only find complete unanimity in a cemetery.

Abel Aganbegyan in the *Guardian*, 27 June 1987

3 The lion and the calf shall lie down together but the calf won't get much sleep. **Woody Allen** *Without Feathers*: 'The Scrolls'

4 Now no man can argue on his knees.

Walter Bagehot *The English Constitution*, Ch. 3

5 A continual dropping in a very rainy day and a contentious woman are alike. **Bible, OT** Proverbs 27:15

6 How agree the kettle and the earthen pot together? For if the one be smitten against the other, it shall be broken.

Bible, Apocrypha Ecclesiasticus 13:2

7 It is hard for thee to kick against the pricks.

Bible, NT Acts of the Apostles 9:5

See also Adorno

8 And if a house be divided against itself, that house cannot stand.

Bible, NT Mark 3:25

9 The reward for conformity is that everyone likes you except yourself.

Rita Mae Brown *Bingo*, Ch. 35

10 He that complies against his will,
Is of his own opinion still. **Samuel Butler 1** *Hudibras*, Pt 3, Canto 3, 547–8

11 Disagreement is a sign of spiritual vitality. It culminates in disagreement with God. Were we to make peace with God, we wouldn't live any more, he would live for us. As long as we assimilate ourselves to him we do not exist, whereas if we resist him, there is no reason for us to exist. **E. M. Cioran** *Tears and Saints*

12 The gentleman agrees with others without being an echo. The small man echoes without being in agreement. **Confucius** *The Analects*, Bk 13, 23

13 In every age and clime we see,
Two of a trade can ne'er agree. **John Gay** *Fables*, Pt 1, 21, 43

14 Disagreement may be the shortest cut between two minds.

Kahlil Gibran *Sand and Foam*

15 Never in any circumstance
Let them induce you to refute.
Wise men fall into ignorance
When with the ignorant they dispute.

Johann Wolfgang von Goethe *Poems and Epigrams*: 'Never in any circumstance'

16 Opposition brings concord. Out of discord comes the fairest harmony.
Heraclitus *Fragments*, 98

17 In a hundred ells of contention, there is not an inch of love.
George Herbert *Jacula Prudentum*

18 Arguments about art are like arguments about opinions. Men cannot understand one another unless they love one another. They can love one another only if they experience the world more in themselves than outside themselves. **Hermann Hesse** *Reflections*, 480: 'Art and the Artist'

19 We may convince *others* by our arguments; but we can only persuade them by their own. **Joseph Joubert** *Pensées*, 106

20 The outcome of every argument is necessarily an insult. Either the truth insults its opponent, or a compromise insults the truth.
David Kipp *Aphorisms*, p. 5

21 A committee is an animal with four back legs.
John Le Carré *Tinker, Tailor, Soldier, Spy*, Pt 3, Ch. 34

22 Agreement is an altogether tiresome constituent of conversation.
Michel de Montaigne *Essays*, Bk 3, Ch. 8

23 I do not believe that any two men, on what are called doctrinal points, think alike, who think at all. It is only those who have not thought who appear to agree. **Thomas Paine** *The Rights of Man*, Pt 2

24 The talent of insinuation is more useful than that of persuasion; as everybody is open to insinuation but scarce any to persuasion.
Cardinal de Retz *Memoirs*, Pt 2, translated by Earl of Chesterfield in *Letters to His Son*, 1810 edn

25 The reason why people so often disagree in discussion is that they say what they do not think. The things we think are not those which cause differences. **Mark Rutherford** *Last Pages from a Journal*: Notes, p. 300

26 When men and women agree, it is only in their conclusions; their reasons are always different. **George Santayana** *The Life of Reason*, Ch. 6

27 We are citizens of an age, as well as of a state; and if it is mistaken, if not inadmissible, for a man to cut himself off from the customs and manners of the circle in which he lives, surely it is no less his duty, when opting for an activity, to submit his decision to the needs and the taste of his century.
Friedrich Schiller *On the Aesthetic Education of Man*: 'Second Letter', 1795

28 It is shades that clash, not colours.
Alexis de Tocqueville quoted in *Wit and Wisdom of Dean Inge*: Preface

29 Orthodoxy is my doxy; heterodoxy is another man's doxy.

William Warburton remark to Lord Sandwich, quoted in Joseph Priestley, *Memoirs*, Vol. 1, p. 372

30 When people agree with me I always feel I must be wrong.

Oscar Wilde *The Critic as Artist*, 2

31 If two men on the same job agree all the time, then one is useless. If they disagree all the time, then both are useless.

Darryl F. Zanuck in the *Observer*, 'Sayings of the Week', 23 October 1949

See also ***Disputes***

Ambitions

1 A man's worth is no greater than the worth of his ambitions.

Marcus Aurelius *Meditations*, Bk 7, 3

2 As in nature things move violently to their place and calmly in their place, so virtue in ambition is violent, in authority settled and calm.

Francis Bacon *Essays*: 'Of Great Place'

3 No bird soars too high if he soars with his own wings.

William Blake *The Marriage of Heaven and Hell*: 'Proverbs of Hell'

4 It is easier to achieve an ambition than to give it up.

Herbert Bluen *Lightning Flashes*

5 'Tis too late to be ambitious. The great mutations of the world are acted, our time may be too short for our designs.

Sir Thomas Browne *Urn Burial*, Ch. 4

6 Well is it known that ambition can creep as well as soar.

Edmund Burke *Third Letter . . . on the Proposals for Peace with the Regicide Directory*

7 Every achievement is a servitude. It compels us to a higher achievement.

Albert Camus *Notebooks 6*, 6 March 1951

8 Ambition, if it be a weed, grows only in the best soil.

Earl of Clarendon in Edward Meryon, *Epitaphs, Personal Anecdotes and Epigrams*: 'Quotations'

9 No one rises so high as he who knows not whither he is going.

Oliver Cromwell to French ambassador Sieur de Bellièvre, who reported it to Cardinal Retz, who found such an attitude to eminence incomprehensible!

10 You never go further than when you no longer know where you are going.

Johann Wolfgang von Goethe *Maxims and Reflections* (Penguin), from *Wilhelm Meister's Journeyman Years*, 901

11 Some people would rather be first in the second rank than second in the first. **Baltasar Gracián** *The Oracle*, 63

12 He who thinks his *Place* below him, will certainly be below his *Place*.

Marquis of Halifax *Maxims of State*

13 Ambition hath no Mean, it is either upon *all four* or upon Tiptoes.

Marquis of Halifax *Moral Thoughts and Reflections*: 'Of Ambition'

14 Ambition is in some sort genius.

William Hazlitt , quoted in Michael Foot, *Debts of Honour*, Ch. 2

15 In these times gain is not just a matter of greed but of ambition.

Joseph Joubert *Pensées*, 245

16 If you were tall, you wouldn't use stilts.

Duc de Lévis *Maximes et réflexions*, 87

17 Violent ambition and suspicion I have always seen going about hand in hand. **Georg Christoph Lichtenberg** *The Lichtenberg Reader*: Aphorisms 1764–70

18 To achieve great things we must live as though we never meant to die. **Marquis de Vauvenargues** *Reflections and Maxims*, 142

19 We are all in the gutter, but some of us are looking at the stars.

Oscar Wilde *Lady Windermere's Fan*, Act 1

20 Ambition is the last refuge of failure.

Oscar Wilde *Phrases and Philosophies for the Use of the Young*

21 Processions that lack high stilts have nothing that catches the eye.

W. B. Yeats *High Talk*

Anger and Aggression

1 Temper seems to pay some attention to reason, but to hear it imperfectly – just as eager servants go darting off before hearing the end of what is said to them. **Aristotle** *Ethics*, Bk 7, vi

2 Anger makes dull men witty, but it keeps them poor.

Francis Bacon *Apothegms*, 5; possibly originally said by Queen Elizabeth to Sir Edward ——

3 A man that studieth revenge keeps his own wounds green.

Francis Bacon *Essays*: 'Of Revenge'

4 A soft answer turneth away wrath: but grievous words stir up anger.
Bible, OT Proverbs 15:1

5 Envy and wrath shorten the life. **Bible, Apocrypha** Ecclesiasticus 30:24

6 All they that take the sword shall perish with the sword.
Bible, NT Matthew 26:52

7 The tigers of wrath are wiser than the horses of instruction.
William Blake *The Marriage of Heaven and Hell*: 'Proverbs of Hell'

8 There is another man within me that's angry with me.
Sir Thomas Browne *Religio Medici*, Pt 1, 9

9 A puritan's a person who pours righteous indignation into the wrong things. **G. K. Chesterton** in the *New York Times*, 30 November 1930

10 He who can control his rising anger as a coachman controls his carriage at full speed, this man I call a good driver; others merely hold the reins. *The Dhammapada*, 222

11 We boil at different degrees.
Ralph Waldo Emerson *Society and Solitude*: 'Eloquence'

12 Anger is one of the sinews of the soul; he that wants it hath a maimed mind. **Thomas Fuller** *The Holy State*, Bk 3, Ch. 8

13 All the while thou studiest Revenge thou art a-tearing thy own Wound open. **Dr Thomas Fuller** *Introductio ad Prudentium*, 1868

14 I'm always furious with myself when others are in the wrong!
Jean Giraudoux *Ondine*, Act 1

15 Good humour will conquer ill humour, but ill humour will conquer it much better. **Fulke Greville** *Maxims, Characters and Reflections*, p. 104

16 Spleen can subsist on any kind of food.
William Hazlitt *Lectures on the English Comic Writers*: 'On Wit and Humour'

17 Good temper is an estate for life.
William Hazlitt *The Plain Speaker*, Vol. 2, p. 106

18 It is hard to fight with anger; for what it wants it buys at the price of soul.
Heraclitus in G. S. Kirk, J. E. Raven and M. Schofield, *The Pre-Socratic Philosophers*, p. 208

19 Anger is a brief madness. **Horace** *Epistles*, 1, ii, 62

20 A man doesn't seize an axe in defence of his wallet, but in defence of his dignity. **Ryszard Kapuściński** *The Emperor*: 'It's Coming . . .'

21 To be angry is to revenge the faults of others upon ourselves.
Alexander Pope *Thoughts on Various Subjects*

22 Anger always thinks it has more power beyond its power.
Publilius Syrus *Moral Sayings*, 643

23 A woman moved is like a fountain troubled,
Muddy, ill-seeming, thick, bereft of beauty.
William Shakespeare *The Taming of the Shrew*, Act 5, Sc. 2, 143

24 The false God changes suffering into violence. The true God changes violence into suffering. **Simone Weil** *Gravity and Grace*: 'Evil'

See also ***Disputes***

Animals and Other Creatures

1 Horses are always horses, riders are not always horsemen.
Alessandro Alvisi *Horse and Man*, 4, 1

2 A man on a horse
has four eyes but not six legs. **Alessandro Alvisi** *Horse and Man*, 4, 8

3 [Animals] are not brethren, they are not underlings; they are other nations caught with ourselves in the net of life and time.
Henry Beston *The Outermost House*: 'Autumn, Ocean and Birds'

4 A robin redbreast in a cage
Puts all Heaven in a rage. **William Blake** *Auguries of Innocence*

5 The fox condemns the trap, not himself.
William Blake *The Marriage of Heaven and Hell*: 'Proverbs of Hell'

6 When thou seest an Eagle, thou seest a portion of Genius; lift up thy head! **William Blake** *The Marriage of Heaven and Hell*: 'Proverbs of Hell'

7 Just as friendship belongs only to man, attachment belongs to animals. **George-Louis de Buffon** *Histoire naturelle*: 'Des animaux'

8 The cat is an unfaithful servant that we are forced to keep to guard us against other even more awkward household enemies that we can't drive away. **George-Louis de Buffon** *Histoire naturelle*: 'Des animaux'

9 Man is the only animal that can remain on friendly terms with the victims he intends to eat, until he eats them.
Samuel Butler 2 *Notebooks*, Ch. 6: 'Mind and Matter'

10 Whenever you observe an animal closely, you feel as if a human being sitting inside were making fun of you.
Elias Canetti *The Human Province*: '1942'

11 A sparrow in the hand is better than a vulture on the wing.
Miguel Cervantes *Wit and Wisdom of Don Quixote*, p. 127

12 The man as can form a ackerate judgment of a animal, can form a ackerate judgment of anythin'. **Charles Dickens** *Pickwick Papers*, Ch. 55

13 Animals are such agreeable friends – they ask no questions, they pass no criticism. **George Eliot** *Scenes of Clerical Life*: 'Mr Gilfil's Love-Story', Ch. 7

14 A monkey is a man minus the voice. **Xavier Forneret** *Sans titre*: 'October'

15 The Love of no Creature (except the ignoble Spaniel) is confirmed by a Cudgel. **Dr Thomas Fuller** *Introductio ad Prudentium*, 2898

16 The higher animals are not larger than the lower because they are more complicated. They are more complicated because they are larger.
J. B. S. Haldane *Possible Worlds*: 'On Being the Right Size'

17 You can't make a silk purse out of a sow's ear, but you can make the most lovely home-made wine.
Merrily Harpur *The Nightmares of Dream Topping*

See also Morton

18 Nothing to be done really about animals. Anything you do looks foolish. The answer isn't in us. It's almost as if we're put here on earth to show how silly they aren't. **Russell Hoban** *Turtle Diary*, 42

19 What cats most appreciate in a human being is not the ability to produce food, which they take for granted – but his or her entertainment value. **Geoffrey Household** *Rogue Male*

20 You kin fool most any actor with promises, but a trained seal takes no chances. **'Kin' Hubbard** *Abe Martin's Wisecracks*, p. 57

21 God created the cat in order to give man the pleasure of caressing the tiger. **Victor Hugo** in *Selected Thoughts from the French*, ed. J. Raymond Solly

22 A camel is a horse designed by a committee.
Alec Issigonis(attrib.) in the *Guardian*, 14 January 1991

23 Cats seem to go on the principle that it never does any harm to ask for what you want. **Joseph Wood Krutch** *Twelve Seasons*: 'February'

24 A donkey appears to me like a horse translated into Dutch.
Georg Christoph Lichtenberg *The Lichtenberg Reader*: Aphorisms 1779–88

25 One disadvantage of being a hog is that at any moment some blundering fool may try to make a silk purse out of your wife's ear.
J. B. Morton ('Beachcomber') *By the Way*, September: Tail-piece

See also Harpur

26 A door is what a dog is perpetually on the wrong side of.
Ogden Nash *A Dog's Best Friend is His Illiteracy*

27 I fear that the animals consider man as a being like themselves that has lost in a most dangerous way its sound animal common sense; they consider him the insane animal, the laughing animal, the weeping animal, the miserable animal. **Friedrich Nietzsche** *The Gay Science*, Bk 3, 224

28 The more I see of men, the more I admire dogs. **Mme de Roland (attrib.)**

29 An oyster may be crossed in love. **R. B. Sheridan** *The Critic*, Act 1, Sc. 2

30 There is no secret so close as that between a rider and his horse.
R. S. Surtees *Mr Sponge's Sporting Tour*, Ch. 31

31 A cat is more intelligent than people believe, and can be taught any crime. **Mark Twain** *Notebook*, 1895

32 There are two things for which animals are to be envied; they know nothing of future evils, or of what people say about them.
Voltaire letter, 1739

Appearances

1 Private faces in public places
Are wiser and nicer
Than public faces in private places. **W. H. Auden** 'Marginalia'

2 He whose face gives no light, shall never become a star.
William Blake *The Marriage of Heaven and Hell*: 'Proverbs of Hell'

3 The world must judge of you by what you seem, not by what you are.
Earl of Chesterfield quoted in Walter Bagehot, *The English Constitution*, Ch. 4

4 There remains behind the eyes something of what they have seen.
Comtesse Diane *Les Glanes de la vie*, p. 29

5 Are people continuously themselves, or simply over and over again so fast that they give the illusion of continuous features – the temporal flicker of old silent film? **Lawrence Durrell** *Justine*, Pt 3, p. 196

6 Worldly faces never look so worldly as at a funeral.
George Eliot *Scenes of Clerical Life*, Ch. 25: 'Janet's Repentance',

7 There is a great difference between painting a face and not washing it. **Thomas Fuller** *Church History*, Bk 7, Sect. 1, 32

8 It's odd how people waiting for you stand out far less clearly than people you are waiting for. **Jean Giraudoux** *Tiger at the Gates*, Act 1

9 Things do not pass for what they are but for what they seem.

Baltasar Gracián *The Oracle*, 99

10 We tolerate shapes in human beings that would horrify us if we saw them in a horse.

W. R. Inge (attrib.)

11 Man is read in his face; God in his creatures.

Ben Jonson *Timber or Discoveries Made Upon Men and Matter*, 59

12 Nothing prevents us from being natural so much as the desire to appear so.

Duc de La Rochefoucauld *Maxims*, 431

13 At 50, everyone has the face he deserves.

George Orwell final entry in *Notebook*, 17 April 1949

14 One must always tell what one sees. Above all, which is more difficult, one must always see what one sees.

Charles Péguy *Basic Verities*: 'The Honest People'

15 He who has seen everything empty itself is close to knowing with what everything is filled.

Antonio Porchia *Voices*

16 And so when studying faces, we do indeed measure them, but as painters, not as surveyors.

Marcel Proust *Remembrance of Things Past: Within a Budding Grove*: 'Elstir'

17 It is our noticing them that puts things in a room, our growing used to them that takes them away again and clears a space for us.

Marcel Proust *Remembrance of Things Past: Within a Budding Grove*: 'Place-names'

18 A man's face as a rule says more, and more interesting things, than his mouth, for it is a compendium of everything his mouth will ever say, in that it is the monogram of all this man's thoughts and aspirations. The mouth, further, expresses only the thoughts of a man, while the face expresses a thought of nature: so that everyone is worth looking at, even if everyone is not worth talking to.

Arthur Schopenhauer *Essays and Aphorisms*: 'On Various Subjects', 9

19 It is only shallow people who do not judge by appearances.

Oscar Wilde *The Picture of Dorian Gray*, Ch. 2

See also ***Eyes; Perceptions***

Art and Artists

1 Every work of art is an uncommitted crime.

Theodor Adorno *Minima Memoralia*, Pt 2, 72

2 Art has a love for chance and chance for art.

Agathon quoted in Aristotle, *Ethics*, Bk 4

3 The object of art is to give life a shape.

Jean Anouilh *The Rehearsal*, Act 1, Sc. 2

4 Art is our chief means of breaking bread with the dead.

W. H. Auden in the *New York Times*, 7 August 1971

5 In my experience, if you have to keep the lavatory door shut by extending your left leg, it's modern architecture.

Nancy Banks-Smith in the *Guardian*, 20 February 1979

6 To be an artist is to fail, as no other dares fail.

Samuel Beckett quoted Philip Auster in conversation with Edmond Jabès, *The Art of Hunger*

7 Art and Religion are, then, two roads by which men escape from circumstance to ecstasy. **Clive Bell** *Art*, Pt 2, Ch. 1

8 No artefact is a work of art if it does not help to humanize us. Without art, visual, verbal and musical, our world would have remained a jungle. **Bernard Berenson** *Italian Painters of the Renaissance*: Preface to 1952 edn

9 From the instant that a work of art begins to sacrifice essence to expression it is on the way to becoming a photograph or cipher.

Bernard Berenson *Notebooks*, undated

10 Every painted image of something is also about the absence of the real thing. All painting is about the presence of absence. This is why man paints. The broken pictorial space confesses the art's wishfulness.

John Berger in *New Statesman and Society*, 15 July 1988

11 The artist is extremely lucky who is presented with the worst possible ordeal which will not actually kill him.

John Berryman interview in *Paris Review*, Winter 1972

12 A great work – a landscape painted so well that the artist disappears in it. **Pierre Boulez** in Joan Peyser, *Boulez*, Ch. 1

13 Illusions are art, for the feeling person, and it is by art that we live, if we do. **Elizabeth Bowen** *The Death of the Heart*, Pt 1, Ch. 7

14 Art is the only thing that can go on mattering once it has stopped hurting. **Elizabeth Bowen** *The Heat of the Day*, Ch. 16

15 Art is meant to disturb. Science reassures. **Georges Braque** *Pensées sur l'art*

16 A sure sign of an amateur is too much detail to compensate for too little life. **Anthony Burgess** in the *Times Literary Supplement*, 18 June 1971

17 The history of art is the history of revivals.

Samuel Butler 2 *Notebooks*, Ch. 8: 'Anachronism'

18 The true work of art is the one that says least.

Albert Camus *Notebooks 3*, June 1938

19 It is art and the artist who remake the world, but always with an underlying protest. **Albert Camus** *Notebooks 4*, June 1944

20 In the fine arts, and even in other matters, it is only what we have not been taught that we know really well.

Nicholas-Sébastien Chamfort *Maxims and Considerations*, 465

21 The artistic temperament is a disease which afflicts amateurs.

G. K. Chesterton *Heretics*, Ch. 17

22 A small artist is content with art; a great artist is content with nothing except everything. **G. K. Chesterton** *Heretics*, Ch. 20

23 An artist will betray himself by some sort of sincerity.

G. K. Chesterton *The Incredulity of Father Brown*: 'The Dagger with Wings'

24 An artist does not jump upstairs. If he does it is a waste of time, because he will have to walk up afterwards. **Jean Cocteau** *Cock and Harlequin*, p. 9

25 There is no more sombre enemy of good art than the pram in the hall. **Cyril Connolly** *Enemies of Promise*, Ch. 14

26 A work that aspires, however humbly, to the condition of art should carry its justification in every line.

Joseph Conrad *The Nigger of the Narcissus*: Preface

27 Art for art's sake, with no purpose, for all purposes pervert art. But art achieves a purpose which is not its own.

Benjamin Constant *Journal intime*, 11 February 1804

28 The title of artist means: one who perceives more than his fellows, and who records more than he has seen.

Edward Gordon Craig *On the Art of the Theatre*: 'The Actor and the Über-Marionette'

29 The artist does not draw what he sees, but what he has to make others see. **Edgar Degas** quoted in *La Renaissance de l'art Français*

30 In painting you must convey the idea of the true by means of the false. **Edgar Degas** quoted in *La Renaissance de l'art français*

See also Picasso

31 One always has to spoil a picture a little in order to finish it.

Eugène Delacroix *Journal*, 13 April 1853

32 Experience ought to teach us two things; first, that we should do a great deal of correcting; secondly, that we must not correct too much.

Eugène Delacroix *Journal*, 8 March 1860

33 *Only* a born artist can endure the labour of becoming one.
Comtesse Diane in Denis Brearley, *From the French*

34 There are two styles of portrait painting; the serious and the smirk.
Charles Dickens *Nicholas Nickleby*, Ch. 10

35 Nature is a haunted house – but Art – a House that tries to be haunted.
Emily Dickinson quoted in Roberto Calasso, *The Ruin of Kasch*: 'Law and Order'

36 A study of family portraits is enough to convert a man to the doctrine of reincarnation. **Arthur Conan Doyle** *The Hound of the Baskervilles*, Ch. 13

37 The more perfect the artist, the more completely separate in him will be the man who suffers and the mind which creates.
T. S. Eliot *Selected Essays*: 'Tradition and the Individual Talent', 2

38 Every artist writes his own autobiography.
Henry Havelock Ellis *The New Spirit*: 'Tolstoi', 11

39 Art is a jealous mistress. **Ralph Waldo Emerson** *The Conduct of Life*: 'Wealth'

40 The artist in his work ought to be like God in creation, invisible and all powerful; everywhere felt but nowhere visible.
Gustave Flaubert letter to Mlle de Chantepie, 18 March 1857

41 All art both generalizes and particularizes; that is tries to flower in all time, but is rooted in one time. **John Fowles** *The Aristos*, Ch. 10, 15

42 Art is significant deformity. **Roger Fry** in Virginia Woolf, *Roger Fry*, Ch. 8

43 A man may be an artist, though he have not his tools about him.
Dr Thomas Fuller *Gnomologia*, 288

44 The artist is not a special kind of man but every man a special kind of artist. **Eric Gill** in *Art*, 1942

45 Principles always become a matter of vehement discussion when practice is at ebb. **George Gissing** *The Private Papers of Henry Ryecroft*, Spring, 20

46 In art the best is good enough. **Johann Wolfgang von Goethe** *Italian Journey*

47 There is no surer way of evading the world than by Art; and no surer way of uniting with it than by Art.
Johann Wolfgang von Goethe *Maxims and Reflections*: 'Literature and Art', 485

48 What is classical is healthy; what is romantic is sick.
Johann Wolfgang von Goethe *Maxims and Reflections* (Penguin), 1030

49 A work of art is just as much a work of nature as a mountain.
Johann Wolfgang von Goethe quoted in Randall Jarrell, *A Sad Heart at the Supermarket*: 'Stories'

50 Artistic communication is quite unlike throwing hand grenades. There must be not only a sender but also a receiver suitably attuned.

E. H. Gombrich *Art and Illusion*, Ch. 11

51 Any picture that produces a moral impression is a bad picture.

Edmond and Jules de Goncourt *Journal*, 7 December 1860

52 Art is the only work open to people who can't get along with others and still want to be special. **Alasdair Gray** *Lanark*, Bk 3, Ch. 1

53 Art is the contemplation of the world in a state of grace.

Hermann Hesse *Reflections*, 467: 'Art and the Artist'

54 The artist's one advantage is this: that his lunacy is not locked up but enjoys a certain standing because of its products.

Hermann Hesse *Reflections*, 501: 'Art and the Artist'

55 An artist is a person who thinks more than there is to think, feels more than there is to feel, and sees more than there is to see.

John Oliver Hobbes *The Artist's Life*: 'Balzac, Turner and Brahms'

56 Art has to move you and design does not, unless it's a good design for a bus.

David Hockney at press conference for his retrospective at the Tate Gallery, London, 25 October 1988

57 Play is older than work, art older than production for use.

Eric Hoffer in Calvin Tomkins, *Eric Hoffer: an American Odyssey*: Aphorisms

58 Each true work of art is the blueprint for the only temple on earth.

Hugo von Hofmannsthal *The Book of Friends*, 4

59 Architecture is the art of how to waste space.

Philip Johnson the *New York Times*, 27 December 1964

60 Illusion based on reality, that is the secret of the fine arts – in fact, of all art. **Joseph Joubert** *Notebooks*, 1802

61 Art as a precursor of scientific thought is second-rate. Art as a successor to scientific thought is trash. Art that remains a precursor of scientific thought which never catches up with it – that's art.

Hans Keller *Maxims and Reflections*, 112

62 Art does not reproduce what we see. Rather, it makes us see.

Paul Klee *Creative Credo*

63 Nature can afford to be prodigal in everything, the artist must be frugal down to the smallest detail. **Paul Klee** *Diaries 1898–1918*, 857

64 Nature is garrulous to the point of confusion; let the artist be truly taciturn. **Paul Klee** *Diaries 1898–1918*, 857

65 Art should be at home everywhere like a fairy tale; and it should know how to deal in good and evil, like the Almighty.

Paul Klee in Felix Klee, *Paul Klee*, Pt 3, 3

66 Artists have a right to be modest and a duty to be vain.

Karl Kraus *Half-Truths and One-and-a-Half Truths*: 'Riddles'

67 Art is not a special sauce applied to ordinary cooking; it is the cooking itself if it is good. **W. R. Lethaby** *Form in Civilization*: 'Art and Workmanship'

68 All living artists compete with the towering dead with their nightingales and psalms. **Elisabeth Lutyens** *A Goldfish Bowl*, Ch. 2

69 The whole of art is an appeal to a reality which is not without us but in our minds. **Desmond MacCarthy** *Theatre*: 'Modern Drama'

70 Art is not a mirror to reflect the world, but a hammer with which to shape it. **Vladimir Mayakovsky** quoted in the *Guardian*, 11 December 1974

71 Less is more.

Ludwig Mies van der Rohe in the *New York Herald Tribune*, 28 June 1959

72 The worst sin that can be committed against the artist is to take him at his word, to see in his work a fulfilment instead of an horizon.

Henry Miller *The Cosmological Eye*: 'An Open Letter to Surrealists Everywhere'

73 A picture was once a rare sort of symbol, rare enough to call for attentive concentration. Now it is the actual experience that is rare, and the picture has become ubiquitous.

Lewis Mumford *Art and Technics*: 'Standardization, Reproduction and Choice'

74 All art deals with the absurd and aims at the simple. Good art speaks truth, indeed *is* truth, perhaps the only truth.

Iris Murdoch *The Black Prince*: 'Bradley Pearson's Foreword'

75 All art is a struggle to be, in a particular sort of way, virtuous.

Iris Murdoch in *Novelists in Interview*, ed. John Haffenden

76 Great artists have no country **Alfred de Musset** *Lorenzaccio*, Act 1, Sc. 5

77 As an *artist*, one has no home in Europe except in Paris.

Friedrich Nietzsche *Ecce Homo*: 'Why I am so Clever', 5

78 All art constantly aspires towards the condition of music.

Walter Pater *The Renaissance*: 'Giorgione'

79 An artist should know all about love and learn to live without it.

Anna Pavlova quoted in the *Guardian*, 5 October 1987

80 The test of a good portrait is that if you take it down, you have the feeling that somebody has left the room.

Tom Phillips interview in the *Observer*, 1 October 1989

81 Art is a lie which makes us realize the truth.

Pablo Picasso in D. Ashton, *Picasso on Art*

82 Everything interesting in art happens at the start. Once past the beginning you're already at the end.

Pablo Picasso in John Berger, *The Success and Failure of Picasso*, p. 54

83 It's far more difficult to disfigure a great work of art than to create one. **Marcel Proust** *Remembrance of Things Past: Cities of the Plain*, Pt 2, Ch. 1

84 But, less disappointing than life, great works of art do not begin by giving us the best of themselves.

Marcel Proust *Remembrance of Things Past: Within a Budding Grove*, p. 119

85 It's the artist's job to create sunshine when there isn't any.

Romain Rolland *Jean Christophe: The Market on 'Change*

86 Artists – by definition innocent – don't steal. But they do borrow without giving back. **Ned Rorem** *Music from Inside Out*: 'Anatomy of Two Songs'

87 The modern painter begins with nothingness. That is the only thing he copies. The rest he invents.

Harold Rosenberg of Jackson Pollock, in the *Guardian*, 23 November 1989

88 All great art is praise.

John Ruskin quoted in 'Ruskin, Turner and the Pre-Raphaelites' exhibition, Tate Gallery, 2000

89 Art, so long as it needs to be a dream, will never cease to prove a disappointment. **George Santayana** *Little Essays*, 51: 'Mere Art'

90 A portrait is a picture in which there is just a tiny little something not quite right about the mouth.

John Singer Sargent in *Anecdotes of Modern Art*, ed. Donald Hall and Pat Corrington-Wykes

91 Architecture in general is frozen music.

Friedrich von Schelling *Die Philosophie der Kunst*, p. 576; also said by Goethe

92 Art should be cold.

Arnold Schoenberg in Artur Schnabel, *My Life and Music*, Pt 2, Ch. 9; but elsewhere ascribed to Stravinsky

93 A cartoonist is someone who does the same thing every day without repeating himself. **Charles Schulz** in the *Guardian*, 8 December 1999

94 It's easier to replace a dead man than a good picture.

George Bernard Shaw *The Doctor's Dilemma*, 2

95 The artist, like the idiot or clown, sits on the edge of the world, and a push may send him over it. **Osbert Sitwell** *The Scarlet Tree*, Bk 4, Ch. 2

96 Nothing is likely about masterpieces, least of all whether there will be any.

Igor Stravinsky and Robert Craft *Conversations with Stravinsky*: 'The Future of Music'

97 A painter should not paint what he sees, but what will be seen.

Paul Valéry *Bad Thoughts and Not So Bad*, S

98 Art can be as spiteful as love. Art and love are potentially criminal – or else they don't exist. **Paul Valéry** *Rhumbs*: 'Pencilled at Random'

99 Know that the secret of the arts is to correct nature.

Voltaire *À M. de Verrière*

100 As long as a thing is useful or necessary to us, or affects us in any way, either for pain or for pleasure, or appeals strongly to our sympathies, or is a vital part of the environment in which we live, it is outside the proper sphere of Art. **Oscar Wilde** *The Decay of Lying*

101 Art itself is really a form of exaggeration; and selection, which is the very spirit of Art, is nothing more than an intensified mode of over-emphasis. **Oscar Wilde** *The Decay of Lying*

102 The great superiority of France over England is that in France every bourgeois wants to be an artist, whereas in England every artist wants to be a bourgeois. **Oscar Wilde** in conversation, from *Epigrams of Oscar Wilde*: 'Art'

103 Art is the only serious thing in the world. And the artist is the only person who is never serious.

Oscar Wilde *For the Instruction of the Over-educated*

104 The moral life of man forms part of the subject matter of the artist, but the morality of art consists in the perfect use of an imperfect medium. **Oscar Wilde** *The Picture of Dorian Gray*: Preface

105 The dominating influence that spawned these arts was the need to impose order on the confusion caused by intelligence.

Edward O. Wilson *Consilience*, Ch. 10

106 A work of art is a corner of creation seen through a temperament.

Émile Zola *Mes Haines*: 'M. H. Taine, Artiste'

B

Beauty

1 Anything in any way beautiful derives its beauty from itself, and asks nothing beyond itself. Praise is no part of it.

Marcus Aurelius *Meditations*, Bk 4, 20

2 There is no excellent beauty that hath not some strangeness in the proportion.

Francis Bacon *Essays*: 'Of Beauty'

3 Beauty in distress is much the most affecting beauty.

Edmund Burke *On the Sublime and Beautiful*, III, 9

4 Though we travel the world over to find the beautiful, we must carry it with us or we find it not.

Ralph Waldo Emerson *Essays*: 'Art'

5 Light (God's eldest daughter!) is a principal beauty in a building.

Thomas Fuller *The Holy State*, Bk 2, Ch. 7

6 Beauty is always the first to hear about the sins of the world.

Jean Giraudoux *Duel of Angels*, Act 1

7 Beauty can never really understand itself.

Johann Wolfgang von Goethe *Maxims and Reflections*: 'Life and Character', 136

8 Beauty in things exists in the mind which contemplates them.

David Hume *Essays*: 'Of Tragedy'

9 This nonsense about beauty being only skin-deep. That's deep enough. What do you want – an adorable pancreas?

Jean Kerr *The Snake Has All the Lines*: 'Mirror, Mirror'

10 A woman who cannot be ugly is not beautiful.

Karl Kraus *Half-Truths and One-and-a-Half Truths*: 'Not for Women'

11 Women don't look for handsome men, they look for men with beautiful women. **Milan Kundera** *The Book of Laughter and Forgetting*, Pt 1, 8

12 Beauty is Nature's coin, must not be hoarded,
But must be current. **John Milton** *Comus*, 739

13 Beauty is in the eye of the beholder.
Proverbial quoted in Margaret Hungerford, *Molly Bawn*, 1, xii

14 I always say beauty is only sin deep. **Saki** *Reginald's Choir Treat*

15 Beauty provoketh thieves sooner than gold.
William Shakespeare *As You Like It*, Act 1, Sc. 3, (113)

16 Every fair from fair sometime declines. **William Shakespeare** *Sonnets*, 18

17 To have been born into a world of beauty, to die amid ugliness, is the common fate of all us exiles. **Evelyn Waugh** *A Little Learning*, p. 33

18 Beauty captivates the flesh in order to obtain permission to pass right to the soul. **Simone Weil** *Gravity and Grace*: 'Beauty'

19 A subject that is beautiful in itself gives no suggestion to the artist. It lacks imperfection. **Oscar Wilde** *For the Instruction of the Over-educated*

Beginnings and Endings

1 We deliberate not about ends, but about means. **Aristotle** *Ethics*, Bk 3, iii

2 Better is the end of a thing than the beginning thereof.
Bible, OT Ecclesiastes 7:8

3 All things on arth hav an end to them, and I kant think ov but phew things now that hain't got two. **Josh Billings** *Wit and Humor*: 'Finis'

4 Nothing arrives on paper as it started, and so much arrived that never started at all. **Elizabeth Bowen** *The Death of the Heart*: 'The World', 1

5 The course of a river is almost always disapproved of by the source.
Jean Cocteau *Cock and Harlequin*, p. 9

6 It is better to be the lichen on a rock than the President's carnation. Only by avoiding the beginning of things can we escape their ending.
Cyril Connolly *The Unquiet Grave*, Ch. 1

7 First things first, second things never.
Shirley Conran *Superwoman*: 'How to be a Working Wife and Mother'

8 The opera ain't over till the fat lady sings.

Dan Cook from baseball commentary on US TV, April 1978, in the *Washington Post*, 11 June 1978

9 Imperfection is an end. Perfection is only an aim.

Ivor Cutler label, in the *Guardian*, 12 August 1999

10 If we are not first, we may as well be last in any pursuit. To be worst is some form of distinction, and implies by the rule of contrary, that we ought to excel in some opposite quality. **William Hazlitt** *Characteristics*, 80

11 He who has begun has half done. Have the courage to be wise.

Horace *Epistles*, 1, ii, 40

12 Infinity is a dreadfully poor place. They can never manage to make ends meet. **Norton Juster** *The Phantom Tollbooth*, Ch. 16

13 There is a goal, but no way; what we call a way is hesitation.

Franz Kafka *Collected Aphorisms*, 26

14 Extremes meet. **Louis-Sébastien Mercier** *Tableau de Paris*, Vol. 4, Ch. 348: heading

15 The last thing we discover in writing a work is what to put first.

Blaise Pascal *Pensées*, 63

16 We are in the middle of a race between human skill as to means and human folly as to ends. **Bertrand Russell** *The Impact of Science on Society*, Ch. 7

17 There's a divinity that shapes our ends,
Rough-hew them how we will. **William Shakespeare** *Hamlet*, Act 5, Sc. 2, 10

18 To the latter end of a fray and the beginning of a feast
Fits a dull fighter and a keen guest.

William Shakespeare *Henry IV*, *Pt 1*, Act 4, Sc. 2, 86

19 Finality is death. Perfection is finality. Nothing is perfect. There are lumps in it. **James Stephens** *The Crock of Gold*, Bk 1, Ch. 4

20 The end may justify the means as long as there is something that justifies the end.

Leon Trotsky quoted in A. Pozzolini, *Antonio Gramsci: An Introduction to His Thought*: Preface

21 What is not quite completed does not yet exist. What isn't completed is less advanced than what is not begun.

Paul Valéry *At Moments*: 'The Beautiful is Negative'

Behaviour

1 You can't ride two horses with one behind.

Woody Allen in film *Broadway Danny Rose*

2 We become charlatans unconsciously and comedians involuntarily.

Henri-Frédéric Amiel *Amiel's Journal*, 13 September 1866

3 The sum of behaviour is – to retain a man's own dignity without intruding upon that of others. **Francis Bacon** *Essays*: 'Of Ceremonies'

4 Whenever I meet anybody they're always on their best behaviour. And when one is on one's best behaviour one isn't always at one's best.

Alan Bennett *Single Spies*: 'A Question of Attribution'

5 Politeness looks well to me in every man, except an undertaker.

Josh Billings *Wit and Humor*: Affurisms: 'Parboils'

6 Behavioural psychology is the science of pulling habits out of rats.

Dr Douglas Busch in Laurence J. Peter, *Peter's Quotations*

7 No people do so much harm as those who go about doing good.

Bishop Mandell Creighton *Life and Letters*, Vol. 2, Ch. 14

8 We must be as courteous to a man as we are to a picture, which we are willing to give the advantage of a good light.

Ralph Waldo Emerson *The Conduct of Life*: 'Behaviour'

9 Everything has two handles, one by which it may be borne, the other by which it may not. If your brother acts unjustly, do not lay hold of the act by the handle of its injustice, for this is the handle which cannot be borne: but rather of the other, that you were brought up together – and you will lay hold of the thing by the handle by which it can be borne. **Epictetus** *The Manual*, 42

10 Because we bring so little is no reason to bring nothing.

P. J. Kavanagh *People and Weather*, 4

11 The majority of men are subjective towards themselves and objective towards all others, terribly objective sometimes, but the real task is in fact to be objective towards oneself and subjective towards all others.

Søren Kierkegaard *Concluding Unscientific Postscript*

12 We may give advice, but we can never prompt behaviour.

Duc de La Rochefoucauld *Maxims*, 378

13 Considering how bad men are, it is wonderful how well they behave.

Salvador de Madariaga *Morning without Noon*, Pt 1, Ch. 14

14 Never descend to the ways of those above you. **George Mallaby** *From My Level*

15 Better one day as a lion than one hundred years as a sheep.
Benito Mussolini quoted in Louis de Bernières, *Captain Corelli's Mandolin*, 35; it echoes a Tibetan proverb

16 There is nothing so dangerous as what pleases both God and men. For those states that please both have one aspect that pleases God and another that pleases men. **Blaise Pascal** *Pensées*, 719

17 Treat me as you should treat me, not as I should be treated.
Antonio Porchia *Voices*

18 Only to those people whom we know we can never lose are we truly unkind. **Arthur Schnitzler** *Aphorismen und Betrachtungen*, p. 66

See also ***Actions***

Beliefs

1 God knows that belief is more important than what we believe.
Elizabeth Bibesco *Haven*: 'Aphorisms'

2 **Prudent.** A man who believes ten per cent of what he hears, a quarter of what he reads, and half of what he sees.
Ambrose Bierce *The Enlarged Devil's Dictionary*

3 Just as every conviction begins as a whim so does every emancipator serve his apprenticeship as a crank. A fanatic is a great leader who is just entering the room. **Heywood Broun** in the *New York World*, 6 February 1928

4 A priest or parson must believe a little in order not to be a hypocrite, and yet, to avoid intolerance, be not quite sure of his belief. The Grand-Vicar can smile at a remark against religion, the Bishop laugh outright, the Cardinal add a few words of his own.
Nicholas-Sébastien Chamfort *Maxims and Considerations*, 22

5 The most bigoted people in the world are the people who have not got any convictions at all. **G. K. Chesterton** in *Black and White*, March 1903

6 Man can be defined as an animal that makes dogmas.
G. K. Chesterton *Heretics*, Ch. 20

7 When men stop believing in God, it isn't that they believe in nothing: they *believe in everything*.
G. K. Chesterton quoted in Umberto Eco, *Foucault's Pendulum*, Ch. 118

See also Foucault

8 The abdication of Belief
Makes the Behaviour small –
Better an *ignis fatuus*
Than no illume at all. **Emily Dickinson** *Complete Poems*, 1551

9 Monotheism, a graceless and unreasonable belief, has its origin in laziness. A single god is an absurdity and a bore.
Norman Douglas *How About Europe?* p. 118

10 A fanatic is a man that does what he thinks th' Lord wud do if He knew th' facts iv th' case.
Finley Peter Dunne *Mr Dooley's Opinions*: 'Casual Observations'

11 One believes in rheumatism and true love only when afflicted by them. **Maria von Ebner-Eschenbach** *Aphorisms*, p. 49

12 Not that the incredulous person doesn't believe in anything. It's just that he doesn't believe in everything.
Umberto Eco *Foucault's Pendulum*, Ch. 7

See also Chesterton

13 The vehemence of the convert is striking. He is making up for having hitherto deceived *himself*. **Michael Frayn** *Constructions*, 245

14 Do not force feelings of any kind, least of all the feeling of conviction.
Sándor Ferenczi *Notes and Fragments*

15 Perhaps ghosts don't believe in men. **Jean Giraudoux** *Intermezzo*, Act 1

16 The believer will fight another believer over a shade of difference: the doubter fights only with himself.
Graham Greene *Monsignor Quixote*, Pt 1, Ch. 4

17 Astrology is true, but the Astrologers cannot find it.
George Herbert *Jacula Prudentum*

18 A creed is an ossified metaphor.
Elbert Hubbard *The Note Book of Elbert Hubbard*, p. 111

19 It is harder for some people to believe that God loves them than to believe that He exists.
Cardinal Basil Hume quoted in his obituary in the *Guardian*, 18 June 1999

20 A belief is like a guillotine, just as heavy, just as light.
Franz Kafka *Collected Aphorisms*, 87

21 Credulity is the man's weakness, but the child's strength.
Charles Lamb *Essays of Elia*. 'Witches and other Night Fears'

22 Convictions are more dangerous enemies to truth than lies.
Friedrich Nietzsche *Human, All Too Human*: 'A Man Alone with Himself', 485

23 Never believe in mirrors or newspapers.

John Osborne *The Hotel in Amsterdam*, Act 1

24 It is necessary to the happiness of man that he be mentally faithful to himself. Infidelity does not consist in believing, or in disbelieving, it consists in professing to believe what one does not believe.

Thomas Paine *The Age of Reason*, Pt 2

25 You can't teach an old dogma new tricks.

Dorothy Parker quoted in R. E. Drennan, *Wit's End*

26 It is natural for the mind to believe and the will to love; therefore if they lack true objects they must attach themselves to false.

Blaise Pascal *Pensées*, 103

27 Atheism, the mark of a strong intellect, but only to a certain point.

Blaise Pascal *Pensées*, 360

28 All beliefs are bald ideas. **Francis Picabia** *Yes No, Poems and Sayings*: 'Sayings'

29 The most positive men are the most credulous.

Alexander Pope *Thoughts on Various Subjects*

30 The facts of life do not penetrate to the sphere in which our beliefs are cherished: they did not engender those beliefs, and they are powerless to destroy them.

Marcel Proust *Remembrance of Things Past: Swann's Way*; quoted in Adam Phillips, *The Beast in the Nursery*, Ch. 4

31 He who believes in nothing still needs a girl to believe in him.

Eugen Rosenstock-Huessy quoted in W. H. Auden, *A Certain World*: 'Belief'

32 To die for one's beliefs is to put too high a price on conjecture.

Bertrand Russell (attrib.)

33 It is difficult to believe in God, not because He is far off, but because He is so near. **Mark Rutherford** *Last Pages from a Journal*: Notes, p. 281

34 Fanaticism consists of redoubling your effort when you have forgotten your aim. **George Santayana** *The Life of Reason*: Introduction

35 I confused things with their names: that is belief.

Jean-Paul Sartre *Words*, Pt 2

36 Knowledge is something which you can use. Belief is something which uses you. **Idries Shah** *Reflections*: 'Belief and Knowledge'

37 A company of believers is like a prisonful of criminals: their intimacy and solidarity are based on what about themselves they can least justify. **John Updike** *In the Beauty of the Lilies*, 4

38 The great mistake of the Marxists and of the whole of the nineteenth century was to think that by walking straight on one mounted upwards into the air. **Simone Weil** *Gravity and Grace*: 'Social Harmony'

39 Believe Things rather than People.
Benjamin Whichcote *Moral and Religious Aphorisms*, 39

40 One can mistrust one's own senses, but not one's own belief.
Ludwig Wittgenstein *Philosophical Investigations*, Pt 2, Sect. 10

41 By night an atheist half believes a God.
Edward Young *Night Thoughts*: 'Night 5', line 176

See also ***Faith***

Big and Small

1 The little things are infinitely the most important.
Arthur Conan Doyle *The Adventures of Sherlock Holmes*: 'A Case of Identity'

2 Large streams from little fountains flow,
Tall oaks from little acorns grow.
David Everett *Lines Written for a School Declamation*

3 If we lived in a featureless desert, we would learn to place the individual grains of sand in a moral and aesthetic hierarchy.
Michael Frayn *Constructions*, 10

4 All things help, said the Wren, when she piss'd in the Sea.
Dr Thomas Fuller *Gnomologia*, 563

5 Size is not grandeur, and territory does not make a nation.
T. H. Huxley *Aphorisms and Reflections*, 110

6 A man would never undertake great things, could he be amused by small. **Dr Samuel Johnson** in James Boswell, *Life of Johnson*, 7 April 1778

7 It is better to have loved a short man, than never to have loved a tall.
Miles Kington 'Cod' Albanian proverb, in the *Independent*, 27 December 1991

8 A single day is enough to make us a little larger, or, another time, a little smaller. **Paul Klee** *The Diaries of Paul Klee 1898–1918*, January 1908

9 Generalization is the death of art. It's in the details that God resides.
Arthur Miller in the *Observer*, 'Sayings of the Week', 9 April 1995

10 We think in generalities, but we live in detail.
Alfred North Whitehead (attrib.)

Birth and Death

1 Death is an acquired trait.

Woody Allen in E. Lax, *Woody Allen and His Comedy*, Ch. 11

2 Man dies when he wants, as he wants, of what he chooses.

Jean Anouilh (attrib.)

3 It is as natural to die as to be born; and to a little infant, the one is as painful as the other. **Francis Bacon** *Essays*: 'Of Death'

4 Revenge triumphs over death; love slights it; honour aspireth to it; grief flieth to it. **Francis Bacon** *Essays*: 'Of Death'

5 The dying man looks at himself in the mirror and says, 'We won't be seeing each other any more.'

Paul Bowles quoted in Ned Rorem, *The Paris Diary*, Pt 1

6 When we attend the funerals of our friends we grieve for them, but when we go to those of other people it is chiefly our own deaths that we mourn for. **Gerald Brenan** *Thoughts in a Dry Season*: 'Death'

7 We all labour against our own cure; for death is the cure of all diseases. **Sir Thomas Browne** *Religio Medici*, Pt 2, 9

8 Genius does not know how to die. Poor women do.

Albert Camus *Notebooks 6*, 1949

9 There's a remedy for everything except death.

Miguel Cervantes *Don Quixote*, Pt 2, 10

10 We can be certain that more than a hundred thousand persons die in the world every day. So that a man who has only lived for thirty years has escaped this tremendous destruction about one thousand, four hundred times. **Nicholas-Sébastien Chamfort** *Maxims and Considerations*, 18

11 The grass grows green on the battlefield, but never on the scaffold.

Winston S. Churchill (attrib.) on the Irish Rebellion, 1916

12 Only rich people *experience* death; poor people expect it; no beggar ever died. Only owners die. **E. M. Cioran** *Tears and Saints*

13 Nothing can equal the everlasting discretion of death.

Joseph Conrad *The Secret Agent*, Ch. 11

14 I think the dying pray at the last not please but thank you as a guest thanks his host at the door. **Annie Dillard** *Pilgrim at Tinker Creek*, Ch. 15

15 He not busy being born
Is busy dying. **Bob Dylan** song: *It's Alright, Ma (I'm Only Bleeding)*

16 Reflect that the chief source of all evils to man as well as of baseness and cowardice, is not death but the *fear* of death.

Epictetus *The Golden Sayings*, 135

17 So death, the most terrifying of ills, is nothing to us, since so long as we exist, death is not with us; but when death comes, then we do not exist. It does not then concern either the living or the dead, since for the former it is not, and the latter are no more. **Epicurus** letter to Menoeceus

18 Death destroys a man; the idea of Death saves him.

E. M. Forster *Howards End*, Ch. 27

19 In the nineteenth century the problem was that God is dead; in the twentieth century the problem is that man is dead.

Erich Fromm *The Sane Society*, Ch. 9

20 We take Death to be before us, but it is behind us; and has already swallowed up all that is past. **Dr Thomas Fuller** *Introductio ad Sapientiam*, 1410

21 For he alone will die who wishes to die, to whom life is intolerable.

Georg Groddeck *The Book of the It*, Letter 13

22 A pregnant woman is of good complexion if the child be male; of ill complexion if the child be female. **Hippocrates** *Aphorisms*, 5, 42

23 Pale Death knocks with impartial foot at poor men's hovels and kings' palaces. **Horace** *Odes*, 1, iv, 13

24 Everyone's afraid of dying but no one is afraid of being dead.

Mgr Ronald Knox quoted by Cardinal Basil Hume in interview in John Mortimer, *In Character*

25 The dead don't die. They look on and help.

D. H. Lawrence letter to J. Middleton Murry on the death of his wife, Katherine Mansfield, 2 February 1923

26 Die before you die. There is no chance after.

C. S. Lewis *Till We Have Faces*, Bk 2, Ch. 2

27 It always saddens me when a man of talent dies, for the earth has more need of such men than Heaven does.

Georg Christoph Lichtenberg *Aphorisms*, Notebook J, 98

28 A man's dying is more the survivors' affair than his own.

Thomas Mann *The Magic Mountain*, Ch. 6, Sect. 8

29 I should like to see funerals banned: we should grieve at someone's birth, not his death. **Charles de Montesquieu** *Persian Letters*, 40

30 When a person dies the angels say, 'what has he sent in advance?' but human beings say, 'what has he left behind?'

Muhammad *The Sayings of Muhammad*: 'Death and the Hereafter'

31 For death is no more than a turning of us over from time to eternity.
William Penn *Reflections and Maxims*, 1, 503

32 We are born, so to speak, twice over; born into existence and born into life; born a human being and born a man. **Jean-Jacques Rousseau** *Émile*, Bk 4

33 Death is that after which nothing is of interest.
V. V. Rozanov *Fallen Leaves*, p. 57

34 Dying is not everything: you have to die in time. **Jean-Paul Sartre** *Words*, Pt 1

35 Once a man has fully grasped his mortality, for him the death throes have already begun. **Arthur Schnitzler** *Aphorismen und Betrachtungen*, p. 247

36 Nothing that is extreme is evil. Death comes to you? It would be dreadful could it remain with you; but of necessity either it does not arrive or else it departs. **Seneca** *Letters from a Stoic*, 90

37 A man can die but once; we owe God a death.
William Shakespeare *Henry IV, Pt 2*, Act 3, Sc. 2, (253)

38 He that dies pays all debts. **William Shakespeare** *The Tempest*, Act 3, Sc. 1, (143)

39 Death must be distinguished from dying with which it is often confounded.
Revd Sydney Smith *Maxims*, in his daughter, Lady Holland's, *Memoirs of Revd Sydney Smith*, Ch. 6

40 The birth you are afraid to take becomes your death.
Chuck Spezzano *Awaken the Gods*, p. 158

41 Death belongs to life as birth does.
The walk is in the raising of the foot as in the laying of it down.
Rabindranath Tagore *Stray Birds*, 268

42 Death is the price paid by life for an enhancement of the complexity of a live organism's structure. **Arnold Toynbee** *Life After Death*

43 Whoever has lived long enough to find out what life is, knows how deep a debt of gratitude we owe to Adam, the first great benefactor of our race. He brought death into the world.
Mark Twain *Pudd'nhead Wilson*, Ch. 3: epigraph

44 Man dies of cold, not of darkness.
Miguel de Unamuno *The Tragic Sense of Life*, Ch. 4

45 Death: a trick played by the inconceivable on the conceivable.
Paul Valéry *Rhumbs*: 'Moralities'

46 Death. An instantaneous state, without past or future. Indispensable for entering eternity. **Simone Weil** *Gravity and Grace*: 'Decreation'

See also ***Immortality; Life and Death***

Body and Soul

1 Outside every fat man there is an even fatter man trying to close in.

Kingsley Amis *One Fat Englishman*, Ch. 3

See also Arnold; Connolly; Orwell; Waugh

2 Inside every fat man there is a man who is starving.

Matthew Arnold as tourist in US, quoted in Randall Jarrell, *A Sad Heart at the Supermarket*: title essay

See also Amis; Connolly; Orwell; Waugh

3 No one hates his body. **St Augustine**

4 You are composed of three parts: body, breath, and mind. The first two merely belong to you in the sense that you are responsible for their care; the last alone is truly yours. **Marcus Aurelius** *Meditations*, Bk 12, 3

5 The fingers must be educated, the thumb is born knowing.

Marc Chagall in *Barnes and Noble Book of Quotations*, ed. Robert I. Fitzhenry: 'Painters'

6 Imprisoned in every fat man a thin one is wildly signalling to be let out. **Cyril Connolly** *The Unquiet Grave*, Ch. 1

See also Amis, Arnold, Orwell, Waugh

7 The Soul unto itself
Is an imperial friend –
Or the most agonizing Spy –
An Enemy – could send –. **Emily Dickinson** *Complete Poems*, 683

8 We even find it painful to be men – real men of flesh and blood, with *our own private bodies*; we're ashamed of it, and we long to turn ourselves into something hypothetical called the average man.

Fyodor Dostoevsky *Notes from the Underground*, Pt 2, 10

9 Life is the sleep of the soul: as soon as a soul is tired, it looks out for a body as a bed; enters into a body in the season of dentition, and sleeps seventy years. **Ralph Waldo Emerson** *Journal*, 1846: 'Life'

10 Plainly the body is a most unsuitable vehicle, let alone companion, for the soul. Consider its vulgar inconveniencies, its shameful habits, its evil communications, always causing mischief. And the soul is an utterly inappropriate companion, or mentor, for the body, always whining, spoiling things, causing mischief. A couple of hangers-on with nothing better to hang on to. But just try to imagine either without the other. **D. J. Enright** *Interplay*, p. 156

11 Only one thing is wrong with our noses. They are too far off the ground to be much use. **Richard Feynman** quoted in the *Independent*, 17 March 1988

12 Whichever school a man may adhere to, the protestant or the philosophical, he continues to eat through the middle years of life with increasing interest. He grows more conscious of his body as it becomes less tolerant. **M. F. K. Fisher** *Serve It Forth*: 'When a Man is Small'

13 No sooner do we come into this world than bits of us start to fall off.
Gustave Flaubert quoted in Julian Barnes, *A History of the World in 10½ Chapters*

14 The hungry Belly thinks the throat cut.
Dr Thomas Fuller *Gnomologia*, 4603

15 Be not nasty in thy Clothes, or about thy Body, in much sweating, belching, biting thy Nails, rubbing thy Teeth, picking thy Nose or Ears, handling any Parts of thy Body which are not usually uncovered.
Dr Thomas Fuller *Introductio ad Prudentium*, 1310

16 Cough and the world coughs with you. Fart and you stand alone.
Trevor Griffiths *The Comedians*, Act 1

17 There's nothing man knows less than his own nose.
Friedrich Hebbel *Diaries*, entry 358, 1836

18 Some of us know with our heads or our hearts that it is not a question of progress or romanticism, of forward or backward, but of outside and inside, that what we dread is not railroads and motorcars, not money or reason, but only forgetfulness of God, the flattening of the soul.
Hermann Hesse *Reflections*, 415

19 As a body everyone is single, as a soul never.
Hermann Hesse *Steppenwolf*: 'Treatise on the Steppenwolf'

20 Is the soul greater than the hum of its parts?
Douglas R. Hofstadter *The Mind's I*, composed with Daniel C. Dennett, 11: 'Reflections'

21 What are our legs but crutches, by means of which, with restless efforts, we go hunting after the things we have not inside ourselves.
William James *A Pluralistic Universe*, Ch. 4

22 A man should have the fine point of his soul taken off to become fit for this world. **John Keats** letter to J. H. Reynolds, 22 November 1817

23 A soul weighs infinitely more than a kingdom, an empire, sometimes even more than the human species.
Jules Michelet *History of France*, IX: Preface

24 Poverty of goods is easily cured; poverty of soul, impossible.
Michel de Montaigne *Essays*, Bk 3, Ch. 10

25 There's a thin man inside every fat man, just as they say there's a statue inside every block of stone. **George Orwell** *Coming up for Air*, 1, 3

See also Amis; Arnold; Connolly; Waugh

26 Life is a slow birth. It would a little too easy to adopt a ready-made soul. **Antoine de Saint-Exupéry** *Flight to Arras*, Ch. 10

27 Of bones, man's body, as is plainly seen,
In all has some two hundred and nineteen;
Of teeth, in number, thirty-two contains,
With full three hundred-five-and-sixty veins.

Code of Health of the School of Salernum *Medical Maxims in Verse Form*: 'Number of Bones, Teeth . . .'

28 Toes are the fingers that have forgotten their past.

Rabindranath Tagore *Stray Birds*, 187

29 What is peculiar in the life of a man consists not in his obedience, but his opposition, to his instincts. In one direction or another he strives to live a supernatural life. **H. D. Thoreau** *Journals*, after 29 July 1850

30 There are two kinds of blood, the blood that flows in the veins and the blood that flows out of them. **Julian Tuwim** *We, the Polish Jews*

31 The body has its end which it does not know; the mind its means of which it is unaware. **Paul Valéry**

32 Enclosing every thin man, there's a fat man demanding elbow-room.

Evelyn Waugh *Officers and Gentlemen*: Interlude

See also Amis; Arnold; Connolly; Orwell

33 Body and soul are not two substances but one. They are man becoming aware of himself in two different ways.

C. F. von Weizsäcker in *Hodder Book of Christian Quotations*, comp. Tony Castle

34 Good men spiritualize their bodies; bad men incarnate their souls.

Benjamin Whichcote quoted in Aldous Huxley, *The Perennial Philosophy*, Ch. 14

35 Those who see any difference between soul and body have neither.

Oscar Wilde *Phrases and Philosophies for the Use of the Young*

36 The human body is the picture of the human soul.

Ludwig Wittgenstein *Philosophical Investigations*, Pt 2, Sect. 4

See also ***The Eyes; Human Nature; The Senses***

Books

1 In a world where books have long lost all likeness to books, the real book can no longer be one. **Theodor Adorno** *Minima Memoralia*, Pt 1, 30

2 Some books are undeservedly forgotten; none are undeservedly remembered. **W. H. Auden** *The Dyer's Hand*, Pt 1: 'Reading'

3 Books will speak plain when counsellors blanch.
Francis Bacon *Essays*: 'Of Counsel'

4 Some books are to be tasted, others to be swallowed, and some few to be chewed and digested. **Francis Bacon** *Essays*: 'Of Studies'

5 Books say: she is this because. Life says: she did this. Books are where things are explained to you; life is where things aren't. I'm not surprised some people prefer books. Books make sense of life. The only problem is that the lives they make sense of are other people's lives, never your own. **Julian Barnes** *Flaubert's Parrot*, 13

6 Books and harlots – footnotes in one are as banknotes in the stockings of the other. **Walter Benjamin** *One-way Street*: 'No. 13'

7 Of making many books there is no end; and much study is a weariness of the flesh. **Bible, OT** Ecclesiastes 12:12

8 On the whole, books are indeed less finite than ourselves. Even the worst among them outlast their authors – mainly because they occupy a smaller amount of physical space than those who penned them.
Joseph Brodsky *On Grief and Reason*: 'How to Read a Book'

9 I don't rightly know what's worse, burning books or not reading them. **Joseph Brodsky** *On Grief and Reason*: 'Immodest'

See also Heine; Rushdie

10 They do most by Books, who could do much without them, and he that chiefly owes himself unto himself, is the substantial Man.
Sir Thomas Browne *Christian Morals*, Pt 2, 5

11 Most contemporary books seem as if they had been made in one day, from yesterday's reading.
Nicholas-Sébastien Chamfort *Maxims and Considerations*, 427

12 Due attention to the inside of books, and due contempt for the outside, is the proper relation between a man of sense and his books.
Earl of Chesterfield *Letters to His Son*, 10 January 1749

13 To write books is to have a certain relation with original sin. For what is a book if not a loss of innocence, an act of aggression, a repetition of our Fall?
E. M. Cioran *The Temptation to Exist*: 'Some Blind Alleys'

14 Contemporary books do not keep. The quality in them which makes for their success is the first to go; they turn overnight.
Cyril Connolly *Enemies of Promise*, Ch. 2

15 Books cannot always please, however good;
Minds are not ever craving for their food.
George Crabbe *The Borough*, Letter 24, 402

16 I cannot tell whether books have brought me closer to things or separated me from them.
Edward Dahlberg *Sorrows of Priapus*: Prologue

17 A great man's book is a compromise between him and his reader.
Eugène Delacroix letter to Balzac, 1832

18 We know that books are not a way of letting someone else think in our place: on the contrary, they are machines that provoke further thought.
Umberto Eco in the *Observer Review*, 18 June 1995

19 Never read any book that is not a year old.
Ralph Waldo Emerson *Society and Solitude*: 'Books'

20 Books are all right but don't let them give you ideas.
D. J. Enright *Interplay*: 'Family Rules, Old Style'

21 Books may change the political climate more than politics shape books.
Michael Foot *Debts of Honour*, Ch. 3

22 The only books that influence us are those for which we are ready, and which have gone a little farther down our particular path than we have yet got ourselves.
E. M. Forster *Two Cheers for Democracy*: 'Books That Influenced Me'

23 I don't think any good book is based on factual experience. Bad books are about things the writer already knew before he wrote them.
Carlos Fuentes in *International Herald Tribune*, 5 November 1991

24 Learning hath gained most by those books by which the printers have lost.
Thomas Fuller *The Holy State*, Bk 3, Ch. 18

25 Some books seem to have been written, not to teach us anything but to let us know that the author knows something.
Johann Wolfgang von Goethe *Maxims and Reflections*: 'Literature and Art', 417

26 A book is never a masterpiece; it becomes one.
Edmond and Jules de Goncourt *Journal*, 23 July 1864

27 Even bad books are books and therefore sacred.
Günter Grass *The Tin Drum*: 'Rasputin and the Alphabet'

28 Few books have more than one thought: the generality indeed have not quite so many. **Julius and Augustus Hare** *Guesses at Truth*, 2

29 Wherever they burn books they will also end up burning people. **Heinrich Heine** *Almansor*, 245; used as inscription on memorial at Dachau concentration camp

See also Brodsky; Rushdie

30 All good books are alike in that they are truer than if they had really happened. **Ernest Hemingway** in *Esquire* magazine, December 1934

31 Not two out of a thousand books can arouse the feeling that not the author but things themselves are speaking to us. **Hermann Hesse** *Reflections*, 393

32 Humanity ought therefore always to carry with it a library of a thousand years as a balancing pole. **T. E. Hulme** *Speculations*, Ch. 1

33 Books are the money of Literature, but only the counters of Science. **T. H. Huxley** *Aphorisms and Reflections*, 102

34 Books are aids to forgetting as frequently as to remembering. **Holbrook Jackson** *Maxims of Books and Reading*, 2

35 No place affords a more striking conviction of the vanity of human hopes, than a public library. **Dr Samuel Johnson** *The Rambler*, 6, 23 March 1751

36 A book that reveals a mind is worth more than one which only reveals its subject. **Joseph Joubert** *Notebooks*, 1807

37 The great inconvenience of new books is that they prevent us from reading old books. **Joseph Joubert** *Notebooks*, 1808

38 Making books is a skilled trade, like making clocks; it needs more than native wit to become an author. **Jean de La Bruyère** *Characters*: 'Of Books', 3

39 Never judge a cover by its book. **Fran Lebowitz** *Metropolitan Life*

40 No book is really worth reading at the age of ten which is not equally (and often far more) worth reading at the age of fifty and beyond. **C. S. Lewis** in *Writer's Quotation Book*, ed. James Charlton

41 A book is a mirror: when a monkey looks in, no apostle can look out. **Georg Christoph Lichtenberg** *The Lichtenberg Reader*: Aphorisms 1775–9

42 A good book is the precious life-blood of a master spirit, embalmed and treasured up on purpose to a life beyond life. **John Milton** *Areopagitica*

43 There is no one thing to be found in books which it is a disgrace not to know. **Sir Walter A. Raleigh (attrib.)**

44 When a new book is published, read an old one.

Samuel Rogers (attrib.)

45 Any real book conveys one idea and one idea only. Its author is a man who is so slow of understanding that he has to write a whole book where common sense is perfectly satisfied with one phrase or slogan.

Eugen Rosenstock-Huessy *The Christian Future or the Modern Mind Outrun*, Ch. 1

46 To burn a book is not to destroy it. One minute of darkness will not make us blind.

Salman Rushdie review of Gabriel García Márquez, *Clandestine in Chile*, in the *Weekend Guardian*, 14–15 October 1989

See also Brodsky; Heine

47 A library is thought in cold storage.

Herbert Samuel in his *Book of Quotations*: 'Books'

48 Buying books would be a good thing if one could also buy the time to read them in; but as a rule the purchase of books is mistaken for the appropriation of their contents.

Arthur Schopenhauer *Essays and Aphorisms*: 'On Books and Writing', 17

49 No furniture so charming as books.

Revd Sydney Smith in his daughter, Lady Holland's, *Memoir*, Vol. 1, Ch. 9

50 Books are good enough in their own way, but they are a mighty bloodless substitute for life.

Robert Louis Stevenson *Virginibus Puerisque*: 'An Apology for Idlers'

51 The worm thinks it strange and foolish
that man does not eat his books.

Rabindranath Tagore *Fireflies*, p. 159

52 A good book is the best of friends, the same today and for ever.

Martin Tupper *Proverbial Philosophy, Series I*: 'Of Reading'

53 Books have the same enemies as man: fire, moisture, animals, the weather – and what's inside them.

Paul Valéry *Odds and Ends*: 'Literature'

54 The most influential books are always those that are not read.

Francis Wheen in the *Guardian*, 14 February 2001

55 In old days books were written by men of letters and read by the public. Nowadays books are written by the public and read by nobody.

Oscar Wilde *For the Instruction of the Over-educated*

56 There is no such thing as a moral or an immoral book. Books are well written, or badly written.

Oscar Wilde *The Picture of Dorian Gray*: Preface

See also ***Literature; Reading; Writing***

Boredom

1 He had the satisfied countenance of a man who has never succeeded in boring himself. **Peter Ackroyd** *The Last Testament of Oscar Wilde*, 24 August 1900

2 Insomnia commands respect while somnolence is boring.
Diana Athill *Stet* Ch. 3

3 Dullness, I now realize, is like halitosis; the sufferer is always the last to know. **Terence Blacker** in the *Independent on Sunday*, 4 August 1991

4 The English send all their bores abroad, and acquired the Empire as a punishment. **Edward Bond** *Narrow Road to the Deep North*, Pt 2, 1

5 Everyone is a bore to someone. That is unimportant. The thing to avoid is being a bore to oneself. **Gerald Brenan** *Thoughts in a Dry Season*: 'Life'

6 The table is the only place where the first hour is never dull.
Jean-Anthelme Brillat-Savarin *The Physiology of Taste*, aphorism 8

7 Society is now one polished horde,
Formed of two mighty tribes, the *Bores* and *Bored*.
Lord Byron *Don Juan*, XIII, 95

8 There is no such thing on earth as an uninteresting subject; the only thing that can exist is an uninterested person.
G. K. Chesterton *Heretics*, Ch. 3

9 When the chord of monotony is stretched most tight, then it breaks with a sound like a song.
G. K. Chesterton *The Napoleon of Notting Hill*, Bk 1, Ch. 1

10 Sameness is in all things the mother of satiety.
Cicero quoted by Peter Abelard, *Sic et Non*

11 Life creates itself in delirium and is undone in ennui.
E. M. Cioran *A Short History of Decay*, 1: 'Dislocation of Time'

12 Boredom is the misfortune of happy people.
Marquise du Deffand quoting Horace Walpole back to him, letter, 21 September 1777

13 Pleasure interrupts boredom, pain puts it to flight.
Comtesse Diane *Les Glanes de la vie*, p. 45

14 There are two ways of living, one of which leads to astonishment and the other to boredom. **Celia Green** *Advice to Clever Children*: 'Aphorisms'

15 Are you bored? Read your pulse! **Friedrich Hebbel** *Diaries*, entry 2968, 1843

16 Some people can stay longer in an hour than others can in a week.
William Dean Howells (attrib.) in *Treasury of Humorous Quotations*, ed. Evan Esar and Nicolas Bentley

17 Politeness is the art of being bored without boredom or (if you prefer) of bearing boredom without being bored. **Joseph Joubert** *Notebooks*, 1800

18 What wonder, then, that the world is regressing, that evil is gaining ground more and more, since boredom is on the increase and boredom is a root of all evil. We can trace this from the very beginning of the world. The gods were bored so they created man.
Søren Kierkegaard *Either/Or*, Pt 1, Ch. 6

19 We often forgive those who bore us, but we cannot forgive those who find us boring. **Duc de La Rochefoucauld** *Maxims*, 304

20 The capacity of human beings to bore one another seems to be vastly greater than that of any other animals. Some of their most esteemed inventions have no other apparent purpose, for example, the dinner party of more than two, the epic poem, and the science of metaphysics. **H. L. Mencken** *Notebooks, Minority Report*, 67

21 Is not life a hundred times too short – to be bored in it?
Friedrich Nietzsche *Beyond Good and Evil*, Pt 7, 227

22 What a bore it is, waking up in the morning always the same person.
Logan Pearsall Smith *Trivia II*: 'Green Ivory'

23 A bore is a man who, when you ask him how he is, tells you.
Bert Leston Taylor *The So-called Human Race*, p. 163

24 When a bore leaves the room you feel as if someone has just come in. ***Tigers Don't Eat Grass: Oriental and Occidental Aphorisms*** 'Bores'

25 Boredom is rage spread thin.
Paul Tillich in *Barnes and Noble Book of Quotations*, ed. Robert I. Fitzhenry: 'Bores'

26 He is an old bore; even the grave yawns for him.
Sir Herbert Beerbohm Tree in Hesketh Pearson, *Beerbohm Tree*, Ch. 21

27 A healthy male adult bore consumes each year one and a half times his own weight in other people's patience.
John Updike *Assorted Prose*: 'Confessions of a Wild Bore'

28 Punctuality is the virtue of the bored. **Evelyn Waugh** *Diaries*, 26 March 1962

29 Monotony is the most beautiful or the most atrocious thing. The most beautiful if it is a reflection of eternity – the most atrocious if it is the sign of an unvarying perpetuity. It is time surpassed or time sterilized.
Simone Weil *Gravity and Grace*: 'The Mysticism of Work'

30 An English peer of the right sort can be bored nearer to the point where mortification sets in, without showing it, than anyone else in the world. **P. G. Wodehouse** *Something Fresh*, Ch. 3

Business

1 Commerce is like war; its result is patent . . . There is as little appeal from figures as from battle. **Walter Bagehot** *The English Constitution*, Ch. 4

2 For the merchant even honesty is a financial speculation.
Charles Baudelaire *Intimate Journals*: 'My Heart Laid Bare', 97

3 The gambling known as business looks with austere disfavour upon the business known as gambling. **Ambrose Bierce** *The Devil's Dictionary*

4 **Incorporation, n.** The act of uniting several persons into one fiction called a corporation, in order that they may be no longer responsible for their actions. **Ambrose Bierce** *The Enlarged Devil's Dictionary*

5 A completely planned economy ensures that when no bacon is delivered, no eggs are delivered at the same time.
Leo Frain in the *Sunday Telegraph*, January 1965

6 Take care to sell your horse before he dies.
The art of life is passing losses on. **Robert Frost** *The Ingenuities of Debt*

7 Business is other people's money.
Mme de Girardin *Marguérites*, Vol. 2, p. 104

8 Men in business are in as much danger from those that work under them, as from those that work against them.
Marquis of Halifax *Political Thoughts and Reflections*: 'Instruments of State Ministers'

9 If I had to give a definition of capitalism I would say: the process whereby American girls turn into American women.
Christopher Hampton *Savages*, Sc. 16

10 Three women make a market. **George Herbert** *Jacula Prudentum*

11 Promise, large promise, is the soul of an advertisement.
Dr Samuel Johnson *The Idler*, no. 40, 20 January 1759

12 Regarded as a means the business man is tolerable; regarded as an end he is not so satisfactory.
John Maynard Keynes *Essays in Persuasion*, 4: 'A Short View of Russia'

13 Economists set themselves too easy, too useless a task if in tempestuous seasons they can only tell us that when the storm is long past the ocean is flat again. **John Maynard Keynes** *A Tract on Monetary Reform*, Ch. 3

14 When you are skinning your customers, you should leave some skin on to grow so that you can skin them again.
Nikita S. Khrushchev addressing British businessmen; quoted in the *Observer*, 'Sayings of the Week', 28 May 1961

15 Advertising may be described as the science of arresting the human intelligence long enough to get money from it.
Stephen Leacock *Garden of Folly*: 'The Perfect Salesman'

16 The best and simplest general type of capital is a well-made ploughshare. **John Ruskin** *Unto This Last*, 73

17 After all, for mankind as a whole there are no exports. We did not start developing by obtaining foreign exchange from Mars or the moon. Mankind is a closed society. **E. F. Schumacher** *Small is Beautiful*, 14

18 If all economists were laid end to end, they would not reach a conclusion. **George Bernard Shaw (attrib.)**

19 Every one lives by selling something.
Robert Louis Stevenson *Across the Plains*, 9: 'Beggars'

20 Nothing is so opposed to poetry – not crime – as business. It is a negation of life. **H. D. Thoreau** *Journal*, 29 June 1852

21 The attributes of a merchant are three hands and two faces.
Tigers Don't Eat Grass: Oriental and Occidental Aphorisms 'Trading'

22 Every business has a belief system – and it is at least as important as its accounting system or its authority system.
Alvin Toffler *The Adaptive Corporation*, Ch. 2

23 Buying and selling is good and necessary; it is very necessary and it may, possibly, be very good; but it cannot be the noblest work of man. **Anthony Trollope** *Dr Thorne*, Ch. 1

24 New York tolerated hypocrisy in private relations; but in business matters it exacted a limpid and impeccable honesty.
Edith Wharton *The Age of Innocence*, Bk 2, Ch. 26

See also ***Money; Work and Leisure***

C

Calm and Unease

1 Things can never touch the soul, for they are external and remain immovable; so that disquiet can arise only from fancies.

Marcus Aurelius *Meditations*, Bk 4, 3

2 Nothing matters very much, and very few things matter at all.

A. J. Balfour (attrib.)

3 Damn braces. Bless relaxes.

William Blake *The Marriage of Heaven and Hell*: 'Proverbs of Hell'

4 Worry is the interest paid on trouble before it falls due.

W. R. Inge in the *Observer*, 'Sayings of the Week', 14 February 1932

5 If you can keep your head when all about you are losing theirs, it's just possible you haven't grasped the situation.

Jean Kerr *Please Don't Eat the Daisies*: Introduction

6 Amnesia is not knowing who one is and wanting desperately to find out. Euphoria is not knowing who one is and not caring. Ecstasy is knowing exactly who one is – and still not caring.

Tom Robbins *Another Roadside Attraction*, Pt 3

Certainty and Doubt

1 Uncertainty is the refuge of hope.

Henri-Frédéric Amiel *Amiel's Journal*, 23 January 1881

2 If a man will begin with certainties, he shall end in doubts; but if he will be content to begin with doubts, he shall end in certainties.

Francis Bacon *The Advancement of Learning*, Bk 1, v, 8

3 Suspicions amongst thoughts are like bats amongst birds, they ever fly by twilight. **Francis Bacon** *Essays*: 'Of Suspicion'

4 We often call a certainty a hope, to bring it luck.

Elizabeth Bibesco *Haven*: 'Aphorisms'

5 If the Sun and Moon should doubt,
They'd immediately go out. **William Blake** *Auguries of Innocence*

6 Unstable and indeterminate ideas are the cause of all the mischief. It is better to be something less and that indisputably.

Nicholas-Sébastien Chamfort *Maxims and Considerations*, 42

7 Truths turn into dogmas the instant that they are disputed. Thus every man who utters a doubt defines a religion. **G. K. Chesterton** *Heretics*, Ch. 20

8 It would be wise to be sceptical even of scepticism.

Arthur C. Clarke *Profiles of the Future*, Ch. 14

9 The testimony of those who doubt the least is, not unusually, that very testimony that ought most to be doubted.

Charles Caleb Colton *Lacon*: 'Doubters'

10 It's the unstable which is solid. You have to base yourself on the uncertain. **Eugène Delacroix** letter to J.-B. Pierret, 19 August 1846

11 Scepticism? Yes, but a saint is a sceptic once in twenty-four hours.

Ralph Waldo Emerson *Journal* 1855: 'Merit Wins'

12 The man who has made up his mind for all contingencies will often be too quick for one who tries to understand.

Pieter Geyl *Debates with Historians*: 'Ranke in the Light of the Catastrophe'

13 Truth tyrannizes; doubt liberates.

Rémy de Gourmont *Selections*: 'The Problem of Style'

14 Two things which cannot be brought to perfection, unless they are learnt in youth, are music and decisiveness. **Sir Arthur Helps** *Brevia*, p. 136

15 Hesitation increases in relation to risk in equal proportion to age.

Ernest Hemingway in A. E. Hotchner, *Papa Hemingway*, Pt 1, Ch. 3

16 There is no more miserable human being than one in whom nothing is habitual but indecision. **William James** *The Principles of Psychology*, Ch. 4

17 Scepticism, then, is not avoidance of option; it is option of a certain particular kind of risk. *Better risk loss of truth than chance of error.*
William James *The Will to Believe*, 10

18 Truth, Sir, is a cow, which will yield such people [sceptics] no more milk, and so they are gone to milk the bull.
Dr Samuel Johnson in James Boswell, *Life of Johnson*, 21 July 1763

19 Despair is an expression of the total personality, doubt only of thought. **Søren Kierkegaard** *Either/Or*, Pt 2, Ch. 2

20 A women's guess is much more accurate than a man's certainty.
Rudyard Kipling *Plain Tales from the Hills*: 'Three and – An Extra'

21 It is hard to decide whether irresolution makes man more miserable or more contemptible; and whether it is always worse to make the wrong decision than to make none. **Jean de La Bruyère** *Characters*: 'Of Man', 5

22 I respect faith, but doubt is what gets you an education.
Wilson Mizner in Alva Johnston, *The Incredible Mizners*, Ch. 4

23 The uncertainties of science are no less relative than the certainties.
Jean Rostand *Pensées d'un biologiste*, p. 129

24 What men really want is not knowledge but certainty.
Bertrand Russell quoted by G. M. Carstairs in the *Listener*, 30 July 1964

25 She believed in nothing; only her scepticism kept her from being an atheist. **Jean-Paul Sartre** *Words*, Pt 1

26 Our doubts are traitors,
And make us lose the good we oft might win,
By fearing to attempt. **William Shakespeare** *Measure for Measure*, Act 1, Sc. 4, 77

27 'Tis a miserable thing to live in suspense; it is the life of a spider.
Jonathan Swift *Thoughts on Various Subjects*

28 We are not sure of sorrow,
And joy was never sure. **A. C. Swinburne** *The Garden of Proserpine*, 10

29 Cleave ever to the sunnier side of doubt.
Alfred, Lord Tennyson *The Ancient Sage*, 68

30 Life is doubt, and faith without doubt is nothing but death.
Miguel de Unamuno *Poesías*

31 Scepticism is the beginning of faith.
Oscar Wilde *The Picture of Dorian Gray*, Ch. 17

See also ***Beliefs; Faith***

Chance, Destiny and Fate

1 Each man the architect of his own fate.

Appius Caecus quoted by Sallust, *De Civitate*, 1, 2

2 If there is a God, all is well; and if chance rules, at least you need not be aimless too. **Marcus Aurelius** *Meditations*, Bk 9, 28

3 If a man look sharply, and attentively, he shall see Fortune: for though she be blind, yet she is not invisible. **Francis Bacon** *Essays*: 'Of Fortune'

4 There is no return game between a man and his stars.

Samuel Beckett *Murphy*: opening words

5 The race is not to the swift, nor the battle to the strong.

Bible, OT Ecclesiastes, 9:11

6 For Fortune lays the Plot of our Adversities in the foundation of our Felicities, blessing us in the first quadrate, to blast more sharply in the last. And since in the highest felicities there lieth a capacity of the lowest miseries, she hath this advantage from our happiness to make us truly miserable. **Sir Thomas Browne** *Christian Morals*, Pt 2, 10

7 I do not believe in a fate that falls on men however they act; but I do believe in a fate that falls on men unless they act.

G. K. Chesterton (attrib.)

8 Who does not believe in Fate proves he has not lived.

E. M. Cioran *Anathemas and Admirations*, 9

9 'Tis a gross error, held in schools,
That Fortune always favours fools. **John Gay** *Fables*, Pt 12, 119

10 He that leaveth nothing to chance will do few things ill, but he will do very few things.

Marquis of Halifax *Miscellaneous Thoughts and Reflections*: 'Of Caution and Suspicion'

11 In general, the greatest reverses of fortune are the most easily borne from a sort of dignity belonging to them.

William Hazlitt *The Life of Napoleon Bonaparte*, Ch. 53

12 He that hath not ill fortune, is troubled with good.

George Herbert *Jacula Prudentum*

13 We are all driven into the same fold. **Horace** *Odes*, xxxviii, 25

14 My fate cannot be mastered; it can only be collaborated with and thereby, to some extent, directed. Nor am I the captain of my soul; I am only its noisiest passenger.

Aldous Huxley *Adonis and the Alphabet*: 'Knowledge and Understanding'

15 Happy is the man who can only do one thing; in doing it, he fulfils his destiny.
Joseph Joubert *Notebooks*, 1819

16 Greater virtues are needed to bear good fortune than bad.
Duc de La Rochefoucauld *Maxims*, 25

17 One is never as fortunate or as unfortunate as one imagines.
Duc de La Rochefoucauld *Maxims*, 49

18 There is no good in arguing with the inevitable. The only argument available with an east wind is to put on your overcoat.
James Russell Lowell *Democracy and Addresses*: 'Democracy'

19 Whoever has perished in a battle could have escaped; whoever returns from it could have remained. All are not dead, but all were there to die.
Joseph de Maistre *The Saint Petersburg Dialogues*, 1

20 We may become the makers of our fate when we have ceased to pose as its prophets.
Karl Popper *The Open Society and Its Enemies*: Introduction

21 There's a special providence in the fall of a sparrow. If it be now, 'tis not to come; if it be not to come, it will be now; if it be not now, yet it will come: the readiness is all.
William Shakespeare *Hamlet*, Act 5, Sc. 2, (232)

22 Hanging and wiving goes by destiny.
William Shakespeare *The Merchant of Venice*, Act 2, Sc. 9, 83

Change and Revolution

1 Times change, and we change with them.
Anon. quoted in William Harrison, *Description of Britain*, 1577, Pt 3, Ch. 3

2 Beware that it be the reformation that draweth on the change; and not the desire of change that pretendeth the reformation.
Francis Bacon *Essays*: 'Of Innovations'

3 A carnival is not a revolution.
Howard Barker in the *Guardian*, 10 February 1986

4 There is in all changes something at once sordid and agreeable, which smacks of infidelity and household removals.
Charles Baudelaire *Intimate Journals*: 'My Heart Laid Bare', 4

5 Neither do men put new wine into old bottles.
Bible, NT Matthew, 9:17

6 **Revolution, n.** In politics, an abrupt change in the form of misgovernment.
Ambrose Bierce *The Devil's Dictionary*

7 Revolutions are celebrated when they are no longer dangerous.
Pierre Boulez interview in the *Guardian*, 13 January 1989

8 Little changes are the enemies of great changes. **Bertolt Brecht** *Quotation*

9 Revolutions are not made with rosewater.
Edward Bulwer-Lytton *The Parisians*, Bk 5, Ch. 7

10 To innovate is not to reform. **Edmund Burke** *A Letter to a Noble Lord*, 1796

11 A state without the means of some change is without the means of its conservation. **Edmund Burke** *Reflections on the Revolution in France*, p. 106

12 A revolution is always carried out against the gods – from that of Prometheus onwards. It is a protest against his destiny, and both tyrants and bourgeois puppets are nothing but pretexts.
Albert Camus *Notebooks 3*, February 1938

13 Posting a letter and getting married are among the few things left that are entirely romantic; for to be entirely romantic a thing must be irrevocable. **G. K. Chesterton** *Heretics*, Ch. 3

14 It is only the most intelligent and the most stupid who are not susceptible to change. **Confucius** *The Analects*, Bk 17, 3

15 Women want men to change, but they don't. Men want women to stay the same but they can't.
Shirley Conran in the *Observer*, 'They said what . . . ?', 24 December 2000

16 A man who reforms himself has contributed his full share towards the reformation of his neighbour. **Norman Douglas** *How About Europe?*, p. 5

17 We cannot reform our forefathers. **George Eliot** *Adam Bede*

18 Men are conservatives when they are least vigorous, or when they are most luxurious. They are conservatives after dinner.
Ralph Waldo Emerson *Essays*: 'New England Reformers'

19 The successful revolutionary is a statesman, the unsuccessful one a criminal. **Erich Fromm** *The Fear of Freedom*, 7

20 All successful revolutions are the kicking in of a rotten door. The violence of revolutions is the violence of men who charge into a vacuum. **J. K. Galbraith** *The Age of Uncertainty*, Ch. 3

21 Coups d'état would go much better if there were seats, boxes, and stalls so that one could see what was happening and not miss anything.
Edmond and Jules de Goncourt *Journal*, December 1851

22 Revolution is the festival of the oppressed.
Germaine Greer *The Female Eunuch*: 'Revolution'

23 After a Revolution, You see the *same Men* in the Drawing-room, and within a week the same Flatterers.
Marquis of Halifax *Political Thoughts and Reflections*: 'Of Courts'

24 It is essential to the triumph of reform that it shall never succeed.
William Hazlitt *Collected Works*, 1904, Vol. 12, p. 213

25 People change and forget to tell each other.
Lillian Hellman *Toys in the Attic*, Act 3

26 You cannot step twice into the same river, for other waters are continually flowing on. **Heraclitus** *Fragments*, 21

27 Change alone is unchanging. **Heraclitus** *Fragments*, 23

28 Revolution just as reformation stands in the churchyard.
Alexander Herzen quoted in Edward Dahlberg, *Alms for Oblivion*: 'Randolph Bourne'

29 In a time of drastic change it is the learners who inherit the future. The learned usually find themselves equipped to live in a world that no longer exists. **Eric Hoffer** *Between the Devil And the Dragon*, Pt 3: Introduction

30 Alteration though it be from worse to better, hath in it inconveniences, and those weighty. **Richard Hooker** *Of the Laws of Ecclesiastical Polity*, Bk 4, 14

31 The revolution chooses its enemies.
Saddam Hussein quoted in the *Guardian*, 10 December 1990

32 Every revolution evaporates, leaving behind only the slime of a new bureaucracy. **Franz Kafka** *The Great Wall of China: Aphorisms, 1917–1919*

33 *Plus ça change, plus c'est la même chose.* – The more things change, the more they are the same. **Alphonse Karr** *Les Guêpes*, January 1849

34 There is nothing stable in the world; uproar's your only music.
John Keats letter to G. and T. Keats, 13 January 1818

35 A riot is at bottom the language of the unheard.
Martin Luther King Jr *Chaos or Community*, Ch. 4

36 If we want things to stay as they are, things will have to change.
Giuseppe di Lampedusa *The Leopard*, Ch. 1

37 Expected revolutions often never revolve.
D. H. Lawrence letter to Willard Johnson, 19 November 1923

38 The revolt of a population injected with needs they are unable to satisfy. **Herbert Marcuse** definition of revolution in *Granta*, 16: 'Warsaw Diary'

39 Human life swings between two poles: movement and settlement.
Lewis Mumford *The City In History*, Ch. 1, 2

40 Revolutionary periods breed crime and genius. Both enjoy an opportunity to thrive. **Napoleon Bonaparte** *Maxims*

41 A revolution is an opinion backed by bayonets.
Napoleon Bonaparte *Maxims*

LIBRARY - CAÑADA COLLEGE

42 An effective revolution requires some degree of stupidity on one side and a measure of light on the other.

Antoine de Rivarol *Notes, réflexions et maximes*: 'Politique'

43 To a mankind that recognizes the equality of man everywhere, every war becomes a civil war. Now every revolution creates two people, two groups as foreign to each other as two nations.

Eugen Rosenstock-Huessy *The Christian Future or the Modern Mind Outrun*, Ch. 2

44 Every reformation must have its victims. You can't expect the fatted calf to share the enthusiasm of the angels over the prodigal's return.

Saki *Reginald on the Academy*

45 Revolutions have never lightened the burden of tyranny; they have only shifted it to another shoulder.

George Bernard Shaw *Man and Superman*: 'The Revolutionist's Handbook': Foreword

46 Man's yesterday may ne'er be like his morrow;
Nought may endure but Mutability.

P. B. Shelley *Mutability*

47 People die when curiosity goes. People have to find out, people have to know. How can there be any true revolution till we know what we're made of?

Graham Swift *Waterland*, 27

48 All change in history, all advance, comes from the non-conformists. If there had been no troublemakers, no Dissenters, we should still be living in caves.

A. J. P. Taylor *The Troublemakers*, 1

49 Fortune does not change men, it only unmasks them.

Tigers Don't Eat Grass: Oriental and Occidental Aphorisms: 'Behaviour'

50 It is always easier to talk about change than to make it. It is easier to consult than to manage.

Alvin Toffler *The Adaptive Corporation*, Ch. 12

51 Revolutions are always verbose.

Leon Trotsky *History of the Russian Revolution*, Pt 2, Ch. 12

52 Insurrection is an art, and like all arts it has its laws.

Leon Trotsky *History of the Russian Revolution*, Pt 3, Ch. 6

53 Revolutions have never succeeded unless the establishment does three-quarters of the work.

Peter Ustinov *Dear Me*, Ch. 15

54 Such is the fate of kings and generals that they are always blamed for what they do and for what they don't do.

Voltaire *The Century of Louis XIV*, Ch. 13

55 A reformer is a guy who rides through a sewer in a glass-bottomed boat.

James J. Walker speech as Mayor of New York, 1928

56 The only way a woman can ever reform a man is by boring him so completely that he loses all possible interest in life.

Oscar Wilde *The Picture of Dorian Gray*, Ch. 8

57 Revolution only needs good dreamers who remember their dreams.

Tennessee Williams *Camino Real*, Block 2

58 The only possible way there'd be an uprising in this country would be if they banned car boot sales and caravanning.

Victoria Wood stage performance at Strand Theatre, London, October 1990

Character

1 Tell me what galls you and I will tell you what you are not.

Henri-Frédéric Amiel *Amiel's Journal*, 8 September 1866

2 Look at the characters of your own associates: even the most agreeable of them are difficult to put up with: and for that matter it's difficult enough to put up with oneself. **Marcus Aurelius** *Meditations*, Bk 5, 10

3 Nature is often hidden; sometimes overcome; seldom extinguished.

Francis Bacon *Essays*: 'Of Nature in Men'

4 A man's nature runs either to herbs, or to weeds; therefore let him seasonably water the one, and destroy the other.

Francis Bacon *Essays*: 'Of Nature in Men'

5 Never ascribe to an opponent motives meaner than your own.

James Barrie 'Courage', rectorial address at St Andrews University, Scotland, 3 May 1922

6 What the English call character. By which they mean the power to refrain. **Alan Bennett** *Single Spies*: 'An Englishman Abroad'

7 A good character precludes a man from taking advantage of many opportunities by which others might profit without being blamed.

Mr Justice Charles J. Darling *Scintillae Juris*, 10

8 Human character, however it may be exalted, or depressed, by a temporary enthusiasm, will return by degrees to its proper and natural level, and will resume those passions which seem the most adapted to its present condition. **Edward Gibbon** *The Decline and Fall of the Roman Empire*, Ch. 15

9 To live in a great idea means to treat the impossible as though it were possible. It is just the same with a strong character; and when an idea and a character meet things arise which fill the world with wonder for thousands of years.

Johann Wolfgang von Goethe *Maxims and Reflections*: 'Life and Character', 239

10 Good temper is an estate for life.

William Hazlitt *The Plain Speaker*: 'On Personal Character'

11 The proper time to influence the character of a child is about a hundred years before he is born. **W. R. Inge** in the *Observer*, 21 July 1929

12 The hell to be endured hereafter, of which theology tells, is no worse than the hell we make for ourselves in this world by habitually fashioning our characters in the wrong way.

William James *The Principles of Psychology*, Vol. 1, Ch. 4

13 A man may be so much of everything, that he is nothing of anything.

Dr Samuel Johnson in James Boswell, *Life of Johnson*, 1783

14 Personality is only ripe when a person has made the truth his own.

Søren Kierkegaard *The Journals*, 1843

15 Men carry their character not seldom in their pockets: you might decide on more than half of your acquaintance, had you will or right to turn their pockets inside out.

Johann Kaspar Lavater *Aphorisms on Man*, 612; William Blake commented: 'I seldom carry money in my pockets; they are generally full of paper'

16 A character is a completely fashioned will.

J. S. Mill quoted in William James, *The Principles of Psychology*, Ch. 4

17 Character drags fortune in its train, and moulds it to its own form.

Michel de Montaigne *Essays*, Bk 1, Ch. 50

18 Tell me to what you pay attention and I will tell you who you are.

José Ortega y Gasset quoted in W. H. Auden, *A Certain World*, p. 306

19 Character is much easier kept than recovered.

Thomas Paine *The American Crisis*, 13

20 Reputation is what you are in the limelight; character what you are in the dark. Many a man's reputation and character would not recognize each other if they met. **His Honour J. Tudor Rees** *Reserved Judgement*, Ch. 21

21 There are only two qualities in the world: efficiency and inefficiency; and only two sorts of people: the efficient and the inefficient.

George Bernard Shaw *John Bull's Other Island*, Act 4

22 Education has for its object the formation of character.

Herbert Spencer *Social Statics*, Pt 2, Ch. 17.4

23 She used to be no better than she ought to be, but she is now.

James Thurber *Men, Women and Dogs*, cartoon caption

See also ***Behaviour***

Charity

1 In charity there is no excess.

Francis Bacon *Essays*: 'Of Goodness and Goodness of Nature'

2 Let not thy left hand know what thy right hand doeth.

Bible, NT Matthew, 6:3

3 Knowledge puffeth up, but charity edifieth. **Bible, NT** Corinthians, 8:1

4 **Charity, n.** An amiable quality of the heart which moves us to condone in others the sins and vices to which ourselves are addicted.

Ambrose Bierce *The Enlarged Devil's Dictionary*

5 Too many people have decided to do without generosity in order to practise charity. **Albert Camus** *The Fall* p. 84

6 I have always heard, Sancho, that doing good to base fellows is like throwing water into the sea. **Miguel Cervantes** *Don Quixote*, Pt 1, Ch. 23

7 Many a person professes to have a good heart, but in truth has only weak nerves. **Maria von Ebner-Eschenbach** *Aphorisms*, p. 32

8 True generosity consists precisely in fighting to destroy the causes which nourish false charity. **Paulo Freire** *Pedagogy of the Oppressed*, Ch. 1

9 The charity which begins at home is pretty sure to end there.

Julius and Augustus Hare *Guesses at Truth*, 1

10 There is as much charity in helping a man down-hill, as in helping him up-hill.

Dr Samuel Johnson in James Boswell, *The Journal of a Tour to the Hebrides*, 23 September 1773

11 Generosity lies less in giving much than in giving at the right moment. **Jean de La Bruyère** *Characters*: 'Of the Heart', 47

12 The generous, who is always just – and the just, who is always generous – may, unannounced, approach the throne of God.

Johann Kaspar Lavater *Aphorisms on Man*, 370; William Blake underlined last part in approval

13 There are only two classes of people, the magnanimous, and the rest.

Marcel Proust *Remembrance of Things Past: Swann's Way*: 'Swann in Love'

14 We reserve our indulgence for the perfect.

Marquis de Vauvenargues *Reflections and Maxims*, 169

15 That person who is not concerned that his brother should not perish, is in great danger of perishing himself.

Bishop Thomas Wilson *Maxims of Piety and Christianity*: 'Charity'

See also ***Giving and Taking; Love; Sympathy***

Children and Adults

1 Only those in the last stage of disease could believe that children are true judges of character. **W. H. Auden** *The Orators*: 'Journal of an Airman'

2 Children sweeten labours; but they make misfortunes more bitter.

Francis Bacon *Essays*: 'Of Parents and Children'

3 A boy does not put his hand into his pocket until every other means of gaining his end has failed. **James Barrie** *Sentimental Tommy*, Ch. 1

4 When we make life difficult for our parents, he said, we make something of ourselves. **Thomas Bernhard** *Gathering Evidence*, 2

5 He who shall teach the child to doubt
The rotting grave shall ne'er get out. **William Blake** *Auguries of Innocence*

6 Being a child is horrible. It is slightly better than being a tree or a piece of heavy machinery but not half as good as being a domestic cat.

Julie Burchill *Damaged Goods*: 'Are You Sitting Comfortably?'

7 The child passes its childhood on to smaller and smaller children.

Elias Canetti *The Secret Heart of the Clock*: '1982'

8 As fathers commonly go, it is seldom a misfortune to be fatherless; and considering the general run of sons, as seldom a misfortune to be childless. **Earl of Chesterfield** *Letters to His Son*, 15 July 1751

9 Children and subjects, though their obligations are certainly the lesser of the two, are much seldomer in the wrong than parents and kings.

Earl of Chesterfield letter to the Bishop of Waterford, 10 October 1753

10 What a wilderness were this sad world,
If man were always man and never child.

Hartley Coleridge quoted in Walter Bagehot, *Literary Studies*: 'Hartley Coleridge'

11 How inimitably graceful children are in general before they learn to dance! **Samuel Taylor Coleridge** *Table Talk*, 1 January 1832

12 Young children have no sense of wonder. They bewilder well but few things surprise them. **Annie Dillard** *An American Childhood*, Pt 2

13 Play with Children but let the Saints alone.
Dr Thomas Fuller *Introductio ad Prudentium*, 12

14 Where yet was ever found a mother,
Who'd give her booby for another? **John Gay** *Fables*, Pt 1, iii, 33

15 Your children are not your children. They are the sons and daughters of Life's longing for itself . . . you may strive to be like them, but seek not to make them like you. **Kahlil Gibran** *The Prophet*: 'Of Children'

16 Childhood is a disease – a sickness that you grow out of.
William Golding in the *Guardian*, 22 June 1990

17 There is always one moment in childhood when the door opens and lets the future in. **Graham Greene** *The Power and the Glory*, Pt 1, Ch. 1

18 In childhood eternity has no meaning – a child has not learnt to hope. **Graham Greene** *A Sort of Life*, 2:1

19 Love is presently out of breath when it is to go up Hill, from the Children to the Parents. **Marquis of Halifax** *Miscellaneous Thoughts and Reflections*

20 Alas! It is not the child, but the boy that generally survives the man.
Sir Arthur Helps *Thoughts in the Cloister and the Crowd*

21 The first service a child doth his father is to make him foolish.
George Herbert *Jacula Prudentum*

22 The growth of flesh is but a blister;
Childhood is health. **George Herbert** *The Temple*: 'Holy Baptism'

23 Children are entertaining because they are easily entertained.
Hugo von Hofmannsthal *The Book of Friends*, 1

24 Childhood's a risk we all take. **David Hughes** *The Pork Butcher*, p. 114

25 One parent is enough to spoil you but discipline takes two.
Clive James *Unreliable Memoirs*, Ch. 1

26 The reason children are the future is not that one day they will be grownups. No, the reason is that mankind is moving more and more in the direction of infancy, and childhood is the image of the future.
Milan Kundera *The Book of Laughter and Forgetting*, Pt 6, 25

27 There are some extraordinary fathers whose sole purpose in life seems to be giving their children good reason not to regret their death.
Jean de La Bruyère *Characters*: 'Of Man', 13

28 Children have neither past nor future; and unlike us, they enjoy the present. **Jean de La Bruyère** *Characters*: 'Of Man', 51

29 Children do not give up their innate imagination, curiosity, dreaminess easily. You have to love them to get them to do that.

R. D. Laing *The Politics of Experience*, Ch. 3

30 Adults are children who have failed to find a substitute for the charm they lost. **Irving Layton** *The Whole Bloody Bird*: 'aphs'

31 Looking after children is one way of looking after yourself.

Ian McEwan *Black Dogs*: Preface

32 Few misfortunes can befall a boy which bring worse consequences than to have a really affectionate mother.

W. Somerset Maugham *A Writer's Notebook*: '1896'

33 A mother loves the child more than the father does, for she knows it's her own, while he only thinks it is. **Menander** *Fragments*, 657 K

34 It is for friends to demand goodness of each other. For father and son to do so seriously undermines the love between them.

Mencius Bk 4, Pt B, 30

35 Men are more careful of the breed of their horses and dogs than of their children. **William Penn** *Reflections and Maxims*, 1, 85

36 Only the child who somewhere feels safe can take risks. Adults are less daring than children because they can never feel safe.

Adam Phillips *Monogamy*, 35

37 The best thing we can learn from children is how to lose interest. The worst thing they learn from adults is how to force their attention.

Adam Phillips *Monogamy*, 96

38 Nothing is astonishing when everything is astonishing: that is the condition of the child.

Antoine de Rivarol *Notes, réflexions et maximes*: 'Philosophe'

39 It's never too late to have a happy childhood.

Tom Robbins *Still Life with Woodpecker*: Epilogue

40 If you wish to raise your children well, treat them as though they were drunk. **Ned Rorem** *The Paris Diary*, Pt 9

41 The most infallible way to make your child miserable is to accustom him to obtain everything he desires.

Jean Jacques Rousseau quoted in *Aphorisms on Education* 1800, 82

42 Adults are obsolete children.

Dr Seuss in L. L. Levinson, *Bartlett's Unfamiliar Quotations*

43 Parents learn a lot from their children about coping with life.

Muriel Spark *The Comforters*, Ch. 6

44 A child becomes an adult when he realizes that he has a right not only to be right but also to be wrong. **Thomas S. Szasz** *The Second Sin*: 'Childhood'

45 Children who play life discern its true law and relations more clearly than men who fail to live it worthily – but think they are wiser by experience. **H. D. Thoreau** *Journal*, 5 May 1846

46 Familiarity breeds contempt – and children.
Mark Twain *Notebooks*, p. 237

47 Never have children, only grandchildren. **Gore Vidal** *Two Sisters*

48 All women become like their mothers. That is their tragedy. No man does. That's his. **Oscar Wilde** *The Importance of Being Earnest*, Act 1

49 Children begin by loving their parents; as they grow older they judge them; sometimes they forgive them.
Oscar Wilde *The Picture of Dorian Gray*, Ch. 5

50 A child has much to learn before it can pretend. (A dog cannot be a hypocrite, but neither can it be sincere.)
Ludwig Wittgenstein *Philosophical Investigations*, Pt 2, Sect. 11

See also ***Family; Relationships; Youth and Age***

Choice

1 A mistake to talk of a bad choice in love, since as soon as there is a choice it can only be a bad one.
Marcel Proust *Remembrance of Things Past: The Fugitive*, p. 700

2 Dullards are law-abiding because they choose not to choose. Outlaws, being less frightened by the bewildering variety of experience, being in fact slightly made for encounters new and extreme, will seek to choose even when no choice readily presents itself.
Tom Robbins *Still Life with Woodpecker*, 71

3 A woman whose dresses are made in Paris and whose marriage has been made in Heaven might be equally biased for and against free imports.
Saki *The Unbearable Bassington*, 9

4 There's small choice in rotten apples.
William Shakespeare *The Taming of the Shrew*, Act 1, Sc. 1, (137)

5 I cannot choose the best. The best chooses me.
Rabindranath Tagore *Stray Birds*, 20

Civilization

1 Theory of true civilization. It does not consist in gas or steam or turntables. It consists in the diminution of Original Sin.

Charles Baudelaire *Intimate Journals*: 'My Heart Laid Bare', 32

2 Civilizations are remembered by their artefacts, not their bank-rates.

Stephen Bayley in the *Observer*, 9 March 1986

3 In cultural matters, it is not demand that creates supply, it is the other way round. **Joseph Brodsky** *On Grief and Reason*: title essay

4 Civilization is a *process of approximation to an ideal state*.

R. G. Collingwood *The New Leviathan*, Pt 3, 34, 5

5 The English, on the strength of a few mechanical discoveries, have mistaken comfort for civilization.

Benjamin Disraeli in W. R. Inge, *The End of an Age*, Ch. 7

6 Civilization has made man, if not always more bloodthirsty, at least more viciously, more horribly bloodthirsty.

Fyodor Dostoevsky *Notes from the Underground*, Pt 1, 7

7 The test of civilization is the power to draw the most benefit out of cities. **Ralph Waldo Emerson** *Journal*, Spring? 1864

8 What a vast difference there is between the barbarism that precedes culture and the barbarism which follows it.

Friedrich Hebbel *Diaries*, undated

9 Civilization is the art of living in cities of such size that everyone does not know everyone else.

Julian Jaynes *The Origin of Consciousness in the Breakdown of the Bicameral Mind* Bk. 2 Ch. 1

10 A decent provision for the poor is the true test of civilization.

Dr Samuel Johnson in James Boswell, *Life of Johnson*, 1770

11 It is so stupid of modern civilization to have given up believing in the devil when he is the only explanation of it.

Mgr Ronald Knox *Let Dons Delight*, Ch. 8

12 We should know how to inherit, because inheriting is culture.

Thomas Mann quoted by Hans Werner Henze, *Music and Politics*

13 The degree of a nation's civilization is marked by its disregard for the necessities of existence. **W. Somerset Maugham** *Our Betters*, Act 1

14 All civilization is simply order, but order repeating itself.

Eugen Rosenstock-Huessy *The Christian Future or the Modern Mind Outrun*, Ch. 4

15 Civilization is a disease produced by the practice of building societies with rotten materials.

George Bernard Shaw *Man and Superman*, 'Maxims for Revolutionists': 'Civilization'

16 Civilization has made the peasantry its pack animal. The bourgeoisie in the long run only changed the form of the pack.

Leon Trotsky *History of the Russian Revolution*, Pt 3, Ch. 1

17 Civilization advances by extending the number of important operations which we can perform without thinking about them.

A. N. Whitehead *An Introduction to Mathematics*, Ch. 5

18 Civilization is hooped together, brought
Under a rule, under the semblance of peace
By manifold illusion. **W. B. Yeats** *Supernatural Songs*: 'Meru'

Comedy and Tragedy

1 Comedy is tragedy interrupted. **Alan Ayckbourn** interview

2 Tragedy is if I cut my finger . . . Comedy is if you walk into an open sewer and die. **Mel Brooks** in Kenneth Tynan, *Show People*

3 Farce may often border on tragedy; indeed farce is nearer tragedy in its essence than comedy is. **Samuel Taylor Coleridge** *Table Talk*, 25 August 1833

4 Farce is the essential theatre. Farce refined becomes high comedy: farce brutalized becomes tragedy.

Edward Gordon Craig *Index to the Story of My Days*

5 Nobody should try to play comedy unless they have a circus going on inside. **Michael Curtiz** in David Niven, *The Moon's a Balloon*, Ch. 11

6 Comedy, like sodomy, is an unnatural act.

Marty Feldman in *The Times*, 9 June 1969

7 Show me a hero and I will write you a tragedy.

F. Scott Fitzgerald *Notebooks*, E

8 Avoiding humiliation is the core of tragedy and comedy.

John Guare in the *Independent*, 17 October 1988

9 We participate in a tragedy; at a comedy we only look.

Aldous Huxley *The Devils of Loudun*, Ch. 11

10 Comedy is a game played to throw reflections upon social life.

George Meredith *The Egoist*: opening words

11 Comedy, we may say, is society protecting itself – with a smile.
J. B. Priestley *George Meredith*

12 Irony is not tragic, it is just a deeply seductive way of getting you to waste your own time.
Jane Stevenson *Several Deceptions*: 'The Colonel and Judy O'Grady'

13 The bad end unhappily, the good unluckily. That is what tragedy means. **Tom Stoppard** *Rosencrantz and Guildenstern are Dead*, Act 2

14 In the best comedy, there is clearly something wrong, but it is secret and unstated – not even implied. Comedy is the public version of a private darkness. **Paul Theroux** *My Secret History*, V, 7

15 Everything must be taken seriously, nothing tragically.
Adolphe Thiers speech in French National Assembly, 24 May 1873

16 And killing time is perhaps the essence of comedy, just as the essence of tragedy is killing eternity.
Miguel de Unamuno *San Manuel Bueno*: Prologue

17 The world is a comedy to those that think, a tragedy to those that feel. **Horace Walpole** letter to the Countess of Upper Ossory, 16 August 1776

See also ***Drama; Laughing Matters; Wit***

Conscience and Consciousness

1 **Philanthropist, n.** A rich [and usually bald] old gentleman who has trained himself to grin while his conscience is picking his pocket.
Ambrose Bierce *The Devil's Dictionary*

2 It requires a considerable amount of unconsciousness to devote oneself unreservedly to anything.
E. M. Cioran *A Short History of Decay*, 6: 'Making Allowances'

3 Consciousness is a symptom of estrangement from life caused by illness. Everything that is *not* nature was revealed to the first sick man when he looked up at the sky for the first time. **E. M. Cioran** *Tears and Saints*

4 If we could buy consciences for what they are worth and sell them at their own valuation, what a profit we should make!
Henri Daumier quoted in J. Raymond Solly, *A Cynic's Breviary*

5 Of consciousness, her awful Mate
The Soul cannot be rid –
As easy as secreting her
Behind the Eyes of God. **Emily Dickinson** *Complete Poems*, 894

6 Solomon's Proverbs, I think, have omitted to say, that as a sore palate findeth grit, so an uneasy consciousness heareth innuendoes.

George Eliot *Middlemarch*, Bk 3, Ch. 31

7 Consciousness, which is the principle of liberty, is not the principle of art. We listen badly to a symphony when we know we are listening. We think badly when we know we are thinking. Consciousness of thinking is not thought. **Rémy de Gourmont** *Selected Writings*

8 Rational consciousness, as we call it, is but one special type of consciousness, whilst all about it, parted from it by the filmiest of screens, there lie potential forms of consciousness entirely different.

William James *The Varieties of Religious Experience*, Lectures 16–17

9 Men never sin so completely and so cheerfully as when they do so for conscience's sake. **Blaise Pascal** *Pensées*, 794

10 When a man is asleep, he has in a circle round him the chain of the hours, the sequence of the years, the order of the heavenly host.

Marcel Proust *Remembrance of Things Past: Swann's Way*: 'Overture'

11 The English have a proverb: 'Conscience makes cowboys of us all.'

Saki *Wratislav*

See also Shakespeare; Wilde

12 Conscience does make cowards of us all;
And thus the native hue of resolution
Is sicklied o'er with the pale cast of thought.

William Shakespeare *Hamlet*, Act 3, Sc. 1, 83

See also Saki; Wilde

13 Most people sell their souls, and live with a good conscience on the proceeds. **Logan Pearsall Smith** *Afterthoughts*, 3

14 The conscience has morbid sensibilities; it must be employed but not indulged, like the imagination or the stomach.

Robert Louis Stevenson *Ethical Studies*, p. 84

15 It is very certain that there may be met with, in public life, a species of conscience which is all bridle and no spurs.

Sir Henry Taylor *The Statesman*, Ch. 9

16 Nothing makes one so vain as being told that one is a sinner. Conscience makes egotists of us all. **Oscar Wilde** *The Picture of Dorian Gray*, Ch. 8

See also Saki; Shakespeare

Courage and Cowardice

1 In civil business; what first? Boldness; what second, and third? Boldness. And yet boldness is a child of ignorance and baseness.

Francis Bacon *Essays*: 'Of Boldness'

2 Are the brave, then, only failed cowards, cowards without the guts to run away? **Julian Barnes** *Staring at the Sun*, Pt 3

See also Fuller; Montaigne; Rochester

3 Cowardice and courage are never without a measure of affectation. Nor is love. Feelings are never true. They play with their mirrors.

Jean Baudrillard *Cool Memories*, Ch. 2

4 Most acts of assent require far more courage than most acts of protest, since courage is clearly a readiness to risk self-humiliation.

Nigel Dennis *Boys and Girls Come Out to Play*

5 Courage is prompted as often by despair as by hope; we have nothing to lose or everything to gain. **Comtesse Diane** *Maxims of Life*, p. 121

6 Many would be cowards if they had courage enough.

Dr Thomas Fuller *Gnomologia*, 3366

See also Barnes; Montaigne; Rochester

7 Few persons have courage enough to appear as good as they really are. **Julius and Augustus Hare** *Guesses at Truth*, 2

8 A woman's as bold as she looks; a man as bold as he feels.

Joseph Joubert *Pensées*, p. 12

9 It requires moral courage to grieve; it requires religious courage to rejoice. **Søren Kierkegaard** *The Journals*, 1840

10 Perfect valour consists in doing without witnesses what one would be capable of doing before the world at large.

Duc de La Rochefoucauld *Maxims*, 216

11 Courage is not simply *one* of the virtues but the form of every virtue at the testing point, which means at the point of highest reality.

C. S. Lewis *The Screwtape Letters*, 29

12 It needs courage to be afraid. **Michel de Montaigne** *Essays*, Bk 3, Ch. 6

See also Barnes; Fuller; Rochester

13 Cowards' hearts beat faster than heroes' but last longer.

Zarko Petan *Aforismi A–Z*

14 For all men would be cowards, if they durst.
John Wilmot, Earl of Rochester *A Satire against Mankind*, 158

See also Barnes; Fuller; Montaigne

15 Of all forms of caution, caution in love is perhaps the most fatal to true happiness. **Bertrand Russell** *The Conquest of Happiness*, Ch. 12

16 People who have more temperament than courage are in a bad way.
Arthur Schnitzler *Aphorismen und Betrachtungen*, p. 268

17 The better part of valour is discretion.
William Shakespeare *Henry IV, Pt 1*, Act 5, Sc. 4, (120)

18 Cowards die many times before their deaths:
The valiant never taste of death but once.
William Shakespeare *Julius Caesar*, Act 2, Sc. 2, 82

19 For courage mounteth with occasion.
William Shakespeare *King John*, Act 2, Sc. 1, 82

20 Anxiety is the unwillingness to play even when you know the odds are for you.
Courage is the willingness to play even when you know the odds are against you. **Thomas S. Szasz** *The Second Sin*: 'Emotions'

21 Fortune favours the brave. **Terence** *Phormio*, 203

22 It takes a valour to open the hearts of men superior to that which opens the gates of cities. **H. D. Thoreau** *Journal*, 1842

23 Except a creature be part coward it is not a compliment to say it is brave; it is merely a loose misapplication of the word.
Mark Twain *Pudd'nhead Wilson*, Ch. 12: epigraph

Creation and Creativity

1 All creation is omniscient – only the individual does not know when he will reach the terminus. **Swami Sri Ananda Acharya** *Aphorisms*, 22

2 Inspiration always comes when a man wishes; but it does not always go when he wishes. **Charles Baudelaire** *Intimate Journals*: 'Rockets', 11

3 Everyone is as God made him, and often a good deal worse.
Miguel Cervantes *Don Quixote*, Pt 2, 4

4 Creative writers are always greater than the causes that they represent. **E. M. Forster** *Two Cheers for Democracy*: 'Gide and George'

5 God is good! He created mankind for me to give me sustenance! said the tape-worm. **Friedrich Hebbel** *Diaries*, entry 3764, 1846

6 Both the revolutionary and the creative individual are perpetual juveniles. The revolutionary does not grow up because he cannot grow, while the creative individual cannot grow up because he keeps growing.
Eric Hoffer *Between the Devil and the Dragon*, Pt 1: Introduction

7 Matter and force are the two names of the one artist who fashions the living as well as the lifeless. **T. H. Huxley** *Aphorisms and Reflections*, 55

8 Only one grain of matter was needed to create the world. But a whole world was needed to create one soul. It is a work that cannot be done with little. **Joseph Joubert** *Notebooks*, 1800

9 Art is a parable of the Creation; it is an example, as the terrestrial is an example of the cosmos. **Paul Klee** in Felix Klee, *Paul Klee*, 15

10 Nothing is lost, nothing is created.
Antoine Lavoisier quoted in Simone Weil, *The Need for Roots*: 'The Growing of Roots'

11 God creates the animals; man creates himself.
Georg Christoph Lichtenberg *The Lichtenberg Reader*: Aphorisms 1775–9

12 The impulse to propagate our race has propagated a lot of other things too. **Georg Christoph Lichtenberg** *The Lichtenberg Reader*: Aphorisms 1775–9

13 Nothing can be created out of nothing.
Lucretius *On the Nature of Things*, Bk 1, 155

14 God, who repented of having created man, never repented of having created woman.
François de Malherbe in J. de Finod, *A Thousand Flashes of French Wit*, p. 177

15 The artist's egoism is outrageous; it must be; he is by nature a solipsist and the world exists only for him to exercise upon it his powers of creation. **W. Somerset Maugham** *The Summing Up*, Ch. 61

16 Politics is the art of the possible; creativity is the art of the impossible.
Ben Okri *A Way of Being Free*: 'The Joys of Storytelling III', 101

17 All I have ever made was made for the present, and with the hope that it will always remain in the present.
Pablo Picasso in John Berger, *The Success and Failure of Picasso*, 1

18 The highest praise of God consists in the denial of him by the atheist who finds creation so perfect that he can dispense with a creator.
Marcel Proust *Remembrance of Things Past: The Guermantes Way*, 2

19 Procreation – is it not also the *utterance* of oneself to the world?
V. V. Rozanov *Fallen Leaves*, p. 84

20 The Creator created not only the world, but he also created possibility itself: therefore he should have created the possibility of a better world than this one. **Arthur Schopenhauer** quoted in D. J. Enright, *Interplay*, p. 146

21 God finds himself by creating. **Rabindranath Tagore** *Stray Birds*, 46

22 God made everything out of nothing. But the nothingness shows through. **Paul Valéry** *Bad Thoughts and Not So Bad*, T

23 God created man and, finding that he was not lonely enough, gave him a wife, so as to make him feel his solitude more keenly.
Paul Valéry *Odds and Ends*: 'Moralities'

See Chekhov on marriage

24 The art of creation
is older than the art of killing. **Andrei Voznesensky** *Poem with a Footnote*

25 We are the products of editing, rather than authorship.
George Wald in *Annals of New York Academy of Sciences*, Vol. 69, 1957: 'The Origin of Optical Activity'

26 The distance between the necessary and the good is the distance between the creature and the creator.
Simone Weil *Gravity and Grace*: 'The Distance Between'

27 Creation employs all its critical faculty within its own sphere. It may not use it in the sphere that belongs to others. It is exactly because a man cannot do a thing that he is the proper judge of it.
Oscar Wilde *The Critic as Artist*, 2

Crime and Punishment

1 Prison is an effective deterrent to those who walk past the gate, not through it. **Roger Attrill** in the *New Statesman*, September 1980

2 Severity breedeth fear, but roughness breedeth hate. Even reproofs from authority ought to be grave and not taunting.
Francis Bacon *Essays*: 'Of Great Place'

3 All punishment is mischief: all punishment in itself is evil.
Jeremy Bentham *Principles of Morals and Legislation*, Ch. 13

4 He that spareth his rod hateth his son. **Bible, OT** Proverbs, 13:24

5 It is better that ten guilty persons escape than one innocent suffer.
Sir William Blackstone *Commentary on the Laws of England*, IV, 27

6 The formula for prison is lack of space counterbalanced by a surplus of time. **Joseph Brodsky** *Less Than One*: title essay

7 How many crimes committed merely because their authors could not endure being wrong! **Albert Camus** *The Fall* p. 16

8 Poverty sets a reduced price on crime.
Nicholas-Sébastien Chamfort *Maxims and Considerations*

9 The terrorist and the policeman both come from the same basket.
Joseph Conrad *The Secret Agent*, Ch. 4

10 Detectives are only policemen with smaller feet.
Marlene Dietrich in Alfred Hitchcock film *Stage Fright*, script by Whitfield Cook *et al.* from S. Jepson, *Man Running*

11 Assassination has never changed the course of history.
Benjamin Disraeli speech in House of Commons, 1 May 1865

12 Like all art and politics, gangsterism is a very important avenue of assimilation into society.
E. L. Doctorow in the *International Herald Tribune*, 1 October 1990

13 Commit a crime and the earth is made of glass.
Ralph Waldo Emerson *Essays*: 'Compensation'

14 Crimes of which a people is ashamed constitute its real history. The same is true of man. **Jean Genet** *The Screens*: notes

15 Most of the crimes which disturb the internal peace of society are produced by the restraints which the necessary but unequal laws of property have imposed on the appetites of mankind, by confining to a few the possession of those objects that are coveted by many.
Edward Gibbon *The Decline and Fall of the Roman Empire*, Ch. 4

16 Men are not hang'd for stealing horses, but that Horses may not be stolen. **Marquis of Halifax** *Political Thoughts and Reflections*: 'Of Punishment'

17 Policing's largely the fine art of getting through biros.
David Hare *Murmuring Judges*, Act 1, Sc. 5

18 A man who has been hanged is not the worst subject for dissection, and a man who deserves to be hanged may be a very amusing companion or topic of discourse. **William Hazlitt** *Characteristics*, 304

19 If you condemn a fish to death, don't throw it in the water.
Friedrich Hebbel *Diaries*, entry 4084, 1847

20 A burglar who respects his art always takes his time before taking anything else. **O. Henry** *Makes the Whole World Kin*

21 The best grafts in the world are built up on copybook maxims and psalms and proverbs and Esau's fables. They seem to kind of hit off human nature.
O. Henry *A Tempered Wind*

22 He that is taken and put into prison or chains is not conquered, though overcome; for he is still an enemy.
Thomas Hobbes *Leviathan*: 'A Review and Conclusion'

23 Keepin' mum about bein' insane till you git all your murderin' done don't count.
'Kin' Hubbard *Abe Martin's Wisecracks*, p. 77

24 When a man knows he is to be hanged in a fortnight, it concentrates his mind wonderfully.
Dr Samuel Johnson in James Boswell, *Life of Johnson*, 19 September 1777

25 The traveller with empty pockets will sing in the thief's face.
Juvenal *Satires*, X, 22

26 Penalties serve to deter those who are not inclined to commit any crimes.
Karl Kraus *Half-Truths and One-and-a-Half Truths*: 'Lord, Forgive the . . .'

27 If poverty is the mother of crime, lack of intelligence is its father.
Jean de La Bruyère *Characters*: 'Of Man', 13

28 Murder, like love-making, is a form of cognition.
Both have been shaken from the same tree.
Irving Layton *The Whole Bloody Bird*: 'aphs'

29 Crimes are created by Parliament; it needs a policeman to make a criminal. You don't become a criminal by breaking the law, but by getting found out.
Edmund Leach *Runaway World*, Ch. 3

30 It's questionable whether, when we break a murderer on the wheel, we aren't lapsing into precisely the mistake of the child who hits the chair he bumps into.
Georg Christoph Lichtenberg *The Lichtenberg Reader*: Aphorisms, 1789

31 'Irregularity' means there's been a crime but you can't prove it. 'Malpractice' means there's been a crime and you can prove it.
Jonathan Lynn and Antony Jay *Yes, Prime Minister*, Vol. 2: 'A Conflict of Interest'

32 Crime is only a left-handed form of human endeavour.
Ben Maddow and John Huston *The Asphalt Jungle*,
film script from novel of W. R. Burnett

33 The one who kills is always his victim's inferior.
Vladimir Nabokov *Pale Fire*: Commentary on lines 597–608

34 The idea of sin and punishment diverted man's anger from his neighbour to himself.
Friedrich Nietzsche *Nietzsche in Outline and Aphorism*: 'Morality'

35 Perhaps we should punish people less for their crime than for the worry of being no different from us, apart from their crime.

Jean Rostand *Pensées d'un biologiste*, p. 26

36 A man can be prevented from stealing but not from being a thief.

Arthur Schnitzler *Aphorismen und Betrachtungen*, p. 127

37 Really premeditated crimes are those that are not committed.

Leonardo Sciascia *1912+1*

38 Crime is only the retail department of what, in wholesale, we call penal law.

George Bernard Shaw *Man and Superman*, 'Maxims for Revolutionists': 'Crime and Punishment'

39 If you strike a child, take care that you strike it in anger, even at the risk of maiming it for life. A blow in cold blood neither can nor should be forgiven.

George Bernard Shaw *Man and Superman*, 'Maxims for Revolutionists': 'How to Beat Children'

40 Assassination is the extreme form of censorship.

George Bernard Shaw *The Shewing-up of Blanco Posnet*: Preface, 'The Limits to Toleration'

41 Where crime is concerned, a good education instils remorse; and foreseen remorse acts as a deterrent. **Stendhal** *Love*, Bk, 1, Ch. 5

42 Those who offend us are generally punished for the offence they give; but we so frequently miss the satisfaction of knowing that we are avenged! **Anthony Trollope** *The Small House at Allington*, Ch. 50

43 The crime is followed by fear and that is its punishment.

Voltaire *Sémiramis*, Act 5, Sc. 1

44 Anyone who has been to an English public school will always feel comparatively at home in prison. **Evelyn Waugh** *Decline and Fall*, Ch. 4

45 When the gods wish to punish us they answer our prayers.

Oscar Wilde *An Ideal Husband*, Act 2

46 I should fancy that murder is always a mistake. One should never do anything one cannot talk about after dinner.

Oscar Wilde *The Picture of Dorian Gray*, Ch. 19

Critics

1 The good critic ought to be master of the three capacities, the three modes of seeing men and things – he should be able simultaneously to see them as they are, as they might be, and as they ought to be.

Henri-Frédéric Amiel *Amiel's Journal*, 7 November 1878

2 Genuine polemics approach a book as lovingly as a cannibal spices a baby.

Walter Benjamin *One-Way Street*: 'Post No Bills'

3 The art of the critic in a nutshell: to coin slogans without betraying ideas.

Walter Benjamin *One-Way Street*: 'Post No Bills'

4 Perhaps the highest function of criticism is to tell people why they like things.

Bernard Berenson *Notebooks*, 11 December 1892

5 **Critic, n.** A person who boasts himself hard to please because nobody tries to please him.

Ambrose Bierce *The Enlarged Devil's Dictionary*

6 To many people dramatic criticism must seem like an attempt to tattoo soap bubbles.

John Mason Brown quoted in Frank Muir, *The Frank Muir Book*

7 He read the books after reviewing them. Thus he already knew what he thought about them.

Elias Canetti *The Secret Heart of the Clock*: '1981'

See also Smith

8 The great critics, of whom there are piteously few, build a home for the truth.

Raymond Chandler letter to Frederick Lewis Allen, 7 May 1948

9 Either criticism is no good at all (a very defensible position) or else criticism means saying about an author the very things that would have made him jump out of his boots.

G. K. Chesterton *Charles Dickens*, Ch. 10

10 Think before you speak is criticism's motto; speak before you think creation's.

E. M. Forster *Two Cheers for Democracy*: 'The Raison d'Être of Criticism'

11 A good critic is one who narrates the adventures of his mind among masterpieces.

Anatole France *Literary Life*, I: 'Dedicatory'

12 Criticism is like Ate: she pursues authors, but she limps.

Johann Wolfgang von Goethe *Maxims and Reflections* (Penguin), 102

13 In this country every criminal has the privilege of being tried by his peers, but an author.

Fulke Greville *Maxims, Characters and Reflections*, p. 250

14 Asking a working writer what he thinks about critics is like asking a lamp-post how it feels about dogs.

Christopher Hampton in the *Sunday Times Magazine*, 16 October 1977

15 To accuse requires less eloquence [such is man's nature] than to excuse. **Thomas Hobbes** *Leviathan*

16 Parodies and caricatures are the most penetrating of criticisms. **Aldous Huxley** *Point Counter Point*, Ch. 28

17 A writer cannot learn about his readers from his critics: they are different races. **Randall Jarrell** *A Sad Heart at the Supermarket*: 'Poets, Critics and Readers'

18 Critics are a kind of Tinkers; that make more faults than they mend ordinarily. **Ben Jonson** *Timber or Discoveries Made Upon Men and Matter*, 129

19 In the arts, the critic is the only independent source of information. The rest is advertising. **Pauline Kael** in *Newsweek*, 24 December 1973

20 Let us consider the critic, therefore, as a *discoverer of discoveries*. **Milan Kundera** in *Review of Contemporary Fiction*, Summer 1989: 'On Criticism, Aesthetics and Europe'

21 A wise scepticism is the first attribute of a good critic. **James Russell Lowell** *Among My Books*: 'Shakespeare Once More'

22 One needs very strong ears to hear oneself freely criticized. **Michel de Montaigne** *Essays*, Bk 3, Ch. 13

23 We should try to judge the work of others by the most that it is, and our own, if not by the least that it is, take the least into consideration. **Marianne Moore** in *Writers at Work, Second Series*, ed. George Plimpton

24 They have a right to censure that have a heart to help: the rest is cruelty, not justice. **William Penn** *Reflections and Maxims*, I, 46

25 When critics get together, they talk about spatial relationships. When painters get together, they talk about turpentine. **Pablo Picasso** quoted by David Mamet in the *Guardian*, 27 August 1999

26 Take heed of critics when they are not fair; resist them even when they are. **Jean Rostand** *The Substance of Man*: 'A Biologist's Thoughts', Ch. 8

27 He who can distinguish a good fruit from a bad with his palate does not have to be able to express the distinction through a chemical formula and does not need the formula to recognize the distinction. **Arnold Schoenberg** *The Theory of Harmony*, Ch. 22

28 I never read a book before reviewing it, it prejudices a man so. **Revd Sydney Smith** in Hesketh Pearson, *The Smith of Smiths*, Ch. 3

See also Canetti

29 The prudent critic will try himself by his achievements rather than by his ideals, and his neighbours, living and dead alike, by their ideals not less than by their achievements.

R. H. Tawney *Religion and the Rise of Capitalism*, Ch. 5

30 A good drama critic is one who perceives what is happening in the theatre of his time. A great drama critic also perceives what is not happening.

Kenneth Tynan *Tynan Right and Left*: Foreword

31 A critic is a man who knows the way but can't drive the car.

Kenneth Tynan in the *New York Times Magazine*, 9 January 1966

32 That is what the highest criticism really is, the record of one's own soul.

Oscar Wilde *The Critic as Artist*, 1

33 The moment criticism exercises any influence, it ceases to be criticism. The aim of the true critic is to try to chronicle his own moods, not to try to correct the masterpieces of others.

Oscar Wilde interview quoted in *Epigrams of Oscar Wilde*: 'Criticism'

See also ***Art and Artists; Drama; Literature; Writing***

Desires

1 Passion is the form in which genius comes to the untalented.

Elizabeth Bibesco *Haven*: 'Aphorisms'

2 He who desires but acts not breeds pestilence.

William Blake *The Marriage of Heaven and Hell*: 'Proverbs of Hell'

3 Sooner murder an infant in its cradle than nurse unacted desires.

William Blake *The Marriage of Heaven and Hell*: 'Proverbs of Hell'

4 All men that are ruined are ruined on the side of their natural propensities. **Edmund Burke** *Two Letters on the Proposals for Peace with the Regicide Directory*

5 The man's desire is for the woman; but the woman's desire is rarely other than for the desire of the man.

Samuel Taylor Coleridge *Table Talk*, 23 July 1827

6 Human longings are perversely obstinate; and to the man whose mouth is watering for a peach, it is no use to offer the largest vegetable marrow. **George Eliot** *Scenes of Clerical Life*: 'Mr Gilfil's Love-Story', Ch. 2

7 Why do we always want what we haven't got? You might equally well ask, wouldn't it be more convenient if we were hungry for the last meal instead of the next one? **Michael Frayn** *Constructions*, 57

8 We are never further from our desires than when we imagine we possess what we desire. **Johann Wolfgang von Goethe** *Elective Affinities*, Pt 2, Ch. 5

9 So true is it that the path of desire, once trodden, remains frequented, that we not only keep wanting what we cannot have but go on wanting what we no longer really want.

Eric Hoffer *Between the Devil and the Dragon*, 1: Introduction

10 Some luck lies in not getting what you thought you wanted but getting what you have, which once you have it you may be smart enough to see is what you would have wanted had you known.

Garrison Keillor *Lake Wobegon Days*: 'Revival'

11 It belongs to the imperfection of everything human that man can only attain his desire by passing through its opposite.

Søren Kierkegaard *The Journals*, 1841

12 And a woman is only a woman, but a good cigar is a smoke.

Rudyard Kipling *The Betrothed*

13 Uncertain wishes express themselves in speech, strong ones in action.

Gustave Le Bon *Hier et demain*

14 Let anyone examine the things he has wished for all his life. If he is happy, it is because the fond hopes have not been realized.

Prince de Ligne quoted in J. Raymond Solly, *A Cynic's Breviary*

15 Our capacity for disgust, let me observe, is in proportion to our desires; that is in proportion to the intensity of our attachment to the things of this world. **Thomas Mann** *The Confessions of Felix Krull*, Pt 1, Ch. 5

16 Perhaps we should remember, before we take flight into grand ideas about human nature – or even worse, the human condition – that there is a difference between having something because you want it, and wanting something because you have it. **Adam Phillips** *Monogamy*, 111

17 We do not succeed in changing things according to our desire, but gradually our desire changes.

Marcel Proust *Remembrance of Things Past: The Sweet Cheat Gone*, Ch. 1

18 What comes by wishing is never truly ours. **Publilius Syrus** *Moral Sayings*, 1

19 You can keep going on much less attention than you crave.

Idries Shah *Reflections*: 'Viability'

20 I want to make this movie so much I'd stab *myself* in the back.

Joel Silver (attrib.) of film *Die Hard*

21 The other day we had a long discourse with [Lady Orkney] about love; and she told us a saying . . . which I thought excellent, that in men, desire begets love, and in women that love begets desire.

Jonathan Swift *Journal to Stella*, 30 October 1712

22 The only difference between a caprice and a life-long passion is that the caprice lasts a little longer. **Oscar Wilde** *The Picture of Dorian Gray*, Ch. 2

23 The wish precedes the event, the will accompanies it.

Ludwig Wittgenstein *Notebooks 1914–16*, 4 November 1916

See also **Emotions**

Differences and Similarities

1 All colours will agree in the dark. **Francis Bacon** *Essays*: 'Of Unity in Religion'

2 In the East the ordeal is one of privation, in the West one of choice.
Saul Bellow *More Die of Heartbreak*

3 Consistency requires you to be as ignorant today as you were a year ago. **Bernard Berenson** *Notebooks*, 1892

4 Without contraries is no progression. Attraction and repulsion, reason and energy, love and hate, are necessary to human existence.
William Blake *The Marriage of Heaven and Hell*: 'The Argument'

5 The cistern contains: the fountain overflows.
William Blake *The Marriage of Heaven and Hell*: 'Proverbs of Hell'

6 Men are close to one another by nature. They only diverge as a result of repeated practice. **Confucius** *The Analects*, Bk 17, 2

7 There is often a greater contrast between the same person at two different ages and two people of the same age. **Comtesse Diane** *Les Glanes de la vie*, p. 115

8 A foolish consistency is the hobgoblin of little minds, adored by little statesmen and philosophers and divines.
Ralph Waldo Emerson *Essays*: 'Self-Reliance'

9 We are so made that we can derive intense enjoyment from a contrast and very little from a state of things.
Sigmund Freud *Civilization and Its Discontents*, Ch. 2

10 Everything is simpler than one can imagine, at the same time more complicated than can be comprehended.
Johann Wolfgang von Goethe *Maxims and Reflections* (Penguin), 1209

11 In the country of the blind the one-eyed man is lucky to escape with his life. **Celia Green** *The Decline and Fall of Science*: 'Aphorisms'

12 Men endeavour to hold to a mathematical consistency in things, instead of recognizing that certain things may both be good and mutually antagonistic. **Thomas Hardy** *Diary*, 8 September 1896

13 The way up and the way down are one and the same.
Heraclitus *Fragments*, 108

14 It is the stretched soul that makes music, and souls are stretched by the pull of opposites – opposite bents, tastes, yearnings, loyalties. Where there is no polarity – where energies flow smoothly in one direction – there will be much doing but no music.
Eric Hoffer *Between the Devil and the Dragon*, 2: Introduction

15 Consistency is contrary to nature, contrary to life. The only completely consistent people are the dead.

Aldous Huxley *Do What You Will*: 'Wordsworth in the Tropics'

See also Agenbegyan in ***Agreement***

16 Some people are different from the rest of us, and so are the rest of us. **Clive James** *Falling Towards England*, Ch. 13

17 If we cannot now end our differences, at least we can help make the world safe for diversity.

President John F. Kennedy address at American University, Washington, 10 June 1963

18 A keeper is only a poacher turned outside in, and a poacher a keeper turned inside out. **Charles Kingsley** *The Water Babies*, Ch. 1

19 East is East, and West is West, and never the twain shall meet.

Rudyard Kipling *The Ballad of East and West*

20 What is food to one man is bitter poison to others.

Lucretius *On the Nature of Things*, IV, 637

21 My dream is of a world in which one respects differences and abolishes frontiers. But we are moving towards a world that respects frontiers and abolishes differences.

Amin Maalouf interview in the *Guardian*, 18 November 1994

22 There's as much difference between us and ourselves as between us and others. **Michel de Montaigne** *Essays*, Bk 2, Ch. 1

23 The quest for righteousness is Oriental, the quest for knowledge, Occidental. **Sir William Osler** *Aphorisms*, 179

24 We would prefer our alternatives to be opposites. It narrows the field, by making a path. **Adam Phillips** *Monogamy*, 104

25 Banks exist to lend banknotes and dictionaries to lend words. But what cannot be borrowed is the distinction between one note and another. **Carl Fredrik Reuterswärd** in *Multi-Media Dictionary of 20th Century Art*

26 You have only to live: you see everything and its opposite.

Charles-Augustin Sainte-Beuve in J. de Finod, *A Thousand Flashes of French Wit*: 'Life and Death'

27 Quite a common observation is: 'It takes all sorts to make a world.' This may well be true: but if it is – where are they all?

Idries Shah *Reflections*: 'The Difference between Saying and Doing'

28 Like all young men, you greatly exaggerate the difference between one young woman and another. **George Bernard Shaw** *Major Barbara*, Act 3

29 If we were not always bringing ourselves into comparison with others, we should know them better.

Revd Sydney Smith quoted by Mrs A. Jameson, *A Commonplace Book*

30 Opposition is so strong a likeness as to remind us of the difference.

H. D. Thoreau *Journal*, 12 February 1840

31 Even consistency though it is much abused is sometimes a virtue.

H. D. Thoreau *Journal*, after 19 April 1851

32 A man finds it almost as difficult to be inconsistent in his language as to be consistent in his conduct.

Alexis de Tocqueville *Democracy in America*, Vol. 2

33 The sage concluded: 'Now I shall sum up my teaching. It is contained in two axioms:
"All different things are identical."
"All identicals are different."'

Paul Valéry *Bad Thoughts and Not So Bad*, A

34 Men differ by what they show, and have in common what they hide.

Paul Valéry *Petites études*: 'Things Human'

Diplomacy

1 An ambassador is not simply an agent: he is also a spectacle. He is sent abroad for show as well as substance.

Walter Bagehot *The English Constitution*, Ch. 4

2 Tact in audacity consists in knowing how far we may go too far.

Jean Cocteau *Cock and Harlequin*, p. 7

3 Diplomacy doesn't go well with consistent contempt.

Joseph Conrad *Victory*, Pt 4, Ch. 5

4 Tact is good taste in action.

Comtesse Diane *Maxims of Life*, p. 71

5 A diplomat is a man who always remembers a woman's birthday but never remembers her age.

Robert Frost in *Treasury of Humorous Quotations*, ed. Evan Esar and Nicolas Bentley

6 Diplomacy – lying in state.

Oliver Herford in Laurence J. Peter, *Peter's Quotations*

7 ***Diplomat***: A man who says 'perhaps' when he means no, as opposed to a woman who says 'perhaps' when she means yes.

Elbert Hubbard *The Roycroft Dictionary*

8 How is the world ruled and led to war? Diplomats lie to journalists and believe these lies when they see them in print.

Karl Kraus *Half-Truths and One-and-a-Half Truths*: 'In this War . . .'

9 The only decent diplomat is a deaf Trappist. **John Le Carré** *A Perfect Spy*, 3

10 The basic rule for the safe handling of Foreign Affairs is that it is simply too dangerous to get involved in diplomacy. Diplomacy is about surviving till the next century – politics is about surviving till Friday afternoon. **Jonathan Lynn and Antony Jay** *Yes, Prime Minister*, Vol. 1: 'A Victory'

11 If an ambassador says yes, it means perhaps; if he says perhaps, it means no; if he ever said no, he would cease to be an ambassador.

K. M. Panikkar in *New Light's Dictionary of Quotations*, compiled Ved Bhushan

12 Diplomacy is letting someone else have your way.

Lester Pearson quoted in the *Observer*, 18 March 1965

13 The tact of a woman excels the skill of men.

Anthony Trollope *Claverings*, Ch. 41

14 A diplomat these days is nothing but a head-waiter who's allowed to sit down occasionally. **Peter Ustinov** *Romanoff and Juliet*, Act 1

15 An ambassador is an honest man sent to lie abroad for the good of his country.

Sir Henry Wotton written in Christopher Fleckmore's album, 1604; quoted in Izaak Walton, *Life of Sir Henry Wotton*

See also ***Politics***

Discovery and Invention

1 They are ill discoverers that think there is no land, when they can see nothing but sea. **Francis Bacon** *The Advancement of Learning*, Bk 1, vii, 5

2 As the births of living creatures at first are ill-shapen, so are all innovations, which are the births of time.

Francis Bacon *Essays*: 'Of Innovations'

3 One invention still lacking: how to reverse explosions.

Elias Canetti *The Human Province*: '1945'

4 The progress of invention is really a threat. Whenever I see a railroad I look for a republic. **Ralph Waldo Emerson** *Journal*, August–September 1866

5 Central heating, French rubber goods, and cookbooks are three amazing proofs of man's ingenuity in transforming necessity into art, and, of these, cookbooks are perhaps most lastingly delightful.

M. F. K. Fisher *Serve It Forth*: 'The Curious Nose'

6 Inventions that are not made, like babies that are not born, are rarely missed. **J. K. Galbraith** *The Affluent Society*, Ch. 9, Sect. 3

7 What you invent you do with love; what you have learnt you do with certainty. **Johann Wolfgang von Goethe** *Maxims and Reflections* (Penguin), 1142

8 Two feelings most difficult to get over: to have found something that has already been found, and not to find something that one should have found. **Johann Wolfgang von Goethe** *Maxims and Reflections* (Penguin), 1149

9 There is no great invention, from fire to flying, which has not been hailed as an insult to some god.

J. B. S. Haldane *Daedalus or Science and the Future*

10 If Galileo had said in verse that the world moved, the Inquisition might have let him alone.

Thomas Hardy in Florence Emily Hardy, *The Life of Thomas Hardy*

11 If you do not expect it, you will not find out the unexpected, for it is trackless and unexplored. **Heraclitus** *Fragments*, 7

12 Everything that is found is always lost again, and nothing that is found is ever lost again. **Russell Hoban** *The Lion of Boaz-Jachin and Jachin-Boaz*, Ch. 2

13 Explorers have to be ready to die lost.

Russell Hoban interview in *The Times*, 1975

14 To find a new country and invade it has always been the same.

Dr Samuel Johnson *The World Displayed*: Introduction

15 It can probably be agreed that discovery is the common task of the thinker and the poet. The former discovers words for his thoughts, and the latter, thoughts for his words. **David Kipp** *Aphorisms*, p. 9

16 The Americans who first discovered Columbus made a bad discovery. **Georg Christoph Lichtenberg** *Aphorisms*, Notebook G, 42

See also Twain

17 One thing about pioneers that you don't hear mentioned is that they are invariably, by their nature, mess-makers.

Robert M. Pirsig *Zen and the Art of Motorcycle Maintenance*, Pt 3, Ch. 21

18 Anyone who tells you he has discovered something new is a fool, or a liar or both. **Mack Sennett** in James Agee, *Agee on Film*, Vol. 1

19 We often discover what *will* do, by finding out what will not do; and probably he who never made a mistake never made a discovery.

Samuel Smiles *Self-Help*, Ch. 11

20 If you took away everything in the world that had to be invented, there'd be nothing left except a lot of people getting rained on.

Tom Stoppard *Enter a Free Man*, Act 1

21 Discovery consists of seeing what everybody has seen and thinking what nobody has thought.

Albert Szent-Györgyi in I. J. Good, *The Scientist Speculates*, p. 15

22 It was wonderful to find America, but it would have been more wonderful to miss it. **Mark Twain** *Pudd'nhead Wilson*, Conclusion: epigraph

See also Lichtenberg

23 Man is absurd in what he seeks, great through what he finds.

Paul Valéry *Odds and Ends*: 'Moralities'

24 It is not the most astonishing or useful discoveries that do the human mind most credit. **Voltaire** *Philosophical Letters*, 12

25 Women have a wonderful instinct about things. They can discover everything except the obvious. **Oscar Wilde** *An Ideal Husband*, Act 2

Disputes

1 A continual dropping in a very rainy day and a contentious woman are alike. **Bible, OT** Proverbs 27:15

2 We are sure to be losers when we quarrel with ourselves; it is a civil war, and in all such contentions, triumphs are defeats.

Charles Caleb Colton *Lacon*: 'Self-Condemnation'

3 A liberal is a man too broad-minded to take his own side in a quarrel.

Robert Frost in *Portable Curmudgeon*, comp. J. Winokur: 'Quotes on "L" '

4 About one fifth of the people are against everything all the time.

Robert Kennedy speech at University of Pennsylvania, 6 May 1964

5 Lovers' quarrels are the renewal of love. **Terence** *Andria*, 555

6 The most violent clashes have always taken place between *very slightly different* doctrines and dogmas. **Paul Valéry** *Odds and Ends*: 'Moralities'

See also ***Agreement and Disagreement***

Drama

1 He is not a dramatist: he has no interest in himself, let alone in other people. **Peter Ackroyd** *The Last Testament of Oscar Wilde*, 10 October 1900

2 A plausible impossibility is always preferable to an unconvincing possibility. **Aristotle** *Poetics*, 24

3 Because you cannot address everybody, you may as well address the impatient. **Howard Barker** in the *Guardian*, 10 February 1986

4 A good actor does not make his entry before the theatre is built.
Jorge Luis Borges *Six Problems of Don Isidro Parodi*, written under the pseudonym H. Bustos Domecq, with Adolfo Bioy Casares

5 In the theatre men rediscover the ferocity of children, but they have lost their clairvoyance. **Jean Cocteau** *Cock and Harlequin*, p. 24

6 The best actors do not let the wheels show.
Henry Fonda in *Barnes and Noble Book of Quotations*, ed. Robert I. Fitzhenry: 'Acting'

7 English actresses are mistresses and French ones clever daughters.
Terry Hands (attrib.) in the *Sunday Times Magazine*, 26 November 1978

8 A gift for dialogue qualifies you to be a playwright no more than a gift for mixing sand and water qualifies you to build cathedrals.
David Hare in the *Independent on Sunday*, 26 May 1991

9 The theatre is the best way of showing the gap between what is said and what is seen to be done, and that is why, ragged and gap-toothed as it is, it has still a far healthier potential than some poorer, abandoned arts.
David Hare in the *Sunday Times Magazine*, 26 November 1978: 'The Playwright as Historian'

10 Starlet is a name for any woman under thirty not actively employed in a brothel.
Ben Hecht in *Hollywood Anecdotes*, ed. Paul F. Boller Jr and Kristin Thompson

11 Drama is life with the dull bits left out.
Alfred Hitchcock (attrib.) in Leslie Halliwell, *The Filmgoer's Book of Quotes*

12 The historian, essentially, wants more documents than he can really use; the dramatist only wants more liberties than he can really take.
Henry James *The Aspern Papers*: Preface to 1909 edn

13 The structure of a play is always the story of how the birds came home to roost. **Arthur Miller** in *Harper's Magazine*, August 1958

14 Seeing people pretending to be someone else helps us actually to be who we are. **Jonathan Miller** interview in the *Observer*, 21 November 1999

15 Actresses will happen in the best regulated families.

Ethel Watts Mumford, Oliver Herford, Addison Mizner *The Entirely New Cynic's Calendar of Revised Wisdom for 1905*: 'February'

16 We English are more violent than we allow ourselves to know. That is why we have the greatest body of dramatic literature in the world.

John Osborne in *The Theatre and Opera-Lover's Quotation Book*

17 In the theatre, the director is God – but unfortunately, the actors are atheists. **Zarko Petan** *Aforismi A–Z*

18 There are lots of reasons why people become actors. Some to hide themselves, and some to show themselves.

Ralph Richardson TV interview with Russell Harty on LWT, September 1975

19 Rehearsing a play is making the word flesh. Publishing a play is reversing the process. **Peter Shaffer** *Equus*: A Note on the Text

20 Opera is the theatre of the absurd set to music.

Godfrey Smith in the *Sunday Times*, 15 November 1987

21 We do on the stage the things that are supposed to happen off. Which is a kind of integrity, if you look on every exit being an entrance somewhere else. **Tom Stoppard** *Rosencrantz and Guildenstern are Dead*, Act 1

See also ***Critics; The Media***

Dreams

1 Germany expresses its daydreams in line, whereas England does so in perspective. **Charles Baudelaire** *Intimate Journals*: 'Rockets', 12

2 For every age is fed on illusions, lest men should renounce life early and the human race come to an end. **Joseph Conrad** *Victory*, Pt 2, Ch. 3

3 If anything is to be really done in the world, it must be done by visionaries; men who see the future, and make the future because they see it. **Benjamin Disraeli** *Falconet*, quoted in Michael Foot, *Debts of Honour*, Ch. 3

4 When one has not even time to dream awake, one has still less time to dream asleep. **Anatole France** *The Crime of Sylvestre Bonnard*, Pt 1: 'The Log'

5 Perhaps we dream because we cannot stand the solitude of sleep.

Michael Frayn *Constructions*, 69

6 Dreams are probably the best proof that we aren't tied as tightly into our skins as we seem. **Friedrich Hebbel** *Diaries*, entry 3045, 1844

7 Deprive the average human being of his life-lie, and you rob him of his happiness. **Henrik Ibsen** *The Wild Duck*, Act 5

8 There are three alternative attitudes to life – to impose one's dreams on it, which is self-love; to let others impose their dreams on one, which is the vice of humility, micromania; and to penetrate both curtains or blankets of dreams with a boiling heart and freezing intellect, in an effort to live one's life rather than die it.

Hans Keller *Maxims and Reflections*, 4

9 When we sleep, dreams make us think that they are real. When we wake, they make us think that we are. **David Kipp** *Aphorisms*, p. 18

10 They pick our dreams as if they were our pockets.

Karl Kraus *Half-Truths and One-and-a-Half Truths*: 'In Hollow Heads'

11 All men dream: but not equally. Those who dream by night in the dusty recesses of their minds wake in the day to find that it was vanity: but the dreamers of the day are dangerous men, for they may act their dream with open eyes, to make it possible.

T. E. Lawrence *Seven Pillars of Wisdom*, Ch. 1

12 Life is a dream; when we sleep we are awake, and when awake we sleep. **Michel de Montaigne** *Essays*, Bk 2, Ch. 12

13 We are waking up when we dream that we are dreaming.

Novalis *Pollen*, 77

14 A dream is a creation of the intelligence, the creator being present but not knowing how it will end.

Cesare Pavese *This Business of Living: Diary 1935–1950*, 22 July 1940

15 One can be demanding of dreams as psycho-analysis is, but one cannot demand a dream. **Adam Phillips** *On Kissing, Tickling and Being Bored*, Ch. 10

16 When we are dreaming are we perhaps ghosts in someone else's dreams? **Arthur Schnitzler** *Aphorismen und Betrachtungen*, p. 268

17 In a dream you are never eighty. **Anne Sexton** *All My Pretty Ones*: 'Old'

18 One can write, think and pray exclusively of others; dreams are all egocentric. **Evelyn Waugh** *Diaries*, 5 October 1962

Dress

1 Lace, like charity, covers a multitude of sinners.

Minna Antrim *The Wisdom of the Foolish*, p. 9

2 To be naked is to be oneself. To be nude is to be seen naked by others, and yet not recognized for oneself . . . Nudity is a form of dress.

John Berger ***et al.*** *Ways of Seeing*

3 Martha Bartlett told me that a lady said to Miss Andrews, 'that the sense of being perfectly dressed gives a feeling of peace which religion could never give'. **Ralph Waldo Emerson** *Journal*, February 1866

4 No woman so naked as one you can see to be naked underneath her clothes. **Michael Frayn** *Constructions*, 25

5 It is madness to put on gloves, when you are stark naked.

Dr Thomas Fuller *Gnomologia*, 2973

6 Those who make their dress a principal part of themselves, will, in general, become of no more value than their dress.

William Hazlitt *Political Essays*: 'On the Clerical Character'

7 Apes are apes, though clothed in scarlet.

Ben Jonson *The Poetaster*, Act 5, Sc. 1

8 As you treat your body, so your house, your domestics, your enemies, your friends. Dress is a table of your contents.

Johann Kaspar Lavater *Aphorisms on Man*, 119

9 The kilt is an unrivalled garment for fornication and diarrhoea.

John Masters quoting a major of Highlanders in *Bugles and a Tiger*

10 Brevity is the Soul of Lingerie.

Dorothy Parker caption for a fashion magazine, in Alexander Woollcott, *While Rome Burns*: 'Our Mrs Parker'

11 Beware of all enterprises which demand new clothes, and not rather a new wearer of clothes. **H. D. Thoreau** *Walden*: 'Economy'

12 Eat according to your means, but dress above them.

Tigers Don't Eat Grass: Oriental and Occidental Aphorisms 'Appearances'

13 She wore far too much rouge last night, and not quite enough clothes. That is always a sign of despair in a woman.

Oscar Wilde *An Ideal Husband*, Act 2

14 One should either be a work of art, or wear a work of art.

Oscar Wilde *Phrases and Philosophies for the Use of the Young*

See also ***Style and Fashion***

Duty

1 When a duty ceases to be a pleasure, then it ceases to exist.
Norman Douglas *How About Europe?*, p. 161

2 The reward of one duty is the power to fulfil another.
George Eliot *Daniel Deronda*, Bk 6, Ch. 46

3 Duty is what no one else will do at the moment.
Penelope Fitzgerald *Offshore*, 1

4 Duty: where one loves what one orders oneself to do.
Johann Wolfgang von Goethe *Maxims and Reflections* (Penguin), from *Wilhelm Meister's Journeyman Years*, 829

5 There are books you must read, but none you ought to read.
Holbrook Jackson *Maxims of Books and Reading*, 10

6 We must make people feel obliged to us according to what they are, not we. **Georg Christoph Lichtenberg** *The Lichtenberg Reader*: Aphorisms 1768–71

7 Demand first what one can do; afterwards, what one ought.
Friedrich Nietzsche *Nietzsche in Outline and Aphorism*: 'New Commandments'

8 You become responsible, for ever, for what you have tamed. You are responsible for your rose. **Antoine de Saint-Exupéry** *The Little Prince*, Ch. 21

9 When a stupid man is doing something he is ashamed of, he always declares that it is his duty. **George Bernard Shaw** *Caesar and Cleopatra*, Act 3

10 There is no duty we so much underrate as the duty of being happy.
Robert Louis Stevenson *Virginibus Puerisque*: 'An Apology for Idlers'

E

Education

1 A teacher affects eternity; he can never tell where his influence stops.
Henry Adams *The Education of Henry Adams*, Ch. 20

2 We can only teach others profitably what they already virtually know.
Henri-Frédéric Amiel *Amiel's Journal*, 6 December 1870

3 Some scribes become wise.
Anon. poet of *Fates of Men* in *Anglo-Saxon Poetry*, selected by R. K. Gordon

4 Education is that which remains, if one has forgotten everything he learnt at school.
Anon. attrib. to 'a wit' in Albert Einstein, *Out of My Later Years*, Ch. 8

5 A professor is one who talks in someone else's sleep.
W. H. Auden in Charles Osborne, *W. H. Auden: The Life of a Poet*, Ch. 3

6 We all love to instruct, though we can teach only what is not worth knowing.
Jane Austen *Pride and Prejudice*, Ch. 44

7 Histories make men wise; poets, witty; the mathematics, subtle; natural philosophy, deep; moral, grave; logic and rhetoric, able to contend.
Francis Bacon *Essays*: 'Of Studies'

8 A schoolmaster should have an atmosphere of awe, and walk wonderingly, as if he was amazed at being himself.
Walter Bagehot *Literary Studies*: 'Hartley Coleridge'

9 Train up a child in the way he should go: and when he is old, he will not depart from it.
Bible, OT Proverbs 22:6

10 **Education, n.** That which discloses to the wise and disguises from the foolish their lack of understanding.
Ambrose Bierce *The Enlarged Devil's Dictionary*

11 Edukashun iz a good thing generally, but most pholks eddukate their prejudices. **Josh Billings** *Wit and Humor*: 'Billings' Proverbs'

12 The better class of Briton likes to send his children away to school until they're old and intelligent enough to come home again. Then they're too old and intelligent to want to.
Malcolm Bradbury *Rates of Exchange*, 5, III

13 Education makes a people easy to lead, but difficult to drive; easy to govern, but impossible to enslave. **Lord Brougham (attrib.)**

14 There are no great teachers, only great pupils.
Hans von Bülow but sometimes attributed to Franz Liszt; quoted BBC Radio 3, 1995

15 He that has less Learning than his Capacity is able to manage, shall have more Use of it, than he that has more than he can master.
Samuel Butler 1 *Genuine Remains*: 'Thoughts upon Various Subjects'

16 All education is magnetized by something tacit and implied, while instruction that is merely explicit sounds shrill and horrid.
Roberto Calasso *The Ruin of Kasch*: 'Talleyrand'

17 That is the difference between good teachers and great teachers: good teachers make the best of a pupil's means: great teachers foresee a pupil's ends. **Maria Callas** in Kenneth Harris, *Kenneth Harris Talking to*: 'Maria Callas'

18 Very different sorts of eternal students: those who always have their nose in a dictionary, and those who keep searching the books of wisdom. But there are also some who prefer to dissolve wisdom with the help of a dictionary. **Elias Canetti** *The Secret Heart of the Clock*: '1981'

19 Education is a sieve as well as a lift. **Sid Chaplin** *The Day of the Sardine*, Ch. 2

20 Education is simply the soul of a society as it passes from one generation to another. **G. K. Chesterton** in the *Observer*, 'Sayings of the Week', 6 July 1924

21 Headmasters have powers at their disposal with which Prime Ministers have never yet been invested. **Winston S. Churchill** *My Early Life*, Ch. 2

22 Certainly the prolonged education indispensable to the progress of society is not natural to mankind. **Winston S. Churchill** *My Early Life*, Ch. 3

23 Pedantry crams our heads with learned lumber, and takes out our brains to make room for it. **Charles Caleb Colton** *Lacon*: 'Pedantry'

24 A man can, indeed, be said to be eager to learn who is conscious, in the course of a day, of what he lacks and who never forgets, in the course of a month, what he has mastered. **Confucius** *The Analects*, Bk 19, 5

25 A private school has all the faults of a public school without any of its compensations. **Cyril Connolly** *Enemies of Promise*, Ch. 19

26 Though academics love bickering they hate rows.

Robertson Davies *The Rebel Angels*: 'The New Aubrey II'

27 Education is a state-controlled manufactory of echoes.

Norman Douglas *How About Europe?*, p. 29

28 By education most have been misled;
So they believe, because they so were bred.
The priest continues what the nurse began,
And thus the child imposes on the man.

John Dryden *The Hind and the Panther*, Pt 3, 389

29 Education is the process of casting false pearls before real swine.

Irwin Edman in Frank Muir, *The Frank Muir Book*

30 The things taught in schools and colleges are not an education but the means of education. **Ralph Waldo Emerson** *Journal*, 15 July 1831

31 There is much to be said for apathy in education.

E. M. Forster *Maurice*, Ch. 1

32 Old professors never die, they merely lose their faculties.

Stephen Fry *The Liar*, 2, V

33 First let a man teach himself, and then he will be taught by others.

Johann Wolfgang von Goethe *Maxims and Reflections*: 'Science', 519

34 We live less and less, and we learn more and more. Sensibility is surrendering to intelligence.

Rémy de Gourmont *Selected Writings*: 'The Value of Education'

35 Many aspire to learn what they can never comprehend, as others pretend to teach what they themselves do not know.

Marquis of Halifax *Moral Thoughts and Reflections*: 'Of Vanity'

36 It is better to be able neither to read nor write than to be able to do nothing else. **William Hazlitt** *Table Talk*: 'On the Ignorance of the Learned'

37 In me school destroyed a great deal, and I know of few men of any stature who cannot say the same. All I learned there was Latin and lying. **Hermann Hesse** *Reflections*, 257: 'Education and Schools'

38 Animals can learn, but it is not by learning that they become dogs, cats, or horses. Only man has to learn to become what he is supposed to be. **Eric Hoffer** *Between the Devil and the Dragon*, Pt 1: Introduction

39 The world's great men have not commonly been scholars, nor its great scholars great men. **Oliver Wendell Holmes** *The Autocrat of the Breakfast Table*, Ch. 6

40 ***Learn***: To add to one's ignorance by extending the knowledge we have of the things that we can never know.

Elbert Hubbard *The Roycroft Dictionary*

41 ***Teacher***: One who makes two ideas grow where only one grew before. **Elbert Hubbard** *The Roycroft Dictionary*

42 It's what we learn after we think we know it all that counts.
'Kin' Hubbard *Abe Martin's Wisecracks*, p. 24

43 The great thing, then, in all education, is to *make our nervous system our ally instead of our enemy*. **William James** *The Principles of Psychology*, Ch. 4

44 Example is always more efficacious than precept.
Dr Samuel Johnson *Rasselas*, Ch. 29

45 He has a deal of learning; but it never lies straight.
Dr Samuel Johnson in James Boswell, *Life of Johnson*, Vol. 4, 225

46 To teach is to learn twice. **Joseph Joubert** *Pensées*

47 The guidance of our mind is of more importance than its progress.
Joseph Joubert *Pensées*, 6

48 What is the principle of education? We do nothing but deceive children. We teach them things we don't believe and subsequently they won't believe. We make them promise to avoid everything they see, which subsequently would give them worldly success.
Prince de Ligne *Mes Écarts*

49 If you educate a man you educate a person, but if you educate a woman you educate a family.
Ruby Manikan in the *Observer*, 'Sayings of the Week', 30 March 1947; echoing Bishop Fénélon's *Treatise on the Education of Girls*

50 The best teacher lodges an intent not in the mind but in the heart.
Anne Michaels *Fugitive Pieces*: 'The Way Station'

51 The acquisition of learning is much more dangerous than that of any other form of food or drink. **Michel de Montaigne** *Essays*, Bk 3, Ch. 12

52 Education costs money, but then so does ignorance.
Claus Moser speech at British Association, Swansea, 20 August 1990

53 Except it be a lover, no one is more interesting as an object of study than a student. **Sir William Osler** *Aphorisms*, 4

54 A great university has a dual function, to teach and to think.
Sir William Osler *Aphorisms*, 51

55 Learning is a compound of memory, imagination, scientific habit and accurate observation concentrated for a long period on the remains of literature – The result of this sustained mental endeavour is not a book but a man. Lessons are not given, they are taken.
Cesare Pavese *This Business of Living: Diary 1935–1950*, 18 August 1946

56 A little learning is a dang'rous thing;
Drink deep, or taste not the Pierian spring:
There shallow draughts intoxicate the brain,
And drinking largely sobers us again. **Alexander Pope** *An Essay on Criticism*, 215

57 'Tis education forms the common mind,
Just as the twig is bent, the tree's inclined.
Alexander Pope *Moral Essays*, Epistle 11, 149

58 Real education must ultimately be limited to men who insist on knowing, the rest is mere sheep-herding. **Ezra Pound** *ABC of Reading*, Ch. 8

59 Education gives us ephemeral knowledge and lasting antipathies.
Jean Rostand *Pensées d'un biologiste*, p. 69

60 For every person wishing to teach there are thirty not wanting to be taught. **W. C. Sellar and R. J. Yeatman** *And Now All This*: Introduction

61 He who can, does. He who cannot, teaches.
George Bernard Shaw *Man and Superman*, 'Maxims for Revolutionists': 'Education' (but he was referring to revolutionaries!)

62 To endeavour, all one's days, to fortify our minds with learning and philosophy, is to spend so much in armour that one has nothing left to defend. **William Shenstone** *Essays on Men and Manners*: 'On Writing and Books'

63 A teacher should have maximal authority and minimal power.
Thomas S. Szasz *The Second Sin*: 'Education'

64 One of the main truths of all education whatsoever – that, if the young are not always right, the old are nearly always wrong.
R. H. Tawney *The Acquisitive Society*, 9

65 Soap and education are not as sudden as a massacre, but they are more deadly in the long run.
Mark Twain *A Curious Dream*: 'The Facts Concerning the Recent Resignation'

66 Cauliflower is nothing but cabbage with a college education.
Mark Twain *Pudd'nhead Wilson*, Ch. 5: epigraph

67 The things we know best are the things we have not learnt.
Marquis de Vauvenargues *Reflections and Maxims*, 488

68 The splendid thing about education is that everyone wants it and, like influenza, you can give it away without losing any of it yourself.
Evelyn Waugh *Essays*, p. 10

69 Education is an admirable thing. But it is as well to remember from time to time that nothing that is worth knowing can be taught.
Oscar Wilde *For the Instruction of the Over-educated*

70 Ignorance is like a delicate exotic fruit; touch it and the bloom is gone. The whole theory of modern education is radically unsound. Fortunately in England, at any rate, education produces no effect whatsoever. **Oscar Wilde** *The Importance of Being Earnest*, Act 1

Emotions

1 Aren't our best feelings poetry of the will? **Honoré de Balzac** *Old Goriot* 154

2 Tears may be intellectual, but they can never be political. They save no man from being shot, no child from being thrown alive into the furnace. **Saul Bellow** *The Dean's December*, Ch. 12

3 Can a man take fire in his bosom, and his clothes not be burned? **Bible, OT** Proverbs 6:27

4 The man who lives without passion does not live; the man who always masters it is only half alive; the man who perishes from it did at least live; the man who recalls it has a future; the man who exorcizes it has nothing more than the past. **Elias Canetti** *The Human Province*: '1946'

5 His passions make man *live*, his wisdom only makes him *last*. **Nicholas-Sébastien Chamfort** *Maxims and Considerations*, 118

6 A sentiment that can be valued has no value. **Nicholas-Sébastien Chamfort** *Maxims and Considerations*, 347

7 Wise people may say what they will, but one passion is never cured but by another. **Earl of Chesterfield** letter to Solomon Dayrolles, 22 June 1753

8 The man who is master of his passions is Reason's slave. **Cyril Connolly** in *Turnstile One*, ed. V. S. Pritchett

9 Everything seems passion to those who have no experience of it. **Claude-Prosper Crébillon** *Les Égarements du cœur et de l'esprit*

10 A man is to be cheated into passion, but to be reasoned into truth. **John Dryden** *Religio Laici*: Preface

11 Our passions do not live apart in locked chambers, but, dressed in their small wardrobe of notions, bring their provisions to a common table and mess together, feeding out of the common store according to their appetite. **George Eliot** *Middlemarch*, Bk 2, Ch. 16

12 Nothing great was ever achieved without enthusiasm. **Ralph Waldo Emerson** *Essays*: 'Circles'

See also Hegel

13 It is not only species of animal that die out, but whole species of feeling. And if you are wise you will never pity the past for what it did not know, but pity yourself for what it did. **John Fowles** *The Magus*, Ch. 24

14 Whatever we mightily love, doth in some sort become a part of ourselves, and cannot hang so loose upon us, as to be separated from us without Trouble, any more than a Limb, that is vitally and by strong Ligaments united to the Body, can be dropped off when we please, or rent from the body without Pain.

Dr Thomas Fuller *Introductio ad Prudentium*, 3152

15 Sentimentality – that's what we call the sentiment we don't share.

Graham Greene in A. Andrews, *Quotations for Speakers and Writers*

See also Maugham

16 Sentiments are for the most part traditional; we feel them because they were felt by those who preceded us.

William Hazlitt *The Life of Napoleon Bonaparte*, Ch. 57

17 Nothing great in the world has been accomplished without passion.

Georg Hegel *The Philosophy of History*: Introduction

See also Emerson

18 The sentimentalist is he who would enjoy without incurring the immense debtorship for a thing done. **James Joyce** *Ulysses*, p. 539

19 A man who has not passed through the inferno of his passions has never overcome them. **C. G. Jung** *Memories, Dreams, Reflections*, Ch. 9, iv

20 One may not regard the world as a sort of metaphysical brothel for emotions. **Arthur Koestler** *Darkness at Noon*: 'The Second Hearing', 7

21 Already between passion and lying there is not a finger's breadth.

Johann Kaspar Lavater *Aphorisms on Man*, 323

22 Sentimentalism is the working off on yourself of feelings you haven't really got. **D. H. Lawrence** *Phoenix*: 'John Galsworthy'

23 It is with our passions as it is with fire and water, they are good servants, but bad masters. **Sir Roger L'Estrange** *Aesop's Fables*, 38

24 A feeling expressed in words is always like music described in words; the expressions are not sufficiently homogeneous with the thing itself.

Georg Christoph Lichtenberg *The Lichtenberg Reader*: Aphorisms 1764–70

25 First feelings are always the most natural.

Louis XIV reported by Mme de Sévigné

26 Sentimentality is the emotional promiscuity of those who have no sentiment. **Norman Mailer** *Cannibals and Christians*, Pt 1: 'My Hope for America'

27 Sentimentality is only sentiment that rubs you up the wrong way.
W. Somerset Maugham *A Writer's Notebook*, 1941

See also Greene

28 One master-passion in the breast,
Like Aaron's serpent, swallows up the rest.
Alexander Pope *An Essay on Man*, Bk 2, 131

29 Reason is the historian, but the emotions are the actors.
Antoine de Rivarol *Notes, réflections et maximes*: 'Philosophe'

30 It is only with the heart that one can see rightly; what is essential is invisible to the eye. **Antoine de Saint-Exupéry** *The Little Prince*, Ch. 21

31 Feelings and understanding may sleep under the same roof, but they run completely different households in the human soul.
Arthur Schnitzler quoted in introduction to *Dream Story*

32 Passion, you see, can be destroyed by a doctor. It cannot be created.
Peter Shaffer *Equus*, Act 2, Sc. 5

33 Love is the only passion which rewards itself in a coin of its own manufacture. **Stendhal** *Love*: 'Various Fragments', 145

34 Inconsistency in matters of feeling is the surest sign of their genuineness. **Leo Tolstoy** *Boyhood*, 23

35 Nothing is serious except passion. The intellect is not a serious thing, and never has been. **Oscar Wilde** *A Woman of No Importance*, Act 1

36 A sentimentalist is simply one who desires to have the luxury of an emotion without paying for it.
Oscar Wilde in conversation; in *Epigrams of Oscar Wilde*: 'Emotions'

See also ***Desires***

Environments

1 Any landscape is a condition of the spirit.
Henri-Frédéric Amiel *Amiel's Journal*, 31 October 1852

2 Comfort came in with the middle classes. **Clive Bell** *Civilization*, Ch. 4

3 Heredity is just environment stored.
Luther Burbank in *A Dictionary of Scientific Quotations*, ed. A. L. Mackay

4 For rich people, the sky is just an extra, a gift of nature. The poor, on the other hand, can see it as it really is: an infinite grace.

Albert Camus *Notebooks 1*, May 1935

5 To be born into this earth is to be born into uncongenial surroundings, hence to be born into a romance. **G. K. Chesterton** *Heretics*, Ch. 14

6 How inappropriate to call this planet Earth when it is quite clearly Ocean. **Arthur C. Clarke** in *Nature*, 8 March 1990

7 Something there is that doesn't love a wall. **Robert Frost** *Mending Wall*

8 One outstandingly important fact regarding Spaceship Earth, and that is that no instruction book came with it.

R. Buckminster Fuller *Operating Manual for Spaceship Earth*, Ch. 4

9 Man is preceded by forest, followed by desert.

Graffito in France during the student revolt, 1968

10 We shall never be content until each man makes his own weather and keeps it to himself.

Jerome K. Jerome *The Idle Thoughts of an Idle Fellow*: 'On the Weather'

11 Cinemas and theatres are always bigger inside than they are outside.

Miles Kington in the *Independent*, 29 March 1989

12 There is only one plant and only one animal, and these two are one. The animal that lives off plants has its roots in the earth, thus the animal that lives off animals does so too.

Georg Christoph Lichtenberg *Aphorisms*, Notebook J, 161

13 I am I plus my surroundings, and if I do not preserve the latter, I do not preserve myself. **José Ortega y Gasset** *Meditations of Quixote*: 'To the Reader'

14 The brilliance of the earth is the brilliance of every paradise.

Wallace Stevens quoted in Adam Phillips, *Darwin's Bones*: 'Prologue'

15 Hills are the earth's gesture of despair for the unreachable.

Rabindranath Tagore *Fireflies*, p. 118

16 A town is saved not by any righteous men in it but by the woods and swamps that surround it. **H. D. Thoreau** *Journal*, after 11 September 1849

17 It has ever been regarded as a crime even among warriors to cut down a nation's trees. **H. D. Thoreau** *Journal*, 27 May 1852

18 In wildness is the preservation of the world.

H. D. Thoreau 'Walking', in *Atlantic Monthly*, June 1862

19 Our species and its ways of thinking are a product of evolution, not the purpose of evolution. **Edward O. Wilson** *Consilience*, Ch. 3

20 The most beautiful thing under the sun, is being under the sun.
Christa Wolf *A Model Childhood*, Ch. 8

See also ***Nature; Places; Town and Country; The World***

Epigrams

1 **Saw, n.** A trite popular saying or proverb. (Figurative and colloquial.) So called because it makes its way into a wooden head.
Ambrose Bierce *The Devil's Dictionary*

2 **Epigram, n.** A short, sharp saying in prose or verse, frequently characterized by acidity or acerbity and sometimes by wisdom.
Ambrose Bierce *The Enlarged Devil's Dictionary*

3 Maxims tew be good should be az sharp az vinegar, as short as pi krust, and az trew az a pair of steelyards.
Josh Billings *Wit and Humor*: Affurisms: 'Nest Eggs'

4 Proverbs are literature on the haff shell.
Josh Billings *Wit and Humor*: 'Billings' Proverbs'

5 Her whole life is an Epigram, smart, smooth, and neatly pen'd,
Platted quite neat to catch applause with a sliding noose at the end.
William Blake *Miscellaneous Poems and Fragments*

6 An aphorism is true where it has fixed the impression of a genuine experience. **F. H. Bradley** *Aphorisms*, 41

7 The great writers of aphorisms read as if they had all known each other very well. **Elias Canetti** *The Human Province*: '1943'

8 France was long a despotism tempered by epigrams.
Thomas Carlyle *The French Revolution*, Pt 1, Bk 1, Ch. 1

9 Most anthologists and collectors of *bons mots* are like people who eat cherries or oysters, picking the best first and ending up eating the lot.
Nicholas-Sébastien Chamfort *Maxims and Considerations*, 1

10 What is an epigram? A dwarfish whole,
It's body brevity, and wit its soul. **Samuel Taylor Coleridge** *On Epigram*

11 No people require maxims so much as the American. The reason is obvious; the country is so vast, the people always going somewhere, from Oregon apple valley to boreal New England – that we do not know

whether to be temperate orchards or sterile climate.

Edward Dahlberg *Alms for Oblivion*: 'Word-Sick and Place-Crazy'

12 You may cram a truth into an epigram; the truth, never.

Norman Douglas *An Almanac 1945*

13 An aphorism is the last link in a long chain of thought.

Maria von Ebner-Eschenbach *Aphorisms*: epigraph

14 I hate your epigrams and pointed saws
Whose narrow truth is but broad falsity. **George Eliot** *Armgart*

15 Windbags can be right. Aphorists can be wrong. It's a tough world.

James Fenton in *The Times*, 21 February 1985

16 Much matter decocted into a few words.

Thomas Fuller *The Worthies of England*, Ch. 2: definition of a proverb

17 A collection of anecdotes and maxims is the greatest treasure for a man of the world – as long as he knows how to introduce the former at a strategic place in his conversation and to remember the latter at the right moment.

Johann Wolfgang von Goethe *Maxims and Reflections*, from *Art and Antiquity*, 190

18 The best grafts in the world are built up on copybook maxims and psalms and proverbs and Esau's fables. They seem to kind of hit off human nature. **O. Henry** *A Tempered Wind*

19 Aphorisms are something like jewels; rarity increases their value, and they are enjoyable only in small doses.

Hermann Hesse *Reflections*: 'Epigraph'

20 Clarity is the virtue of maxims. Maxims are charming, they are useful, educational, witty, informative – but they are never true. Because the opposite of every maxim is also true.

Hermann Hesse *Reflections*, 336: 'Knowledge and Consciousness'

21 ***epigram***: A dash of wit and a jigger of wisdom, flavoured with surprise. **Elbert Hubbard** *The Roycroft Dictionary*

22 Everything that is exact is short. **Joseph Joubert** *Notebooks*, 1804

23 Maxims, because what is isolated can be seen better.

Joseph Joubert *Notebooks*, 1808

24 One cannot dictate an aphorism to a typist. It would take far too long. **Karl Kraus** *Half-Truths and One-and-a-Half Truths*: 'Riddles'

25 An aphorism never coincides with the truth: it is either a half-truth or one-and-a-half truths.

Karl Kraus *Half-Truths and One-and-a-Half Truths*: 'Riddles'

26 An aphorism
should be
like a burr;
sting,
stick,
and leave
a little soreness
afterwards.

Irving Layton *The Whole Bloody Bird*: 'aphs'

27 An epigram is only a wisecrack that's played at Carnegie Hall.

Oscar Levant in *Coronet* magazine, September 1968

28 I have jotted down a host of little thoughts and sketches, but they are awaiting not so much a final revision as a few more glimpses of the sun that will make them blossom.

Georg Christoph Lichtenberg *Aphorisms*, Notebook B, 55

29 The art of newspaper paragraphing is
to stroke a platitude until it purrs like an epigram.

Don Marquis in the *New York Sun*: 'The Sun Dial'

30 Anyone can tell the truth, but only very few of us can make epigrams.

Somerset Maugham *A Writer's Notebook*, 1896

31 There are aphorisms that, like airplanes, stay up only while they are in motion.

Vladimir Nabokov *The Gift*, Ch. 1

32 If, with the literate, I am
Impelled to try an epigram,
I never seek to take the credit;
We all assume that Oscar said it.

Dorothy Parker *Oscar Wilde*

33 A virtue of aphorisms: they're too short to bore.

Joseph Prescott *Aphorisms and Other Observations, Third Series*: 'Literature'

34 Nothing is so dangerous for the state as those who would govern kingdoms with maxims found in books.

Cardinal Richelieu *Political Testament*, I.8

35 Two things can echo: a mountain and an aphorism.

Colin Ross *Adecarcinoma and Other Poems*, aphorism 100

36 A proverb is one man's wit and all men's wisdom.

Lord John Russell (attrib.) in R. J. Mackintosh, *Sir James Mackintosh*, Vol. 2, Ch. 7

37 An aphorism ought to be entirely isolated from the surrounding world like a little work of art and complete in itself like a hedgehog.

Friedrich von Schlegel *Dialogue on Poetry and Literary Aphorisms*, 206

38 If one shakes an aphorism, a lie will fall out and a banality remain.

Arthur Schnitzler *Aphorismen und Betrachtungen*, p. 132

39 In the heart of every aphorism, no matter how new or indeed paradoxical its demeanour, there beats an ancient truth.

Arthur Schnitzler *Aphorismen und Betrachtungen*, p. 133

40 It is the nature of aphoristic thinking to be always in a state of concluding, a bid to have the final word is inherent in all phrase-making.

Susan Sontag in introduction to R. Barthes, *Selected Writings*

41 As Rochefoucauld his maxims drew
From Nature I believe them true.
They argue no corrupted mind
In him – the fault is in mankind.

Dean Swift *Verses on His Own Death*

42 Few maxims are true in every respect.

Marquis de Vauvenargues *Reflections and Maxims*, 111

43 There must in the nature of human things be a mental language common to all nations, which uniformly grasps the substance of things feasible in human social life, and expresses it with as many diverse modifications as these same things may have diverse aspects. A proof of this is afforded by proverbs or maxims of vulgar wisdom, in which substantially the same meanings find as many diverse expressions as there are nations ancient and modern.

Giambattista Vico *The New Science*, 161

44 He would stab his best friend for the sake of writing an epigram on his tombstone.

Oscar Wilde *Vera, or the Nihilists*, Act 2

Equality

1 If a man is genuinely superior to his fellows the first thing that he believes in is the equality of man.

G. K. Chesterton *Heretics*, Ch. 17

2 The trouble with treating people as equals is that the first thing you know they may be doing the same thing to you.

Peter De Vries *The Prick of Noon*, Ch. 1

3 What is a communist? One who hath yearnings
For equal division of unequal earnings.

Ebenezer Elliott *Epigram*

4 Capitalism depends on the fundamental principle of inequality, some will do better than others, but will only in the long term in a democracy if most people have an equal chance to aspire to that inequality.

Charles Handy *The Age of Paradox*, Ch. 2

5 There are few people quite above, or completely below, par.

William Hazlitt *Characteristics*, 51

6 Equality without freedom creates a more stable social pattern than freedom without equality.

Eric Hoffer *Between the Devil and the Dragon*, Pt 4, 2: 'The Free Poor'

7 Society cannot exist without inequality of wealth, and inequality of wealth cannot exist without religion.

Napoleon Bonaparte quoted in John Fowles, *The Aristos*, Ch. 7, 50

8 All animals are equal, but some animals are more equal than others.

George Orwell *Animal Farm*, Ch. 10

9 I believe in equality. Bald men should marry bald women.

Fiona Pitt-Kethley interview in the *Guardian*, 21 November 1990

10 Men are born equal. By the next day they no longer are.

Jules Renard *Journal 1887–1910*, 12 September 1907

11 In the ashes all men are levelled. We're born unequal, we die equal.

Seneca *Letters from a Stoic*, 91

12 We must be thoroughly democratic, and patronize everybody without distinction of class. **George Bernard Shaw** *John Bull's Other Island*, Act 2

13 How unfair it is that those who have less are always adding to the possessions of those who have more

Terence in Sagittarius and Daniel George, *The Perpetual Pessimist*, 27 April

14 The principle of equality does not destroy the imagination, but lowers its flight to the level of the earth.

Alexis de Tocqueville *Democracy in America*, Vol. 2, Pt 3, Ch. 11

15 We who are liberal and progressive know that the poor are our equals in every sense except that of being equal to us.

Lionel Trilling *The Liberal Imagination*: 'Princess Casamassima'

Excess

1 Speaking in a perpetual hyperbole is comely in nothing but in love.

Francis Bacon *Essays*: 'Of Love'

2 The road of excess leads to the palace of wisdom.

William Blake *The Marriage of Heaven and Hell*: 'Proverbs of Hell'

3 You never know what is enough unless you know what is more than enough. **William Blake** *The Marriage of Heaven and Hell*: 'Proverbs of Hell'

4 The faults of great authors are generally excellencies carried to excess. **Samuel Taylor Coleridge** *Miscellanies*, p. 149

5 This woman did not fly to extremes; she lived there.

Quentin Crisp *The Naked Civil Servant*, Ch. 3

6 The Way to think we have enough, is to desire to have too much.

Dr Thomas Fuller *Introductio ad Prudentium*, 2609

7 An exaggeration is a truth that has lost its temper.

Kahlil Gibran *Sand and Foam*

8 Too much is sometimes enough for a woman.

Edmond and Jules de Goncourt *Idées et sensations*

9 Thou shalt not carry moderation unto excess.

Arthur Koestler last entry in his final notebook; in George Mikes, *Arthur Koestler: The Story of a Friendship*

See also Wilde

10 'Tis not the eating, nor 'tis not the drinking, that is to be blamed, but the excess.

John Selden *Table Talk*, 54

11 They are as sick that surfeit with too much, as they that starve with nothing.

William Shakespeare *The Merchant of Venice*, Act 1, Sc. 2, (5)

12 It is no mean happiness therefore to be seated in the mean: superfluity comes sooner by white hairs, but competency lives longer.

William Shakespeare *The Merchant of Venice*, Act 1, Sc. 2, (7)

13 Better to be carried away in any direction, and become a prodigal son or lost sheep, than not be carried away at all.

Francis Stuart quoted in his obituary in the *Guardian*, 4 February 2000

14 Moderation is a fatal thing, Lady Hunstanton. Nothing succeeds like excess.

Oscar Wilde *A Woman of No Importance*, Act 3

See also Koestler

Existence

1 One thing hastens into being, another hastens out of it.

Marcus Aurelius *Meditations*, Bk 6, 15

2 There are only three proper beings: the priest, the warrior, the poet. To know, to kill and to create.

Charles Baudelaire *Intimate Journals*: 'My Heart Laid Bare', 13

3 The isness of things is well worth studying; but it is their whyness that makes life worth living.

William Beebe quoted in Konrad Lorenz, *On Aggression*, Ch. 2

4 So far as we are human, what we do must be either evil or good; so far as we do evil or good, we are human; and it is better in a paradoxical way, to do evil than to do nothing: at least we exist.

Anthony Burgess quoted in D. J. Enright, *Interplay*, p. 233

5 Perhaps every breath you take is someone else's last.

Elias Canetti *The Human Province*: '1950'

6 To exist is a habit I do not despair of acquiring.

E. M. Cioran *The Temptation to Exist*

7 Into this Universe, and *Why* not knowing
Nor *Whence*, like Water willy-nilly flowing:
And out of it, as Wind along the Waste,
I know not *Whither*, willy-nilly blowing.

Edward Fitzgerald *The Rubáiyát of Omar Khayyám*, Edn 1, 29

8 I am is I was not, I might not have been, I may not be, I shall not be.

John Fowles *The Aristos*, Ch. 1, 24

9 Man is the only animal for whom his own existence is a problem he has to solve. **Erich Fromm** *Man for Himself*, Ch. 3

10 The whole art of living consists in giving up existence in order to exist. **Johann Wolfgang von Goethe** *Maxims and Reflections*: 'Life and Character', 192

11 Nothing exists except by virtue of a disequilibrium, an injustice. All existence is a theft paid by other existences; no life flowers except on a cemetery. **Rémy de Gourmont** *Selected Writings*: 'The Dissociation of Ideas'

12 We are too late for the gods, too early for Being. Being's poem, just begun, is man. **Martin Heidegger** *Poetry, Language and Thought*, 1

13 You are what you think and not what you think you are.

Elbert Hubbard *The Philosophy of Elbert Hubbard*: 'Epigrams'

14 Life exists in the universe only because the carbon atom possesses certain exceptional properties. **Sir James Jeans** *The Mysterious Universe*, Ch. 1

15 All beings come from little, and little is needed for them to come to nothing. **Joseph Joubert** *Notebooks*, 1802

16 As far as we can discern, the sole purpose of human existence is to kindle a light in the darkness of mere being.

C. G. Jung *Memories, Dreams, Reflections*, Ch. 11

17 He, who has frequent moments of complete existence, is a hero, though not laurelled; is crowned, and without crowns, a king: he only who has enjoyed immortal moments can reproduce them.

Johann Kaspar Lavater *Aphorisms on Man*, 507; William Blake underlined and commented: 'O that men would seek immortal moments! O that men would converse with God!'

18 One does what one is: one becomes what one does.

Robert Musil *Kleine Prosa*

19 The cradle rocks above an abyss, and common sense tells us that our existence is but a brief crack of light between two eternities of darkness. Although the two are identical twins, man, as a rule, views the prenatal abyss with more calm than the one he is heading for (at forty-five hundred heartbeats an hour). **Vladimir Nabokov** *Speak, Memory*, Ch. 1, 1

20 Better not to have lived than to leave no traces of your existence.

Napoleon Bonaparte quoted in introduction to Cardinal de Retz, *Memoirs*, Vol. 1, 1917 edn

21 Existence is really an imperfect tense that never becomes a present.

Friedrich Nietzsche *The Use and Abuse of History*, Sect. 1

22 I know perfectly well that I don't want to do anything; to do something is to create existence – and there's quite enough existence as it is.

Jean-Paul Sartre *Nausea*: 'One hour later'

23 One is still what one is going to cease to be and already what one is going to become. One lives one's death, one dies one's life.

Jean-Paul Sartre *Saint Genet*, Bk 2: 'The Melodious Child . . .'

24 Anything one is remembering is a repetition, but existing as a human being, that is being, listening and hearing is never repetition.

Gertrude Stein quoted in David Lodge, *Changing Places*, Ch. 5

25 Unless all existence is a medium of Revelation, no particular revelation is possible. **William Temple** *Nature, Man and God*, Lecture 12

26 We're all in this together by ourselves.

Lily Tomlin in *Hammer and Tongues*, ed. Michèle Brown and Ann O'Connor: 'Life'

27 What resembles nothing does not exist.

Paul Valéry *Bad Thoughts and Not So Bad*, P

28 We have to be nothing in order to be in our right place in the whole.

Simone Weil *Gravity and Grace*: 'Decreation'

29 If the world could
have had the chance
of not existing, existence could have existed.

Wols *Aphorisms and Pictures*, p. 9

See also ***Birth and Death; Life and Death***

Experience

1 Experience is a good teacher, but she sends in terrific bills.

Minna Antrim *Naked Truth and Veiled Illusions*

See also Heine

2 Nothing can happen to any man that nature has not fitted him to endure. **Marcus Aurelius** *Meditations*, Bk 5, 18

3 To a great experience one thing is essential, an experiencing nature.

Walter Bagehot *Estimates of Some Englishmen and Scotsmen*: 'Shakespeare – the Individual'

4 You should make a point of trying every experience once, except incest and folk-dancing.

Arnold Bax *Farewell to My Youth*: 'Cecil Sharp'; he was quoting a 'sympathetic Scot'

5 We go through life expecting to be tasted while we are being swallowed. **Elizabeth Bibesco** *Haven*: 'Aphorisms'

6 Experience isn't interesting till it begins to repeat itself – in fact, till it does that, it hardly *is* experience.

Elizabeth Bowen *The Death of the Heart*, Pt 1, Ch. 1

7 To most men, experience is like the stern light of a ship, which illumines only the track it has passed. **Samuel Taylor Coleridge** *Table Talk*, p. 434

8 Not all need experience, but all need the fruit of experience.

Bishop Mandell Creighton *Life and Letters*, Vol. 2

9 There are two things that experience teaches us: the first is that we should correct heavily; the second, that it should not be too heavily.

Eugène Delacroix *Journal*, 8 March 1860

10 Experience only serves us to give others useless advice.

Comtesse Diane *Maxims of Life*, p. 75

11 Some of us learn to make the best of a bad job. Few learn to make the best of a good one. **Norman Douglas** *An Almanac 1945*

12 If we had no experience of a world external to us, we should have no experience of ourselves, either. Our relationship to the world is that intimate! **Michael Frayn** *Constructions*, 262

13 Life should serve up its feast of experience in a series of courses.

William Golding *Close Quarters*, 17

14 We cannot afford to forget any experience, not even the most painful. **Dag Hammarskjöld** *Markings*

15 Experience is a good school, but the fees are high.

Heinrich Heine in *Wit and Wisdom of Dean Inge*: Preface

See also Antrim

16 A moment's insight is sometimes worth a life's experience.

Oliver Wendell Holmes *The Professor at the Breakfast Table*, Ch. 10

17 Experience is not what happens to a man; it is what a man does with what happens to him. **Aldous Huxley** *Texts and Pretexts*: Introduction

18 Now you can reach forty and get no nearer a real grief than the television news. **P. J. Kavanagh** *People and Weather*, 4

19 We read fine things but never feel them to the full until we have gone the same steps as the author. **John Keats** letter to J. H. Reynolds, 3 May 1818

20 A desk is a dangerous place from which to watch the world.

John Le Carré *The Honourable Schoolboy*, 4

21 If you want knowledge, you must take part in the practice of changing reality. If you want to know the taste of a pear, you must change the pear by eating it yourself. **Mao Zedong** *On Practice*, July 1937

22 Experience dulls the edges of all our dogmas. **Gilbert Murray (attrib.)**

23 To experience anything as beautiful means: to experience it necessarily wrongly.

Friedrich Nietzsche quoted in Susan Sontag, *On Photography*: 'A Brief Anthology of Quotations'

24 One can learn from experience, but one cannot be taught by it.

Adam Phillips *On Kissing, Tickling and Being Bored*, Ch. 10

25 Experience is like the pole-star: it only guides man in the evening and rises when he is going to rest.

Charles-Augustin Sainte-Beuve in J. R. Solly, *Selected Thoughts from the French*

26 Taste all, and hand the knowledge down.

Gary Snyder *Turtle Island*: 'Ethnobotany'

27 You can only experience fear if you are trying to live in the future –
You can only experience guilt if you are trying to live in the past.

Chuck Spezzano *Awaken the Gods*, p. 110

28 Who is old enough to have learned from experience?

H. D. Thoreau *Journal*, 20 March 1842

29 Events play cat-and-mouse with our ideas. They belong to a quite different species and even when seeming to bear out our preconceptions are never quite as we expected. Foresight is a dream from which the event awakens us. **Paul Valéry** *Bad Thoughts and Not So Bad*, H

30 A man is more than a serial succession of occasions of experience.

A. N. Whitehead *Adventures of Ideas*, Ch. 13

31 Experience is the name everyone gives to their mistakes.

Oscar Wilde *Lady Windermere's Fan*, Act 3

32 We can have in life but one great experience at best, and the secret of life is to reproduce that experience as often as possible.

Oscar Wilde *The Picture of Dorian Gray*, Ch. 17

Eyes

1 The splinter in your eye is the best magnifying-glass.

Theodor Adorno *Minima Memoralia*, Pt 1, 29

2 Look twice for a just appraisal; look once, for a sense of beauty.

Henri-Frédéric Amiel *Amiel's Journal*, 26 December 1852

3 It is not possible to look and listen with equal attention and, in any competition, the eyes have it.

Nancy Banks-Smith in the *Guardian*, 23 March 1990

4 Seeing through is rarely seeing into. **Elizabeth Bibesco** *Haven*: 'Aphorisms'

5 Surely in vain the net is spread in the sight of the bird.

Bible, OT Proverbs 1:17

6 A fool sees not the same tree that a wise man sees.

William Blake *The Marriage of Heaven and Hell*: 'Proverbs of Hell'

7 He must be blind indeed who cannot see through a sieve.

Miguel Cervantes *Wit and Wisdom of Don Quixote*, p. 104

8 We would know much more about things if we weren't intent on discerning them too precisely. For, surely, an object can only be comprehensible when viewed at an angle of forty-five degrees.

Johann Wolfgang von Goethe *Maxims and Reflections* (Penguin), from *Wilhelm Meister's Journeyman Years*, 501

9 Look at yourself with one eye, listen to yourself with the other.

Eugene Ionesco *Improvisation*

See also Klee

10 Description only excites curiosity: seeing satisfies it.

Dr Samuel Johnson in James Boswell, *Life of Johnson*, Vol. 4, 199

11 One eye sees, the other feels. **Paul Klee** *Diaries, 1898–1918*, no. 937 (1914)

See also Ionesco

12 'How is it going?' a blind man asked a cripple. 'As you see,' the cripple replied. **Georg Christoph Lichtenberg** *Aphorisms*, Notebook E, 71

13 The person who looks in through an open window never sees all the things that are seen by someone who looks in through a closed window.

Max Ophuls in radio talk, quoted in Roberto Calasso, *The Ruin of Kasch*: 'Behind the Window Pane'

14 Great is his faith who dares believe his own eyes.

Coventry Patmore *The Rod, the Root and the Flower*: 'Aurea Dicta' 16

15 Two mirrors facing each other; that means confusion for the short-sighted, and infinity for the long-sighted.

Arthur Schnitzler *Aphorismen und Betrachtungen*, p. 252

16 Observation is an old man's memory.

Jonathan Swift *Thoughts on Various Subjects*, p. 285

17 The looking-glass reveals us as we are to ourselves; the wine-glass reveals us as we are to others. **Sydney Tremayne** *Tatlings*, p. 11

See also ***Appearances; Perceptions; The Senses***

Faith

1 The wish to call down fire from heaven is rarely absent in pure zeal for a pure cause. **Walter Bagehot** *Literary Studies*: 'The First Edinburgh Reviewers'

2 A faith is something you die for; a doctrine is something you kill for: there is all the difference in the world.
Tony Benn in the *Observer*, 'Sayings of the Week', 16 April 1989

See also Hesse

3 Faith is the substance of things hoped for, the evidence of things not seen. **Bible, NT** Hebrews 11:1

4 **Faith, n.** Belief without evidence in what is told by one who speaks without knowledge, of things without parallel.
Ambrose Bierce *The Devil's Dictionary*

5 Methinks there be not impossibilities enough in Religion for an active faith. **Sir Thomas Browne** *Religio Medici*, Pt 1, 9

6 To believe only possibilities is not faith, but mere philosophy.
Sir Thomas Browne *Religio Medici*, Pt 1, 48

7 You can do very little with faith, but you can do nothing without it.
Samuel Butler 2 *Notebooks*, Ch. 21: 'Faith'

8 We dignify our faith when we can cross oceans with it – though most prefer ships. **Emily Dickinson** letter to Mrs Anthon, 1861

9 'Faith' is a fine invention
When gentlemen can *see*!
But *Microscopes* are prudent
In an Emergency! **Emily Dickinson** *Complete Poems*, 185

10 The faith that stands on authority is not faith.
Ralph Waldo Emerson *Essays*: 'The Over-Soul'

11 We're all unbelievers within our own faiths.
Graham Greene in Martin Amis, *Visiting Mrs Nabokov*

12 I hold that it is permissible for each one of us to die for his faith, but not to kill for his faith. **Hermann Hesse** *Reflections, 66*

See also Benn

13 Most often when we renounce a faith, we do not cast it off, but swallow it; we substitute the self for the abandoned holy cause.
Eric Hoffer in Calvin Tomkins, *Eric Hoffer: an American Odyssey*: Aphorisms

14 The true way leads along a tight-rope, which is not stretched aloft but just above the ground. It seems designed more to trip one than to be walked along. **Franz Kafka** *Collected Aphorisms*, 1

15 Faith is the highest passion in a human being. Many in every generation may not come that far, but none comes further.
Søren Kierkegaard *Fear and Trembling*: Epilogue

16 Faith may be defined briefly as an illogical belief in the occurrence of the improbable. **H. L. Mencken** *Prejudices, Third Series*: 'Types of Men', 3

17 Bigots: they sleep with God on a Sunday and deceive Him the rest of the week. **Jules Renard** *Journal 1887–1910*, 14 September 1903

18 The ungodly are usually the pious in revolt.
Antoine de Rivarol *Notes, réflexions et maximes*: 'Philosophe'

19 Faith has need of all the truth.
Pierre Teilhard de Chardin *The Appearance of Man*, Ch. 2

20 Faith is the state of being ultimately concerned.
Paul Tillich *Dynamics of Faith*, Ch. 1

21 He had not that perfect faith in mankind which is the surest evidence of a simple mind. **Anthony Trollope** *Mr Scarborough's Family*, Ch. 32

22 Martyrs create faith more than faith creates martyrs.
Miguel de Unamuno *The Tragic Sense of Life*, Ch. 9

See also ***Beliefs; Trust***

Fame

1 Fame is like a river, that beareth up things light and swollen, and drowns things weighty and solid. **Francis Bacon** *Essays*: 'Of Praise'

2 The world beats a path past his door.
Guy Bellamy *The Sinner's Congregation*, Ch. 7

3 A good name is better than precious ointment; and the day of death than the day of one's birth. **Bible, OT** Ecclesiastes 7:1

4 Children and the building of a city continue a man's name; but a blameless wife is counted above them both.
Bible, Apocrypha Ecclesiasticus 40:19

5 A good life hath but few days: but a good name endureth for ever.
Bible, Apocrypha Ecclesiasticus 51:13

6 A man is known by the company that he organizes.
Ambrose Bierce *The Devil's Dictionary*

7 The celebrity is a person who is known for his well-knownness.
Daniel Boorstin *The Image*, Ch. 2

See also Lasch

8 Stars are not the people who are best at what they do; they are merely the people who want it most. **Julie Burchill** in the *Guardian*, 13 November 1999

9 Fame sweeps in double the amount that envy cuts away.
Elias Canetti *The Secret Heart of the Clock*: '1980'

10 Celebrity: the advantage of being known by those who do not know you. **Nicholas-Sébastien Chamfort** *Maxims and Considerations*, 135

11 Being a personality is not the same as having a personality.
Alan Coren in the *Mail on Sunday*, 12 March 1989

12 Fame is a fickle food
Upon a shifting plate. **Emily Dickinson** *Complete Poems*, 1659

13 If a man can write a better book, preach a better sermon, or make a better mouse-trap than his neighbour, though he build his house in the woods, the world will make a beaten path to his door.
Ralph Waldo Emerson lecture noted down by Sarah Yule in her *Borrowings*; also attrib. Elbert Hubbard

14 The combination of a desire for glory and an inability to endure the monotony it entails puts many people in the asylum. Glory comes from the unchanging din-din-din of a supreme gift.

F. Scott Fitzgerald *Notebooks*, O

15 Fame is a powerful aphrodisiac.

Graham Greene in the *Radio Times*, 10 September 1964

16 Those only deserve a monument who do not need one – that is, who have raised themselves a monument in the minds and memories of men. **William Hazlitt** *Characteristics*, 388

17 It is a mark of many famous people that they cannot part with their brightest hour. **Lillian Hellman** *Pentimento*: 'Theatre'

18 How many people live on the reputation of the reputation they might have made!

Oliver Wendell Holmes *The Autocrat at the Breakfast Table*, Ch. 3

19 I'm afraid of losing my obscurity. Genuineness only thrives in the dark. Like celery. **Aldous Huxley** *Those Barren Leaves*, Pt 1, Ch. 1

20 Men have a solicitude about fame; and the greater share they have of it, the more afraid they are of losing it.

Dr Samuel Johnson in James Boswell, *Life of Johnson*, 1763

21 It is very rarely that an author can be hurt by his critics. Reputation cannot be blown out, but it often dies in the socket.

Dr Samuel Johnson in James Boswell, *Life of Johnson*, Vol. 3, 423

22 The only important attribute of celebrity is that it is celebrated; no one can say why. **Christopher Lasch** *The Culture of Narcissism*, Ch. 2

See also Boorstin

23 From the moment prestige is called in question it ceases to be prestige. The gods and men who have kept their prestige for long have never tolerated discussion. For the crowd to admire, it must be kept at a distance. **Gustave Le Bon** *The Crowd*, Ch. 3

24 When smashing monuments, save the pedestals – they always come in handy. **Stanislaw Lec** *Unkempt Thoughts*, p. 50

25 Popularity . . . is a razor in the hands of a child.

Prince de Ligne *Mes Écarts posthumes*

26 Awards are like piles. Sooner or later every bum has one.

Maureen Lipman in the *Independent*, 'Quotes of the Week', 31 July 1999

27 A dead writer can at least be illustrious without any strain on himself.

Marcel Proust *Remembrance of Things Past: The Guermantes Way*, 2

28 Bore a little hole in the head on my statue, so that the birds can take a drink. **Jules Renard** *Journal 1887–1910*, 10 December 1899

29 As regards calumny, any attack which does not injure a reputation serves to strengthen it.

Cardinal de Retz quoted in J. Raymond Solly, *A Cynic's Breviary*

30 It is easier to gain fame than to retain it.

Artur Schnabel *My Life and Music*, Pt 2, Ch. 4

31 He that filches from me my good name
Robs me of that which not enriches him,
And makes me poor indeed. **William Shakespeare** *Othello*, Act 3, Sc. 3, 159

32 Martyrdom is the only way in which a man can become famous without ability. **George Bernard Shaw** in Preface to 1908 reprint of *Fabian Essays*

33 To famous men all the earth is a sepulchre. **Thucydides** *History*, II, 43, iii

34 The only man who wasn't spoilt by being lionized was Daniel.

Sir Herbert Beerbohm Tree in Hesketh Pearson, *Beerbohm Tree*, Ch. 12

35 Celebrity is a mask that eats into the face. One can either see or be seen. **John Updike** *Self-Consciousness*, Ch. 6

36 Fame should be obtained as a by-product. **Paul Valéry** *Analecta*, 23

37 One can survive anything now except death, and live down anything except a good reputation. **Oscar Wilde** *A Woman of No Importance*, Act 1

See also ***Praise and Blame***

Family

1 He that hath wife and children, hath given hostages to fortune; for they are impediments to great enterprises, either of virtue, or mischief.

Francis Bacon *Essays*: 'Of Marriage and Single Life'

2 The joys of parents are secret, and so are their griefs and fears.

Francis Bacon *Essays*: 'Of Parents and Children'

3 Grandfathers are our teachers, our real philosophers. They are the people who pull open the curtain that others are always closing. When we are with them, we see things as they really are – not just the auditorium but the stage and all that goes on behind the scenes. For thousands of years grandfathers have taken it upon themselves to create the devil where otherwise there would have only been God.

Thomas Bernhard *Gathering Evidence*: 'A Child'

4 A wise son maketh a glad father: but a foolish son is the heaviness of his mother. **Bible, OT** Proverbs 10:1

5 People are thankful to their forebears because they never knew them.

Elias Canetti *The Human Province*: '1943'

6 If one is not going to take the necessary precautions to avoid having parents, one must undertake to bring them up.

Quentin Crisp *The Naked Civil Servant*, Ch. 5

7 There are times when parenthood seems nothing but feeding the mouth that bites you. **Peter De Vries** *The Tunnel of Love*, Ch. 5

8 The family is a collection of people who defend each other as a group but attack each other as individuals. **Comtesse Diane** *Les Glanes de la vie*

9 It is a melancholy truth that even great men have their poor relations. **Charles Dickens** *Bleak House*, Ch. 28

10 Accidents will occur in the best-regulated families.

Charles Dickens *David Copperfield*, Ch. 28

11 Family quarrels are bitter things. They don't go according to any rules. They're not like aches or pains; they're more like splits in the skin that won't heal because there's not enough material.

F. Scott Fitzgerald *Notebooks*, O

12 One would be in less danger
From the wiles of the stranger
If one's own kin and kith
Were more fun to be with. **Ogden Nash** *Family Court*

13 All men are brothers, but thank God, they aren't all brothers-in-law.

Anthony Powell *At Lady Molly's*, Ch. 4

14 For there is no friend like a sister
In calm or stormy weather. **Christina Rossetti** *Goblin Market*, line 562

15 Families naturally prefer widows to unmarried mothers, but only just. **Jean-Paul Sartre** *Words*, Pt 1

16 The family that prays together stays together.

Al Scalpone slogan of Roman Catholic Rosary Crusade, first broadcast 6 March 1947; in Father Patrick Peyton, *All for Her*

17 When our relatives are at home, we have to think of all their good points or it would be impossible to endure them. But when they are away, we console ourselves for their absence by dwelling on their vices. **George Bernard Shaw** *Heartbreak House*, Act 1

18 As a rule there is only one person an English girl hates more than she hates her eldest sister; and that's her mother.

George Bernard Shaw *Man and Superman*, Act 2

19 All happy families resemble one another, each unhappy family is unhappy in its own way. **Leo Tolstoy** *Anna Karenina*, Pt. 1, Ch. 1

20 Maturity is the assimilation of the features of every ancestor.
Derek Walcott 'The Muse of History', in *Is Massa Day Done?*, ed. Orde Coombs

21 Fathers should be neither seen nor heard. That is the only proper basis for family life. **Oscar Wilde** *An Ideal Husband*, Act 4

See also **Children and Adults; Relationships**

Faults

1 The greatest mistake is trying to be more agreeable than you can be.
Walter Bagehot *Biographical Studies*, p. 294

2 To slip upon a pavement is better than to slip with the tongue; so the fall of the wicked shall come speedily. **Bible, Apocrypha** Ecclesiasticus 20:18

3 Every man haz a weak side, and sum hav two or three.
Josh Billings *Wit and Humor*: Affurisms, 'Glass Dimonds'

4 I think most men had rather be charged with malice than with making a blunder. **Josh Billings** *Wit and Humor*: Affurisms, 'Lobstir Sallad'

5 From a worldly point of view there is no mistake so great as that of being always right. **Samuel Butler 2** *Notebooks*, p. 250

6 The chapter of knowledge is very short, but the chapter of accidents is very long. **Earl of Chesterfield** letter to Solomon Dayrolles, 16 February 1753

7 Half our mistakes in this life arise from feeling where we ought to think, and thinking where we ought to feel.
John Churton Collins *Maxims and Reflections*

8 We do not admire our faults as much as our virtues, but we enjoy them more. **Comtesse Diane** *Les Glanes de la vie*

9 Errors look so very ugly in people of small means – one feels they are taking quite a liberty in going astray; whereas people of fortune may naturally indulge in a few delinquencies.
George Eliot *Scenes of Clerical Life*: 'Janet's Repentance', Ch. 25

10 There's nothing kills a man so soon as having nobody to find fault with but himself. **George Eliot** *Silas Marner*, Ch. 17

11 God punishes man's faults by letting him live.
Xavier Forneret *Sans titre, par un homme noir, blanc de visage*

12 Those see nothing but faults that seek for nothing else.

Dr Thomas Fuller *Gnomologia*, 5021

13 We are far readier to admit to shortcomings in our behaviour than in our ideas. **Johann Wolfgang von Goethe** *Maxims and Reflections*: 'Science', 529

14 We confess our faults in the plural, and deny them in the singular.

Fulke Greville *Maxims, Characters and Reflections*, p. 27

15 We don't ask others to be faultless; we only ask that their faults should not incommode our own. **Gyp** quoted in J. Raymond Solly, *A Cynic's Breviary*

16 The World is beholden to *generous Mistakes* for the greatest Part of the Good that is done to it.

Marquis of Halifax *Moral Thoughts and Reflections*: 'Of the World'

17 Every error under the sun seems to arise from thinking that you are right yourself because you are yourself, and other people wrong because they are not you. **Thomas Hardy** *Diary*, March or April 1884

18 The confession of our failings is a thankless office. It savours less of sincerity or modesty than of ostentation. It seems as if we thought our weaknesses as good as other people's virtues.

William Hazlitt *Characteristics*, 43

19 The only people, scientific or other, who never make mistakes are those who do no thinking. **T. H. Huxley** *Aphorisms and Reflections*, 136

20 The vulgar mind always mistakes the exceptional for the important.

W. R. Inge *More Lay Thoughts of a Dean*, Pt 4, Ch. 1

21 Generally it is our failures that civilize us. Triumph confirms us in our habits. **Clive James** *Unreliable Memoirs*, Ch. 6

22 There is no harm in being sometimes wrong – especially if one is promptly found out. **John Maynard Keynes** *Essays in Biography*

23 The trouble with mistakes is that there are as many people who learn too much from them as there are who learn nothing at all.

David Kipp *Aphorisms*, p. 12

24 She only lacked a flaw to be perfect.

Karl Kraus *Half-Truths and One-and-a-Half Truths*: 'Not for Women'

25 Any view of knowledge that leaves error in the mind will have its truth in no other place. We *make* mistakes; we don't think mistakes.

John William Miller *The Philosophy of History*, Ch. 35, iii

26 Perversion is an idea of an object, not conforming to its nature.

Bhagwān Shree Patanjali *Aphorisms of Yoga*, 1, 8

27 There are some faults which are better indicators of a good character than some virtues.
Cardinal de Retz *Memoirs*, Pt 2

28 And oftentimes excusing of a fault
Doth make the fault the worse by the excuse.
William Shakespeare *King John*, Act 4, Sc. 2, 30

29 If you want a person's faults, go to those who love him. They will not tell you, but they know.
Robert Louis Stevenson *Familiar Studies of Men and Books*, p. 159

30 The able man is the one who makes mistakes according to the rules.
Paul Valéry *Bad Thoughts and Not So Bad*, Q

31 Nowadays people die of a sort of creeping common sense, and discover when it is too late that the only things one never regrets are one's mistakes.
Oscar Wilde *The Picture of Dorian Gray*, Ch. 3

32 The physician can bury his mistakes, but the architect can only advise his client to plant vines.
Frank Lloyd Wright in the *New York Times Magazine*, 4 October 1953

Fears

1 Terror is as much a part of the concept of truth as runniness is of the concept of jam.
Jean Baudrillard *Cool Memories*, Ch. 5

2 There is no fear in love; but perfect love casteth out fear.
Bible, NT 1 John 4:18

3 Often the fear of one evil leads us into a worse.
Nicolas Boileau *L'Art poétique*, I, 64

4 No passion so effectually robs the mind of all its powers of acting and reasoning as fear.
Edmund Burke *On the Sublime and the Beautiful*, II, ii

5 Fear has many eyes and can see things underground.
Miguel Cervantes *Don Quixote*, Pt 1, 20

6 We often pretend to fear what we really despise, and more often to despise what we really fear.
Charles Caleb Colton *Lacon*: 'Fear and Contempt'

7 Dread is a sympathetic antipathy and an antipathetic sympathy.
Søren Kierkegaard in *Søren Kierkegaard Anthology*, selected by W. H. Auden, Ch. 1

8 The source of fear is in the future, and a person freed of the future has nothing to fear.
Milan Kundera *Slowness*, 1

9 He who fears dangers does not perish by them.

Leonardo da Vinci *Selections from the Notebooks*, Ch. 6, II

See also Livy

10 Fear governs the world, and hope consoles it.

Duc de Lévis *Maximes et réflexions*, 5

11 The less fear there is, the less is the danger. **Livy** *History of Rome*, Bk 22.5

See also Leonardo

12 Fear sometimes arises from deficient judgement as much as from deficient courage. **Michel de Montaigne** *Essays*, Bk 3, Ch. 6

13 Fear finds it more natural to consult than to decide.

Cardinal de Retz *Memoirs*, Pt 2

14 Fear cannot be without hope nor hope without fear.

Benedict Spinoza *On Ethics*

15 My fears are as good prophets as my hopes.

H. D. Thoreau *Journal*, 19 March 1842

16 Fear won't always save you but it will take some of the pressures off your luck. **Tobias Wolff** *In Pharaoh's Army*: 'Close Calls'

See also ***Calm and Unease***

Fiction and Fact

1 Parcels have always exercised an odd fascination for me – one always expects something of a sensational nature, and one is always disappointed. In that respect they resemble the modern novel.

Peter Ackroyd *The Last Testament of Oscar Wilde*, 14 August 1900

2 Fact is richer than diction.

J. L. Austin *Philosophical Papers*: 'A Plea for Excuses', 1961

3 Myth is neither a lie nor a confession; it is an inflexion.

Roland Barthes *Mythologies*: 'Myth Today'

4 All stories, before they are narrated, begin with the end.

John Berger *Story for Aesop*

5 You can't get at the truth by writing history; only the novelist can do that.

Gerald Brenan when invited to write the Spanish volume in the *Oxford History of Europe*, quoted in the *Times Literary Supplement*, 28 November 1986

6 History is in the shit sense. You have left it behind you. Fiction is piss: a stream of past events but not behind you, because they never really happened. **Brigid Brophy** *In Transit*, Sect. 1, 1

7 Every story of two is always a story of three: two pairs of hands grab the same thing at the same time and pull in opposite directions.
Roberto Calasso *The Marriage of Cadmus and Harmony*, Ch. 6

8 A good novel tells us the truth about its hero; but a bad novel tells us the truth about its author. **G. K. Chesterton** *Heretics*, Ch. 15

9 Fairy tales are the only true accounts that man has ever given of his destiny. **G. K. Chesterton** in *The World*, 3 May 1902

10 You must look at facts because they look at you.
Winston S. Churchill speech in House of Commons, 7 May 1925

11 The novel, whatever else it may be, is partly a notice board.
E. M. Forster *Two Cheers for Democracy*: 'Anonymity: an Inquiry'

12 By its very nature, the novel indicates that we are becoming. There is no final solution. There is no last word.
Carlos Fuentes in the *Guardian*, 24 February 1989

13 Fiction was invented the day Jonah arrived home and told his wife that he was three days late because he had been swallowed by a whale.
Gabriel García Márquez in the *Guardian*, 30 January 1999

14 The most mediocre novel is still better than mediocre readers, indeed the worst novel still participates in some way in the excellence of the genre as a whole.
Johann Wolfgang von Goethe *Maxims and Reflections* (Penguin), 1406

15 Every novelist has something in common with a spy: he watches, he overhears, he seeks motives and analyses character, and in his attempt to serve literature he is unscrupulous. **Graham Greene** *A Sort of Life*, Ch. 7

16 The only part of a story that is true is the part the listener believes.
Hermann Hesse *Reflections*, 400: 'Reality and Imagination'

17 Great novels are always a little more intelligent than their authors. Novelists who are more intelligent than their books should go into another line of work. **Milan Kundera** *The Art of the Novel*: 'Jerusalem Address'

18 There is no life that can be recaptured wholly; as it was. Which is to say that all biography is ultimately fiction. **Bernard Malamud** *Dubin's Lives*, 1

19 A novelist is, like all mortals, more fully at home on the surface of the present than in the ooze of the past. **Vladimir Nabokov** *Strong Opinions*, 20

20 Novels arise out of the shortcomings of history.
Novalis *Fragmente und Studien 1799–1800*, 7, 3

21 Stories are always a form of resistance.

Ben Okri *A Way of Being Free*: 'The Joys of Storytelling III', 60

22 All our stories are about what happens to our wishes. About the world as we would like it to be, and the world as it happens to be, irrespective of our wishes and despite our hopes.

Adam Phillips *The Beast in the Nursery*: Introduction

23 A novel is a mirror walking along a main road.

Stendhal *Scarlet and Black*, Ch. 49

24 The ancient historians gave us delightful fiction in the form of fact; the modern novelist presents us with dull facts in the guise of fiction.

Oscar Wilde *The Decay of Lying*

25 The good ended happily, and the bad unhappily. That is what Fiction means. **Oscar Wilde** *The Importance of Being Earnest*, Act 2

26 A woman must have money and a room of her own if she is to write fiction. **Virginia Woolf** *A Room of One's Own*, Ch. 1

See also ***History; Writing***

Flattery

1 The arch-flatterer, with whom all the petty flatterers have intelligence, is a man's self. **Francis Bacon** *Essays*: 'Of Love'

2 Flattery is a Juggler, and no Kin unto Sincerity.

Sir Thomas Browne *Christian Morals*, Pt 1, 23

3 Flattery corrupts both the receiver and the giver.

Edmund Burke *Reflections on the Revolution in France*

4 Every woman is infallibly to be gained by every sort of flattery, and every man by one sort or other.

Earl of Chesterfield *Letters to His Son*, 16 March 1752

5 Envy is the sincerest form of flattery.

John Churton Collins in the *English Review*, April 1914, p. 95

6 Flattery is often a traffic of mutual meanness, where, although both parties intend deception, neither are deceived; since words that cost little are exchanged for hopes that cost less.

Charles Caleb Colton *Lacon*: 'Flattery'

7 He who cannot love must learn to flatter or he won't succeed.

Johann Wolfgang von Goethe *Maxims and Reflections*: 'Life and Character', 145

8 Flattery won't hurt you if you don't swaller it.

'Kin' Hubbard *Abe Martin's Wisecracks*, p. 53

See also Stevenson

9 Just praise is only a debt, but flattery is a present.

Dr Samuel Johnson *The Rambler*, 155, 10 September 1751

10 The flatterer does not think highly enough of himself or of others.

Jean de La Bruyère *Characters*: 'Of Opinions', 90

11 All flatterers live at the expense of those who listen to them.

Jean de La Fontaine *Fables*, I, 2: 'The Crow and the Fox'

12 If we never flattered ourselves the flattery of others could do us no harm. **Duc de La Rochefoucauld** *Maxims*, 152

13 What gives flattery so much charm is that it appears to confirm our own judgement. **Duc de Lévis** *Maxims, Precepts and Reflections*

14 It is possible to be below flattery, as well as above it.

Thomas Babington Macaulay *The History of England*, Ch. 2

15 Flattery is all right – if you don't inhale.

Adlai Stevenson TV broadcast, 30 March 1952

See also Hubbard

16 No syren did ever so charm the ear of the listener, as the listening ear has charmed the soul of the syren. **Sir Henry Taylor** *The Statesman*, Ch. 31

17 The most perfect form of flattery is to tell people what they think of themselves. **Sydney Tremayne** *Tatlings*, p. 39

18 If humans did not flatter each other, society would not exist.

Marquis de Vauvenargues *Reflections and Maxims*, 589

19 Women are never disarmed by compliments. Men always are. That is the difference between the sexes. **Oscar Wilde** *An Ideal Husband*, Act 1

See also ***Praise and Blame***

Food and Drink

1 You *can* have your cake and eat it; the only trouble is you get fat.

Julian Barnes *Flaubert's Parrot*, Ch. 7

2 For when the wine is in, the wit is out. **Thomas Becon** *Catechism*, 375

3 Wine is a mocker, strong drink is raging: and whosoever is deceived thereby is not wise. **Bible, OT** Proverbs 20:1

4 **Teetotaller, n.** One who abstains from strong drink, sometimes totally, sometimes tolerably totally. **Ambrose Bierce** *The Devil's Dictionary*

5 Grub first, then ethics. **Bertolt Brecht** *The Threepenny Opera*, Act 2, Sc. 1

6 Animals feed: man eats: only the man of intellect knows how to eat.
Jean-Anthelme Brillat-Savarin *The Physiology of Taste*: Aphorisms, II

7 Tell me what you eat: I will tell you what you are.
Jean-Anthelme Brillat-Savarin *The Physiology of Taste*: Aphorisms, IV

See also Feuerbach

8 The discovery of a new dish does more for the happiness of mankind than the discovery of a star.
Jean-Anthelme Brillat-Savarin *The Physiology of Taste*: Aphorisms, IX

9 First parents of the human race, whose gourmandism is historical, you lost all that for an apple, what would you not have done for a truffled turkey? But in the earthly paradise there were no cooks or confectioners. **Jean-Anthelme Brillat-Savarin** *The Physiology of Taste*: Aphorisms, Ch. 27

10 Freedom and Whisky gang thegither!
Robert Burns *The Author's Earnest Cry and Prayer*, 185

11 The healthy stomach is nothing if not conservative. Few radicals have good digestions. **Samuel Butler 2** *Notebooks*, Ch. 6: 'Indigestion'

12 Eating is touch carried to the bitter end.
Samuel Butler 2 quoted in W. H. Auden, *A Certain World*: 'Eating'

13 Hunger is the best sauce in the world.
Miguel Cervantes *Don Quixote*, Pt 2, 5

14 Society is composed of two great classes – those who have more dinners than appetite, and those who have more appetite than dinners.
Nicholas-Sébastien Chamfort *Maxims and Considerations*, 194

15 We're less hungry when warm, and less warm when hungry. It's the stomach that controls climate. **Malcolm de Chazal** *Sens plastique*, p. 42

16 No animal ever invented anything so bad as drunkenness – or so good as drink. **G. K. Chesterton** *All Things Considered*: 'Wine When It Is Red'

17 A sober man may become a drunkard through being a coward. A brave man may become a coward through being a drunkard.
G. K. Chesterton *Charles Dickens*, Ch. 8

18 It does not so very much matter whether a man eats a grilled tomato or a plain tomato; it does very much matter whether he eats a plain tomato with a grilled mind. **G. K. Chesterton** *Heretics*, Ch. 10

19 Gluttony is an emotional escape, a sign something is eating us.
Peter De Vries *Comfort Me with Apples*, Ch. 15

20 In the Proverbs of Solomon you will find the following words, ' "May we never want a friend in need, nor a bottle to give him!" When found, make a note of.' **Charles Dickens** *Dombey and Son*, Ch. 15

21 Doctors are always working to preserve our health and cooks to destroy it, but the latter are the more often successful.
Denis Diderot quoted in J. Raymond Solly, *A Cynic's Breviary*

22 The cocktail-party – as the name suggests – was originally invented by dogs. They are simply bottom-sniffings raised to the rank of formal ceremonies. **Lawrence Durrell** *Justine*, Pt 3, p. 171

23 There is this to be said in favour of drinking, that it takes the drunkard first out of society, then out of the world.
Ralph Waldo Emerson *Journal*, July 1866

24 A man is what he eats.
Ludwig Feuerbach *Blätter für Literarische Unterhaltung*, 12 November 1850

See also Brillat-Savarin

25 Gastronomic perfection can be reached in these combinations: one person dining alone, usually upon a couch or a hillside; two persons, of no matter what sex or age, dining in a good restaurant; six people, of no matter what sex or age, dining in a good home.
M. F. K. Fisher *An Alphabet for Gourmets*: 'From A to Z: The Perfect Dinner'

26 If the days are short, an early evening meal seems to cut them in two, leaving the second part hanging lifeless on the hardly realized beginning, and if they are long, they are made twice as monotonously hot by the tired interruption of cooked food. **M. F. K. Fisher** *Serve It Forth*: 'Meals for Me'

27 The Grape that can with Logic absolute
The Two-and-Seventy jarring Sects confute.
Edward Fitzgerald *The Rubáiyát of Omar Khayyám*, Edn 1, 43

28 Leeks are the asparagus of the poor. **Anatole France** *Crainquebille*, Ch. 2

29 I gladly accept all the ups and downs of human life, from birth to death. I even accept family meals. **Jean Giraudoux** *Amphitryon*, Act 1

30 We can eat the apple, not the apple tree.
Friedrich Hebbel *Diaries*, entry 2856, 1843

31 There is always hope for a man who, when sober, will not concede or acknowledge that he was ever drunk.

O. Henry *The Rubaiyat of a Scotch Highball*

32 Drink not the third glass which thou canst not tame
When once it is within thee.

George Herbert *The Temple*: 'The Church Porch', Verse 5

33 It is better to be full of drink than full of food.

Hippocrates *Aphorisms*, 2, 11

34 Man wants but little drink below,
But wants that little strong.

Oliver Wendell Holmes *A Song of Other Days* (parody of Oliver Goldsmith)

35 Malt does more than Milton can
To justify God's ways to man. **A. E. Housman** *A Shropshire Lad*, 62

36 Wouldn't it be awful if spinach hain't really healthful after all th' trouble it takes t' git the sand out of it?

'Kin' Hubbard *Abe Martin's Wisecracks*, p. 56

37 He who does not mind his belly, will hardly mind anything else.

Dr Samuel Johnson in James Boswell, *Life of Johnson*, 5 August 1763

38 There is nothing which has yet been contrived by man, by which so much happiness is produced as by a good tavern or inn.

Dr Samuel Johnson in James Boswell, *Life of Johnson*, 21 March 1776

39 This is one of the disadvantages of wine, it makes a man mistake words for thoughts. **Dr Samuel Johnson** in James Boswell, *Life of Johnson*, 28 April 1778

40 He devours crumbs that fall from his own table; this means that he is indeed better satisfied than anyone else for a while, but he forgets how to eat at the table itself; but this means that there are then no more crumbs either. **Franz Kafka** *Collected Aphorisms*, 73

41 A hungry stomach has no ears.

Jean de La Fontaine *Fables*, IX, 18: 'The Kite and the Nightingale'

42 To eat is a necessity, but to eat intelligently is an art.

Duc de La Rochefoucauld quoted in M. F. K. Fisher, *Serve It Forth*: 'When A Man Is Small'

43 If you're going to America, bring your own food.

Fran Lebowitz *Social Studies*: 'Fran Lebowitz's Travel Hints'

44 The downfall of most diets is that they restrict your intake of food.

Fran Lebowitz *Social Studies*: 'The High Stress Diet'

45 However great the dish that holds the turbot, the turbot is still greater than the dish. **Martial** *Epigrams*

46 You're not drunk if you can lie on the floor without holding on.
Dean Martin quoted in Paul Dickson, *Official Rules*

47 At a dinner party one should eat wisely but not too well, and talk well but not too wisely. **W. Somerset Maugham** *A Writer's Notebook*, 1896

48 I've made it a rule never to drink by daylight and never to refuse a drink after dark. **H. L. Mencken** in the *New York Post*, 18 September 1945

49 Kissing don't last: cookery do. **George Meredith** *The Ordeal of Richard Feverel*, Ch. 28

50 No man is lonely while eating spaghetti.
Robert Morley quoted in Jonathon Green, *Consuming Passions*

51 A meal for two is enough for three, a meal for three is enough for four. **Muhammad** *The Sayings of Muhammad*: 'Food and Etiquette'

52 The belly is the reason man does not so easily take himself for a god.
Friedrich Nietzsche *Beyond Good and Evil*: 'Maxims and Interludes', 141

53 The English have three vegetables and two of them are cabbage.
Walter Page quoted in Jonathon Green, *Consuming Passions*

54 There are two reasons for drinking: one is, when you are thirsty, to cure it; the other, when you are not thirsty, to prevent it.
Thomas Love Peacock *Melincourt*, Ch. 16

55 Eat therefore to live, and do not live to eat.
William Penn *Reflections and Maxims*, I, 59

56 *In vino veritas*. – Truth comes out in wine.
Pliny the Elder proverbial adaptation of *Natural History*, Bk 14, 28

57 Coffee, which makes the politician wise,
And see through all things with his half-shut eyes.
Alexander Pope *The Rape of the Lock*, lines 117–18

58 At Meals to sipping only, cling perforce,
And, for health's sake, drink not between each course.
Code of Health of the School of Salernum *Medical Maxims in Verse Form*: 'Method of Eating and Drinking'

59 Drunkenness is nothing but a state of self-induced insanity.
Seneca *Letters from a Stoic*, 83

60 'Tis an ill cook that cannot lick his own fingers.
William Shakespeare *Romeo and Juliet*, Act 4, Sc. 2, (6)

61 Grass will carry you through times of no money better than money through times of no dope.
Gilbert Shelton motto in strip cartoon 'Fabulous Furry Freak Brothers'

62 There are two things that will be believed of any man whatsoever, and one of them is that he has taken to drink. **Booth Tarkington** *Penrod*, Ch. 10

63 The human desire for food and sex is relatively equal. If there are armed rapes why should there not be armed hot dog thefts?
John Kennedy Toole *A Confederacy of Dunces*, Ch. 7, 1

Fools and Folly

1 Nothing is more characteristic of a man than the manner in which he behaves towards fools. **Henri-Frédéric Amiel** *Amiel's Journal*, 17 December 1854

2 A fool knows more in his own house than a wise body in another man's. **Anon.** in George Herbert, *Outlandish Proverbs*

3 There is in human nature generally more of the fool than of the wise.
Francis Bacon *Essays*: 'Of Boldness'

4 As a dog returneth to his vomit, so a fool returneth to his folly.
Bible, OT Proverbs 26:11

5 A man that hideth his foolishness is better than a man that hideth his wisdom. **Bible, Apocrypha** Ecclesiasticus 41:15

6 If the fool would persist in his folly he would become wise.
William Blake *The Marriage of Heaven and Hell*: 'Proverbs of Hell'

7 A fool always finds a greater fool to admire him.
Nicolas Boileau *L'Art poétique*, I, 232

8 There are more Fools than Knaves in the World, else the Knaves would not have enough to live on.
Samuel Butler 1 *Genuine Remains*: 'Thoughts upon Various Subjects'

9 The university brings out all abilities, including stupidity.
Anton Chekhov *Notebooks 1894–1902*

10 His soul will never starve for exploits or excitements who is wise enough to be made a fool. To be 'taken in' everywhere is to see the inside of everything. **G. K. Chesterton** (attrib.)

11 A fool often fails because he thinks what is difficult is easy, and a wise man because he thinks what is easy is difficult.
John Churton Collins in the *English Review*, April 1914, p. 100

12 A fool must now and then be right, by chance.
William Cowper *Conversation*, 96

13 If a fool can see his own folly, he in this at least is wise; but the fool who thinks he is wise, he indeed is the real fool. ***The Dhammapada*** 63

14 Stupidity consists in wanting to reach conclusions. We are a thread, and we want to know the whole cloth.

Gustave Flaubert letter to Louis Bouilhet, 4 September 1850, Damascus

15 There are no fools so troublesome as those that have wit.

Benjamin Franklin *Poor Richard's Almanack*, 1741

16 Most fools think they are only ignorant.

Benjamin Franklin *Poor Richard's Almanack Improved*, 1748

17 Often the cockloft is empty in those whom nature hath built many storeys high. **Thomas Fuller** *The Holy and the Profane State*, Bk 5, Ch. 18, Sect. 9

18 To commit a Folly, makes not a Fool, but not to know how to hide it. **Dr Thomas Fuller** *Introductio ad Prudentium*, 2675

19 Poppycock is not simply nonsense; it may be sense in the wrong place. **Johann Wolfgang von Goethe** *Goethe's Opinions*, p. 57

20 If he is a fool who at forty applies to Hippocrates for health, still more is he one who then applies to Seneca for wisdom.

Baltasar Gracián *The Art of Worldly Wisdom*, 36

21 Some men have just sense enough to prove their want of it.

Fulke Greville *Maxims, Characters and Reflections*, p. 75

22 A fool hath no dialogue within himself, the first thought carrieth him without the reply of a second.

Marquis of Halifax *Moral Thoughts and Reflections*: 'Of Folly and Fools'

23 I am always afraid of a fool: one cannot be sure that he is not a knave as well. **William Hazlitt** *Characteristics*, 225

24 Folly is as often owing to a want of proper sentiments as to a want of understanding. **William Hazlitt** *Characters of Shakespeare's Plays*: 'Cymbeline'

25 Mingle some brief folly with your wisdom. To forget it in due place is sweet. **Horace** *Odes*, xii, 27

26 A fool and his books are soon parted.

Holbrook Jackson *Maxims of Books and Reading*, 13

27 As foolish as it must seem to the crab when he sees man walking forwards. **Georg Christoph Lichtenberg** *Aphorisms*, Notebook D, 22

28 There are two sorts of fool: those who doubt nothing and those who doubt everything. **Prince de Ligne** *Mes Écarts*

29 A fellow who is always declaring he's no fool usually has his suspicions. **Wilson Mizner** in A. Andrews, *Quotations for Speakers and Writers*

30 A learned fool is more foolish than an ignorant fool.

Molière *Les Femmes savantes*, Act 4, Sc. 3

31 Seriousness is stupidity sent to college.

P. J. O'Rourke *Give War a Chance*: 'A Serious Problem'

32 Some women can be fooled all the time – all women can be fooled some of the time but the same woman can't be fooled by the same man in the same way more than half the time. **Helen Rowland** *A Guide to Men*: 'Intermezzo'

33 Against stupidity the gods themselves struggle in vain.

Friedrich von Schiller *The Maid of Orleans*, Act 3, Sc. 6

34 A fool leads a thankless and anxious life, given over wholly to the future.

Seneca *Letters from a Stoic*, 15, quoting a 'striking maxim which comes from the Greek'

35 A fool and his words are soon parted, for so should the proverb run.

William Shenstone *Essays on Men and Manners*: 'On Reserve'

36 You can fool too many of the people too much of the time.

James Thurber *Fables for Our Time*: 'The Owl Who Was God'

37 A fool and his money are soon married.

Tigers Don't Eat Grass: Oriental and Occidental Aphorisms 'Fools'

38 Stupidity is not seeing what another man sees; weakness, being unable to do what another man can do. **Paul Valéry** *Analecta*, 35

39 There is no sin except stupidity. **Oscar Wilde** *The Critic as Artist*, II

40 In examinations the foolish ask questions that the wise cannot answer. **Oscar Wilde** *Phrases and Philosophies for the Use of the Young*

41 But there comes a moment in everybody's life when he must decide whether he'll live among human beings or not – a fool among fools or a fool alone. **Thornton Wilder** *The Matchmaker*, Act 4

See also ***Madness and Sanity; Wisdom***

Forgiveness

1 We read that we ought to forgive our enemies; but we do not read that we ought our friends.

Francis Bacon *Apothegms*, 143; quoting Cosimo Medici, Duke of Florence

2 The cut worm forgives the plough.

William Blake *The Marriage of Heaven and Hell*: 'Proverbs of Hell'

3 Once a woman has forgiven her man, she must not reheat his sins for breakfast. **Marlene Dietrich** *Marlene Dietrich's ABC*: 'Forgiveness'

4 We do not quite forgive a giver.
Ralph Waldo Emerson *Essays: Second Series*: 'Gifts'

5 Forgive, O Lord, my little jokes on Thee
And I'll forgive Thy great big one on me. **Robert Frost** *Cluster of Faith*

6 Nobody ever forgets where he buried a hatchet.
'Kin' Hubbard in *Indianapolis News*, 4 January 1925

7 The public seldom forgive twice.
Johann Kaspar Lavater *Aphorisms on Man*, 606; William Blake commented, 'Let us take their example'

8 Jews ask forgiveness of man, not God, which is rough on us because man is a harder con than God any day.
John Le Carré *The Tailor of Panama*, Ch. 6

9 People will sometimes forgive you the good you have done them, but seldom the harm they have done you.
W. Somerset Maugham *A Writer's Notebook*, 1933

10 Men would never offend God if they knew how ready He is to forgive them. **Coventry Patmore** *The Rod, the Root and the Flower*: 'Aurea Dicta', 42

11 To err is human, to forgive, divine.
Alexander Pope *An Essay on Criticism*, 525

12 The stupid neither forgive nor forget; the naïve forgive and forget; the wise forgive but do not forget.
Thomas S. Szasz *The Second Sin*: 'Personal Conduct'

13 Society often forgives the criminal; it never forgives the dreamer.
Oscar Wilde *The Critic as Artist*, 2

14 It costs more to revenge than to bear with injuries.
Bishop Thomas Wilson *Maxims of Piety and Christianity*: 'Injuries'

Freedom and Tyranny

1 It is part of the mechanism of domination to forbid recognition of the suffering it produces. **Theodor Adorno** *Minima Memoralia*, Pt 1, 38

2 Under conditions of tyranny, it is far easier to act than to think.
Hannah Arendt quoted in W. H. Auden, *A Certain World*: 'Tyranny'

3 There is no method by which men can be both free and equal.
Walter Bagehot in the *Economist*, 5 September 1863

4 Despotism accomplishes great things illegally; liberty does not even go to the trouble of accomplishing the smallest things legally.
Honoré de Balzac *La Peau de chagrin*, Ch. 3

5 Freedom is nothing but the distance
between the hunter and the hunted. **Bei Dao** *The August Sleeper*

6 Abstract liberty, like other mere abstractions, is not to be found.
Edmund Burke speech on conciliation with America, 22 March 1775

7 The true danger is when liberty is nibbled away, for expedience, and by parts. **Edmund Burke** letter to the Sheriffs of Bristol, 3 April 1777

8 Liberty, too, must be limited in order to be possessed.
Edmund Burke letter to the Sheriffs of Bristol 3 April 1777

9 Scorn is the first victory over the world; detachment the last, the supreme. The interval separating them is identified with the path leading from liberty to liberation. **E. M. Cioran** *Anathemas and Admirations*, 9

10 Tyrants are always assassinated too late; that is their great excuse.
E. M. Cioran quoted in W. H. Auden, *A Certain World*: 'Tyranny'

11 There is no limit to tyranny when it seeks to obtain the signs of consensus. **Benjamin Constant** *On the Spirit of Conquest and Usurpation*

12 Censors tend to do what only psychotics do: they confuse reality with illusion. **David Cronenberg** *Cronenberg on Cronenberg*, Ch. 5

13 All men would be tyrants if they could.
Daniel Defoe *The Kentish Petition*: addenda, 11

14 The world exists, as I understand it, to teach the science of liberty, which begins with the liberty from fear.
Ralph Waldo Emerson *The Fugitive Slave Law*

15 No man can rob us of our free will. **Epictetus** *Moral Discourses*, II, 22

16 Whosoever will be free, let him not desire or dread that which is within the power of others either to deny or inflict; otherwise he is a slave.
Epictetus *Moral Discourses*, IV, 2

17 To live under constraint is a misfortune, but there is no constraint to live under constraint. **Epicurus** quoted in Seneca, *Letters to a Stoic*, 12

18 The *sense* of liberty is a message read between the lines of constraint. Real liberty is as transparent, odourless and tasteless as water.
Michael Frayn *Constructions*, 85

19 Liberation, a human phenomenon, cannot be achieved by semi-humans.
Paulo Freire *Pedagogy of the Oppressed*, Ch. 1

20 Man has achieved *freedom from*, without yet having *freedom to* – to be himself, to be productive, to be fully awake.
Erich Fromm *The Fear of Freedom*, 4

21 The interpretation of our reality through patterns not our own serves only to make us ever more unknown, ever less free, ever more solitary.
Gabriel García Márquez epigraph to Rana Kabbani, *Europe's Myths of Orient*

22 O Freedom, what liberties are taken in thy name!
Daniel George in Sagittarius and Daniel George, *The Perpetual Pessimist*, 30 June

23 Everything that frees our spirit without giving us control of ourselves is ruinous.
Johann Wolfgang von Goethe *Maxims and Reflections*: 'Life and Character', 33

24 When a Despotick Prince hathe bruised all his subjects with a slavish Obedience, all the force he can use cannot subdue his own fears.
Marquis of Halifax *The Character of a Trimmer*

25 The history of the world is none other than the progress of the consciousness of freedom.
Georg Hegel *The Philosophy of History*: Introduction

26 Unless freedom is universal it is only extended privilege.
Christopher Hill *The Century of Revolution*, Ch. 20

27 It is better for a man to go wrong in freedom than to go right in chains.
T. H. Huxley *Aphorisms and Reflections*, 315

28 It is better to die on your feet than to live on your knees!
Dolores Ibárruri ('La Pasionaria') Republican slogan broadcast in the Spanish Civil War, but coined by Emiliano Zapata in Mexico in 1910; in Hugh Thomas, *The Spanish Civil War*, Ch. 16

29 One should never put on one's best trousers to go out to battle for freedom and truth.
Henrik Ibsen *An Enemy of the People*, Act 5

30 If men have to choose between chaos and despotism they will generally choose despotism.
W. R. Inge *The End of an Age*, Ch. 4

31 The tree of liberty must be refreshed from time to time with the blood of patriots and tyrants. It is its natural manure.
Thomas Jefferson letter to W. S. Smith, 13 November 1787

32 A country governed by a despot is an inverted cone.
Dr Samuel Johnson in James Boswell, *Life of Johnson*, Vol. 3, 283

33 A cage went in search of a bird.
Franz Kafka *Collected Aphorisms*, 16

34 It's often safer to be in chains than to be free.
Franz Kafka *The Trial*, 8

35 It is better that a man should tyrannize over his bank balance than over his fellow citizens.

John Maynard Keynes *The General Theory of Employment*, Bk 6, Ch. 24

36 Aren't people absurd! They never use the freedoms they do have but demand those they don't have; they have freedom of thought, they demand freedom of speech. **Søren Kierkegaard** *Either/Or*, Pt 1, Ch. 1

37 So long as the state exists there is no freedom. When there is freedom there will be no state **Vladimir Ilyich Lenin** *The State and Revolution*, Ch. 5, Sect. 4

38 I believe that man is in the last resort so free a being that his right *to be* what he believes himself to be cannot be contested.

Georg Christoph Lichtenberg *Aphorisms*, Notebook L, 98

39 Freedom is always and exclusively freedom for the one who thinks differently. **Rosa Luxemburg** *The Russian Revolution*, Sect. 4

40 There is only one cure for the evils which newly acquired freedom produces; and that is freedom.

Thomas Babington Macaulay *Literary Essays*: 'Milton'

41 Man in general, if reduced to himself, is too wicked to be free.

Joseph de Maistre *Four Chapters on Russia*, Ch. 1

42 The liberty of the individual must be thus far limited; he must not make himself a nuisance to other people. **John Stuart Mill** *On Liberty*, Ch. 3

43 As good almost kill a man as kill a good book; who kills a man kills a reasonable creature, God's image; but he who destroys a good book, kills reason itself, kills the image of God, as it were in the eye.

John Milton *Areopagitica*

44 The singing bird forgets its cage.

Cardinal József Mindszenty quoted in the *Observer*, 5 May 1991

45 Liberty is the right to do everything which the laws allow.

Charles de Montesquieu *Of the Spirit of the Laws*, XI, 3

46 If liberty means anything at all, it means the right to tell people what they do not want to hear.

George Orwell 'The Freedom of the Press': proposed preface to *Animal Farm*

47 I sometimes think that the price of liberty is not so much eternal vigilance as eternal dirt. **George Orwell** *The Road to Wigan Pier*, Ch. 4

48 Tyranny is the wish to obtain by one means what can only be had by another. **Blaise Pascal** *Pensées*, 244

49 What is freedom of expression? Without the freedom to offend, it ceases to exist. **Salman Rushdie** in the *Weekend Guardian*, 10 February 1990

50 No human being, however great, or powerful, was ever so free as a fish.
John Ruskin quoted in Sagittarius and Daniel George, *The Perpetual Pessimist*, 11 December

51 A nation has no character until it is free.
Mme de Staël *De la Littérature*, Pt 1, Ch. 5

52 The worst evil of being in prison, he thought, is that one can never bar one's door. **Stendhal** *Scarlet and Black*, Ch. 44

53 My definition of a free society is a society where it is safe to be unpopular. **Adlai Stevenson** speech in Detroit, 7 October 1952

54 Emancipation from the bondage of the soil
is no freedom for the tree. **Rabindranath Tagore** *Fireflies*, p. 243

55 Despots themselves do not deny that freedom is excellent; but they only want it for themselves, and maintain that everyone else is totally unworthy of it. **Alexis de Tocqueville** *The Ancien Régime and the Revolution*, p. 75

56 He who seeks in liberty for anything other than itself, is born to be a servant. **Alexis de Tocqueville** *The Ancien Régime and the Revolution*, p. 217

57 There is nothing more tyrannical than a strong popular feeling among a democratic people. **Anthony Trollope** *North America*, I, 11

Friends and Enemies

1 A man often hopes that his friends are more sincere than himself.
William Allingham *By the Way*, Notes 151

2 Business, you know, may bring money, but friendship hardly ever does. **Jane Austen** *Emma*, Ch. 34

3 There is little friendship in the world, and least of all between equals.
Francis Bacon *Essays*: 'Of Followers'

4 The perfect interlocutor, the friend, is he not the one who constructs around you the greatest possible resonance? Cannot friendship be defined as a space with sonority?
Roland Barthes *A Lover's Discourse*: 'mutisme/silence'

5 A man that hath friends must shew himself friendly: There is a friend that sticketh closer than a brother. **Bible, OT** Proverbs 18:24

6 A faithful friend is the medicine of life. **Bible, Apocrypha** Ecclesiasticus 6:16

7 Forsake not an old friend; for the new is not comparable to him; a new friend is as new wine; when it is old, thou shalt drink it with pleasure.
Bible, Apocrypha Ecclesiasticus 9:10

8 While your friend holds you affectionately by both your hands you are safe because you can watch both his. **Ambrose Bierce** *The Devil's Dictionary*

9 **Acquaintance, n.** A person whom we know well enough to borrow money from, but not well enough to lend to.
Ambrose Bierce *The Enlarged Devil's Dictionary*

10 Opposition is true friendship.
William Blake *The Marriage of Heaven and Hell*: 'A Memorable Fancy: Opposition'

11 The bird a nest, the spider a web, man friendship.
William Blake *The Marriage of Heaven and Hell*: 'Proverbs of Hell'

12 He that wrestles with us strengthens our nerves, and sharpens our skill. Our antagonist is our helper.
Edmund Burke *Reflections on the Revolution in France*, p. 278

13 If an enemy is drowning, and the water is up to his waist, pull him out; if up to his chin, push him in.
Baldassare Castiglione *The Courtier*, Bk 3, citing a proverb

14 There are few vices as likely to diminish the number of a man's friends, as can an excessive possession of fine qualities.
Nicholas-Sébastien Chamfort *Maxims and Considerations*, 110

15 Women only give to friendship what they borrow from love.
Nicholas-Sébastien Chamfort *Maxims and Considerations*, 403

16 I have three kinds of friends: those who love me, those who pay no attention to me, and those who detest me.
Nicholas-Sébastien Chamfort quoted in Georg Christoph Lichtenberg, *Aphorisms*, Notebook K, 53

17 Most people enjoy the inferiority of their best friend.
Earl of Chesterfield *Letters to His Son*, 9 July 1750

18 We make our friends; we make our enemies; but God makes our next-door neighbour. **G. K. Chesterton** *Heretics*, Ch. 14

19 Affection may not be love, but it is at least its cousin.
J. M. Coetzee *Disgrace*, 1

20 In prosperity our friends know us; in adversity we know our friends.
John Churton Collins in the *English Review*, April 1914

21 There are some men whose enemies are to be pitied much, and their *friends* more. **Charles Caleb Colton** *Lacon*: 'Pity'

22 Fate chooses your relations, you choose your friends.
Abbé Jacques Delille *Malheur et pitié*, I

See also Kingsmill

23 Friendship is less fragile than love, because it is never involuntary.
Comtesse Diane *Les Glanes de la vie*, p. 17

24 The true friend overlooks nothing but forgives you everything.
Comtesse Diane *Maxims of Life*, p. 119

25 To find a friend one must close one eye. To keep him – two.
Norman Douglas *An Almanac 1945*

26 The falling out of faithful friends, renewing is of love.
Richard Edwardes *Amantium Irae*

27 The only reward of virtue is virtue; the only way to have a friend is to be one. **Ralph Waldo Emerson** *Essays*: 'Friendship'

28 There is no little enemy. **Benjamin Franklin** *Poor Richard's Almanack*, 1733

29 Thou hast no greater enemies than within thyself.
Dr Thomas Fuller *Introductio ad Prudentium*, 3054

30 Friendship increases in visiting friends; but in visiting them seldom.
Dr Thomas Fuller *Introductio ad Sapientiam*, 287

31 Friendship is a disinterested commerce between equals: love, an abject intercourse between tyrants and slaves.
Oliver Goldsmith *The Good-Natured Man*, Act 1

32 In times of prosperity, a man never has friends because he disowns them; in adversity, they disown him. **Baltasar Gracián** *The Oracle*, 114

33 There is more Skill necessary to keep a friend, than there is to reclaim an Enemy. **Marquis of Halifax** *Moral Thoughts and Reflections*: 'Of Friendship'

34 It is good to have some friends both in heaven and hell.
George Herbert *Jacula Prudentum*

35 When the ways of friends converge, the whole world looks like home for an hour. **Hermann Hesse** *Reflections*, 593: 'Happiness'

36 It is easier to love humanity as a whole than to love one's neighbour.
Eric Hoffer *Between the Devil and the Dragon*, Pt 5, 2

37 We have fewer friends than we imagine but more than we know.
Hugo von Hofmannsthal *The Book of Friends*, 1

38 Never explain – your friends do not need it and your enemies will not believe you anyway. **Elbert Hubbard** *Motto Book*

39 There are three classes of friends: some are like food which thou canst not dispense with, others like medicine which is needful occasionally, and others like an illness which thou dost never want.
Solomon Ibn Gabirol *Choice of Pearls*, 261

40 If a man does not make new acquaintance as he advances through life, he will soon find himself alone. A man, Sir, should keep his friendship *in constant repair*. **Dr Samuel Johnson** in James Boswell, *Life of Johnson*, 1755

41 A friend may be often found and lost: but an *old friend* never can be found, and nature has provided that he cannot easily be lost.
Dr Samuel Johnson letter to Mrs Thrale, 13 November 1783

42 Friends are God's apology for relations.
Hugh Kingsmill *The Best of Hugh Kingsmill*, ed. Michael Holroyd: Introduction

See also Delille

43 Even a paranoid can have enemies.
Henry Kissinger in *Time* magazine, 24 January 1977; also attrib. Delmore Schwartz

44 True love is rare; true friendship still rarer.
Jean de La Fontaine in J. de Finod, *A Thousand Flashes of French Wit*, p. 122

45 It is more shameful to distrust one's friends than to be deceived by them. **Duc de La Rochefoucauld** *Maxims*, 84

46 In the misfortunes of our best friends, we always find something not unpleasing. **Duc de La Rochefoucauld** *Withdrawn Maxims*, 583

47 Be not the fourth friend of him who had three before and lost them.
Johann Kaspar Lavater *Aphorisms on Man*, 305; William Blake underlined and expressed his approval: 'An excellent rule'

48 The qualities of your friends will be those of your enemies: cold friends, cold enemies – half friends, half enemies – fervid enemies, warm friends.
Johann Kaspar Lavater *Aphorisms on Man*, 518; William Blake commented: 'Very Uneasy indeed, but *truth*'

49 Nothing in the world is rarer than a person one can always put up with. **Giacomo Leopardi** *Pensieri*, 76

50 We picture lovers face to face but friends side by side; their eyes look ahead. **C. S. Lewis** *The Four Loves*, Ch. 4

51 Levin wanted friendship and got friendliness; he wanted steak and they offered spam. **Bernard Malamud** *A New Life*, Sect. vi

52 The most disagreeable thing that your worst enemy says to your face does not approach what your best friend says behind your back.
Alfred de Musset quoted in J. Raymond Solly, *A Cynic's Breviary*

53 Better to have open enemies than hidden friends.
Napoleon Bonaparte *Maxims*

54 'Our neighbour is not our neighbour but our neighbour's neighbour' – thus thinks every people.

Friedrich Nietzsche *Beyond Good and Evil*: 'Maxims and Interludes', 162

55 Addiction is a friendship without a friend.

Connie Palmen *The Friendship*, Pt 3, Ch. 7

56 Homosexuals, like Jews, often find themselves numbered among their enemies' best friends. **Frederic Raphael** in *3: Radio Three Magazine*, October 1982

57 There are no such things as friends: there are moments of friendship.

Jules Renard *Journal 1887–1910*, 4 January 1894

58 To like and dislike the same things, that is indeed true friendship.

Sallust *Catiline*, Ch. 20

59 A friend in need is a friend to be avoided.

Anon. in Herbert Samuel *Book of Quotations*, 'Maxims'

60 Friendship is almost always the union of a part of one mind with a part of another; people are friends in spots.

George Santayana *Soliloquies in England*: 'Friendships'

61 Friendship is constant in all other things
Save in the office and affairs of love.

William Shakespeare *Much Ado About Nothing*, Act 2, Sc. 1, 184

62 Do not love your neighbour as yourself. If you are on good terms with yourself it is an impertinence; if on bad, an injury.

George Bernard Shaw *Man and Superman*, 'Maxims for Revolutionists': 'The Golden Rule'

63 We need two kinds of acquaintances, one to complain to, while we boast to the others. **Logan Pearsall Smith** *Afterthoughts*, 3

64 Some great misfortune to portend,
No enemy can match a friend. **Jonathan Swift** *On the Death of Dr Swift*, 119

65 Do not insult your friend by lending him merits from your own pocket. **Rabindranath Tagore** *Stray Birds*, 105

66 My friend is he who can make a good guess at me. – hit me on the wing. **H. D. Thoreau** *Journal*, 22 September 1852

67 My friend is one whom I meet, who takes me for what I am. A stranger takes me for something else than I am. We do not speak – we cannot communicate till we find that we are recognized.

H. D. Thoreau *Journal*, 23 October 1852

68 I do not believe that friends are necessarily the people you like best, they are merely the people who got there first.

Peter Ustinov *Dear Me*, Ch. 5

69 If our friends do us a service, we think they owe it to us by virtue of being a friend. It never strikes us that they do not owe us their friendship. **Marquis de Vauvenargues** *Reflections and Maxims*, 179

70 Friendship is a supernatural harmony, a union of opposites.
Simone Weil *Waiting on God*: 'Forms of the Implicit Love of God'

71 Friendship is far more tragic than love. It lasts longer.
Oscar Wilde *For the Instruction of the Over-educated*

72 The absence of old friends one can endure with equanimity. But even a momentary separation from anyone to whom one has just been introduced is almost unbearable. **Oscar Wilde** *The Importance of Being Earnest*, Act 2

73 A man cannot be too careful in the choice of his enemies.
Oscar Wilde *The Picture of Dorian Gray*, Ch. 1

74 Friendship can be purchased only by friendship. A man may have authority over others; but he can never have their heart but by giving his own. **Bishop Thomas Wilson** *Maxims of Piety and Christianity*: 'Friendship'

The Future

1 That period of time in which our affairs prosper, our friends are true and our happiness is assured. **Ambrose Bierce** *The Enlarged Devil's Dictionary*

2 For some reason, the past doesn't radiate such immense monotony as the future does. Because of its plenitude, the future is propaganda. So is grass. **Joseph Brodsky** *Less Than One*: title essay

3 You can never plan the future by the past.
Edmund Burke *Letter to a Member of the National Assembly*

4 Though we ourselves have come too late, we will be envied by our immediate successors, and still more by our remote descendants. In their eyes we shall have the look of privileged characters, and rightly so, for everyone wants to be as far as possible from the future.
E. M. Cioran *Anathemas and Admirations*, 7

5 The future belongs to the suburbs of the globe.
E. M. Cioran *The Temptation to Exist*: 'On a Winded Civilization'

6 The future is a mirror with no glass.
Xavier Forneret *Sans titre, par un homme noir, blanc de visage*

7 The only certain thing about the future is that it will surprise even those who have seen furthest into it.
E. J. Hobsbawm *The Age of Empire, 1875–1914*: final sentence

8 Tomorrow is an old deceiver, and his cheat never grows stale.
Dr Samuel Johnson letter to Mrs Thrale, 24 May 1773

9 The only reason people want to be masters of the future is to change the past. **Milan Kundera** *The Book of Laughter and Forgetting*, Pt 1, 17

10 I detest posterity – every king hates his heir.
Ouida *Wisdom, Wit, and Pathos*: 'Chandos'

11 When we are planning for posterity we ought to remember that virtue is not hereditary. **Thomas Paine** *Common Sense*, Ch. 4

12 The future is only the past again. Only the cynic knows the future because he has seen it all before. **Adam Phillips** *Monogamy*, 95

13 The future is only the past again, entered through another gate.
Arthur Wing Pinero *The Second Mrs Tanqueray*, Act 4

14 He is a bad man who does not pay to the future at least as much as he has received from the past.
A. W. Pollard in the *Observer*, 'Sayings of the Week', 31 July 1927

15 Tomorrow is yesterday's pupil. **Publilius Syrus** *Moral Sayings*, 146

16 Are you not the future of all the memories stored within you? The future of a past? **Paul Valéry** *Bad Thoughts and Not So Bad*, P

17 Normal people think of the past, clever people think of the present, only stupid people think of the future.
Vietnamese saying quoted in the *Guardian*, 16 December 1992

See also ***Past and Present***

G

Games and Sports

1 Boxing's just show business with blood.

Frank Bruno in the *Observer*, 'Sayings of the Week', 24 November 1991

2 People are governed with the head; kindness of heart is little use in chess. **Nicholas-Sébastien Chamfort** *Maxims and Considerations*, 522

3 There is a passion for hunting something deeply implanted in the human breast. **Charles Dickens** *Oliver Twist*, Ch. 10

4 There's a fine line between boxing and chaos.

Gordon Fink applying for the revoking of Mike Tyson's boxing licence for biting his opponent's ear; *Newsweek*, 21 July 1997

5 To behold the Englishman at his *best* one should watch him play tip-and-run. **Ronald Firbank** *The Flower Beneath the Foot*, Ch. 14

6 The bigger they come, the harder they fall.

Bob Fitzsimmons before his fight with J. Jeffries, San Francisco, 9 June 1899

7 Chess, Game of: simulates military tactics. All the great generals were good chess-players. Too serious for a game, too frivolous for a science. **Gustave Flaubert** *The Dictionary of Received Ideas*

8 Exercise is bunk. If you are healthy, you don't need it: if you are sick, you shouldn't take it. **Henry Ford (attrib.)**

9 Life is what we make it as Whist is what we make it; but not as Chess is what we make it; which ranks higher as a purely intellectual game than either whist or Life.

Thomas Hardy Notebook, 1 May 1902, in Florence Emily Hardy, *The Life of Thomas Hardy*, Ch. 26

10 Cricket is first and foremost a dramatic spectacle. It belongs with the theatre, ballet, opera and the dance. **C. L. R. James** *Beyond a Boundary*, Ch. 16

11 I am sorry I have not learnt to play at cards. It is very useful in life: it generates kindness, and consolidates society.

Dr Samuel Johnson in James Boswell, *The Journal of a Tour to the Hebrides*, 11 November 1773

12 Man is a gaming animal. He must always be trying to get the better in something or other. **Charles Lamb** *Essays of Elia*: 'Mrs Battle's Opinions on Whist'

13 I never did like working out – it bears the same relationship to real sport as masturbation does to real sex. **David Lodge** *Therapy*, 1, p. 25

14 Man only plays when he is fully a human being, and is only fully human when he plays.

Friedrich von Schiller *On the Aesthetic Education of Man*, 15

15 The world can be divided into people that read, people that write, people that think, and fox-hunters.

William Shenstone *Essays on Men and Manners*: 'On Writing and Books'

16 Most sorts of diversion in men, children, and other animals, are an imitation of fighting. **Jonathan Swift** *Thoughts on Various Subjects*, p. 281

17 Solitaire is the only thing in life that demands absolute honesty.

Hugh Wheeler *A Little Night Music*, book to musical by Stephen Sondheim

18 The English country gentleman galloping after a fox – the unspeakable in full pursuit of the uneatable. **Oscar Wilde** *A Woman of No Importance*, Act 1

Genius

1 To do easily what is difficult for others is the mark of talent. To do what is impossible for talent is the mark of genius.

Henri-Frédéric Amiel *Amiel's Journal*, 17 December 1856

2 Geniuses are the luckiest of mortals because what they must do is the same as what they most wanted to do.

W. H. Auden Foreword to Dag Hammarskjöld, *Markings*

3 We see the contrast between the genius which does what it must and the talent which does what it can.

Maurice Baring *Outline of Russian Literature*, Ch. 3

4 We define genius as the capacity for productive reaction against one's training. **Bernard Berenson** *The Decline of Art*

5 Improvement makes strait roads; but the crooked roads without Improvement are roads of Genius.

William Blake *The Marriage of Heaven and Hell*: 'Proverbs of Hell'

6 A genius, in the sense that a genius is a man who has *two* great ideas.
J. Bronowski *The Ascent of Man*, Ch. 13

7 Genius is nothing but a great aptitude for patience. Style is the man himself. **George-Louis de Buffon** in Hérault de Séchelles, *Voyage à Montbar*

8 Talent, lying in the understanding, is often inherited; genius, being the action of reason and imagination, rarely or never.
Samuel Taylor Coleridge *Table Talk*, 21 May 1830

9 Whom the gods wish to destroy they first call promising.
Cyril Connolly *Enemies of Promise*, Ch. 13

10 Few people can see genius in someone who has offended them.
Robertson Davies *The Enthusiasms of Robertson Davies*: 'Dylan Thomas and Hector Berlioz'

11 What moves men of genius, or rather, what inspires their work, is not new ideas, but their obsession with the idea that what has already been said has still not been said enough. **Eugène Delacroix** *Journal*, 15 May 1824

12 Mediocrity knows nothing higher than itself, but talent instantly recognizes genius. **Arthur Conan Doyle** *The Valley of Fear*, Ch. 1

13 Genius points the way, talent takes it.
Maria von Ebner-Eschenbach *Aphorisms*, p. 52

14 Genius is one per cent inspiration and ninety-nine per cent perspiration. **Thomas Alva Edison** newspaper interview, 1903; recorded in *Life*, Ch. 24

15 It's always seemed to me a sort of clever stupidity only to have one sort of talent – almost like a carrier pigeon.
George Eliot *The Mill on the Floss*, Bk 5, Ch. 3

16 To believe what is true for you in your own private heart is true for all men – that is genius. **Ralph Waldo Emerson** *Essays*: 'Self-Reliance'

17 The difference between talent and genius, is, that talent says things which he has never heard but once, and genius things which he has never heard. **Ralph Waldo Emerson** *Journal*, March–April 1843

18 There is no greater consolation for mediocrity than that the genius is not immortal.
Johann Wolfgang von Goethe *Maxims and Reflections*: 'Life and Character', 273

19 A broadminded man of genius strives to be in advance of his century; a talented man of obstinate nature often wants to retard his century.
Johann Wolfgang von Goethe *Maxims and Reflections* (Penguin), 1010

20 True genius walks along a line, and perhaps our greatest pleasure is in seeing it so often near falling, without being ever actually down.
Oliver Goldsmith *The Bee*: 'The Characteristics of Greatness'

21 A genius creates harmony between the world he lives in and the world that lives in him. **Hugo von Hofmannsthal** *The Book of Friends*, 4

22 A man of genius has been seldom ruined but by himself.

Dr Samuel Johnson in James Boswell, *Life of Johnson*: letter to Joseph Baretti, 21 December 1762

23 The true genius is a mind of large general powers, accidentally determined to some particular direction.

Dr Samuel Johnson *Lives of the English Poets*: 'Cowley'

24 Talent is stimulated towards the imitation or development of other people's thoughts; genius is stimulated towards their contradiction.

Hans Keller *Maxims and Reflections*, 66

25 Who in the same given time can produce more than many others has vigour; who can produce more and *better*, has talents; who can produce what none else can, has genius.

Johann Kaspar Lavater *Aphorisms on Man*, 23; William Blake underlined the last part in approval

26 Woe to the genius in countries where there are no earthquakes.

Georg Christoph Lichtenberg *Aphorisms*, Notebook L, 64

27 Everyone is a genius at least once a year. The real geniuses simply have their bright ideas closer together.

Georg Christoph Lichtenberg *The Lichtenberg Reader*: Aphorisms 1779–88

28 Genius is talent provided with ideals.

W. Somerset Maugham *A Writer's Notebook*, 1892

29 Genius does what it must, and talent does what it can.

Owen Meredith *Last Words of a Sensitive Second-Rate Poet*

30 There are two kinds of genius: the kind which above all begets and wants to beget, and the kind which likes to be fructified and give birth. **Friedrich Nietzsche** *Beyond Good and Evil*: 'Peoples and Fatherlands', 248

31 The scorn of genius is the most arrogant and the most boundless of all scorns. **Ouida** *Wisdom, Wit, and Pathos*: 'Moths'

32 Genius and evil-doing
Don't go together. **Alexander Pushkin** *Mozart and Salieri*

33 If you have great talents, industry will improve them: if you have but moderate abilities, industry will supply their deficiency.

Sir Joshua Reynolds *Discourses*, 2

34 Every real genius has to be naïve.

Friedrich von Schiller *On Naïve and Sentimental Poetry*

35 Genius can thus be defined as an exceptional consciousness of things, and therefore also of their antithesis, one's own self.

Arthur Schopenhauer *Essays and Aphorisms*: 'On Philosophy and the Intellect', 23

36 When a true genius appears in the world, you may know him by this sign that the dunces are all in confederacy against him.

Jonathan Swift *Thoughts on Various Subjects*, p. 274

37 The peculiarity of a work of genius is the absence of the speaker from his speech – He is but the medium. You behold a perfect work, but you do not behold the worker. **H. D. Thoreau** *Journal*, 27 August 1852

38 Talent without genius comes to little. Genius without talent is *nothing*. **Paul Valéry** *At Moments*: 'The Beautiful is Negative'

39 Caricature is the tribute mediocrity pays to genius.

Oscar Wilde lecture in America; in *Epigrams of Oscar Wilde*, ed. Alvin Redman

Giving and Taking

1 There are only two places in which one pays for giving something away: public lavatories and brothels.

Charles Baudelaire *Intimate Journals*: 'Rockets', 12

2 Gifts must affect the receiver to the point of shock.

Walter Benjamin *One-Way Street*: 'Fancy Goods'

3 There are things we want to give and things we want to give away.

Elizabeth Bibesco *Haven*: 'Aphorisms'

4 It is harder to cut our gains than our losses.

Elizabeth Bibesco *Haven*: 'Aphorisms'

5 Cast thy bread upon the waters: for thou shalt find it after many days.

Bible, OT Ecclesiastes 11:1

6 Men do not despise a thief, if he steal to satisfy his soul when he is hungry. **Bible, OT** Proverbs 6:30

7 Be not made a beggar by banqueting upon borrowing, when thou hast nothing in thy purse; for thou shalt lie in wait for thine own life, and be talked on. **Bible, Apocrypha** Ecclesiasticus 18:33

8 It is more blessed to give than to receive. **Bible, NT** John 20:35

9 **Hand, n.** A singular instrument worn at the end of a human arm and commonly thrust into somebody's pocket.

Ambrose Bierce *The Devil's Dictionary*

10 He who has suffered you to impose on him, knows you.
William Blake *The Marriage of Heaven and Hell*: 'Proverbs of Hell'

11 The conveyance of money from its rightful owners to others without claim on it should not be viewed as generosity. **Cicero** *Offices*, 1, 14

12 And herein lies the chief enjoyment to be had from the making of gifts; that, whereas the quiet and continued possession of anything is not a striking manner of asserting dominion over it, the fact that you part with any property proclaims that you possess it, and your bestowing it on some one of your choice involves the pleasure of refusing it to all whom you do not endow. **Mr Justice Charles J. Darling** *Scintillae Juris*, 1

13 You don't have to be as rich to give as you do to lend.
Comtesse Diane *Maxims of Life*, p. 93

14 Never ask a man f'r annything unless ye can make him think ye're li'ble to take it annyhow. **Finley Peter Dunne** *Dissertations of Mr Dooley*

15 Everything you really possess was given to you.
Maria von Ebner-Eschenbach *Aphorisms*, p. 42

16 One must be poor to know the luxury of giving.
George Eliot *Middlemarch*, Bk 2, Ch. 17

17 To whom nothing is given, of him can nothing be required.
Henry Fielding *Joseph Andrews*, Bk 2, Ch. 8

18 Having, not being, governs our time. **John Fowles** *The Aristos*, Ch. 8, 3

19 What belongs to a man he cannot get rid of, even though he throws it away.
Johann Wolfgang von Goethe *Maxims and Reflections*: 'Life and Character', 311

20 You must not be much surprised at the ingratitude of those to whom you have given nothing but money.
Sir Arthur Helps *Essays and Aphorisms*: 'Social Government'

21 It is better to give books than to lend them.
Holbrook Jackson *Maxims of Books and Reading*, 13

22 It is a sad woman who buys her own perfume.
Lena Jeger in the *Observer*, 'Sayings of the Week', 20 November 1955

23 There are people who can never forgive a beggar for their not having given him anything. **Karl Kraus** *Half-Truths and One-and-a-Half Truths*: 'Lord, forgive the . . .'

24 'Presents', I often say, 'endear absents.'
Charles Lamb *Essays of Elia*: 'A Dissertation upon Roast Pig'

25 The human species, according to the best theory I can form of it, is composed of two distinct races, *the men who borrow* and *the men who lend.* **Charles Lamb** *Essays of Elia*: 'The Two Races of Men'

26 Say not you know another entirely, till you have divided an inheritance with him.

Johann Kaspar Lavater *Aphorisms on Man*, 157; William Blake underlined the last part in approval, followed by two exclamation marks

27 You beg as you question; you give as you answer.

Johann Kaspar Lavater *Aphorisms on Man*, 419; William Blake underlined and commented, 'Excellent!'

28 Who gives a trifle meanly is meaner than the trifle.

Johann Kaspar Lavater *Aphorisms on Man*, 475

29 Both the honest man and the scoundrel simply confuse *mine* and *thine*. The honest man regards the former as if it were the latter; the scoundrel does the opposite.

Georg Christoph Lichtenberg *The Lichtenberg Reader*: Aphorisms 1779–88

30 It is a good maxim to ask of no one more than he can give without inconvenience to himself. **W. Somerset Maugham** *A Writer's Notebook*, 1894

31 What has been received no longer counts. We love only the liberality to come. **Michel de Montaigne** *Essays*, Bk 3, Ch. 6

32 Giving is a pleasure not so easily forgotten as receiving; the one to whom we have given becomes necessary to us, that is, we love him.

Cesare Pavese *This Business of Living, Diary 1935–1950*, 27 May 1941

33 I know what I have given you. I do not know what you have received.

Antonio Porchia *Voices*

34 *La propriété c'est le vol.* – Property is theft.

Joseph Proudhon *Qu'est-ce que la propriété?*, Ch. 1

35 He gives the poor twice as much good who gives quickly: [becomes proverbial saying: He gives twice who gives promptly].

Publilius Syrus *Moral Sayings*, 274

36 Gifts are best given to those with the best memories.

Publilius Syrus *Moral Sayings*, 491

37 The woman who can sacrifice a clean unspoiled penny stamp is probably unborn. **Saki** *The Unbearable Bassington*, Ch. 1

38 If you give what can be taken, you are not really giving.
Take what you are given, not what you want to be given.
Take what is given:
Give what cannot be taken. **Idries Shah** *Reflections*: 'Giving and Taking'

39 Neither a borrower, nor a lender be;
For loan oft loses both itself and friend,
And borrowing dulls the edge of husbandry.

William Shakespeare *Hamlet*, Act 1, Sc. 3, 75

40 The robbed that smiles steals something from the thief.

William Shakespeare *Othello*, Act 1, Sc. 2, 208

41 Self-sacrifice enables us to sacrifice other people without blushing.

George Bernard Shaw *Man and Superman*, 'Maxims for Revolutionists': 'Self-sacrifice'

42 The proverb warns that, 'You should not bite the hand that feeds you.' But maybe you should, if it prevents you from feeding yourself.

Thomas S. Szasz *The Second Sin*: 'Control and Self-control'

43 Love's gift cannot be given,
it waits to be accepted. **Rabindranath Tagore** *Fireflies*, p. 271

44 One who would thrive by seeking favours from the great, should never trouble them for small ones. **Sir Henry Taylor** *The Statesman*, Ch. 14

45 You cannot rob a man of anything which he will miss.

H. D. Thoreau *Journal*, 5 July 1840

46 When a man has money to burn the chronic borrower is a match for it. **Sydney Tremayne** *Tatlings*, p. 56

47 There are many things that we would throw away if we were not afraid that others might pick them up. **Oscar Wilde** *The Picture of Dorian Gray*, Ch. 4

See also **Charity**

Gods

1 He who created us without our help will not save us without our consent. **St Augustine (attrib.)**

2 Nothing human can be done without reference to the divine, and conversely. **Marcus Aurelius** *Meditations*, Bk 3, 13

3 God is the eternal confidant, in that tragedy of which each of us is the hero. **Charles Baudelaire** *Intimate Journals*: 'My Heart Laid Bare', 43

4 Even if God did not exist, religion would still be holy and divine. God is the only being who, in order to rule, does not even need to exist.

Charles Baudelaire *Intimate Journals*: 'Rockets', 1

5 God is no respecter of persons. **Bible, NT** John 10:34

6 A God who let us prove his existence would be an idol.
Dietrich Bonhoeffer *No Rusty Swords*, Pt 2, Ch. 1

7 An atheist is a man who has no invisible means of support.
John Buchan quoted in H. E. Fosdick, *On Being a Real Person*, Ch. 10

8 God was a mistake. But it is hard to decide whether too early or too late. **Elias Canetti** *The Human Province*: '1948'

9 The most difficult thing for one who does not believe in God: that he has no one to give thanks to. More than for one's time of need, one needs a God for giving thanks. **Elias Canetti** *The Secret Heart of the Clock*: '1982'

10 Man appoints and God disappoints. **Miguel Cervantes** *Don Quixote*, Pt 2, 22

11 It is only the uselessness of the first Flood which prevents God from sending a second.
Nicholas-Sébastien Chamfort quoted in J. Raymond Solly, *A Cynic's Breviary*

12 Without God, all is night, and with him light is useless.
E. M. Cioran *Tears and Saints*

13 It is the final proof of God's omnipotence that he need not exist in order to save us. **Peter De Vries** *The Mackerel Plaza*, Ch. 2

14 The God of the Christians is a father who is a great deal more concerned about his apples than he is about his children.
Denis Diderot *Addition aux pensées philosophiques*

15 One needs a tremendous ignorance to approach God. I have always known too much, I suppose. **Lawrence Durrell** *Justine*, Pt 2, p. 118

16 God can no more do without us than we can do without him.
Meister Eckhart *Fragments*

See also Silesius

17 The dice of God are always loaded.
Ralph Waldo Emerson *Essays*: 'Compensation'

18 Heartily know,
When half-gods go
The gods arrive. **Ralph Waldo Emerson** *Journal*

19 God is a circle whose centre is everywhere and whose circumference is nowhere.
Empedocles quoted in *Roman de la Rose*, anon. thirteenth-century French poem

See also Silesius

20 If there is an active god he has, since 1914, paid very poor wages.

John Fowles *The Aristos*, Ch. 15

21 God is not Dead but Alive and Well and working on a Much Less Ambitious Project.

Graffito in a Greenwich pub; in the *Guardian*, 'London Letter', 27 November 1975

22 Men pretend to serve God Almighty who doth not need it, but make use of him because they need him.

Marquis of Halifax *Political Thoughts and Reflections*: 'Religion'

23 *Dieu me pardonnera, c'est son métier*. – God will pardon me, it is His trade.

Heinrich Heine last words – which echo Catherine the Great – quoted in Edmond and Charles Goncourt, *Journal*, 23 February 1863

24 One who says no to himself cannot say yes to God.

Hermann Hesse *Reflections*, 289: 'Religion and the Church'

25 We are all children in the kindergarten of God.

Elbert Hubbard *The Philosophy of Elbert Hubbard*: 'Epigrams'

26 An honest God is the noblest work of man.

R. G. Ingersoll *Gods*, Pt 1 (parodying Pope)

27 'Twas only fear first in the world made gods.

Ben Jonson *Sejanus*, Act 2, Sc. 2

28 It is not hard to know God, provided you do not tax yourself by defining him.

Joseph Joubert *Thoughts and Maxims*, 1838, quoted in Matthew Arnold, *Essays in Criticism, Series 1*

29 He who is always the same, and never the same, resembles God.

Johann Kaspar Lavater *Aphorisms on Man*, 354

30 Let none turn over books, or roam the stars in quest of God, who sees him not in man.

Johann Kaspar Lavater *Aphorisms on Man*, 408; William Blake underlined the last part in approval

31 Gods are no more likely to achieve their private ambitions than are mere men who suffer the slings and arrows of outrageous fortune, but gods have much more fun. **Edmund Leach** *Runaway World*, Ch. 6

32 God is love but get it in writing. **Gypsy Rose Lee (attrib.)** catchphrase

33 The dramatist changes the props but keeps the players. The Almighty does the reverse.

Thomas McKeown in *Perspectives in Biology and Medicine*, Spring 1983

34 We owe God more love than we owe ourselves, and we know Him less; and yet we talk our fill about Him. **Michel de Montaigne** *Essays*, Bk 3, Ch. 8

35 Which is it? Is man only God's mistake or God only man's mistake?
Friedrich Nietzsche *Twilight of the Idols*: 'Maxims and Arrows', 7

36 Man is not worthy of God; but he is not incapable of being made worthy. **Blaise Pascal** *Pensées*, 4, 84

37 There is a very good saying that if triangles invented a god, they would make him three-sided. **Charles de Montesquieu** *Persian Letters* 59

38 God is really only another artist. He invented the giraffe, the elephant, and the cat. He has no real style. He just goes on trying other things.
Pablo Picasso in Françoise Gilot and Carlton Lake, *Life with Picasso*, Pt 1

39 The highest praise of God consists in the denial of him by the atheist who finds creation so perfect that he can dispense with a creator.
Marcel Proust *Remembrance of Things Past: The Guermantes Way*, 2

40 God is very economical, don't you think? Wastes nothing. Yet also the opposite. **Ralph Richardson** in Kenneth Tynan, *Show People*

41 Remind yourself every day that *now* is in your hands, but *tomorrow* is in the hands of God, and that He Who gave you this morning has not bound Himself with the promise to give you the evening too.
Lorenzo Scupoli *Unseen Warfare*, ed. Nicodemus *et al.*, Ch. 20

42 Beware of the man whose god is in the skies.
George Bernard Shaw *Man and Superman*, 'Maxims for Revolutionists': 'Religion'

43 God is the circle's centre
for those who dare embrace Him.
for those who merely stand in awe
He is the circle's rim.
Angelus Silesius *The Book of Angelus Silesius*: 'Of the one and the many'

See also Empedocles

44 The eye by which I see God is the same eye by which he sees me.
Angelus Silesius quoted in Henri-Frédéric Amiel, *Amiel's Journal*, 1 October 1849

45 I know that without me God cannot live for an instant: if I perish he must give up the ghost.
Angelus Silesius quoted in Arthur Schopenhauer, *Essays and Aphorisms*: 'On Ethics', 6

See also Eckhart

46 The only excuse for God is that he does not exist.
Stendhal quoted in J. Hick, *Evil and the God of Love*: Preface

47 If you talk to God, you are praying; if God talks to you, you have schizophrenia. If the dead talk to you, you are a spiritualist; if God talks to you, you are a schizophrenic. **Thomas S. Szasz** *The Second Sin*: 'Schizophrenia'

48 The modern world is not seriously inconvenienced by rendering to God the things which are God's. They are not numerous, nor are they of the kind which it misses. **R. H. Tawney** *The Acquisitive Society*, 11

49 It is a mistake to suppose that God is only, or even chiefly, concerned with religion. **William Temple** in R. V. C. Bodley, *In Search of Serenity*, Ch. 12

50 Man proposes but God disposes. **Thomas à Kempis** *Imitation of Christ*, 19

51 If God were not a necessary Being of himself, He might almost seem to be made for the use and benefit of mankind. **John Tillotson** *Sermons*, 93

52 God is a sort of burglar. As a young man you knock him down; as an old man you try to conciliate him, because he may knock you down.
Sir Herbert Beerbohm Tree quoted in Hesketh Pearson, *Beerbohm Tree*, Ch. 21

53 God is always on the side of the big battalions.
attrib. Marshal Turenne and later quoted in a letter by Comte Bussy-Rasbutin in 1677 and by Voltaire in his *Piccini Notebooks, 1735–50*. He emended it to: 'God is on the side not of the big battalions, but of the best shots.'

54 If God did not exist, it would be necessary to invent Him.
Voltaire *Epître* 96: 'À l'auteur du livre des trois imposteurs'

55 If God made us in His image, we have certainly returned the compliment. **Voltaire** *Le Sottisier*, 32

56 Only he who loves God with a supernatural love can look upon means simply as means. **Simone Weil** *Gravity and Grace*: 'Metaxu'

57 Wretched is the man that knows every thing but God.
Bishop Thomas Wilson *Maxims of Piety and Christianity*: 'Learning'

58 A God all mercy is a God unjust.
Edward Young *Night Thoughts*: 'Night 4', 233

See also ***Beliefs; Faith; Religion***

Good and Evil

1 Good can imagine Evil, but Evil cannot imagine Good.
W. H. Auden *A Certain World*: 'Imagination'

2 This disappointment serves you right. You would rather hope for goodness tomorrow than practise it today. **Marcus Aurelius** *Meditations*, Bk 8, 23

3 The sinner sins against himself; the wrongdoer wrongs himself, becoming the worse by his own action.
Marcus Aurelius *Meditations*, Bk 9, 4

4 Where everything is bad it must be good to know the worst.
F. H. Bradley *Appearance and Reality*: Preface

5 The wickedness of the world is so great you have to run your legs off to avoid having them stolen from under you.
Bertolt Brecht *The Threepenny Opera*, Act 1, Sc. 3

6 Tread softly and circumspectly in this funambulatory track and narrow path of goodness. **Sir Thomas Browne** *Christian Morals*, I, 1: opening words

7 A thing may look specious in theory, and yet be ruinous in practice; a thing may look evil in theory, and yet be in practice excellent.
Edmund Burke speech on the impeachment of Warren Hastings, 19 February 1788

8 When bad men combine, the good must associate; else they will fall, one by one, an unpitied sacrifice in a contemptible struggle.
Edmund Burke *Thoughts on the Cause of the Present Discontents*

9 One cannot resist evil, but one can resist good.
Anton Chekhov *Notebooks, 1894–1902*, p. 17

10 All saints have a past and all sinners have a future.
Anton Chekhov quoted in *The Week*, 13 June 1998

11 Evil comes at leisure like the disease; good comes in a hurry like the doctor. **G. K. Chesterton** *The Man Who Was Orthodox*

12 The good are not so good as they think themselves, the wicked as the good think them. **Bishop Mandell Creighton** *Life and Letters*, Vol. 2, Ch. 14

13 It's easy to see the faults in people I know; it's hardest to see the good. Especially when the good isn't there. **Will Cuppy (attrib.)**

14 All you need is a healthy nose, for we smell good and evil much quicker than we understand them. **Edward Dahlberg** *Alms for Oblivion*: 'Western Fable'

15 The good shine far away, like the Himalayan mountains: but the wicked are in darkness like arrows thrown in the night. *The Dhammapada* 304

16 There is so much goodness in real life. Do let us keep it out of our books. **Norman Douglas** *An Almanac, 1945*

17 It is easier to be good for *everybody*, than to be good for *somebody*.
Alexandre Dumas, the younger in J. de Finod, *A Thousand Flashes of French Wit*, p. 86

18 One has to do good for it to exist in the world.
Maria von Ebner-Eschenbach *Aphorisms*, p. 24

19 The first condition of human goodness is something to love; the second, something to reverence.
George Eliot *Scenes of Clerical Life*: 'Janet's Repentance', Ch. 10

20 The first lesson of history is the good of evil. Good is a good doctor, but Bad is a better. **Ralph Waldo Emerson** *Journal*, 1855, in *Conduct of Life*

21 I am by Nature made for my own good; not my own evil.
Epictetus *The Golden Sayings*, 129

22 In later life, we are never quite as good as we hoped; nor quite as bad, either. **Michael Frayn** *Constructions*, 149

23 What after all
Is a halo? It's only one more thing to keep clean.
Christopher Fry *The Lady's Not for Burning*, Act 1

24 Man and nature have such different views about the good of the world. **George Gissing** *Our Friend the Charlatan*, Ch. 21

25 Malice is a greater Magnifying-Glass than Kindness.
Marquis of Halifax *Moral Thoughts and Reflections*: 'Of Malice and Envy'

26 It was when Lucifer first congratulated himself upon his angelic behaviour that he became the tool of evil.
Dag Hammarskjöld *Markings*, 1–7, November 1956

27 I believe in the theoretical benevolence, and practical malignity of man. **William Hazlitt** *Aphorisms on Man*, 46

28 We as often repent the good we have done as the ill.
William Hazlitt *Characteristics*, 127

29 If goodness were only a theory, it were a pity it should be lost to the world. **William Hazlitt** *Characteristics*, 308

30 There is so much good in the worst of us,
And so much bad in the best of us,
That it hardly becomes any of us
To talk about the rest of us.
Edward Wallis Hoch *Good and Bad* (authorship not absolutely certain)

31 The way o' the transgressor hain't so hard if he can jist manage to involve the right people.
'Kin' Hubbard *Abe Martin's Broadcast*: 'Crime Notes'

32 Good is that which makes for unity; Evil is that which makes for separateness. **Aldous Huxley** *Ends and Means*, Ch. 15

33 The only good in man is his young feelings and his old thoughts.
Joseph Joubert *Notebooks*, 1798

34 Everything better is purchased at the price of something worse.
C. G. Jung quoted by W. L. Webb in the *Guardian*, 27 December 1984

35 To those who are good to me, I am good. To those who are not good to me, I am good in order to make them good. **Lao Tzu** Tao Te Ching, v, 49

36 You are not very good if you are not better than your best friends imagine you to be. **Johann Kaspar Lavater** *Aphorisms on Man*, 536

37 It is as dangerous to overestimate
the goodness of people
as to underestimate their stupidity. **Irving Layton** *The Whole Bloody Bird*: 'aphs'

38 Burning stakes do not lighten the darkness.
Stanislaw Lec *Unkempt Thoughts*

39 Man is almost always as wicked as he has to be.
Giacomo Leopardi *Pensieri*, 109

40 We no more become bad by thinking of badness than we become triangular by thinking about triangles. **C. S. Lewis** *A Preface to 'Paradise Lost'*, Ch. 12

41 All except the best men would rather be called wicked than vulgar.
C. S. Lewis quoted in the *Guardian*, 21 August 1980

42 Benevolence brings honour; cruelty, disgrace. Now people who dwell in cruelty while disliking disgrace are like those who are content to dwell in a low-lying place while disliking dampness.
Mencius Bk 2, Pt A, 4

43 To be proved true, violence need only occur once. But good is proved true by repetition. **Anne Michaels** *Fugitive Pieces*: 'Terra Nullius'

44 People will endlessly conceal from themselves that good is only good if one is good for nothing. The whole history of philosophy, the whole of theology, is this act of concealment.
Iris Murdoch *The Time of the Angels*, Ch. 17

45 I see better things and approve; I follow the worse.
Ovid *Metamorphoses*, Bk 7, 20

46 There are only two kinds of men: the righteous who think themselves sinners, and the sinners who think themselves righteous.
Blaise Pascal *Pensées*, 681

47 Every evil is some good spelt backwards.
Coventry Patmore *The Rod, the Root and the Flower*: 'Knowledge and Science', 26

48 We are all capable of evil thoughts, but only very rarely of evil deeds. We can all do good deeds, but very few can think good thoughts.
Cesare Pavese *This Business of Living: Diary 1935–1950*, 3 November 1938

49 It is always a temptation to see how bad one can be, but only to find out how good one is at being bad. Don Juan was nothing if not conscientious. **Adam Phillips** *Monogamy*, 99

50 How very different is the nature of the necessary from the nature of the good.
Plato *The Republic*, 493: C

51 Evil is the product of the ability of humans to make abstract that which is concrete.
Jean-Paul Sartre in *New Society*, 31 December 1970

52 Every good human quality is related to a bad one into which it threatens to pass over; and every bad quality is similarly related to a good one.
Arthur Schopenhauer *Essays and Aphorisms*: 'On Ethics', 4

53 There is nothing either good or bad, but thinking makes it so.
William Shakespeare *Hamlet*, Act 2, Sc. 2, (259)

54 Wisdom and goodness to the vile seem vile;
Filths savour but themselves.
William Shakespeare *King Lear*, Act 4, Sc. 2, 38

55 A bad man is not so bad as a worse.
George Bernard Shaw *Dramatic Opinions*; quoted in W. Burton Baldry, *Topical Epigrams*, Sect. 17

56 Nothing can harm a good man, either in life or after death.
Socrates quoted in Plato, *Apology*, 42

57 He who is too busy doing good finds no time to be good.
Rabindranath Tagore *Stray Birds*, 184

58 'Tis only noble to be good.
Kind hearts are more than coronets,
And simple faith than Norman blood.
Alfred, Lord Tennyson *Lady Clara Vere de Vere*

59 The weak sometimes want to be thought wicked, but the wicked want to pass for good.
Marquis de Vauvenargues *Reflections and Maxims*, 192

60 The best is the enemy of the good.
Voltaire *Philosophical Dictionary*: 'Dramatic Art'; but derived from an Italian proverb

61 Evil is the shadow of good. All real good, possessing solidity and thickness, projects evil. Only imaginary good does not project it.
Simone Weil *Gravity and Grace*: 'Contradictions'

62 We are drawn towards a thing because we believe it is good. We end by being chained to it because it has become necessary.
Simone Weil *Gravity and Grace*: 'Illusions'

63 Only he who loves God with a supernatural love can look upon means simply as means.
Simone Weil *Gravity and Grace*: 'Metaxu'

64 Blessed are the pure in heart for they have so much more to talk about.
Edith Wharton in *John O'London's Weekly*, 10 April 1932

65 The fact of the instability of evil is the moral order of the world.
A. N. Whitehead in Victor Gollancz, *A Year of Grace*, p. 7

66 One can always be kind to people about whom one cares nothing.
Oscar Wilde *The Picture of Dorian Gray*, Ch. 8

Governments

1 Democracy means government by discussion but it is only effective if you can stop people talking. **Clement Attlee** speech at Oxford, 14 June 1957

2 It is a certain sign of a wise government and proceeding when it can hold men's hearts by hopes, when it cannot by satisfaction.
Francis Bacon *Essays*: 'Of Seditions and Troubles'

3 Whatever is unnecessary in government is pernicious.
Walter Bagehot *The English Constitution*, Ch. 4

4 Fascism is not in itself a new order of society. It is the future refusing to be born. **Aneurin Bevan** in Michael Foot, *Aneurin Bevan*, Vol. 1, Ch. 10

5 Ministers fall like buttered bread: usually good side up.
Ludwig Börne *Aphorismen*

6 Government is a contrivance of human wisdom to provide for human *wants*. Men have a right that these wants should be provided for by this wisdom. **Edmund Burke** *Reflections on the Revolution in France*, p. 151

7 A perfect democracy is therefore the most shameless thing in the world. **Edmund Burke** *Reflections on the Revolution in France*, p. 191

8 All government, indeed every human benefit and enjoyment, every virtue, and every prudent act, is founded on compromise and barter.
Edmund Burke speech on conciliation with America, 22 March 1775

9 One of democracy's achievements; extending to everyone the privilege of access to things that no longer exist.
Roberto Calasso *The Ruin of Kasch*: 'The Organization Wouldn't Like It'

10 The only good government . . . is a bad one in a hell of a fright.
Joyce Cary *The Horse's Mouth*, Ch. 32

11 It is a pleasant thing to govern, even though it is only a flock of sheep.
Miguel Cervantes *Wit and Wisdom of Don Quixote*, p. 203

12 Democracy means government by the uneducated, while aristocracy means government by the badly educated.
G. K. Chesterton in the *New York Times*, 1 February 1931

13 It has been said that democracy is the worst form of government except all those other forms that have been tried from time to time.

Winston S. Churchill speech in House of Commons, 11 November 1947

14 Government is not founded on property (taken merely as such, in the abstract); it is founded on *unequal property*.

Samuel Taylor Coleridge *Table Talk*, 20 March 1831

15 Democracy becomes a government of bullies tempered by editors.

Ralph Waldo Emerson *Journal*, 1846: 'New England's Shame'

16 Two cheers for Democracy: one because it admits variety and two because it permits criticism. Two cheers are quite enough; there is no occasion to give three. **E. M. Forster** *Two Cheers for Democracy*: 'What I Believe'

17 The state does not want to be, it wants to survive.

John Fowles *The Aristos*, Ch. 9, 131

18 Decision by majorities is as much an expedient as lighting by gas.

W. E. Gladstone speech in House of Commons, 1858

19 The private sector is that part of the economy the Government controls and the public sector is the part that nobody controls.

James Goldsmith in the *Observer*, 'Sayings of the Week', 25 March 1979

20 A government that is big enough to give you all you want is big enough to take it all away.

Senator Barry Goldwater speech at West Chester, Pennsylvania, 21 October 1964

21 In an autocracy, one person has his way; in an aristocracy, a few people have their way; in a democracy, no one has his way.

Celia Green *The Decline and Fall of Science*: 'Aphorisms'

22 In corrupted Governments the Place is given for the sake of the Man; in good ones the Man is chosen for the sake of the Place.

Marquis of Halifax *Political Thoughts and Reflections*: 'Of Fundamentals'

23 A Minister of State must have a spirit of liberal Economy, not a restrained Frugality. **Marquis of Halifax** *Political Thoughts and Reflections*: 'Of Ministers'

24 The best party is but a kind of conspiracy against the rest of the nation. They put everybody else out of their protection. Like the Jews to the Gentiles, all others are the offscourings of the world.

Marquis of Halifax *Political Thoughts and Reflections*: 'Of Parties'

25 Where the people are generally dissatisfied, there is no commonwealth. **James Harrington** *Aphorisms Political*, nos. 1 and 12

26 The one cannot survive against the all, so the all unite against the one – the criminal. That's the origin of the state.

Friedrich Hebbel *Diaries*, entry 3947, 1847

27 He that goeth about to persuade a multitude that they are not so well governed as they ought to be, shall never want attentive and favourable hearers. **Richard Hooker** *Of the Laws of Ecclesiastical Polity*, Bk 1, Sect. 1

28 Universal suffrage almost inevitably leads to government by mass bribery, an auction of the worldly goods of the unrepresented minority.

W. R. Inge *The End of an Age*, Ch. 1

29 The punishment of bad princes is to be thought worse than they are.

Joseph Joubert *Thoughts and Maxims*, 195

30 Democracy means the permission to be everyone's slave.

Karl Kraus *Half-Truths and One-and-a-Half Truths*: 'Lord, forgive the . . .'

31 Communism is Soviet power plus the electrification of the whole country.

Vladimir Ilyich Lenin at Congress of Soviets, 22 December 1920; slogan promoting the electrification programme

32 To govern is to choose.

Duc de Lévis *Maximes et réflexions: Maximes politiques*, 24

33 In a free society the state does not administer the affairs of men. It administers justice among men who conduct their own affairs.

Walter Lippman *The Good Society*, Ch. 12

34 In government, a clarification is not to make things clear, it's to put you in the clear.

Jonathan Lynn and Antony Jay *Yes, Prime Minister*, Vol. 2: 'A Tangled Web'

35 Every nation has the government that it deserves.

Joseph de Maistre to le Chevalier de —— on the subject of Russia, 15 August 1811

36 A constitution that is made for all nations is made for none.

Joseph de Maistre *Considerations on France*, Ch. 6

37 The government burns down whole cities while the people are forbidden to light lamps. **Mao Zedong (attrib.)**

38 There is, in public affairs, no state so bad, provided it has age and stability on its side, that it is not preferable to change and disturbance. **Michel de Montaigne** *Essays*, Bk 2, Ch. 17

39 There are bad examples that are worse than crimes; and more States have perished through the violation of their customs than of their laws.

Charles de Montesquieu *Considerations of the Causes of Roman Greatness and Decadence*

40 Republics come to an end through luxury; monarchies through poverty. **Charles de Montesquieu** *Of the Spirit of the Laws*, Bk 7, Ch. 4

41 Man's capacity for evil makes democracy necessary and man's capacity for good makes democracy possible.
Reinhold Niebuhr *The Children of Light and the Children of Darkness*: Foreword

42 Every government is a parliament of whores. The trouble is, in a democracy the whores are us. **P. J. O'Rourke** *Parliament of Whores*: last words

43 Government, even in its best state, is but a necessary evil; in its worst state, an intolerable one. **Thomas Paine** *Common Sense*, Para. 2

44 It is even more damaging for a minister to say foolish things than to do them. **Cardinal de Retz** *Memoirs*, Pt 2

45 Democracy is like a hobby-horse: it will carry you nowhere unless you use your own legs.
Herbert Samuel in the *Observer*, 'Sayings of the Week', 27 March 1927

46 Democracy substitutes election by the incompetent many for appointment by the corrupt few.
George Bernard Shaw *Man and Superman*, 'Maxims for Revolutionists': 'Democracy'

47 City government is of the people, by the rascals, for the rich.
Lincoln Steffens quoted in *The Times*, 18 July 1977

48 What deserves admiration in America is the form of government and not the society. Elsewhere it is the government that does the harm. They have reversed the parts in Boston, and the government plays the hypocrite in order not to shock society. **Stendhal** *Love*: 'Various Fragments', 55

49 It's not the voting that's democracy, it's the counting.
Tom Stoppard *Jumpers*, Act 1

50 He who has once advanced by a stride will not be content to advance afterwards by steps. Public servants, therefore, like racehorses, should be well fed with regard, but not to fatness.
Sir Henry Taylor *The Statesman*, Ch. 23

51 Experience shows that the most dangerous moment for a bad government is usually just as it's starting on reform.
Alexis de Tocqueville *The Ancien Régime and the Revolution*, Bk 3, Ch. 4

52 A democratic government is the only one in which those who vote for a tax escape the obligation to pay it.
Alexis de Tocqueville *Democracy in America*, Vol. 1, Pt 2, Ch. 5

53 Friend of all, and each man's enemy – there you have the State!
Paul Valéry *Rhumbs*: 'Moralities'

54 Governments must conform to the nature of the men governed.
Giambattista Vico *The New Science*, Bk 1, Para. 246

55 The art of government is to make two thirds of the nation pay all it possibly can pay for the benefit of the other third.

Voltaire quoted in Walter Bagehot, *The English Constitution*, Ch. 6

56 Government is a dangerous servant and a fearful master.

George Washington quoted in W. R. Inge, *The End of an Age*, Ch. 4

57 Democracy is the recurrent suspicion that more than half the people are right more than half of the time.

E. B. White in the *New Yorker*, 3 July 1944

See also ***Politics and Politicians***

Gratitude and Ingratitude

1 Once you have done a man a service what more do you want? Is it not enough to have obeyed the laws of your own nature, without expecting to be paid for it? That is like the eye demanding a reward for seeing, or the feet for walking. **Marcus Aurelius** *Meditations*, Bk 9, 42

2 There is such a thing as low gratitude.

Nicholas-Sébastien Chamfort *Maxims and Considerations*, 583

3 We are never so grateful to the person who does us a good turn as to the one who could do us harm but doesn't.

Maria von Ebner-Eschenbach *Aphorisms*, p. 65

4 Maybe the only thing worse than having to give gratitude constantly all the time, is having to accept it.

William Faulkner *Requiem for a Nun*, Act 2, Sc. 1

5 Most People return small Favours, acknowledge middling ones, and repay great ones with Ingratitude.

Benjamin Franklin *Poor Richard's Almanack (Improved)*, 1751

6 Ingratitude is always a kind of weakness. I have never known competent people to be ungrateful.

Johann Wolfgang von Goethe *Maxims and Reflections* (Penguin), from *Art and Antiquity*, 86

7 Gratitude turns sour like milk, unless the jug it's contained in is not kept scrupulously clean. **Rémy de Gourmont** *Dernières pensées inédites*

8 People are always saying thank you so they can forget what they said it for. **Lillian Hellman** *Toys in the Attic*, Act 3

9 There are minds so impatient of inferiority that their gratitude is a species of revenge, and they return benefits, not because recompense is a pleasure, but because obligation is a pain.

Dr Samuel Johnson *The Rambler*, 87

10 Ingratitude is often disproportionate to the benefaction received.

Karl Kraus *Half-Truths and One-and-a-Half Truths*: 'Lord, forgive the . . .'

11 One's over-great haste to repay an obligation is a kind of ingratitude.

Duc de La Rochefoucauld *Maxims*, 226

12 Gratitude looks to the past and love to the present; fear, avarice, lust and ambition look ahead. **C. S. Lewis** *The Screwtape Letters*, 15

13 A blessing, repeated once too often, becomes a curse.

Lewis Mumford *Art and Technics*: 'Standardization, Reproduction and Choice'

14 Applause is a receipt, not a bill.

Artur Schnabel in explanation of his refusal to give encores, in I. Kolodin, *The Musical Life*: 'Ovation and Triumph'

15 If you pick up a starving dog and make him prosperous, he will not bite you. This is the principal difference between a dog and a man.

Mark Twain *Pudd'nhead Wilson*, Ch. 16, epigraph

16 Gratitude is a necessity of all life; it is love looking at the past as faith is love intending the future. **Charles Williams** *The Forgiveness of Sins*, Ch. 6

Greatness

1 All rising to a great place is by a winding stair.

Francis Bacon *Essays*: 'Of Great Place'

2 Nations have great men only despite themselves – just like families. They make every effort not to have them. This means that a great man, in order to exist, must have a power of attack greater than the power of resistance developed by millions of individuals.

Charles Baudelaire *Intimate Journals*: 'Rockets', 7

3 A first-class man subsists on the matter he destroys, just as the stars do. **Saul Bellow** *The Bellarosa Connection*

4 Great things are done when men and mountains meet;
This is not done by jostling in the street. **William Blake** *Gnomic Verses*

5 It is the nature of all greatness not to be exact.

Edmund Burke first speech on conciliation with America, 19 April 1774

6 There is a great man who makes every man feel small. But the real great man is the man who makes every man feel great.

G. K. Chesterton *Charles Dickens*, Ch. 1

7 It is not the clear-sighted who rule the world. Great achievements are accomplished in a blessed, warm fog. **Joseph Conrad** *Victory*, Pt 2, Ch. 3

8 There are great men enough to cite us to aim at true greatness, but not enough to make us fancy that God could not execute His purposes without them. **Julius and Augustus Hare** *Guesses at Truth*, 2

9 Great men don't take over from each other like sentries.

Friedrich Hebbel *Diaries*, entry 3121, 1844

10 A man would never undertake great things, could he be amused by small. **Dr Samuel Johnson** in James Boswell, *Life of Johnson*, Vol. 3

11 The great are often reproached with having failed to do much they could have done. They might reply: just think of the evil we could have done and did *not* do. **Georg Christoph Lichtenberg** *Aphorisms*, Notebook L, 1

12 Only when a man will not do some things is he capable of doing great things. **Mencius** Bk 4, Pt B, 8

13 One must never forget that the greatest man is nothing but an animal disguised as a god. **Francis Picabia** *Yes No, Poems and Sayings*: 'Airings'

14 It's great to be great but it's greater to be human.

Will Rogers *Autobiography*, Ch. 15

15 Rightly to be great
Is not to stir without great argument,
But greatly to find quarrel in a straw
When honour's at the stake. **William Shakespeare** *Hamlet*, Act 4, Sc. 4, 53

16 In heaven an angel is nobody in particular.

George Bernard Shaw *Man and Superman*, 'Maxims for Revolutionists': 'Greatness'

17 Nothing is more clearly seen by little men than the littleness of great men. **Sir Henry Taylor** *The Statesman*, Ch. 4

18 The great man dies twice; once as a man and once as a great man.

Paul Valéry *Notebook B*, 1910

19 In order to carry out great enterprises, one must live as if one will never have to die. **Marquis de Vauvenargues** *Reflections and Maxims*, 142

See also ***Big and Small***

Greetings and Partings

1 The heart may think it knows better: the senses know that absence blots people out. We have really no absent friends.

Elizabeth Bowen *The Death of the Heart*, Pt 1, Ch. 1

2 Absence only kills love if it was ill to start with.

Comtesse Diane *Maxims of Life*, p. 47

3 Parting is all we know of heaven,
And all we need of hell.

Emily Dickinson *Complete Poems*, 1732

4 It is a maxim of the wise to leave things before things leave them.

Baltasar Gracián *The Oracle*, 110

5 He who returns has never left.

Pablo Neruda *Adioses*, quoted in Adam Phillips, *On Kissing, Tickling and Being Bored*, Ch. 10

6 Thus we live, for ever taking leave.

Rainer Maria Rilke *Duino Elegies*, 7

7 A man never knows *how* to say goodbye; a woman never knows *when* to say it.

Helen Rowland *A Guide to Men*: 'First Interlude'

8 Every parting is a foretaste of death, and every reunion a foretaste of resurrection. That is why even people who are indifferent to one another rejoice so much when they meet again after twenty or thirty years.

Arthur Schopenhauer *Essays and Aphorisms*: 'On Psychology', 4

9 Unbidden guests
Are often welcomest when they are gone.

William Shakespeare *Henry VI, Pt 1*, Act 2, Sc. 2, 55

10 When I arrive somewhere my small suitcase is almost invisible, going away again seems to need a lorry.

Wols *Aphorisms and Pictures*, p. 33

Habit and Customs

1 Chaos often breeds life, when order breeds habit.

Henry Adams *The Education of Henry Adams*, Ch. 16

2 Small habits, well pursued betimes,
May reach the dignity of crimes.

Eulogius in Sagittarius and Daniel George, *The Perpetual Pessimist*, 27 March

3 Custom, then, is the great guide of human life.

David Hume *An Enquiry Concerning Human Understanding*, Sect. 5, Pt 1

4 Could the young but realize how soon they will become mere walking bundles of habits, they would give more heed to their conduct while in the plastic state. **William James** *The Principles of Psychology*, Ch. 4

5 We are all convention; convention carries us away, and we neglect the substance of things. We hold on to the branches, and let go of the trunk and the body. **Michel de Montaigne** *Essays*, Bk 2, Ch. 17

6 What is most resistant to salvation is not sin but habit.

Charles Péguy *Basic Verities*: 'Sinners and Saints'

7 Do not change the established form of things
For custom is the soul of government. **Alexander Pushkin** *Boris Godunov*

8 All men more or less are buried partially in the grave of custom, and of some of them we see only a few hairs upon the crown above ground.

H. D. Thoreau *Journal*, after 24 July 1846

9 A man may have no bad habits and have worse.

Mark Twain *Following the Equator*, Vol. 1, Ch. 1

10 Rigid, the skeleton of habit alone upholds the human frame.

Virginia Woolf *Mrs Dalloway*, p. 62

Happiness and Unhappiness

1 To happiness the same applies as to truth: one does not have it, but is in it. **Theodor Adorno** *Minima Memoralia*, Pt 2, 72

2 There will always be a lost dog somewhere that will prevent me from being happy. **Jean Anouilh** *The Restless Heart*, Act 3

3 Prosperity is the blessing of the Old Testament, adversity is the blessing of the New. **Francis Bacon** *Essays*: 'Of Adversity'

4 Prosperity is not without many fears and distastes; and adversity is not without comforts and hopes. **Francis Bacon** *Essays*: 'Of Adversity'

5 All material happiness is based on figures.
Honoré de Balzac *La Maison Nucingen, scènes de la vie parisienne*, Vol. 3, p. 17

6 To be happy is to become aware of oneself without fright.
Walter Benjamin *One-way Street*: 'Fancy Goods'

7 Human happiness means only asking of others as much as they can give. **Tristan Bernard** *Contes, répliques et bons mots*: 'Le Morale'

8 Calamities are of two kinds: misfortune to ourselves, and good fortune to others. **Ambrose Bierce** *The Devil's Dictionary*

9 When you find a man who iz very solisitus about the well-fare of everyboddy, yu kan safly put him down az one who isz hunting for a misfortune. **Josh Billings** *Wit and Humor*: Affurisms, 'Glass Dimonds'

10 For in all adversity of fortune the worst sort of misery is to have been happy. **Boethius** *The Consolation of Philosophy*, Bk 2, Prose 4

11 It is only possible to live happily ever after on a day to day basis.
Margaret Bonnano *A Certain Slant of Light*, Ch. 16

12 Everyone chases after happiness
But happiness is running after them.
Bertolt Brecht *The Song of the Super-inadequacy of Human Striving*

13 Content may dwell in all Stations. To be low, but above contempt, may be high enough to be Happy. **Sir Thomas Browne** *Christian Morals*, Pt 1, 27

14 Certainly there is no happiness within this circle of flesh, nor is it in the optics of these eyes to behold felicity. The first day of our jubilee is death. **Sir Thomas Browne** *Religio Medici*, Pt 1, 43

15 The Greeks said grandly in their phrase,
'Let no one be called happy till his death'
to which I add, –

Let no one till his death
Be called unhappy. **Elizabeth Barrett Browning** *Aurora Leigh*, Bk 5

See also Solon

16 Happiness or misery consists in a certain arrangement of organs.
E. M. Cioran *Anathemas and Admirations*, Ch. 5

17 There is no greater grief than to recall a time of happiness when in misery. **Dante Alighieri** *The Divine Comedy: Inferno*, 5, 121

18 Unhappiness is best defined as the difference between our talents and our expectations.
Edward de Bono in the *Observer*, 'Sayings of the Week', 12 June 1977

19 Misfortune among the happy,
fortune among the unfortunate
is misfortune. **Hasan Dewran** *A Thousand Winds May Make a Storm*, p. 73

20 Happiness is a branch on which you can land but not make your nest. **Comtesse Diane** *Les Glanes de la vie*, p. 76

21 A great obstacle to happiness is expecting too much happiness.
Bernard Le Bovier de Fontenelle *Du Bonheur*

22 Much is won if we succeed in transforming hysterical misery into common unhappiness. **Sigmund Freud** quoted in Graham Greene, *A Sort of Life*, 4, 2

23 Happiness Makes up in Height What It Lacks in Length.
Robert Frost title of poem

24 God never intended his creatures to be happy; all he meant them to have were a few compensations. Such as fishing, love and dotage.
Jean Giraudoux *Intermezzo*, Act 1

25 The happiest man is one who can link the end of his life with its beginning.
Johann Wolfgang von Goethe *Maxims and Reflections* (Penguin), from *Art and Antiquity*, 140

26 Happiness is a how, not a what: a talent, not an object.
Hermann Hesse *Reflections*, 589

27 Happiness can be possessed only as long as it is unseen.
Hermann Hesse *Reflections*, 601

28 Happiness was the state of those who lived in the continuous present. That was a state not then part of the British Empire.
Veronica Horwell building on Quentin Crisp, in the *Guardian*, 22 November 1999

29 ***Happiness***: something which might have happened yesterday, but which will never happen tomorrow. **Elbert Hubbard** *The Roycroft Dictionary*

30 Happiness is like coke – something you get as a by-product in the process of making something else. **Aldous Huxley** *Point Counter Point*, Ch. 30

31 If a man talks of his misfortunes, there is something in them that is not disagreeable to him. **Dr Samuel Johnson** in James Boswell, *Life of Johnson*, 1780

32 Some deny the existence of misery by pointing to the sun; he denies the existence of the sun by pointing to misery.
Franz Kafka *Collected Aphorisms*, 17 January 1920

33 Happiness comes uninvited; and the moment you are conscious that you are happy, you are no longer happy.
J. Krishnamurti *The Penguin Krishnamurti Reader*: 'Questions and Answers'

34 Most men devote the greater part of their lives to making their remaining years unhappy. **Jean de La Bruyère** *Characters*: 'Of Man', 102

35 We envy the happiness of other people mainly because we believe in it. **Irving Layton** *The Whole Bloody Bird*: 'aphs'

36 Most troubles only come because we go halfway to meet them.
Duc de Lévis *Maximes et Réflexions*, in J. Raymond Solly, *Selected Thoughts from the French*: 'Fortunes'

37 Let anyone examine the things he has wished for all his life. If he is happy, it is because his fond hopes have not been realized.
Prince de Ligne quoted in J. Raymond Solly, *A Cynic's Breviary*

38 The misfortunes hardest to bear are those which never come.
James Russell Lowell speech in Birmingham, England, 6 October 1884

39 Cheerfulness is a quiet condition; glee, on the other hand, is only desperation on a good day. **Aidan Mathews** *Lipstick on the Host*: title story

40 Men are the only animals who devote themselves assiduously to making one another unhappy. **H. L. Mencken** *Notebooks, Minority Report*, 93

41 Ask yourself whether you are happy and you cease to be so.
John Stuart Mill *Autobiography*, Ch. 5

42 If unhappiness develops the forces of the mind, happiness alone is salutary to the body.
Marcel Proust *Remembrance of Things Past: Time Regained*, Ch. 2, p. 774

43 Alas! Why is it that when your cup of happiness is full somebody always jogs your elbow! **Helen Rowland** *A Guide to Men*: 'Syncopations'

44 Men who are unhappy, like men who sleep badly, are always proud of the fact. **Bertrand Russell** *The Conquest of Happiness*, Ch. 1

45 Really high-minded people are indifferent to happiness, especially other people's.

Bertrand Russell *The Conquest of Happiness*; quoted in Michael Foot, *Debts of Honour*, Ch. 6

46 The most effective consolation in every misfortune and every affliction is to observe others who are more unfortunate than we: and everyone can do this. But what does that say for the condition of the whole?

Arthur Schopenhauer *Essays and Aphorisms*: 'On the Suffering of the World', 3

47 He is not happy who does not think himself happy.

Seneca *Letters*, 40, 21

48 Call no man happy till he dies, he is at best fortunate.

Solon quoted in Herodotus, *Histories*, I, 32

See also Browning

49 Happiness is an imaginary condition, formerly often attributed by the living to the dead, now usually attributed by adults to children, and by children to adults. **Thomas S. Szasz** *The Second Sin*: 'Emotions'

50 Grief can take care of itself; but to get the full value of a joy you must have somebody to divide it with. **Mark Twain** *Following the Equator*, Vol. 2, Ch. 12

51 What interests me isn't the happiness of every man, but that of each man. **Boris Vian** *Mood Indigo*

52 Happiness is no laughing matter. **Archbishop Whately** *Apophthegms*, 1865

53 Pleasure is the only thing one should live for. Nothing ages like happiness. **Oscar Wilde** *Phrases and Philosophies for the Use of the Young*

54 Who never knew the price of happiness will not be happy.

Yevgeny Yevtushenko *Lies*

Hatreds

1 How hatred is by far the longest pleasure;
Men love in haste, but they detest at leisure. **Lord Byron** *Don Juan*, XIII, 6

2 It is weakness of character, or lack of ideas, it is all, in a word, that can prevent them from living with themselves, which saves so many people from misanthropy.

Nicholas-Sébastien Chamfort *Maxims and Considerations*, 270

3 You must embrace the man you hate, if you cannot be justified in knocking him down. **Earl of Chesterfield** *Letters to His Son*, 15 January 1753

4 Violent antipathies are always suspicious, and betray a secret affinity. **William Hazlitt** *Table Talk*: 'On Vulgarity and Affectation'

5 Many people believe that they are attracted by God or by nature, when they are only repelled by man.
W. R. Inge *More Lay Thoughts of a Dean*, Pt 4, Ch. 1

6 Keep him at least three paces distant who hates bread, music, and the laugh of a child.
Johann Kaspar Lavater *Aphorisms on Man*, 328; William Blake underlined and commented: 'The best in the book!'

7 For what man hates, he takes seriously.
Michel de Montaigne *Essays*, Bk 1, Ch. 50

8 No woman ever hates a man for having been in love with her; but many a woman hates a man for being a friend to her.
Alexander Pope *Thoughts on Various Subjects*, 90

9 *Hatred* is a thing of the heart, *contempt* a thing of the head.
Arthur Schopenhauer *Essays and Aphorisms*: 'On Psychology', 11

10 Malice is like a game of poker or tennis; you don't play it with anyone who is manifestly inferior to you. **Hilde Spiel** *The Darkened Room*, Ch. 9

11 We despise many things so as not to despise ourselves.
Marquis de Vauvenargues *Reflections and Maxims*, 196

See also ***Love***

Health and Illness

1 In psychoanalysis nothing is true except the exaggerations.
Theodor Adorno *Minima Memoralia*, Pt 1, 29

2 The new definition of psychiatry is the care of the id by the odd.
Anon. in M. B. Strauss, *Familiar Medical Quotations*

3 Despise no new accident in your body, but ask opinion of it. In sickness, respect health principally; and in health, action.
Francis Bacon *Essays*: 'Of Regimen of Health'

4 Health and good estate of body are above all gold, and a strong body above infinite wealth. **Bible, Apocrypha** Ecclesiasticus 30:15

5 Honour a physician with the honour due unto him for the uses which you may have of him: for the Lord hath created him.

Bible, Apocrypha Ecclesiasticus 38:1

6 A fool is he, of little skill,
Who tests the urine of the ill
And says: 'Wait, sir, and be so kind,
The answer in my books I'll find.'
And while he thumbs the folios,
The patient to the bone yard goes. **Sebastian Brant** *The Ship of Fools*, 55

7 The paranoid is on his way to nowhere. Everything external becomes a part of his inner labyrinth. He cannot escape himself. He loses himself without forgetting himself. **Elias Canetti** *The Secret Heart of the Clock*: '1983'

8 A doctor used to say: 'Only heirs pay really well.'

Nicholas-Sébastien Chamfort *Maxims and Considerations*, 582

9 A doctor is called, but a nurse is sent for.

Anton Chekhov *Notebooks 1894–1902*, p. 75

10 Without illness there is no absolute knowledge. Illness is the primary cause of history; sin, only a secondary one. **E. M. Cioran** *Tears and Saints*

11 It is with diseases of the mind as with those of the body; we are half dead before we understand our disorder, and half cured when we do.

Charles Caleb Colton *Lacon*: 'Disease'

12 The health of a writer should not be too good, and perfect only in those periods of convalescence when he is not writing.

Cyril Connolly *Enemies of Promise*, Ch. 16

13 Psychoanalysis is a permanent fad. **Peter De Vries** *Forever Panting*: opening words

14 The best doctor is the one you run after and that you can't find.

Denis Diderot in J. Raymond Solly, *Selected Thoughts from the French*: 'Doctors – Medicine'

15 Diseases are not interested in those who want to die.

Lawrence Durrell *Justine*, Pt 1, p. 50

16 Every physician almost hath his favourite disease.

Henry Fielding *Tom Jones*, Bk 2, Ch. 9

17 Hygiene: Must always be 'carefully maintained'. Prevents illness except when it causes it. **Gustave Flaubert** *The Dictionary of Received Ideas*

18 Early to bed and early to rise, makes a man healthy, wealthy and wise. **Benjamin Franklin** *Poor Richard's Almanack*, 1735

19 Much Virtue in Herbs, little in Men.

Benjamin Franklin *Poor Richard's (Improved) Almanack*, 1755

20 Psychoanalysis meets the optimism of favourable conditions where its practice is not needed – ie among the healthy.

Sigmund Freud letter to Oscar Pfister, 18 January 1909

21 In neurosis, a piece of reality is avoided by a kind of flight, in psychosis it is reconstructed.

Sigmund Freud *Neurosis and Psychosis*, Standard Edition, Vol. 19: 'The Loss of Reality'

22 Commonly physicians, like beer, are best when they are old; and lawyers, like bread, when they are young and new.

Thomas Fuller *The Holy State, and the Profane State*, Bk 2, Ch. 1

23 Much of the world's work, it has been said, is done by men who do not feel quite well. Marx is a case in point.

J. K. Galbraith *The Age of Uncertainty*, Ch. 3

24 Psychoanalysis, we know, is the science of suspicion; it lives by the conviction that things are not what they appear to be.

Peter Gay *Freud for Historians*, Ch. 2, 3

25 Anybody who goes to see a psychiatrist ought to have his head examined. **Sam Goldwyn (attrib.)** but probably invented by one of his staff

26 The resistance of the patient to the doctor is the objective of every treatment. **Georg Groddeck** *The Book of the It*, Letter 14

27 A physician cannot cure a disease, but he can change its mode of expression.

Thomas Hardy Diary, 9 May 1890, in Florence Emily Hardy, *The Early Years of Thomas Hardy*, Ch. 18

28 The Physician owes all to the patient, but the patient owes nothing to him but a little money. **George Herbert** *Jacula Prudentum*

29 Desperate cases need the most desperate remedies.

Hippocrates *Aphorisms*, 1, 6

30 Sneezing supervening on an attack of hiccoughs relieves that condition. **Hippocrates** *Aphorisms*, 6, 13

31 There are three factors in the practice of medicine; the disease, the patient and the physician. The physician is the servant of the science, and the patient must do what he can to fight the disease with the assistance of the physician. **Hippocrates** *Epidemics*, 1, 2

32 Healing is a matter of time but it is sometimes also a matter of opportunity. **Hippocrates** *Precepts*, 1

33 Disease generally begins that equality that death completes.

Dr Samuel Johnson *The Rambler*, 48, 1 September 1750

34 There is a degree of bad health that makes us happy.

Joseph Joubert *Notebooks*, 1809

35 Psychoanalysis is that mental illness of which it believes itself to be the cure. **Karl Kraus** *Half-Truths and One-and-a-Half Truths*: 'In hollow heads'

36 How sickness enlarges the dimensions of a man's self to himself.

Charles Lamb *Last Essays of Elia*: 'The Convalescent'

37 Telling someone he looks healthy isn't a compliment – it's a second opinion. **Fran Lebowitz** *Social Studies*: 'People'

38 *Non est vivere, sedere vita est.* – Life is not living, but being in health.

Martial *Epigrams*, Bk 6, 70

39 If the medicine does not make the head swim, the illness will not be cured. **Mencius** Bk 3, Pt A, 1, quoting *The Book of History*

40 Illness is in part what the world has done to a victim, but in a larger part it is what the victim has done with his world, and with himself.

Karl Menninger quoted in Susan Sontag, *Illness as Metaphor*, Ch. 6

41 One could call every illness an illness of the soul. **Novalis** *Pollen*, 384

42 A physician who treats himself has a fool for a patient.

Sir William Osler *Aphorisms*, 60

43 A symptom, of course, is always a state of conviction.

Adam Phillips *On Kissing, Tickling and Being Bored*, Ch. 11

44 As soon as he ceased to be mad he became merely stupid. There are maladies which we must not seek to cure because they alone protect us from others that are more serious.

Marcel Proust *Remembrance of Things Past: The Guermantes Way*, Ch. 1

45 In the pathology of nervous diseases, a doctor who doesn't talk too much nonsense is a half-cured patient, just as a critic is a poet who has stopped writing verse and a policeman a burglar who has retired from practice.

Marcel Proust *Remembrance of Things Past: The Guermantes Way*, Ch. 1

46 To believe in medicine would be the height of folly, if not to believe in it were not a greater folly still.

Marcel Proust *Remembrance of Things Past: The Guermantes Way*, Ch. 2

47 Illness is the night-side of life, a more onerous citizenship. Everyone who is born holds dual citizenship, in the kingdom of the well and in the kingdom of the sick. Although we all prefer to use only the good passport, sooner or later each of us is obliged, at least for a spell, to identify ourselves as citizens of that other place.

Susan Sontag *Illness as Metaphor*: opening words

48 When I want to take a rest
I am ill.
Just imagine how ill
I shall be when
Dead. **Marin Sorescu** *The Biggest Egg in the World*: 'When I want to take a rest'

49 Someone once defined a psychoanalyst as a nonswimmer working as a lifeguard. **Thomas S. Szasz** *The Second Sin*: 'Professionalism'

50 Formerly when religion was strong and science weak, men mistook magic for medicine; now; when science is strong and religion weak, men mistake medicine for magic.
Thomas S. Szasz *The Second Sin*: 'Science and Scientism'

51 Disease is in fact the *rule* of our terrestrial life – and the prophecy of a *celestial* one. **H. D. Thoreau** *Journal*, 13 September 1851

52 Neurosis is the way of avoiding non-being by avoiding being.
Paul Tillich *The Courage to Be*, Pt 2, Ch. 7

53 We are all ill: but even a universal sickness implies an idea of health.
Lionel Trilling *The Liberal Imagination*: 'Art and Neurosis'

54 A neurosis is a secret you don't know you're keeping.
Kenneth Tynan in Kathleen Tynan, *Life of Kenneth Tynan*, Ch. 19

55 Illness suspends our virtues and our vices.
Marquis de Vauvenargues *Reflections and Maxims*

56 Most men would prefer a month's mental distress to a month's serious neuralgia. It is in our bodies that the secrets exist.
Charles Williams *The Forgiveness of Sins*, Ch. 1

See also ***Body and Soul; Madness and Sanity***

Heaven and Hell

1 That's what hell will be like, small chat to the babbling of Lethe about the good old days when we wished we were dead.
Samuel Beckett *Embers*

2 One was asked, 'What is Hell?' and he answered, 'It is Heaven – that has come too late.' **F. H. Bradley** *Aphorisms*, 99

3 Hell is a special favour reserved to those who have much requested it. **Albert Camus** *Notebooks 6*

4 Hell is paved with good intentions, but heaven goes in for something more dependable. Solid gold. **Joyce Cary** *The Horse's Mouth*, Ch. 22

5 Heaven can do whatever it likes without anybody being able to interfere with it, especially when it is raining.
Miguel Cervantes *The Mayors of Daganco*

6 The devil tempts us not – 'tis we tempt him,
Beckoning his soul with opportunity. **George Eliot** *Felix Holt*, Ch. 47

7 The cherubim know most; the seraphim love most.
Ralph Waldo Emerson *Essays*: 'Intellect'

8 In a real dark night of the soul it is always three o'clock in the morning, day after day. **F. Scott Fitzgerald** *The Crack-up*: 'Handle with Care', March 1936

9 Paradise, as described by the theologians, seems to me too musical: I confess I should be incapable of listening to a cantata which lasted ten thousand years.
Théophile Gautier in J. de Finod, *A Thousand Flashes of French Wit*, p. 34

10 The fear of hell is hell itself, and the longing for paradise is paradise itself. **Kahlil Gibran** *Spiritual Sayings*

11 One loves the earth in detail, but heaven *en bloc*.
Jean Giraudoux *Amphitryon*, Act 2

12 Many might go to heaven with half the labour they go to hell, if they would venture their industry the right way.
Ben Jonson *Timber or Discoveries Made Upon Men and Matter*, 27

13 The doors of heaven and hell are adjacent and identical: both green, both beautiful. **Nikos Kazantzakis** *The Last Temptation*, Ch. 18

14 The attempt to externalize the kingdom of heaven in a temporal shape must end in disaster. It cannot be created by charters and constitutions nor established by arms. Those who set out for it alone will reach it together, and those who seek it in company will perish by themselves. **Hugh Kingsmill** *The Poisoned Crown, The Genealogy of Hitler*

15 The devil is an optimist if he thinks he can make people worse.
Karl Kraus *Half-Truths and One-and-a-Half Truths*: 'Lord, forgive the . . .'

16 Those who consider the Devil to be a partisan of Evil and angels to be warriors for Good accept the demagogy of the angels. Things are clearly more complicated. **Milan Kundera** *The Book of Laughter and Forgetting*, Pt 2, Ch. 4

17 There is wishful thinking in Hell as well as on earth.
C. S. Lewis *The Screwtape Letters*: Preface

18 Probably no invention came more easily to man than inventing Heaven. **Georg Christoph Lichtenberg** *The Lichtenberg Reader*: Aphorisms 1793–9

19 Hell hath no limits, nor is circumscribed
In one self place; for where we are is hell,
And where hell is, must we ever be.
Christopher Marlowe *Doctor Faustus*, Act 2, Sc. 1

20 Better to reign in hell than serve in heav'n.
John Milton *Paradise Lost*, Bk 1, 263

21 If it depended on my choice,
I think it might be great
To have a place in Paradise;
Better yet – outside the gate.
Friedrich Nietzsche *The Gay Science*: Prelude, 'Joke, Cunning and Revenge', 57

22 Every beloved object is the focus of a paradise. **Novalis** *Pollen*, 32

23 Better the devil you know than an angel you don't.
Adam Phillips *On Kissing, Tickling and Being Bored*, Ch. 2

24 If you go to Heaven without being naturally qualified for it, you will not enjoy yourself there. **George Bernard Shaw** *Man and Superman*, Act 3

25 Hell is paved with good intentions, not with bad ones.
George Bernard Shaw *Man and Superman*, 'Maxims for Revolutionists': 'Good Intentions'

26 Heaven, as conventionally conceived, is a place so inane, so dull, so useless, so miserable, that nobody has ever ventured to describe a whole day in heaven, though plenty of people have described a day at the seaside. **George Bernard Shaw** *Misalliance*: Preface

27 Sometimes
The Devil is a gentleman. **P. B. Shelley** *Peter Bell the Third*, 81

See also ***Good and Evil***

Heroes

1 No hero is mortal till he dies. **W. H. Auden** *A Short Ode to a Philologist*

2 Unhappy the land that has no heroes . . . No. Unhappy the land that is in need of heroes. **Bertolt Brecht** *The Life of Galileo*, 13

3 Every hero becomes a bore at last.
Ralph Waldo Emerson *Representative Men*: 'Uses of Great Men'

4 The fame of heroes owes little to the extent of their conquests and all to the success of the tributes paid to them. **Jean Genet** *Prisoner of Love*, Pt 1

5 Heroes are men who glorify a life which they can't bear any longer.
Jean Giraudoux *Duel of Angels*, Act 3

6 What with making their way and enjoying what they have won, heroes have no time to think. But the sons of heroes – ah, they have all the necessary leisure. **Aldous Huxley** *Music at Night*: 'Vulgarity in Literature'

7 Claret is the liquor for boys; port for men; but he who aspires to be a hero . . . must drink brandy.
Dr Samuel Johnson in James Boswell, *Life of Johnson*, 7 April 1779

8 God sometimes sends a famine, sometimes a pestilence, and sometimes a hero for the chastisement of mankind; none of them, surely, for our admiration.
Walter Savage Landor quoted in Sagittarius and Daniel George, *The Perpetual Pessimist*, 24 January

9 The extreme of heroism, alike in foe or friend, is indistinguishable from despair. **Frederic Manning** *Her Privates We*, 1

10 Thoughts of heroes were as good as warming-pans.
George Meredith *Beauchamp's Career*, Ch. 4

History

1 Few people wish they could read
The lost annals
Of a cudgelled people. **W. H. Auden** *City Without Walls*, p. 58

2 Antiquities are history defaced, or some remnants of history which have casually escaped the shipwreck of time.
Francis Bacon *The Advancement of Learning*, Bk 2, ii, 1

3 Much of history is necessarily of little value, – the superficies of circumstance, the scum of events.
Walter Bagehot *Literary Studies*: 'Thomas Babington Macaulay'

4 History is a record of what happens to have been recorded. The fewer the records the more delighted the historian.
Bernard Berenson *Diary*, 18 August 1952

5 History must not be written with bias, and both sides must be given, even if there is only one side.
John Betjeman *First and Last Loves*: 'Love is Dead'

6 **History, n.** An account mostly false, of events mostly unimportant, which are brought about by rulers mostly knaves and soldiers mostly fools. **Ambrose Bierce** *The Enlarged Devil's Dictionary*

7 English history is all about men liking their fathers, and American history is all about men hating their fathers and trying to burn down everything they ever did. **Malcolm Bradbury** *Stepping Westward*, Bk 2, Ch. 5

8 Repetition is the invisible step backward that accompanies every act. Historians distinguish themselves above all by their ability to combine that step with their account of actions, of visible acts.
Roberto Calasso *The Ruin of Kasch*: 'The Demon of Repetition'

9 In history, there seems to be only a negative learning. One notes what one has done to others in order to hold it against them.
Elias Canetti *The Human Province*: '1969'

10 Of necessity, the more contemporary history becomes the more it becomes contemporary hearsay.
David Cannadine in *New Society*, 6 December 1984

11 History is the essence of innumerable biographies.
Thomas Carlyle *Critical and Miscellaneous Essays*: 'On History'

12 History is irony, the Mind's jeer down through men and events. Today this belief triumphs, tomorrow, vanquished, it will be dismissed and replaced. **E. M. Cioran** *A Short History of Decay*, 5

13 All history is the history of thought.
R. G. Collingwood *Autobiography*, Ch. 10

14 The reconstruction of worlds is one of the historian's most important tasks. He undertakes it, not from a strange urge to dig up archives and sift through old paper, but because he wants to talk with the dead.
Robert Darnton *The Literary Underground of the Old Regime*, p. v

15 We are never completely contemporaneous with our present. History advances in disguise; it appears on stage wearing the mask of the preceding scene, and we tend to lose the meaning of the play.
Régis Debray *Revolution in the Revolution?*, Ch. 1

16 History is philosophy drawn from examples.
Dionysius of Halicarnassus *Ars Rhetorica*, 11.2

17 Everything which could possibly enter into the most disordered of imaginations might well be said of the history of the world.
Feodor Dostoevsky *Notes from the Underground*

18 We have been told so often that history is indifferent, but we always take its parsimony or plenty as somehow planned; we never really listen. **Lawrence Durrell** *Justine*, Pt 2, p. 112

19 History is the endless repetition of the wrong way of living, and it'll start again tomorrow, if it's moved from here today.

Lawrence Durrell in the *Listener*, 20 April 1978

20 History teaches us that men and nations behave wisely once they have exhausted all other alternatives.

Abba Eban speech in London, 16 December 1970

21 The historical sense, which is a sense of the timeless as well as of the temporal and of the timeless and of the temporal together.

T. S. Eliot *Tradition and the Individual Talent*, 1

22 There is no history. There is only Biography.

Ralph Waldo Emerson *Journal*, 28 May 1839

23 Many historians have heard the music of the past but have transcribed it for penny whistle. **Peter Gay** *Freud for Historians*, Ch. 2, 3

24 History is not like a novel where everything is true.

Martin Gilbert in the *Guardian*, January 1998

25 History is a novel which did take place; a novel is history that could take place. **Edmond and Jules de Goncourt** *Idées et sensations*

26 History repeats itself: historians repeat each other.

Philip Guedalla *Supers and Supermen*: 'Some Historians'

27 The true theatre of history is therefore the temperate zone.

Georg Hegel *The Philosophy of History*: Introduction

28 History is a child building a sandcastle by the sea, and that child is the whole majesty of man's power in the world. **Heraclitus** *Fragments*, 24

29 If the past cannot teach the present and the father cannot teach the son, then history need not have bothered to go on, and the world has wasted a great deal of time. **Russell Hoban** *The Lion of Boaz-Jachin and Jachin-Boaz*, Ch. 1

30 Historians have been drug dealers to the addicts of national self-affirmation. **E. J. Hobsbawm** quoted in *The Week*, 30 May 1998

31 Histories do not break off clean, like a glass rod; they fray, stretch, and come undone, like a rope. **Robert Hughes** *The Shock of the New*, Ch. 8

32 To all but the saints, who anyhow have no need of them, the lessons of history are totally unavailing. **Aldous Huxley** *Grey Eminence*, Ch. 8

33 Distrust is a necessary qualification of a student of history.

Dr Samuel Johnson 'Review of the Account of the Conduct of the Duchess of Marlborough'

34 There is history that remembers and history that arises from a need to forget. **Christopher Lasch** in the *Times Higher Educational Supplement*, 6 February 1987

35 The unhistorical are usually, without knowing it, enslaved to a fairly recent past. **C. S. Lewis** *They Asked for Paper*, Ch. 1

36 For history's a twisted root
With art its small, translucent fruit
And never the other way round. **Archibald MacLeish** *Ars Poetica*

37 History, like a badly constructed concert hall, has occasional dead spots where the music can't be heard.
Archibald MacLeish in the *Observer*, 'Sayings of the Week', 12 February 1967

38 Hegel says somewhere that all great events and personalities in world history reappear in one way or another. He forgot to add: the first time as tragedy, the second as farce. **Karl Marx** *The Eighteenth Brumaire of Louis Napoleon*, Pt 1

39 Science understands the particular only via the universal. History has no antecedent universals. It is the true empiricism.
John William Miller *The Philosophy of History*, Ch. 35

40 Partial histories are totally impossible. Each history must be a world-history, and only in relation to the whole history is the historical treatment of a particular situation possible. **Novalis** *Pollen*, 301

41 It is impossible to write ancient history because we do not have enough sources, and impossible to write modern history because we have far too many. **Charles Péguy** *Clio*

42 Happy people have no history.
History is the study of man's ill luck. **Raymond Queneau** *Une Histoire modèle*

43 The history of the world is the judgement seat of the world.
Friedrich von Schiller *Resignation*

44 A historian is a prophet looking backwards.
Friedrich von Schlegel *The Athenaeum*, I: 'Fragments'

45 History has always been a favourite study of those who want to learn something without being put to the effort demanded by the true sciences, which require the exercise of reason.
Arthur Schopenhauer *Essays and Aphorisms*: 'On Various Subjects', 4

46 Clio, the Muse of History, is as thoroughly infected with lies as a streetwalker is with syphilis.
Arthur Schopenhauer *Essays and Aphorisms*: 'On Various Subjects', 4

47 There are those who fashion history and those who contemplate it; there are those who make things happen and those who ask why.
Graham Swift *Waterland*, 26

48 History gets thicker as it approaches recent times.
A. J. P. Taylor *English History, 1914–1945*: Bibliography

49 It is commonly said that history is a history of war – but it is at the same time a history of development. **H. D. Thoreau** *Journal*, 29 July 1852

50 History is a gallery of pictures in which there are few originals and many copies. **Alexis de Tocqueville** *The Ancien Régime and the Revolution*, p. 133

51 Historians are like deaf people who go on answering questions that no one has asked them.
Leo Tolstoy quoted in Manning Clark, *A Discovery of Australia*: 'Being an Historian'

52 In the course of history those who have not had their heads cut off and those who have not caused others' heads to fall leave no trace behind. You have a choice of being a victim, a tyrant, or a nobody.
Paul Valéry *Bad Thoughts and Not So Bad*, H

53 History is just the portrayal of crimes and misfortunes.
Voltaire *L'Ingénu*, Ch. 10

54 He had no idea how time could be reworded
Which is the historian's task. **Derek Walcott** *Omeros*, Ch. 18, 1

55 The past can only be told as it truly *is*, not *was*.
Immanuel Wallerstein *The Modern World System*, Vol. 1, Ch. 9

56 History is lived forward but it is written in retrospect.
Veronica Wedgwood quoted in Salman Rushdie, *The Jaguar Smile*: Epilogue

57 Human history becomes more and more a race between education and catastrophe. **H. G. Wells** *The Outline of History*, Ch. 40, 4

58 Now it is on the whole more convenient to keep history and theology apart. **H. G. Wells** *A Short History of the World*, Ch. 37

59 It is sometimes very hard to tell the difference between history and the smell of a skunk.
Rebecca West epigraph to *Voices from the Great War*, ed. Peter Vansittart

60 Anybody can make history. Only a great man can write it.
Oscar Wilde *The Critic as Artist*, 1

See also ***Past and Present; Time***

Honesty and Dishonesty

1 Be so true to thyself, as thou be not false to others.
Francis Bacon *Essays*: 'Of Wisdom for a Man's Self'

2 For the merchant even honesty is a financial speculation.
Charles Baudelaire *Intimate Journals*: 'My Heart Laid Bare', 97

3 Open not thine heart to every man, lest he requite thee with a shrewd turn.
Bible, Apocrypha Ecclesiasticus 8:19

4 Policy – 'honesty is the best policy', but policy iz not alwus the best honesty.
Josh Billings *Wit And Humor*: 'Billings' Lexicon'

5 Most Men owe their Misfortunes rather to their Want of Dishonesty than Wit.
Samuel Butler 1 *Genuine Remains*, p. 474

6 They are honest and truthful as long as it is unnecessary.
Anton Chekhov *Notebooks 1894–1902*, p. 61

7 But to live outside the law, you must be honest.
Bob Dylan song: *Absolutely Sweet Marie*

8 Integrity has few intimates. While many praise her, they do not, however, admit her to their homes; others follow her even in danger; there the false deny her and politicians affect not to know her.
Baltasar Gracián *The Oracle*, 29

9 A word is not like a Bone, that being broken and well set again, is said to be sometimes stronger in that very part.
Marquis of Halifax *The Anatomy of an Equivalent*

10 A Man that should call every thing by its right Name, would hardly pass the Streets without being knock'd down as a common Enemy.
Marquis of Halifax *Miscellaneous Thoughts and Reflections*

11 There is however more *Wit* requisite to be an honest Man, than there is to be a Knave.
Marquis of Halifax *Moral Thoughts and Reflections*: 'Of Cunning'

12 Sincerity has to do with the connection between our words and thoughts, and not between our belief and actions.
William Hazlitt *Sketches and Essays*: 'On Cant and Hypocrisy'

13 You lose more of yourself than you redeem
Doing the decent thing.
Seamus Heaney *Station Island*, XII

14 The boldest among people who deserve to be called good – in the vigorous sense – will seldom be quite sincere.
John Oliver Hobbes *Letters from a Silent Study*: 'Private Opinions'

15 Some folks think they're honest 'cause they return one lost glove.
'Kin' Hubbard *Abe Martin's Broadcast*: 'The Country Newspaper'

16 Integrity without knowledge is weak and useless, and knowledge without integrity is dangerous and dreadful.
Dr Samuel Johnson *Rasselas*, Ch. 41

17 Honesty is praised and starves.
Juvenal *Satires*, I, 74

18 Civility is not a sign of weakness, and sincerity is always subject to proof. **President John F. Kennedy** Inaugural Address, 20 January 1961

19 Even those honest enough to admit to being wrong a thousand times are not honest enough to admit even once to being stupid.
David Kipp *Aphorisms*, p. 4

20 A good man, for all his modesty, cannot prevent people saying about him what an insecure man is capable of saying about himself.
Jean de La Bruyère *Characters*: 'Of Society and Conversation', 21

21 Who comes as he goes, and is present as he came and went, is sincere.
Johann Kaspar Lavater *Aphorisms on Man*, 586; William Blake underlined in approval

22 All really frank people are amusing and would remain so if they could remember that other people may sometimes want to be frank and amusing too. **Ada Leverson** *The Twelfth Hour*, Ch. 9

23 Doctrinaires are the vultures of principle. They feed upon principle after it is dead. **David Lloyd George** quoted by Dingle Foot in the *Guardian*, 17 January 1963

24 I don't think you want too much sincerity in society. It would be like an iron girder in a house of cards. **W. Somerset Maugham** *The Circle*, Act 1

25 The best way to keep one's word is not to give it.
Napoleon Bonaparte *Maxims*

26 An honest man's the noblest work of God.
Alexander Pope *An Essay on Man*, Bk 3, 248

27 A little sincerity is a dangerous thing, and a great deal of it is absolutely fatal. **Oscar Wilde** *The Critic as Artist*, 2

See also ***Hypocrisy***

Hope and Despair

1 Hope is a good breakfast, but it is a bad supper.
Francis Bacon *Apothegms*, 36

2 Hope deferred maketh the heart sick. **Bible, OT** Proverbs 13:12

3 God put self-pity by the side of despair like the cure by the side of the disease. **Albert Camus** *Notebooks 1*, May 1935

4 Exactly the instant when hope ceases to be reasonable it begins to be useful. **G. K. Chesterton** *Heretics*, Ch. 12

5 'Hope' is the thing with feathers –
That perches in the soul –
And sings the tunes without the words –
And never stops – at all –. **Emily Dickinson** *Complete Poems*, 254

6 It is perfection, to be without hope. **Douglas Dunn** *The Dilemma*

7 What we call our despair is often only the painful eagerness of unfed hope. **George Eliot** *Middlemarch*, Bk 5, Ch. 51

8 The Worldly Hope men set their Hearts upon
Turns Ashes – or it prospers; and anon,
Like Snow upon the Desert's dusty face,
Lighting a little Hour or two – is gone.
Edward Fitzgerald *The Rubáiyát of Omar Khayyám*, Edn 1, 14

9 He that lives upon Hope, dies fasting.
Benjamin Franklin *Poor Richard's Almanack*, 1736

10 Despair is the price one pays for setting oneself an impossible aim.
Graham Greene *The Heart of the Matter*, Bk 1, Pt 1, Ch. 2

11 Hope is generally a wrong guide, though it is very good company by the way. **Marquis of Halifax** *Moral Thoughts and Reflections*: 'Of Hope'

12 Cease to hope and you will cease to fear.
Hecato Stoic writer, quoted in Seneca, *Letters to a Stoic*, 5

See also Hesse

13 Hope is the poor man's bread. **George Herbert** *Jacula Prudentum*

14 We are uneasy only as long as we have hope.
Hermann Hesse *Reflections*, 453

See also Hecato

15 We must rediscover the distinction between hope and expectation.
Ivan D. Illich *Deschooling Society*, Ch. 7

16 The natural flights of the human mind are not from pleasure to pleasure, but from hope to hope. **Dr Samuel Johnson** *The Rambler*, No. 2

17 The fact that there is nothing other than a spiritual world deprives us of our hope and gives us our certainty. **Franz Kafka** *Collected Aphorisms*, 62

18 Don't despair, not even over the fact that you don't despair.
Franz Kafka *The Diaries of Franz Kafka*, 21 July 1913

19 Hope is the feeling you have that the feeling you have isn't permanent. **Jean Kerr** *Finishing Touches*, Act 3

20 If there were nothing eternal in a man, he could not despair at all; if despair could consume his self, then there would be no despair at all.

Søren Kierkegaard *The Sickness Unto Death*, Pt 1

21 Do not expect too much of the end of the world.

Stanislaw Lec *Aforyzmy, Fraszki*

22 Man is a victim of dope
In the incurable form of hope. **Ogden Nash** *Goodbye, Old Year*

23 It makes all the difference in life, whether hope is left, or – left out!

Ouida *Wisdom, Wit, and Pathos*: 'Under Two Flags'

24 Hope springs eternal in the human breast;
Man never is, but always to be blessed. **Alexander Pope** *An Essay on Man*, I, 95

25 Blessed is the man who expects nothing.

Alexander Pope letter to Fortescue, 23 September 1725

26 For hope is but the dream of those that wake.

Matthew Prior *Solomon*, Bk 3, 102

27 No one can feel responsible and desperate simultaneously.

Antoine de Saint-Exupéry *Flight to Arras*, Ch. 24

28 Human life begins on the other side of despair.

Jean-Paul Sartre *The Flies*, Act 3, Sc. 2

29 Hope is the confusion of the desire for a thing with its probability.

Arthur Schopenhauer *Essays and Aphorisms*: 'On Psychology', 6

30 Despair has often won battles. **Voltaire** *La Henriade*, Canto 10

House and Home

1 For a man's house is his castle. **Sir Edward Coke** *Institutes*, III, 73

2 Many a man who thinks to found a home discovers that he has merely opened a tavern for his friends. **Norman Douglas** *South Wind*, Ch. 24

3 'Home is the place where, when you have to go there,
They have to take you in.'
'I should have called it
Something you somehow haven't to deserve.'

Robert Frost *The Death of the Hired Man*

4 A house is a machine for living in. **Le Corbusier** *Vers une architecture*, p. ix

5 Have nothing in your houses that you do not know to be useful, or believe to be beautiful. **William Morris** *The Beauty of Life*

See also Environments

Human Nature

1 We have to stand upright ourselves, not be set up.

Marcus Aurelius *Meditations*, Bk 3, 5

2 Men must know that, in this theatre of Man's' life, it is reserved only for God and angels to be lookers on.

Francis Bacon *The Advancement of Learning*: Bk 2, vii, 5

3 In brief, we are all monsters, that is a composition of man and beast.

Sir Thomas Browne *Religio Medici*, Pt 1, 9

4 There is surely a piece of divinity in us, something that was before the elements, and owes no homage unto the sun.

Sir Thomas Browne *Religio Medici*, Pt 2, 11

5 Man is a noble animal, splendid in ashes, and pompous in the grave.

Sir Thomas Browne *Urn Burial*, Ch. 5

6 In the natural, as in the social order, we ought not to wish to be more than we can be. **Nicholas-Sébastien Chamfort** *Maxims and Considerations*, 138

7 Mankind is not a tribe of animals to which we owe compassion. Mankind is a club to which we owe our subscription.

G. K. Chesterton in the *Daily News*, 10 April 1906

8 Alone of all creatures he is not self-sufficient, even while he is supreme. He dare not sleep in his own skin.

G. K. Chesterton in *Hearst's International*, June 1922

9 Man on this earth is an unforeseen accident which does not stand close investigation. **Joseph Conrad** *Victory*, Pt 3, Ch. 3

10 He is the most ridiculous beast on earth and the reason is his mind and his pudendum. **Edward Dahlberg** *Sorrows of Priapus*: Prologue

11 What is this thing, a man? They spend half a lifetime verifying, and pulling to pieces bit by bit, something that has already been discovered. During the other half, they lay the foundations of an edifice that never rises above the level of the ground.

Eugène Delacroix *Journal*, 2 February 1824

12 Man is a social animal who dislikes his fellow men.

Eugène Delacroix *Journal*, 17 November 1852

13 What is man, when you come to think upon him, but a minutely set, ingenious machine for turning, with infinite artfulness, the red wine of Shiraz into urine? **Isak Dinesen** *Seven Gothic Tales*: 'The Dreamers'

14 The best definition of man is the ungrateful biped.

Fyodor Dostoevsky *Notes from the Underground*, Pt 1, 8

15 The meaning of man's life consists in proving to himself every minute that he's a man and not a piano key.

Fyodor Dostoevsky *Notes from the Underground*, Pt 1, 8

16 Men are but children of a larger growth.

John Dryden *All for Love*, Act 4, Sc. 1

17 Things are in the saddle,
And ride mankind. **Ralph Waldo Emerson** *Ode inscribed to W. H. Canning*

18 One definition of man is 'an intelligence served by organs'.

Ralph Waldo Emerson *Society and Solitude*: 'Works and Days', 1870

19 There are only the pursued, the pursuing, the busy, and the tired.

F. Scott Fitzgerald *The Great Gatsby*, Ch. 4

20 Mankind are very odd Creatures: One half censure what they practise, the other half practise what they censure; the rest always say and do as they ought. **Benjamin Franklin** *Poor Richard's (Improved) Almanack*, 1752

21 Every Man thinks he deserves better than indeed he doth; therefore thou can'st not oblige Mankind better than by speaking well. Man is the greatest Humorist and Self-flatterer in the world.

Dr Thomas Fuller *Introductio ad Prudentium*, 2527

22 It may be remarked that man is the only animal that can live and multiply in every country from the equator to the Poles. The hog appears to approach nearest to our species in that privilege.

Edward Gibbon quoted in Sagittarius and Daniel George, *The Perpetual Pessimist*, 22 May

23 Man's a ribald – Man's a rake,
Man is Nature's sole mistake. **W. S. Gilbert** *Princess Ida*, Act 2

24 Man cannot live on the human plane; he must be either above or below it. **Eric Gill** *Autobiography*: Conclusion

25 Man would be the finest creature in the world if only he weren't too fine for it.

Johann Wolfgang von Goethe *Maxims and Reflections*: 'Life and Character', 89

26 The human being is a blind man who dreams he can see.
Friedrich Hebbel *Diaries*, entry 244, 1836

27 If it were not for the beast within us we would be castrated angels.
Hermann Hesse *Reflections*, 28

28 Most human beings have an almost infinite capacity for taking things for granted. **Aldous Huxley** *Themes and Variations*: 'Variations on a Philosopher'

29 We need words to keep us human. Being human is an accomplishment like playing an instrument. It takes practice.
Michael Ignatieff *The Needs of Strangers*: Conclusion

See also Novalis

30 Men are like wine. Some turn to vinegar, but the best improve with age. **Pope John XXIII** in Gerald Brenan, *Thoughts in a Dry Season*: 'Life'

31 A human being must always be treated as an end, not as a means.
Immanuel Kant in W. R. Inge, *The End of an Age*, Ch. 4

32 Humanity does not pass through phases as a train passes through stations: being alive, it has the privilege of always moving yet never leaving anything behind. **C. S. Lewis** *The Allegory of Love*, Ch. 1

33 Man is never more serious than when he is exasperated or praises himself. **Georg Christoph Lichtenberg** *The Lichtenberg Reader*: Aphorisms, 1775

34 In order to distinguish mankind from the other animals, instead of claiming he's the only one that reasons, I'd rather we said: he's the animal that unceasingly deceives or is deceived. **Prince de Ligne** *Mes Écarts*

35 The long-sought missing link between animals and the really humane being is ourselves. **Konrad Lorenz** epigraph to Christa Wolf, *Accident*

36 I'll give you my opinion of the human race in a nutshell . . . Their heart's in the right place, but their head is a thoroughly inefficient organ. **W. Somerset Maugham** *The Summing Up*, 55

37 We are a fatally flawed species, living in a world that we can only say was designed by hindsight, not by foresight.
Jonathan Miller interview in the *Guardian*, 12 September 1998

38 The life of every man is an endlessly repeated performance of the life of man. **Edwin Muir** *An Autobiography*, Ch. 1

39 Human affairs are not serious, but they have to be taken seriously.
Iris Murdoch *Henry and Cato*, Pt 2: 'The Great Teacher'

40 Man is always worse than most people suspect, but also generally better than most people dream.
Reinhold Niebuhr quoted in the *Guardian*, 15 July 1988

41 To become human is an art. **Novalis** *Pollen*, 198

See also Ignatieff

42 Man is the only creature that consumes without producing.
George Orwell *Animal Farm*, Ch. 1

43 Our nature is one of movement; to be completely still is to be dead.
Blaise Pascal *Pensées*, 198

44 Man goes nowhere. Everything comes to man, like tomorrow.
Antonio Porchia *Voices*

45 Man is the measure of all things.
Protagoras quoted by Plato in *Theaetetus*, 160 D

46 Human beings were invented by water as a device for transporting itself from one place to another.
Tom Robbins *Another Roadside Attraction*, p. 28

47 Humans are the most advanced of mammals – although a case could be made for dolphins – because they seldom grow up.
Tom Robbins *Still Life with Woodpecker*, 1, 12

48 Plants grow in two directions, upwards to the light, and downward into the dark. Therefore man is a plant.
Colin Ross *Adecarcinoma and Other Poems*, aphorism 51

49 The becoming of man is the history of the exhaustion of his possibilities. **Susan Sontag** *Styles of Radical Will*: 'Thinking against oneself'

50 Men are cruel, but Man is kind. **Rabindranath Tagore** *Stray Birds*

51 As a species, taking all in all, we are still too young, too juvenile, to be trusted. **Lewis Thomas** *Late Night Thoughts*: 'Seven Wonders'

52 We are all alike – on the inside.
Mark Twain in B. DeVoto, *Mark Twain in Eruption*: 'Andrew Carnegie'

53 The human skin divides the world into two kinds of space: on one side, light; on the other, fright. **Paul Valéry** *Bad Thoughts and Not So Bad*, P

54 A man is more complex, infinitely more so, than his thoughts.
Paul Valéry *Odds and Ends*, II

55 Men first feel necessity, then look for utility, next attend to comfort, still later amuse themselves with pleasure, thence grow dissolute in luxury, and finally go mad and waste their substance.
Giambattista Vico *The New Science*, Bk 1, Para. 241

56 We are no more Second Causes; and our Sufficiency is only in God, who is the First. A Second Cause is no Cause, divided from the First.
Benjamin Whichcote *Moral and Religious Aphorisms*, 530

57 It is because Humanity has never known where it was going that it has been able to find its way. **Oscar Wilde** *The Critic as Artist*, 1

58 It is only the superficial qualities that last. Man's deeper nature is soon found out. **Oscar Wilde** *Phrases and Philosophies for the Use of the Young*

59 We're all of us guinea pigs in the laboratory of God. Humanity is just a work in progress. **Tennessee Williams** *Camino Real*, Block 12

60 Of all things one finds on earth
man is the most inconvenient. **Wols** *Aphorisms and Pictures*, p. 23

See also ***Body and Soul; Character; Individuals; The Mind; The Self; The Senses***

Hypocrisy

1 The hypocrite is too ambitious; not only does he want to appear virtuous before others, he wants to convince himself.
Hannah Arendt *On Revolution*, Ch. 2

2 It is the wisdom of the crocodiles, that shed tears when they would devour. **Francis Bacon** *Essays*: 'Of Wisdom for a Man's Self'

3 Prisons are built with stones of Law, Brothels with bricks of Religion.
William Blake *The Marriage of Heaven and Hell*: 'Proverbs of Hell'

4 That vice pays homage to virtue is notorious; we call it hypocrisy.
Samuel Butler 2 *The Way of All Flesh*, Ch. 19

5 Mental hypocrisy: Whenever a truth threatens, he hides behind a thought. **Elias Canetti** *The Secret Heart of the Clock*: '1975'

6 We ought to see far enough into a hypocrite to see even his sincerity.
G. K. Chesterton *Heretics*, Ch. 5

7 The beginning of self-deception is when we begin to find *reasons* for our *propensities*. **Edward Fitzgerald** *Polonius*: 'Hypocrisy'

8 The true hypocrite is the one who ceases to perceive his deception, the one who lies with sincerity.
André Gide *Journal of 'The Counterfeiters'*, Second Notebook, August 1921

9 The meaning of all which is that Man is the only hypocrite in the creation; or that he is composed of two natures, the ideal and the physical, the one of which is always trying to keep a secret from the other. **William Hazlitt** *Aphorisms on Man*, 65

10 No man is a hypocrite in his pleasures.

Dr Samuel Johnson in James Boswell, *Life of Johnson*, 1784

11 It is as easy to deceive ourselves without noticing it as it is hard to deceive others without their noticing.

Duc de La Rochefoucauld *Maxims*, 115

12 Hypocrisy is a tribute vice pays to virtue. **Duc de La Rochefoucauld** *Maxims*, 218

13 Trust him with none of thy individualities who is, or pretends to be, two things at once. **Johann Kaspar Lavater** *Aphorisms on Man*, 49

14 Hypocrisy is the most difficult and nerve-racking vice that any man can pursue; it needs an unceasing vigilance and a rare detachment of spirit. It cannot, like adultery or gluttony, be practised at spare moments; it is a whole time job. **W. Somerset Maugham** *Cakes and Ale*, Ch. 1

15 The ready tear means treachery not grief.

Publilius Syrus *Moral Sayings*, 536

16 There is plenty of humbug in hell.

George Bernard Shaw *Man and Superman*, Act 3

17 Hypocrisy is as easily known to a man himself, as he knows whether he is awake or asleep; in health or sick: for what does a man know, if he knows not what he means!

Benjamin Whichcote *Moral and Religious Aphorisms*, 88

18 Is insincerity such a terrible thing? I think not. It is merely a method by which we can multiply our personalities.

Oscar Wilde *The Picture of Dorian Gray*, Ch. 11

See also **Lies**

Ideals

1 The idealist walks on tiptoe, the materialist on his heels.

Malcolm de Chazal *Sens plastique*, Vol. 2

2 The value of ideals lies in the experiences to which they lead.

John Dewey *Art as Experience*, quoted in Adam Phillips, *Darwin's Bones*: Epilogue

3 The idealistic male with a cult of principles is the curse of Europe. He will die for his principles; no harm in that. He will persecute others for his principles and that is what makes him such a nuisance.

Norman Douglas *How About Europe?*, p. 87

4 If you cannot catch a bird of paradise, better take a wet hen.

Nikita S. Khrushchev in *Time* magazine, 6 January 1958

5 An idealist is someone who
has convinced himself other people
are less nasty than
himself.

Irving Layton *The Whole Bloody Bird*: 'aphs'

6 An idealist is one who on noticing that a rose smells better than a cabbage concludes that it will also make better soup.

H. L. Mencken *A Book of Burlesques*: Sententiae

7 The idealist conceals facts from himself; the liar from others.

Friedrich Nietzsche *Nietzsche in Outline and Aphorism*: 'Morality'

Ideas

1 One of the greatest pains to human nature is the pain of a new idea.
Walter Bagehot *Physics and Politics*: 'The Age of Discussion'

See also Barker

2 Ideology is the outcome of pain.
Howard Barker in the *Guardian*, 10 February 1986

See also Bagehot

3 An original idea is an idea of which we have forgotten the author.
George Bedborough *Narcotics and Stimulants*

4 If you board the wrong train, it is no use running along the corridor in the other direction. **Dietrich Bonhoeffer** *The Way to Freedom*

5 All ideas in the arts derive from nature's productions: God has created and man imitates. **George-Louis de Buffon** *Histoire naturelle*: 'Premier discours'

6 It doesn't matter how new an idea *is*: what matters is how new it *becomes*. **Elias Canetti** *The Secret Heart of the Clock*: '1981'

7 A man is not necessarily intelligent because he has plenty of ideas, any more than he is a good general because he has plenty of soldiers.
Nicholas-Sébastien Chamfort *Maxims and Considerations*, 446

8 Ideas are the source of everything; they produce facts, which only act as their envelope.
François-René de Chateaubriand *Histoire de France*, Vol. 1: 'Analyse raisonée, éducation'

9 Ideas are dangerous, but the man to whom they are most dangerous is the man of no ideas. **G. K. Chesterton** *Heretics*, Ch. 20

10 There will be nothing to choose between headless practice and legless theory. **Régis Debray** *Revolution in the Revolution?*: Introduction

11 If at first an idea isn't totally absurd, there's no hope for it.
Albert Einstein (attrib.)

12 No grand idea was ever born in a conference, but a lot of foolish ideas have died there. **F. Scott Fitzgerald** *Notebooks*, N

13 Anyone who shrinks from ideas ends by having nothing but sensations. **Johann Wolfgang von Goethe** *Maxims and Reflections*: 'Life and Character', 93

14 Hypotheses are scaffolding erected in front of a building and then dismantled when the building is finished. They are indispensable for the workman, but you mustn't mistake the scaffolding for the building.
Johann Wolfgang von Goethe *Maxims and Reflections* (Penguin), 1222

15 He who is afraid of ideas in the end also lacks concepts.

Johann Wolfgang von Goethe *Maxims and Reflections* (Penguin), from *Art and Antiquity*, 128

16 Unless you're a scientist, it's much more important for a theory to be shapely, than for it to be true. **Christopher Hampton** *The Philanthropist*, Sc. 1

See also Whitehead

17 It is better to entertain an idea than to take it home to live with you for the rest of your life. **Randall Jarrell** *Pictures from an Institution*, Pt 4, Ch. 9

18 Neither in the arts, nor in logic, nor in life should an idea in any way be treated as a thing. **Joseph Joubert** *Notebooks*, 1814

19 To the liberal ideas of the age must be opposed the moral ideas of all ages. **Joseph Joubert** *Thoughts and Maxims*, 248

20 It is with ideas as with umbrellas, if left lying about they are peculiarly liable to change of ownership.

Thomas Kettle from his wife's memoir; in *A Book of Irish Quotations*, ed. Sean McMahon; but other claimants

21 In a war of ideas it is people who get killed.

Stanislaw Lec *Unkempt Thoughts*, p. 105

22 An idea isn't responsible for the people who believe in it.

Don Marquis in the *New York Sun*: 'The Sun Dial'

23 When we are tired we are attacked by ideas we conquered long ago.

Friedrich Nietzsche in *The Faber Book of Aphorisms*, ed. W. H. Auden and Louis Kronenberger

24 What can be done with fewer assumptions is done in vain with more.

William of Occam quoted by Edward O. Wilson, *Consilience*, Ch. 4

25 The English approach to ideas is not to kill them, but to let them die of neglect. **Jeremy Paxman** in the *Independent*, 'Quotes of the Week', 24 October 1998

26 Ideas come to us as the substitutes for griefs, and griefs, at the moment when they change into ideas, lose some part of their power to injure our heart. **Marcel Proust** *Remembrance of Things Past: Time Regained*, p. 268

27 A powerful idea communicates some of its power to the man who contradicts it.

Marcel Proust *Remembrance of Things Past: Within a Budding Grove*: 'Madame Swann at Home'

28 Good ideas may fail but are not lost. **Publilius Syrus** *Moral Sayings*, 84

29 You can't massacre an idea, you cannot run tanks over hope.

Ronald Reagan of Chinese repression of student demonstrations; Churchill Lecture at Guildhall, London, 13 June 1989

30 It's much easier to cope with the abstract than with the concrete; there's no direct, personal involvement – and you can keep an abstract idea steady in your mind whereas real things are usually in a state of flux and always changing. It's safer to play around with a man's wife than with his clichés. **Tom Robbins** *Another Roadside Attraction*, Pt 4, p. 260

31 Theory is often just practice with the hard bits left out.
J. M. Robson in *The Library*, 1985, VI, 7

32 To love an idea is to love a little more than one should.
Jean Rostand 'Carnets d'un biologiste', p. 181

33 What a terrible curse is an idea in the head of an ignorant man!
Mark Rutherford *Last Pages from a Journal*: Notes, p. 276

34 Agreeable ideas arise, in proportion as they are drawn from inanimates, from vegetables, from animals, and from human beings.
William Shenstone *Essays on Men and Manners*: 'Books and Writers'

35 Ideas that enter the mind under fire remain there securely and for ever. **Leon Trotsky** *My Life*, Ch. 35

36 A serious man has few ideas. A man of many ideas cannot be serious.
Paul Valéry *Bad Thoughts and Not So Bad*, I

37 Our ideas are less perfect than language.
Marquis de Vauvenargues *Reflections and Maxims*, 458

38 It is more important that a proposition be interesting than that it be true. **A. N. Whitehead** *Adventures of Ideas*, Ch. 16

See also Hampton

39 An idea that is not dangerous is unworthy of being called an idea at all. **Oscar Wilde** *The Critic as Artist*, 2

See also ***Mind; Thought***

Idleness and Energy

1 To spend too much time in studies is sloth.
Francis Bacon *Essays*: 'Of Studies'

2 Sauntering is a science: it is the gastronomy of the eye.
Honoré de Balzac in J. Raymond Solly, *Selected Thoughts from the French*: 'Miscellaneous'

3 Go to the ant, thou sluggard, consider her ways, and be wise.
Bible, OT Proverbs 6:6

4 As vinegar to the teeth, and as smoke to the eyes, so is the sluggard to them that send him. **Bible, OT** Proverbs 10:26

5 I prefer a ded man to a thoroly lazy one, yu kan bury the ded one, and thus utilize space. **Josh Billings** *Life and Adventures of Josh Billings*, p. 86

6 Hurry alwuss steps on itself – dispatch steps on the other phellow.
Josh Billings *Life and Adventures of Josh Billings*, p. 90

7 Energy is the only life, and is from the body; and reason is the bound or outward circumference of energy. Energy is eternal delight!
William Blake *The Marriage of Heaven and Hell*: 'The Voice of the Devil'

8 We desire the idleness of a wicked man, and the silence of a fool.
Nicholas-Sébastien Chamfort *Maxims and Considerations*, 36

9 If you wish to have little spare time, do nothing.
Anton Chekhov *Notebooks 1894–1902*, p. 39

10 Idleness is only the refuge of weak minds.
Earl of Chesterfield *Letters to His Son*, 20 July 1749

11 Laziness is the hallmark of idealism.
Norman Douglas *How About Europe?*, p. 90

12 The believing we do something when we do nothing is the first illusion of tobacco. **Ralph Waldo Emerson** *Journal*, 1859

13 Time and again we cling to the things we have learned to love; we call this fidelity, but it is only inertia. **Hermann Hesse** *Reflections*, 185

14 It is impossible to enjoy idling thoroughly unless one has plenty of work to do. **Jerome K. Jerome** *Idle Thoughts of an Idle Fellow*: 'On Being Idle'

15 Grief is a species of idleness.
Dr Samuel Johnson in James Boswell, *Life of Johnson*, Vol. 3

16 Laziness is the supreme virtue of the ungifted.
Hans Keller *Maxims and Reflections*, 63

17 He alone has energy that cannot be deprived of it.
Johann Kaspar Lavater *Aphorisms on Man*, 352

18 No human being believes that any other human being has a right to be in bed when he himself is up.
Robert Lynd in *Apt and Amusing Quotations*, ed. G. F. Lamb: 'Bed'

19 Celerity is never more admired
Than by the negligent. **William Shakespeare** *Antony and Cleopatra*, Act 2, Sc. 7, 24

20 Too swift arrives as tardy as too slow.
William Shakespeare *Romeo and Juliet*, Act 2, Sc. 6, 15

21 It is better to have loafed and lost than never to have loafed at all.
James Thurber *Fables for Our Time*: 'The Courtship of Arthur and Al'

22 The chief attraction of military service has consisted and will consist in this compulsory and irreproachable idleness.
Leo Tolstoy *War and Peace*, 7, Ch. 1

23 The lazy are always keen to do something.
Marquis de Vauvenargues *Reflections and Maxims*, 467

24 The condition of perfection is idleness: the aim of perfection is youth. **Oscar Wilde** *Phrases and Philosophies for the Use of the Young*

25 Procrastination is the thief of time.
Edward Young *Night Thoughts*: 'Night I', 393

See also ***Work and Leisure***

Images and Imagination

1 As your repeated imaginations, so will your mind be, for the soul is dyed by its imaginations.
Marcus Aurelius quoted by Joseph Brodsky in *Grief and Reason*: 'Essay of Homage'

2 It is often said that men are ruled by their imaginations; but it would be truer to say they are governed by the weakness of their imaginations.
Walter Bagehot *The English Constitution*: 'The Monarchy'

3 [Of photography] The art of making the object appear, the subject disappear. **Jean Baudrillard** in the *Observer, Life*, 15 February 1998

4 Photography, because it stops the flow of life, is always flirting with death. **John Berger** in *New Society*, 22/29 December 1983

5 What is now proved was once only imagined.
William Blake *The Marriage of Heaven and Hell*: 'Proverbs of Hell'

6 To have frequent recourse to narrative betrays great want of imagination. **Earl of Chesterfield** *Letters to His Son*, 19 October 1748

7 The Fancy is indeed no other than a mode of memory emancipated from the order of time and space.
Samuel Taylor Coleridge *Biographia Literaria*, Ch. 13

8 Where there is no imagination there is no horror.
Arthur Conan Doyle *A Study in Scarlet*, Ch. 5

9 An imaginary cause is capable of producing the most serious and mischievous effects. **Edward Gibbon** *The Decline and Fall of the Roman Empire*, Ch. 12

10 All artistic discoveries are discoveries not of likenesses but of equivalences which enable us to see reality in terms of an image and an image in terms of reality. **E. H. Gombrich** *Art and Illusion*, Ch. 10

11 To transform the outside world by magic without going mad – that is our aim. It's not easy, but on the other hand, there isn't much competition. **Hermann Hesse** *Reflections*, 433

12 Men are only great as they have sympathy. Imagination is sympathy in motion. **Elbert Hubbard** *The Note Book of Elbert Hubbard*, p. 183

13 He who has imagination without learning has wings but no feet.
Joseph Joubert *Thoughts and Maxims*, 53

14 The pleasures of the imagination are as it were only drawings and models which are played with by poor people who cannot afford the real thing. **Georg Christoph Lichtenberg** *Aphorisms*, Notebook C, 38

15 My body is that part of the world which my thoughts are able to change. Even *imaginary* illnesses can become real ones. In the rest of the world my hypotheses cannot disturb the order of things.
Georg Christoph Lichtenberg *Aphorisms*, Notebook J, 234

16 It's imagination that loses battles.
Joseph de Maistre *St Petersburg Nights*: Seventh Conversation

17 Glamour is a youth's form of blindness that lets in light, incoherent colour, but nothing defined. Like the rainbow, it is a once uplifting vision that moves away the closer you come to it.
Arthur Miller *Timebends*, 8

18 Imagination, the supreme delight of the immortal; and the immature, should be limited. In order to enjoy life, we should not enjoy it too much. **Vladimir Nabokov** *Speak Memory*, Ch. 1, 1

19 Bias and attachment are for the imagination what fog, blinding light, and coloured spectacles are for the eyes. **Novalis** *Pollen*, 206

20 The life of nations no less than that of men is lived largely in the imagination.
Enoch Powell said in 1946; epigraph to Martin J. Wiener, *English Culture and the Decline of the Industrial Spirit, 1850–1980*

21 The lunatic, the lover, and the poet,
Are of imagination all compact.
William Shakespeare *A Midsummer Night's Dream*, Act 5, Sc. 1, 7

22 A photograph is not only an image (as a painting is an image), an interpretation of the real; it is also a trace, something directly stencilled off the real, like a footprint or a death mask.
Susan Sontag *On Photography*

23 When we're afraid we shoot. But when we're nostalgic we take pictures.
Susan Sontag *On Photography*

24 Skill without imagination is craftsmanship and gives us many useful objects such as wickerwork picnic baskets. Imagination without skill gives us modern art.
Tom Stoppard *Artist Descending a Staircase*

25 Vision is the art of seeing things invisible.
Jonathan Swift *Thoughts on Various Subjects*, p. 286

26 An imaginative man is apt to see, in his life, the story of his life.
Sir Henry Taylor *The Statesman*, Ch. 5

27 In children memory is most vigorous, and imagination is therefore excessively vivid, for imagination is nothing but extended or compounded memory.
Giambattista Vico *The New Science*, Bk 1, Para. 211

28 Fantasy is more primary than reality, and the enrichment of fantasy with the world's riches depends on the experience of illusion.
D. W. Winnicott *The Family and Individual Development*: 'Transitional Objects'

See also ***Art and Artists; Perceptions***

Imitation and the Inimitable

1 To refrain from imitation is the best revenge.
Marcus Aurelius *Meditations*, Bk 6, 6

2 The difference between a bad artist and a good is, that the bad artist *seems* to copy a great deal, the good one *does* copy a great deal.
William Blake in Alexander Gilchrist, *Life of William Blake*, Vol. 1, Ch. 29

3 The advantage of having imitators is that at last they cure you of yourself.
Jorge Luis Borges quoted by Philip Roth in the *Independent*, 2 September 1990

4 Art does not imitate life if only for fear of clichés.
Joseph Brodsky *Less Than One*: 'Keening Muse'

5 An original writer is not one who imitates nobody, but one whom nobody can imitate.
François-René de Chateaubriand *Génie du Christianisme*

6 Imitation is the sincerest form of flattery.
Charles Caleb Colton *Lacon*: 'Imitation'

7 Immature poets imitate; mature poets steal.
T. S. Eliot *Selected Essays*, 'Philip Massinger'

See also Stravinsky

8 Every man is a borrower and a mimic, life is theatrical and literature a quotation. **Ralph Waldo Emerson** *Society and Solitude*: 'Success'

9 Nothing is repeated, and everything is unparalleled.
Edmond and Jules de Goncourt *Journal*, 15 April 1867

10 It is amazing how much phoniness is needed to produce a grain of originality. **Eric Hoffer** *Between the Devil and the Dragon*, 2: Introduction

11 When people are free to do as they please, they usually imitate each other. Originality is deliberate and forced, and partakes of the nature of a protest. **Eric Hoffer** *The Passionate State of Mind*, Aphorism 33

12 What is originality? Undetected plagiarism.
W. R. Inge *Assessments and Anticipations*, Ch. 31

13 He who abandons his claim to be unique is even less bearable when he claims to be representative. **Clive James** *Falling Towards England*: Preface

14 Contemporaries live from second hand to mouth.
Karl Kraus *Half-Truths and One-and-a-Half Truths*: 'Lord, forgive the . . .'

15 A strict observer is one who would be an atheist under an atheistic king. **Jean de La Bruyère** *Characters*: 'Of Fashion', 21

16 To do the opposite of something is also a form of imitation, namely an imitation of its opposite.
Georg Christoph Lichtenberg *Aphorisms*, Notebook D, 96

17 Anticipatory plagiarism occurs when someone steals your original idea and publishes it a hundred years before you were born.
Robert Merton epigraph to John D. Barrow, *Theories of Everything*

18 If you steal from one author it's plagiarism. If you steal from many it's research. **Wilson Mizner** in A. Johnston, *The Legendary Mizners*, Ch. 4

19 Parody is just originality in a second-hand suit.
Eugenio Montale quoted in the *Listener*, 7 June 1990

20 Nature diversifies and imitates, art imitates and diversifies.
Blaise Pascal *Pensées*, 27

21 Great art is always an invention that begins as an imitation.
Octavio Paz *Convergences*

22 A thought goes walking about the world, and lodges in several people's heads in such quick succession, that they are sure to quarrel in the end as to who gave it house room at first.
Thomas Sheridan in Edward Meryon, *Epitaphs, Personal Anecdotes and Epigrams*: 'Quotations'

23 It is easier to copy than to think, hence fashion. Besides a community of originals is not a community. **Wallace Stevens** *Adagia*, 2

24 A good composer does not imitate; he steals.
Igor Stravinsky in Peter Yates, *Twentieth Century Music*, Pt 1, Ch. 8

See also Eliot

25 The part of a man which is inimitable by others is precisely the part which he himself is incapable of 'imitating'. The inimitable *in* me is inimitable *by* me. **Paul Valéry** *Rhumbs*: 'Literature'

26 Paradox though it may seem – and paradoxes are always dangerous things – it is none the less true that life imitates art far more than art imitates life. **Oscar Wilde** *The Decay of Lying*

27 Born Originals, how comes
it to pass that we die
Copies? **Edward Young** epigraph to Jacob Golomb, *Inauthenticity and Authenticity*

Immortality

1 Eternal nothingness is OK if you're dressed for it.
Woody Allen *Getting Even*: 'My Philosophy'

2 The roaring of lions, the howling of wolves, the raging of the stormy sea, and the destructive sword, are portions of eternity, too great for the eye of man. **William Blake** *The Marriage of Heaven and Hell*: 'Proverbs of Hell'

3 Rational existences in Heaven perish not at all, and but partially on Earth. That which is thus once will in some way be always: the first Living human Soul is still alive, and all Adam hath found no Period.
Sir Thomas Browne *Christian Morals*, Pt 3, 23

4 Thus we are men and we know not how: there is something in us that can be without us, and will be after us.
Sir Thomas Browne *Religio Medici*, Pt 1, 35

5 To himself everyone is an immortal; he may know that he is going to die, but he can never know that he is dead.
Samuel Butler 2 *Notebooks*, Ch. 23: 'Ignorance of Death'

6 The meanest man is immortal and the mightiest movement is temporal, not to say temporary. **G. K. Chesterton** in *Blackfriars*, January 1923

7 The only secret people keep
Is Immortality. **Emily Dickinson** *Complete Poems*, 1748

8 Somebody once said millions long for immortality who don't know what to do with themselves on a rainy Sunday afternoon.
Susan Ertz *Anger in the Sky*, Ch. 5

9 The best metempsychosis is for us to appear again in others.
Johann Wolfgang von Goethe *Maxims and Reflections*: 'Science'

10 He had decided to live for ever or die in the attempt.
Joseph Heller *Catch-22*, Ch. 3

11 There was one who was astonished how easily he moved along the road of eternity; the fact is that he was racing along it downhill.
Franz Kafka *Collected Aphorisms*, 38

12 All that is not eternal is eternally out of date.
C. S. Lewis *The Four Loves*, Ch. 6

13 The majority of the elements we are composed of are potentially immortal. Dying is a collective phenomenon.
Jean Rostand *Pensées d'un biologiste*, p. 53

14 Eternity is time,
Time eternity.
To see the two as opposites
Is mind's perversity.
Angelus Silesius *The Book of Angelus Silesius*: 'Of Time and Eternity'

15 Eternity is a terrible thought. I mean, where's it going to end?
Tom Stoppard *Rosencrantz and Guildenstern are Dead*, Act 2

16 As if you could kill time without injuring eternity.
H. D. Thoreau *Walden*: 'Economy'

17 In fact we do not try to picture the afterlife, nor is it our selves in our nervous tics and optical flecks that we wish to perpetuate; it is the self as the window on the world that we can't bear to think of shutting.
John Updike *Self-Consciousness*, Ch. 6

18 It's because human reason alone is incapable of demonstrating the immortality of the soul that religion has had to reveal it to us.
Voltaire *Philosophical Letters*, Letter 13

Individuals

1 No individual entirely agrees with any other, or he would cease to be an individual. **William Allingham** *By the Way*: Notes, 149

2 You cannot own me. You can only borrow me. God owns me.
Martin Allwood *Something Like Aphorisms*: 'Religion and Morals'

3 We carry within us the wonders we seek without us: there is all Africa and her prodigies in us. **Sir Thomas Browne** *Religio Medici*, Pt 1, 15

4 It is we, individual men and women, who should be the measure of all things, not made to measure for something else.
Charles Handy *The Age of Paradox*: Preface

5 A man may be so much of everything, that he is nothing of anything.
Dr Samuel Johnson in James Boswell, *Life of Johnson*, 19 September 1783

6 The definition of the individual was: a multitude of one million divided by one million. **Arthur Koestler** *Darkness at Noon*: 'The Grammatical Fiction', 2

7 Every human being is a whole colony.
Pablo Picasso in Françoise Gilot and Carlton Lake, *Life with Picasso*, Pt 1

8 For the biologist there are no classes, there are only individuals.
Jean Rostand *Pensées d'un biologiste*, p. 19

9 Biology denies the individual any essential attribute that is not common to all beings. Whether he likes it or not, he drags them round with him like a huge army of beggars. And he has to share with them everything he calls his own. **Jean Rostand** *Pensées d'un biologiste*, p. 88

10 The sectarian thinks
that he has the sea
ladled into his private pond. **Rabindranath Tagore** *Fireflies*, p. 209

See also ***Human Nature; The Self***

Innocence and Guilt

1 He that maketh haste to be rich shall not be innocent.
Bible, OT Proverbs 28:20

2 Unto the pure all things are pure. **Bible, NT** Titus 1:15

3 Sacrifice does not serve to expiate guilt, as the textbooks say. Sacrifice is guilt – the only one. **Roberto Calasso** *The Ruin of Kasch*: 'Elements of Sacrifice'

4 A man is not to aim at innocence, any more than he is to aim at hair; but he is to keep it. It is inestimable as a basis or accompaniment of his ability, but nothing alone. **Ralph Waldo Emerson** *Journal*, 1855: 'Niebuhr'

5 What we call real estate – the solid ground to build a house on – this is the broad foundation on which nearly all the guilt of the world exists. **Nathaniel Hawthorne** *The House of Seven Gables*, Ch. 17

6 There are things we regret before we do them, and still do.

Friedrich Hebbel *Diaries*, entry 1195, 1838

7 Guilt is of course not an emotion in the Celtic countries, it is simply a way of life – a kind of gleefully painful social anaesthetic.

A. L. Kennedy *So I Am Glad*, p. 36

8 When a man points a finger at someone else, he should remember that four of his digits are pointing at himself. **Louis Nizer** *My Life in Court*

9 It is innocence that is full and experience that is empty. It is innocence that wins and experience that loses.

Charles Péguy *Basic Verities*: 'Innocence and Experience'

10 Guilt, by reminding us what we mustn't do, shows us what we may want; it shows us our moral sense, the difference between what we want, and what we want to want. **Adam Phillips** *Monogamy*, 45

11 How extraordinary it is that one feels most guilt about the sins one is unable to commit. **V. S. Pritchett** *Midnight Oil*, Ch. 10

12 The silence often of pure innocence
Persuades when speaking fails.

William Shakespeare *The Winter's Tale*, Act 2, Sc. 2, 41

13 Purity is the power to contemplate defilement.

Simone Weil *Gravity and Grace*: 'Attention and Will'

Intellect and Intelligence

1 Advice to intellectuals: let no one represent you.

Theodor Adorno *Minima Memoralia*, Pt 2, 83

2 Cleverness is serviceable for everything, sufficient for nothing.

Henri-Frédéric Amiel *Amiel's Journal*, 16 February 1868

3 An intellectual – one educated beyond the bounds of common sense.

Anon. in P. and J. Holton, *Quote and Unquote*

4 To the man-in-the-street, who, I'm sorry to say,
Is a keen observer of life,
The word 'Intellectual' suggests straight away
A man who's untrue to his wife. **W. H. Auden** *The Orators*: epigraph

5 The sad thing about artificial intelligence is that it lacks artifice and therefore intelligence. **Jean Baudrillard** *Cool Memories*, Ch. 4

6 Intellectuals are people who believe that ideas are of more importance than values. That is to say, their own ideas and other people's values.

Gerald Brenan *Thoughts in a Dry Season*: 'Life'

7 An intellectual is someone whose mind watches itself.

Albert Camus *Notebooks, 1935–42*

8 Among the most sinister phenomena in intellectual history is the avoidance of the concrete. **Elias Canetti** *Conscience of Words*: 'Power and Survival'

9 Intelligence is almost useless to someone who has no other quality.

Alexis Carrel *Man the Unknown*, Ch. 4, 6

10 There is a road from the eye to the heart that does not go through the intellect. **G. K. Chesterton** *The Defendant*

11 There is nothing in the will or in action that was not already in the intellect. **A. Ciezkowski** *Prolegomena zur Historiosophie*, p. 121

12 It is a terrible thing for an intellectual when he encounters an idea as a reality. **Robertson Davies** *Rebel Angels*: 'The New Aubrey II'

13 We should take care not to make the intellect our god; it has, of course, powerful muscles, but no personality.

Albert Einstein *Out of My Later Years*, Ch. 50

14 The test of a first-rate intelligence is the ability to hold two opposed ideas in the mind at the same time, and still retain the ability to function. **F. Scott Fitzgerald** *The Crack-up*, February 1936, p. 69

15 The most dangerous form of stupidity is a sharp intellect.

Hugo von Hofmannsthal *The Book of Friends*, 2

16 *Intelligence*: The grand inquisitor that tortures from every truth the confession that it lies, and from every lie a confession of its divine necessity. **Elbert Hubbard** *The Roycroft Dictionary*

17 We are thinking beings, and we cannot exclude the intellect from participating in any of our functions.

William James *The Varieties of Religious Experience*, Ch. 18

18 The only means of strengthening one's intellect is to make up one's mind about nothing – to let the mind be a thoroughfare for all thoughts. **John Keats** letter to G. and G. Keats, 17–27 September 1819

19 Desire to appear clever often prevents our becoming so.

Duc de La Rochefoucauld *Maxims*, 199

20 To conceal ingenuity is ingenuity indeed.

Duc de La Rochefoucauld *Maxims*, 245

21 In France intellectuals are usually incapable of opening an umbrella.
André Malraux in Bruce Chatwin, *What am I Doing Here?*: 'André Malraux'

22 Military intelligence is a contradiction in terms.
Groucho Marx in A. Spiegelman and B. Schneider, *Whole Grains*

23 Cynicism is intellectual dandyism. **George Meredith** *The Egoist*, Ch. 7

24 A truly intelligent man feels what other people can only know.
Charles de Montesquieu *Essay on the Causes That Can Affect Minds and Characters*, Pt 2

25 Two heads are better than one: but this refers only to asparagus.
W. Pett Ridge *Name of Garland*, in W. Burton Baldry, *Topical Epigrams*, Sect. 31

26 A smart girl is one who knows how to play tennis, piano and dumb.
Lynn Redgrave in the *Guardian*, 22 May 1992

27 Life is known to be a process of combustion; intellect is the light produced by this process.
Arthur Schopenhauer *Essays and Aphorisms*: 'On Philosophy and the Intellect', 12

28 Intellect is a magnitude of intensity, not a magnitude of extension: which is why in this respect one man can confidently take on ten thousand and a thousand fools do not make one wise man.
Arthur Schopenhauer *Essays and Aphorisms*: 'On Philosophy and the Intellect', 20

29 Interpretation is the revenge of the intellect upon art.
Susan Sontag in *Evergreen Review*, December 1964

See also ***The Mind; Wisdom***

J

Jealousy

1 Neither can he that mindeth but his own business find much matter for envy. For envy is a gadding passion, and walketh the streets and doth not stay home. **Francis Bacon** *Essays*: 'Of Envy'

2 The dullard's envy of brilliant men is always assuaged by the suspicion that they will come to a bad end. **Max Beerbohm** *Zuleika Dobson*, Ch. 4

3 The ear of jealousy heareth all things.
Bible, Apocrypha Wisdom of Solomon, 1:10

4 Jealousy is no more than feeling alone among smiling enemies.
Elizabeth Bowen *The House in Paris*, Pt 1, Ch. 8

5 Thou shalt not covet, but tradition
Approves all forms of competition. **Arthur Hugh Clough** *The Latest Decalogue*

6 Anger and jealousy can no more bear to lose sight of their objects than love. **George Eliot** *The Mill on the Floss*, Bk 1, Ch. 10

7 Man is jealous because of his *amour propre*; woman is jealous because of her lack of it. **Germaine Greer** *The Female Eunuch*: 'Egotism'

8 Envy, among other ingredients, has a mixture of the love of justice in it. We are more angry at undeserved than at deserved good fortune.
William Hazlitt *Characteristics*, 19

9 The covetous spends more than the liberal. **George Herbert** *Jacula Prudentum*

10 Jealousy is a kind of civil war in the soul, where judgement and imagination are at perpetual jars. **William Penn** *Reflections and Maxims*, II, 291

11 Jealousy does not even go with love, it is merely served up with it, as there is pepper provided for those who cannot do without it when

they're eating melon but certainly, whoever knows this fruit will leave it alone. **Rainer Maria Rilke** letter quoted in Hilde Spiel, *The Darkened Room*, Ch. 9

12 Jealousy is the fear of apprehension of superiority; envy our uneasiness under it. **William Shenstone** *Essays on Men and Manners*: title essay

13 Moral indignation is jealousy with a halo.
H. G. Wells *The Wife of Sir Isaac Harman*, Ch. 9

14 Plain women are always jealous of their husbands, beautiful women never are. **Oscar Wilde** *A Woman of No Importance*, Act 1

Judgement

1 The world makes an oracle of its judgement.
Walter Bagehot *Literary Studies*: 'The First Edinburgh Reviewers'

2 A negative judgement gives you more satisfaction than praise, provided it smacks of jealousy. **Jean Baudrillard** *Cool Memories*, Ch. 5

3 No man can justly censure or condemn another, because indeed no man truly knows another. **Sir Thomas Browne** *Religio Medici*, Pt 2, 4

4 We judge other people by what they say and do, ourselves by what we think and intend. **Comtesse Diane** *Maxims of Life*, p. 49

5 Many complain of their Memory, few of their Judgement.
Benjamin Franklin *Poor Richard's Almanack*

See also Fuller; La Rochefoucauld

6 All complain of want of Memory, but none of want of Judgement.
Dr Thomas Fuller *Gnomologia*, 509

See also Franklin; La Rochefoucauld

7 Nothing is more unsatisfactory than a mature judgement adopted by an immature mind.
Johann Wolfgang von Goethe quoted in Edward Fitzgerald, *Polonius*: 'A Persian Legend'

8 The seat of knowledge is in the head; of wisdom, in the heart. We are sure to judge wrong if we do not feel right.
William Hazlitt *Characteristics*, 388

9 Everybody complains of his memory, but nobody of his judgement.
Duc de La Rochefoucauld *Maxims*, 89

See also Franklin; Fuller

10 Passing judgement on people, or characters in a book, means making silhouettes of them.

Cesare Pavese *This Business of Living: Diary 1935–1950*, 18 October 1939

11 A judge passes judgement on himself as much as on the accused.

Publilius Syrus *Moral Sayings*, 698

12 It is much more difficult to judge oneself than to judge others.

Antoine de Saint-Exupéry *The Little Prince*, Ch. 10

13 Commonly we say a judgement falls on a man for something in him we cannot abide. **John Selden** *Table Talk*, 67

See also ***Critics; Justice; Opinions; Prejudice***

Justice

1 Military justice is to justice as military music is to music.

Anon. in Max Ophuls's film *The Memory of Justice*

2 A judge ought to prepare his way to a just sentence as God useth to prepare his way, by raising valleys and taking down hills.

Francis Bacon *Essays*: 'Of Judicature'

3 Judges don't age. Time decorates them.

Enid Bagnold *The Chalk Garden*, Act 2

4 As the judge of the people is himself, so are his officers; and what manner of man the ruler of the city is, such are all they that dwell therein. **Bible, Apocrypha** Ecclesiasticus, 10:2

5 A good parson once said that where mystery begins religion ends. Cannot I say, as truly at least, of human laws, that where mystery begins justice ends? **Edmund Burke** *A Vindication of Natural Society*

6 All witnesses should be kept as far as possible away from subjects with which they are specially conversant; for juries have no more relish than other people for being instructed.

Mr Justice Charles J. Darling *Scintillae Juris*, 6

7 Justice is too good for some people, and not good enough for the rest.

Norman Douglas *How About Europe?*, p. 197

8 Human impartiality, whether judicial or not, can hardly escape being more or less loaded. **George Eliot** *Felix Holt*, Ch. 46

9 *Fiat justitia et pereat mundus.* – Let justice be done, though the world perish. **Emperor Ferdinand I** motto

10 Justice is the sanction of established injustice.

Anatole France *Crainquebille*, Ch. 4

11 If it were not for injustice, men would not know justice.

Heraclitus quoted in John Fowles, *The Aristos*: Appendix

12 The injustice done to an individual is sometimes of service to the public.

'Junius' *Letters*, 41

13 The duty of judges is to dispense justice; their profession is to delay it. Some of them know their duty, and practise their profession.

Jean de La Bruyère *Characters*: 'Of Certain Customs', 33

14 Love of justice in most men is no more than the fear of suffering injustice.

Duc de La Rochefoucauld *Maxims*, 78

15 How strange that it is easier for us to be just toward men than toward God!

Joseph de Maistre *The Saint Petersburg Dialogues*, 1

16 Justice without power is powerless; power without justice is tyranny.

Blaise Pascal *Pensées*, 285

17 Use every man after his desert and who should 'scape whipping?

William Shakespeare *Hamlet*, Act 2, Sc. 2, (561)

18 There can be no Justice without an audience.

Paul Valéry *Bad Thoughts and Not So Bad*, H

19 Nothing is more severe than justice.

Marquis de Vauvenargues *Reflections and Maxims*, 479

See also ***Equality; Judgement; Laws***

Kings, Queens and Rulers

1 The benefits of a good monarch are almost invaluable, but the evils of a bad monarch are almost irreparable.

Walter Bagehot *The English Constitution*, Ch. 3

2 Kings will be tyrants from policy, when subjects are rebels from principle.

Edmund Burke *Reflections on the Revolution in France*, p. 172

3 Even with a true king it is bound to take a generation for benevolence to become a reality.

Confucius *The Analects*, Bk 13, 12

4 A weak prince will always be governed by his domestics.

Edward Gibbon *The Decline and Fall of the Roman Empire*, Ch. 3

5 Rulers like to be assisted but not to be outshone, and they prefer that advice should appear to be rather a reminder of something they have forgotten than a light upon something that is beyond their understanding.

Baltasar Gracián *The Oracle*, 7

6 Monarchy is lik'd by the People, for the Bells and the Tinsel, the outward Pomp and gilding, and there must be milk for the Babes, since the greatest part of Mankind are, and ever will be, included in this List.

Marquis of Halifax *The Character of a Trimmer*

7 A People may let a King fall, yet still remain a People; but if a King let his People slip from him, he is no longer King.

Marquis of Halifax *Maxims of State*

8 A prince who will not undergo the difficulty of understanding, must undergo the danger of trusting.

Marquis of Halifax *Political Thoughts and Reflections*: 'On Princes'

9 The first ground of Prerogative was to enable a Prince to do good, not to do every thing. **Marquis of Halifax** *Political Thoughts and Reflections*: 'Religion'

10 A born leader of men is somebody who is afraid to go anywhere by himself. **Clifford Hanley** in conversation; in *Scottish Quotations*, compiled by Alan Bold

11 A king has less right than anyone else to be an individual.
Friedrich Hebbel *Diaries*, entry 3370, 1845

12 The true leader is always led.
C. G. Jung quoted in the *Guardian Weekly*, 30 October 1976

13 The court does not make a man happy; it prevents him from being happy elsewhere. **Jean de La Bruyère** *Characters*: 'Of the Court', 8

14 A prince who is skilled in government, uses men's faults to curb their vices. **Duc de Lévis** *Maximes et réflexions: Maximes politiques*, 56

15 A king commands that, on pain of life imprisonment, everyone shall regard a stone as a diamond. **Georg Christoph Lichtenberg** *Aphorisms*, Notebook D, 19

16 The greatest virtue in a prince is to know his subjects.
Martial *Epigrams*, Bk 8, 15

17 Rulers are given to employing those that they can teach rather than those from whom they can learn. **Mencius** Bk 2, Pt B, 2

18 The silence of the people is the lesson of kings.
Comte de Mirabeau speech to the French Constituent Assembly, 15 July 1789

19 For who is unhappy at not being a king except a dethroned king?
Blaise Pascal *Pensées*, 268

20 A king is a thing men have made for their own sakes, for quietness' sake. Just as if in a family one man is appointed to buy the meat.
John Selden *Table Talk*, 71

21 Uneasy lies the head that wears a crown.
William Shakespeare *Henry IV, Pt 2*, Act 3, Sc. 1, (31)

22 Kings are not born: they are made by artificial hallucination.
George Bernard Shaw *Man and Superman*, 'Maxims for Revolutionists': 'Royalty'

23 The two maxims of any great man at court are, always to keep his countenance, and never to keep his word.
Jonathan Swift *Thoughts on Various Subjects*, p. 286

24 All kings is mostly rapscallions.
Mark Twain *The Adventures of Huckleberry Finn*, Ch. 23

25 The Roman rulers' greatest failing made them all-conquering; they became masters of the world because they were unhappy at home.
Voltaire *Philosophical Letters*, Letter 8

Knowledge and Ignorance

1 The fox knows many things and the hedgehog knows one big thing.

Archilochus in *Anthologia Lyrica Graeca*, ed. E. Diehl

2 If you dissemble sometimes your knowledge of that you are thought to know, you shall be thought, another time, to know that you know not.

Francis Bacon *Essays*: 'Of Discourse'

3 For knowledge itself is power. **Francis Bacon** *Religious Meditations*: 'Of Heresies'

4 Knowledge is the confirmation of what we knew before we found out.

Elizabeth Bibesco *Haven*: 'Aphorisms'

5 **Connoisseur, n.** A specialist who knows everything about something and nothing about anything else. **Ambrose Bierce** *The Enlarged Devil's Dictionary*

6 It is better to know nothing than to know what ain't so.

Josh Billings *Wit and Humor*, 'Proverb'

7 To Generalize is to be an Idiot. To Particularize is the Alone Distinction of Merit. General Knowledges are those Knowledges that idiots possess.

William Blake *Marginalia* to Sir Joshua Reynolds, *Discourses*, II

8 An expert is a man who has made all the mistakes, which can be made, in a very narrow field.

Niels Bohr quoted by Edward Teller, 10 October 1972, US Embassy, London

9 I always did think that cleverness was the art of hiding ignorance.

Shelland Bradley *An American Girl in India*, in W. Burton Baldry, *Topical Epigrams*, Sect. 4

10 An expert is one who knows more and more about less and less.

Nicholas Murray Butler commencement address, Columbia University

See also Mayo

11 Spontaneity is only a term for man's ignorance of the gods.

Samuel Butler 2 *Erewhon*, Ch. 25

12 The worst people; those who know everything and believe they do.

Elias Canetti *The Human Province*: '1961'

13 I know nothing of what I have learned, I have divined the little I still know.

Nicholas-Sébastien Chamfort *Maxims and Considerations*, 336

14 The more you know the less the better.

Billy Connolly *Gullible's Travels*: 'Thoughts'

15 A department does not know so much as some of its servants. Being a dispassionate organism, it can never be perfectly informed.

Joseph Conrad *The Secret Agent*, Ch. 5

16 It is a universal condition of mankind to want to know.

Hernán Cortés in J. H. Elliott, *Spain and Its World 1500–1700*, p. 31

17 All true knowledge contradicts common sense.

Bishop Mandell Creighton *Life and Letters*, Vol. 2

18 Do not think what you want to think until you know what you ought to know. **John Crow** 'Crow's Law', in R. V. Jones, *Most Secret War*, Ch. 9

19 It is better to be un-informed than ill-informed.

Keith Duckworth in Graham Robson, *Cosworth: The Search for Power*

20 You have to know something in order to be able to conceal that you know nothing. **Maria von Ebner-Eschenbach** *Aphorisms*, p. 59

21 No one knows enough, many know too much.

Maria von Ebner-Eschenbach *Aphorisms*, p. 63

22 He who tells all he knows, will also tell *more* than he knows.

Edward Fitzgerald *Polonius*: 'A Handful of Arrows'

23 One must learn to think well before learning to think; afterwards it proves too difficult.

Anatole France in *The Faber Book of Aphorisms*, ed. W. H. Auden and Louis Kronenberger

24 Men and melons are hard to know.

Benjamin Franklin *Poor Richard's Almanack*, 1733

25 A neurosis would seem to be the result of ignorance, – a not knowing about mental events that one ought to know of.

Sigmund Freud *Introductory Lectures*

26 Those who pretend to know more than others, are mostly more ignorant than those who pretend to know nothing.

Dr Thomas Fuller *Introductio ad Prudentium*, 2748

27 It's what we don't know that gets us safely through life, not what we know. **Jean Giraudoux** *Intermezzo*, Act 3

28 You really only know when you know little; doubt grows with knowledge.

Johann Wolfgang von Goethe *Maxims and Reflections* (Penguin), from *Art and Antiquity*, 281

29 The craziest thing is that everyone imagines he has got to pass on what people have imagined they knew.

Johann Wolfgang von Goethe *Maxims and Reflections* (Penguin), from *Wilhelm Meister's Journeyman Years*, 583

30 Destiny bestows on the ignorant the reins of government,
You are learned and erudite – that is your sin.

Hafez quoted in M. and R. Farmanfarmian, *Blood and Oil*, Ch. 10

31 The knowledge that is got without Pains, is kept without Pleasure.
Marquis of Halifax *Miscellaneous Thoughts and Reflections*

32 An expert is someone who knows some of the worst mistakes that can be made in his subject, and how to avoid them.
Werner Heisenberg *Physics and Beyond*, Ch. 17

33 Knowledge has no worse enemy than wanting to know, than learning.
Hermann Hesse *Reflections*, 271

34 It cannot be expected that one knows everything but that by knowing one thing he knows about all things.
Hugo von Hofmannsthal *The Book of Friends*, 2

35 It's what we learn after we think we know it all that counts.
'Kin' Hubbard *Abe Martin's Wisecracks*, p. 24

36 Knowledge is acquired when we succeed in fitting a new experience into the system of concepts based upon our old experiences.
Aldous Huxley *Adonis and the Alphabet*: 'Knowledge and Understanding'

37 Most ignorance is vincible ignorance. We don't know because we don't want to know.
Aldous Huxley in *The Faber Book of Aphorisms*, ed. W. H. Auden and Louis Kronenberger

38 The known is finite, the unknown infinite; intellectually we stand on an islet in the midst of an illimitable ocean of inexplicability. Our business in every generation is to reclaim a little more land, to add something to the extent and solidity of our possessions.
T. H. Huxley in F. Darwin, *Life of Charles Darwin*, Vol. 2, p. 179

39 A man may choose whether he will have abstemiousness and knowledge, or claret and ignorance.
Dr Samuel Johnson in James Boswell, *Life of Johnson*, Vol. 3, 335

40 To know: it is to see inside oneself.
Joseph Joubert *Notebooks*, 1800

41 If we knew perfectly what was happening in heaven, we would be more free of it. And if we knew perfectly what existed on earth, perhaps we would no longer be mortal.
Joseph Joubert *Notebooks*, 1805

42 He runs after facts like a beginner learning to skate, who is furthermore practising somewhere where it is forbidden.
Franz Kafka *Collected Aphorisms*, 67

43 Erudition can produce foliage without bearing fruit. There are a great many shallow heads who are astonishingly knowledgeable. What we have to discover for ourselves leaves behind in our mind a pathway that can also be used on another occasion.
Georg Christoph Lichtenberg *Aphorisms*, Notebook C, 26

44 So that means you need to know things even when you don't need to know them. You need to know them not because you need to know them but because you need to know whether or not you need to know. And if you don't need to know you still need to know so that you know that there was no need to know.

Jonathan Lynn and Antony Jay *Yes, Prime Minister*, Vol. 2: 'Man Overboard'

45 Specialist – a man who knows more and more about less and less.

Charles H. Mayo in *Modern Hospital*, September 1938, but he did not claim it as his own; elsewhere attrib. to Nicholas Butler

See also Butler

46 This 'know ourself' is a silly proverb in some ways;
to know the man next door's a much more useful rule.

Menander *Fragments*: from *Thrasyleon*

47 I am wary of the intuition, the wisdom of globe-trotters: true knowledge is sedentary. **François Mitterrand** *The Wheat and the Chaff*, Pt 2, 8 December 1975

48 I am sufficiently proud of my knowing something to be modest about my not knowing all. **Vladimir Nabokov** *Lolita*

See also Nietzsche; Pascal

49 It is better to know nothing than know everything by halves.

Friedrich Nietzsche *Nietzsche in Outline and Aphorism*: 'New Commandments'

See also Nabokov; Pascal

50 It is very much better to know something about everything than to know all about something. **Blaise Pascal** *Pensées*, 42

See also Nabokov; Nietzsche

51 Know then thyself, presume not God to scan;
The proper study of mankind is man. **Alexander Pope** *An Essay on Man*, Bk 2, 1

52 Our knowledge can only be finite, while our ignorance must necessarily be infinite. **Karl Popper** *Conjectures and Refutations*

53 Everybody is ignorant, only on different subjects.

Will Rogers *The Illiterate Digest*: 'Defending My Soup Plate Position'

54 When will crowds out knowledge we call the result obstinacy.

Arthur Schopenhauer *Essays and Aphorisms*: 'On Psychology', 10

55 The more you look at 'common knowledge', the more you realize that it is more likely to be common than it is to be knowledge.

Idries Shah *Reflections*: 'Common Knowledge'

56 People who think they know all are often insufferable – rather like those who imagine they know nothing.

Idries Shah *Reflections*: 'Thinking That One Knows'

57 On the death of some men the world reverts to ignorance.

Wallace Stevens *Adagia*, 2

58 Men's ignorance is made as useful as their knowledge. If one knew more, he would admire less.

H. D. Thoreau *Journal*, 15 January 1853

59 Knowledge does not keep any better than fish.

A. N. Whitehead *The Aims of Education*, Pt 3, Ch. 4

60 The sure way of knowing nothing about life is to try to make oneself useful.

Oscar Wilde *The Critic as Artist*, 2

61 Knowledge is in the end based on acknowledgement.

Ludwig Wittgenstein *On Certainty*, Sect. 378

See also ***Education; The Mind; Wisdom***

Language

1 No iron can stab the heart with such force as a full stop put just at the right place. **Isaac Babel** *Guy de Maupassant*

2 Never express yourself more clearly than you can think.
Niels Bohr quoted in the *Observer*, 31 May 1998

3 You always feel braver in another language.
Anita Brookner in the *Observer*, 7 August 1988

4 A language in which one is not allowed to create new words is in danger of suffocating: it constricts me.
Elias Canetti *The Secret Heart of the Clock*: '1976'

5 All slang is metaphor and all metaphor is poetry.
G. K. Chesterton *The Defendant*: 'A Defence of Slang'

6 Language compensates for the inadequacy of remedies and cures most of our diseases. The chatterbox does not haunt pharmacies.
E. M. Cioran *Anathemas and Admirations*, 9

7 No one is ever capable of swearing properly in any language other than their own. **Ben Elton** *Stark*: 'Love Among the Radicals'

8 Language is fossil poetry. **Ralph Waldo Emerson** *Essays*: 'The Poet'

9 Language is like a cracked kettle on which we beat out tunes for bears to dance to, while all the time we long to move the stars to pity.
Gustave Flaubert *Madame Bovary*, Pt 1, Ch. 12

10 What do I mean by a phrase? A clutch of words that gives you a clutch at the heart. **Robert Frost** interview in the *Saturday Evening Post*, 16 November 1960

11 The style of an author should be the image of his mind, but the choice and command of language is the fruit of exercise.

Edward Gibbon *Miscellaneous Works*, Bk 1, p. 145

12 Anyone who doesn't know foreign languages knows nothing of his own.

Johann Wolfgang von Goethe *Maxims and Reflections* (Penguin), from *Art and Antiquity*, 91

13 Language grows by introducing new words but a language consisting only of new words and a new syntax would be indistinguishable from gibberish. **E. H. Gombrich** *Art and Illusion*, Ch. 9

14 If language had been the creation, not of poetry, but of logic, we should only have one. **Friedrich Hebbel** quoted in W. H. Auden, *A Certain World*, p. 226

15 Man acts as though *he* were the shaper and master of language while in fact *language* remains the master of man.

Martin Heidegger *Poetry, Language, Thought*: 'Building, Dwelling, Thinking'

16 After all, when you come right down to it, how many people speak the same language even when they speak the same language?

Russell Hoban *The Lion of Boaz-Jachin and Jachin-Boaz*, Ch. 27

17 Every language is a temple in which the soul of those who speak it is enshrined. **Oliver Wendell Holmes** *The Professor at the Breakfast Table*, Ch. 2

18 I am always sorry when any language is lost, because languages are the pedigree of nations.

Dr Samuel Johnson in James Boswell, *The Journal of a Tour to the Hebrides*, 18 September 1773

19 Language is a form of human reason and has its reasons which are unknown to man. **Claude Lévi-Strauss** *The Savage Mind*, Ch. 9

20 We do not think good metaphors are anything very important, but I think a good metaphor is something even the police should keep an eye on. **Georg Christoph Lichtenberg** *Aphorisms*; Notebook E, 91

21 A gentleman need not know Latin, but he should at least have forgotten it. **Brander Matthews** advice to Dr Joseph Shipley

22 No language has been invented comprehensible to both the living and the dead. **Czesław Milosz** *Undressing Justine*

23 Grammar, which can govern even kings.

Molière *Les Femmes savantes*, Act 2, Sc. 6

24 American is the language in which people say what they mean as Italian is the language in which they say what they feel. English is the language in which what a character means or feels has to be deduced from what he or she says, which may be quite the opposite.

John Mortimer in the *Mail on Sunday*, 26 March 1989

25 Duplicity lies at the heart of language: only Trappists avoid the trap.
Frederic Raphael in the *Sunday Times*, 31 May 1987

26 What is not clear is not French.
Antoine de Rivarol *On the Universality of the French Language*

27 Nobody ever makes up nicknames, a nickname is your real identity, jumping out from behind you like an afreet.
Robert Robinson *Dog Chairman*: 'Nicknames'

28 Slang is a language that rolls up its sleeves, spits on its hands and goes to work. **Carl Sandburg** in the *New York Times*, 13 February 1959

29 Languages have been, throughout history, zones of silence to other men and razor-edges of division. **George Steiner** *After Babel*, Ch. 2

30 Language is the main instrument of man's refusal to accept the world as it is. **George Steiner** *After Babel*, Ch. 3

31 Man invented language to satisfy his deep need to complain.
Lily Tomlin quoted in Steven Pinker, *The Language Instinct*, Ch. 2

32 The universal principle of etymology in all languages: words are carried from bodies and from the properties of bodies to express the things of the mind and spirit. The order of ideas must follow the order of things. **Giambattista Vico** *The New Science*, Bk 1, Paras. 237–8

33 A language is a dialect that has an army and a navy.
Max Weinreich *History of the Yiddish Language*

34 We have really everything in common with America nowadays, except, of course, language. **Oscar Wilde** *The Canterville Ghost*, 1

35 Language is a labyrinth of paths. You approach from *one* side and you know your way about; you approach the same place from another side and no longer know your way about.
Ludwig Wittgenstein *Philosophical Investigations*, Pt 1, Sect. 203

36 It is in language that an expectation and its fulfilment make contact.
Ludwig Wittgenstein *Philosophical Investigations*, Pt 1, Sect. 445

See also ***Words; Writing***

Laughing Matters

1 If it bends, it's funny; if it breaks, it's not funny.

Woody Allen in film *Crimes and Misdemeanours*

2 The absurd is born of this confrontation between the human need and the unreasonable silence of the world.

Albert Camus *The Myth of Sisyphus*: 'Absurd Walls'

3 There is nothing sillier than a silly laugh. **Catullus** *Carmina*, 39

4 Of all days, the day on which one has not laughed is the one most surely wasted. **Nicholas-Sébastien Chamfort** *Maxims and Considerations*, 80

5 Humorists are not happy men . . . they burn while Rome fiddles.

Cyril Connolly *Enemies of Promise*, Ch. 16

6 Ridicule is a wolf that only kills those who are afraid of it.

Comtesse Diane *Les Glanes de la vie*, p. 85

7 'Tis a good thing to laugh at any rate; and if straw can tickle a man, it is an instrument of happiness. **John Dryden** *A Parallel of Poetry and Painting*

8 The clever man finds almost everything ridiculous, the wise man almost nothing. **Johann Wolfgang von Goethe** *Elective Affinities*, Pt 2, Ch. 4

9 The longer and more carefully we look at a funny story the sadder it becomes.

Nikolai Gogol quoted in Milan Kundera, *The Art of the Novel*: 'Sixty-three Words'

10 Throughout history it has always been the absurd that makes the most martyrs. **Edmond and Jules de Goncourt** *Journal*, 31 October 1860

11 Man is the only animal that laughs and weeps; for he is the only animal that is struck with the difference between what things are, and what they ought to be. **William Hazlitt** *Lectures on the English Comic Writers*, 1

12 A man's got to take a lot of punishment to write a really funny book.

Ernest Hemingway letter to William B. Smith Jr, 6 December 1924

13 The privilege of absurdity; to which no living creature is subject, but man only. **Thomas Hobbes** *Leviathan*, Pt 1, Ch. 5

14 Laughter is an affection arising from the sudden transformation of a strained expectation into nothing.

Immanuel Kant *Critique of Judgement*, p. 223

15 We should laugh before being happy, for fear of dying without ever having laughed at all. **Jean de La Bruyère** *Characters*: 'Of the Heart', 63

16 A good laugh is the best pesticide. **Vladimir Nabokov** *Strong Opinions*, Ch. 9

17 There is only one step from the sublime to the ridiculous.

Napoleon Bonaparte remark in December 1812 to the Polish ambassador, De Pradt, on his retreat from Moscow

See also Paine

18 The aim of a joke is not to degrade the human being but to remind him that he is already degraded.

George Orwell *Collected Essays*: 'Funny but Not Vulgar'

19 The sublime and the ridiculous are often so nearly related that it is difficult to class them separately. One step above the sublime makes the ridiculous; and one step above the ridiculous makes the sublime again. **Thomas Paine** *The Age of Reason*: 2, note

See also Napoleon

20 Failure to understand a joke has never yet made anyone find it less amusing.

Marcel Proust *Remembrance of Things Past: Within a Budding Grove*, Bk 1, p. 621

21 Everything is funny as long as it's happening to somebody else.

Will Rogers *The Illiterate Digest*: 'Warning to Jokers'

22 The world loved man when he smiled. The world became afraid of him when he laughed. **Rabindranath Tagore** *Stray Birds*, 299

23 Humour is counterbalance. Laughter need not be cut out of anything, since it improves anything. The power that created the poodle, the platypus and people has an integrated sense of both comedy and tragedy. **James Thurber** letter to Frances Glennon, June 1959

24 Humour . . . is emotional chaos remembered in tranquillity.

James Thurber in the *New York Post*, 29 February 1960

25 Laughter would be bereaved if snobbery died.

Peter Ustinov *Dear Me*; in the *Observer*, 'Sayings of the Week', 13 March 1955

See also ***Comedy and Tragedy; Wit***

Laws

1 It were better to live where nothing is lawful, than where all things are lawful. **Francis Bacon** *Apothegms*, 160; attrib. to a Roman senator

2 One Law for the Lion and Ox is Oppression.

William Blake *The Marriage of Heaven and Hell*: 'A Memorable Fancy: One Law'

3 Laws, like houses, lean on one another.

Edmund Burke *A Tract on the Property Laws*, Ch. 3, Pt 1

4 When you break the big laws, you do not get liberty; you do not even get anarchy. You get the small laws.

G. K. Chesterton in the *Daily News*, 29 July 1905

5 The good of the people is the chief law. **Cicero** *De Legibus*, 3, iii

6 Law and equity are two things which God hath joined, but which man has put asunder. **Charles Caleb Colton** *Lacon*: 'Law and Equity'

7 One with the law is a majority.

President Calvin Coolidge speech of acceptance as Republican vice-presidential candidate in US election, 27 July 1920

8 All laws, even the most democratic, are designed to prevent equality – which is chaos. **Mr Justice Charles J. Darling** *Scintillae Juris*, 1

9 All laws are made by old men. Young men and women lean towards exceptions; old men alone affect the rule.

Johann Wolfgang von Goethe *Goethe's Opinions*, p. 4

10 If one had to study all laws, one would have no time at all to transgress them.

Johann Wolfgang von Goethe *Maxims and Reflections* (Penguin), from *Art and Antiquity*, 207

11 Laws are merely rough police methods; they insure justice by cultivating injustice. **Rémy de Gourmont** *Selections*: 'The Velvet Path'

12 If it be true that the wisest Men generally make the Laws, it is as true, that the strongest often Interpret them.

Marquis of Halifax *The Character of a Trimmer*

13 Laws are generally not understood by three Sorts of Persons, *viz.* By those that make them, by those that execute them, and by those that suffer, if they break them.

Marquis of Halifax *Political Thoughts and Reflections*: 'Of Laws'

14 The Law is not the same at morning and at night.

George Herbert *Jacula Prudentum*

15 The Lawyers earn their bread in the sweat of their browbeating.

James Huneker *Painted Veils*; in *Quotable Lawyer*, ed. D. Shrager and E. Frost

16 The Law and Morality are, naturally enough, brothers-in-law rather than natural brothers. **Hans Keller** *Criticism*, Pt 1, Ch. 3

17 Men have sympathies, laws do not. **Napoleon Bonaparte** *Maxims*

18 Where laws end, tyranny begins.
William Pitt, Earl of Chatham speech on the case of John Wilkes, 9 January 1770

19 Order is heaven's first law. **Alexander Pope** *An Essay on Man*, Bk 3, 49

20 A precedent embalms a principle.
William Scott, Lord Stowell opinion while Advocate-General in 1788; quoted by Benjamin Disraeli in House of Commons, 22 February 1848

21 Lawyers are the only persons in whom ignorance of the law is not punished. ***Tigers Don't Eat Grass: Oriental and Occidental Aphorisms*** 'Law'

22 Laws should never be in contradiction to usages; for, if the usages are good, the laws are valueless.
Voltaire in J. de Finod, *A Thousand Flashes of French Wit*, p. 55

*See also **Justice; Rules***

Lies and Deceit

1 It is not the lie that passeth through the mind, but the lie that sinketh in and settleth in it, that doth the hurt. **Francis Bacon** *Essays*: 'Of Truth'

2 If a ruler harken to lies, all his servants are wicked.
Bible, OT Proverbs 289:12

3 Some men are not liars because they always speak the truth, and others because they never do. **F. H. Bradley** *Aphorisms*, 64

4 The real history of consciousness starts with one's first lie.
Joseph Brodsky *Less than One*, Sect. 1

5 The best liar is he who makes the smallest amount of lying go the longest way. **Samuel Butler 2** *The Way of All Flesh*, Ch. 39

6 And, after all, what is a lie?
'Tis but the truth in masquerade. **Lord Byron** *Don Juan*, XI, 37

7 To *live* signifies to believe and to hope – to lie and to lie *to oneself*.
E. M. Cioran *A Short History of Decay*, 1: 'The Imminent Lie'

8 I am a lie who always speaks the truth. **Jean Cocteau** *Opéra: le paquet rouge*

9 Propaganda is that branch of the art of lying which consists in very nearly deceiving your friends without quite deceiving your enemies.
F. M. Cornford *Microcosmographia Academica*: Preface to 1922 edn

10 All lies walk on crutches. **Comtesse Diane** *Les Glanes de la vie*, p. 175

11 Our memories are stronger than our imaginations – which is what makes lying such a difficult profession. **Comtesse Diane** *Maxims of Life*, p. 25

12 If you take in a lie, you must take in all that belongs to it.
Ralph Waldo Emerson *English Traits*

13 Man's mind is so formed that is far more susceptible to falsehood than to truth. **Desiderius Erasmus** *Praise of Folly*, Ch. 45

14 He deceived himself before ever he deceived others. After all, it is in the ability to deceive oneself that the greatest talent is shown, is it not?
Anatole France *The Crime of Sylvestre Bonnard*, Ch. 3

15 One is never deceived, one deceives oneself.
Johann Wolfgang von Goethe *Maxims and Reflections* (Penguin), from *Wilhelm Meister's Journeyman Years*, 681

16 We are oftener deceived by being told some truth than no truth.
Fulke Greville *Maxims, Characters and Reflections*, p. 31

17 We are never deceived by those we'd like to be.
Sacha Guitry *N'écoutez pas, mesdames*, Act 2

18 Many men *swallow* the being cheated, but no man could ever endure to *chew* it. **Marquis of Halifax** *Miscellaneous Thoughts and Reflections*: 'Cheats'

19 Always divide people into two groups. Those who live by what they know to be a lie, and those who live by what they believe, falsely, to be the truth. **Christopher Hampton** *The Philanthropist*, Sc. 6

20 A person who does not tell lies will not believe that others tell them. From old habit, he cannot break the connection between words and things. **William Hazlitt** *Aphorisms on Man*, 38

21 Some people find more reassurance in someone else's lie than in their own truth. **Friedrich Hebbel** *Diaries*, entry 911, 1837

22 A lie is far dearer than the truth. It costs the whole man.
Friedrich Hebbel *Diaries*, entry 2126, 1840

23 Even when he cheated he couldn't win, because the people he cheated against were always better at cheating too. **Joseph Heller** *Catch-22*, Ch. 4

24 We lie loudest when we lie to ourselves.
Eric Hoffer *Between the Devil and the Dragon*, 2: Introduction

25 Those whom their virtue retains from deceiving others are often disposed by vanity to deceive themselves.
Dr Samuel Johnson in James Boswell, *Life of Johnson*, Vol. 8, 39

26 The lie in the Soul is a true lie.
Benjamin Jowett Introduction to his translation of Plato's *Republic*

27 Unless a man feels he has a good enough memory, he should never venture to lie. **Michel de Montaigne** *Essays*, Bk 1, Ch. 9

See also Sidney

28 You only lie to two people in your life: your girl friend and the police. Everybody else you tell the truth to. **Jack Nicholson** in *Vanity Fair*, April 1994

29 The art of living is the art of knowing how to believe lies. The fearful thing is that, not knowing what truth may be, we can still recognize a lie. **Cesare Pavese** *This Business of Living: Diary 1935–1950*, 5 January 1938

30 An excuse is worse and more terrible than a lie; for an excuse is a lie guarded. **Alexander Pope** *Thoughts on Various Subjects*, 74

31 Tell the truth sometimes, so that you can believe yourself when you are lying. **Jules Renard** *Journal 1887–1910*, 12 March 1893

32 Because I alone can perfectly forge my signature.
Jan Richman *Why I'm the Boss*

33 Any lie contains some truth by the fact of being uttered.
Ned Rorem *An Absolute Gift*, Ch. 2

34 For one man's chin is as rough as another's, and one man's lies as smooth as another's. **Helen Rowland** *The Sayings of Mrs Solomon*, Ch. 5

35 A liar begins with making falsehood appear like truth, and ends with making truth itself appear like falsehood.
William Shenstone *Essays on Men and Manners*: title essay

36 Liars ought to have good memories.
Algernon Sidney *Discourses Concerning Government*, Ch. 2, 15

See also Montaigne

37 If you want to be thought a liar, always tell the truth.
Logan Pearsall Smith *Afterthoughts*, 4

38 A lie is an abomination unto the Lord, and a very present help in trouble. **Adlai Stevenson** speech, Springfield, Illinois, January 1951

39 One of the most striking differences between a cat and a lie is that a cat has only nine lives. **Mark Twain** *Pudd'nhead Wilson*, Ch. 7

40 We sometimes swallow our own lies, so as not to have to contradict them, and practise self-deceit in order to deceive others.
Marquis de Vauvenargues *Reflections and Maxims*, 592

41 He will lie even when it is inconvenient, the sign of a true artist.
Gore Vidal *Two Sisters*

42 After all, what is a fine lie? Simply that which is its own evidence. If a man is sufficiently unimaginative to produce evidence in support of a lie, he might just as well speak the truth at once.

Oscar Wilde *The Decay of Lying*

43 Nothing is so difficult as not deceiving oneself.

Ludwig Wittgenstein *Culture and Value*, 1938 entry

See also ***Trust and Mistrust; Truth and Error***

Life and Death

1 Most men who live long die some years before their funerals.

William Allingham *By the Way*: Notes, 165

2 Life loves the liver of it.

Maya Angelou *Conversations with Maya Angelou*, ed. Jeffrey M. Elliot

3 What is there in dying? You've got to begin by living. That's not so funny, and it lasts longer. **Jean Anouilh** *Romeo and Jeannette*, Act 3

4 Remember that the sole life a man can lose is the life he is living now; and what is more, he can have no other life except the one he loses.

Marcus Aurelius *Meditations*, Bk 2, 14

5 The art of living is more like wrestling than dancing, in as much as it, too, demands a firm and watchful stance against any unexpected onset. **Marcus Aurelius** *Meditations*, Bk 7, 61

6 You find when you are giving up the ghost,
That those who loved you best despised you most. **Hilaire Belloc** *Discovery*

7 Life is rather like a tin of sardines – we're all of us looking for the key.

Alan Bennett in stage review *Beyond the Fringe*

8 Life is a One Way Street. **Bernard Berenson** *Notebooks*, 5 September 1950

9 The dead are the imagination of the living.

John Berger *And Our Faces, My Heart, Brief as Photos*

10 A living dog is better than a dead lion. **Bible, OT** Ecclesiastes 9:4

11 For we are born at all adventure: and we shall be hereafter as though we had never been: for the breath of our nostrils is as smoke, and a little spark in the moving of our heart.

Bible, Apocrypha The Wisdom of Solomon 2:2

12 For everything that lives is holy, life delights in life.

William Blake *America*, 71

13 There is so much trouble in coming into this world, and so much more, as well as meanness, in going out of it, that 'tis hardly worth while to be here at all. **Lord Bolingbroke** letter to Swift

14 Life is a pure flame, and we live by an invisible Sun within us.
Sir Thomas Browne *Urn Burial*, Ch. 5

15 Life is one long process of getting tired.
Samuel Butler 2 *Notebooks*, Ch. 1: 'Life', 7

16 Life is the art of drawing sufficient conclusions from insufficient premises. **Samuel Butler 2** *Notebooks*, Ch. 1: 'Life', 9

17 To live is like to love – all the reason is against it, and all healthy instinct for it. **Samuel Butler 2** *Notebooks*, Ch. 14: 'Life and Love'

18 Life is like playing a violin solo in public and learning the instrument as one goes along.
Samuel Butler 2 speech at the Somerville Club, 27 February 1895

19 The only choice then to be made is the most aesthetically satisfying form of suicide: marriage, and a forty-hour week; or a revolver.
Albert Camus *Notebooks 2*, 10 October 1937

20 Life is a disease from which sleep gives us alleviation every sixteen hours. Sleep is a palliative, Death is the remedy.
Nicholas-Sébastien Chamfort *Maxims and Considerations*, 113

21 Life is a tragedy when seen in close-up, but a comedy in long-shot.
Charlie Chaplin quoted in his obituary in the *Guardian*, 28 December 1977

22 To *live* signifies to believe and to hope – to lie and to lie *to oneself*.
E. M. Cioran *A Short History of Decay*, 1: 'The Imminent Lie'

23 Thou shalt not kill; but needst not strive
Officiously to keep alive. **Arthur Hugh Clough** *The Latest Decalogue*

24 Suicide is the worst form of murder, because it leaves no opportunity for repentance. **John Churton Collins** *Life and Memoirs*: Appendix

25 The shortest life is long enough, if it lead to a better; and the longest life is too short, if it do not. **Charles Caleb Colton** *Lacon*: 'Death'

26 Life is a maze in which we take the wrong turning before we have learnt to walk. **Cyril Connolly** *The Unquiet Grave*, Ch. 1

27 Life is too short to stuff a mushroom. **Shirley Conran** *Superwoman*: epigraph

28 Life is an incurable disease. **Abraham Cowley** *To Dr Scarborough*

29 However many ways there may be of being alive, it is certain there are vastly more ways of being dead.
Richard Dawkins *The Blind Watchmaker*, Ch. 1

30 If one considered life as a simple loan, one would perhaps be less exacting.
Eugène Delacroix journal

31 In distress and crises,
in abandonment,
don't take your own life,
no, give even more of it.
Hasan Dewran *A Thousand Winds May Make a Storm*: 'New Leaders'

32 If you attempt suicide you are a criminal: if you succeed you are a lunatic.
Norman Douglas *How About Europe?*, p. 163

33 I have always thought that the dead think of us as dead. They have rejoined the living after this trifling excursion into quasi-life.
Lawrence Durrell *Justine*, Pt 3, p. 202

34 We are always getting ready to live, but never living.
Ralph Waldo Emerson *Journals*, 13 April 1834

35 Live as if you were already living for the second time, and as if you had made the mistakes you are about to make now.
Viktor Frankel quoted in his obituary in the *Independent*, 5 September 1997

36 But life and death
Is cat and dog in this double-bed of a world.
Christopher Fry *A Phoenix Too Frequent*

37 The great part of our life ill spent, is Time only, not Life.
Dr Thomas Fuller *Introductio ad Sapientiam*, 131

38 For life and death are one, even as the river and sea are one.
Kahlil Gibran *The Prophet*: 'Of Death'

39 God hasn't granted us much, after all: a couple of yards of air between heaven and hell! And it's not a very attractive proposition, life, with hands to be washed all the time, and noses to be blown, and your hair falling out!
Jean Giraudoux *Ondine*, Act 3

40 The suicide has judged by the laws of chance – so many odds against one, that to live will be more miserable than to die. His sense of mathematics is greater than his sense of survival.
Graham Greene *The Comedians*, Pt 1, Ch. 4

41 We are all of us resigned to death: it's life we aren't resigned to.
Graham Greene *The Heart of the Matter*, Bk 3, Pt 2, Ch. 2

42 Successful suicide is often only a cry for help which hasn't been heard in time.
Graham Greene *A Sort of Life*, 3, 3

43 There are strange courses in life, some of which look like circles.
Georg Groddeck *The Unknown Self*, p. 46

44 In the last analysis, it is our conception of death which decides our answers to all the questions that life puts to us.

Dag Hammarskjöld *Diaries*, 1958

45 That is the art of living that your price shall suit everybody.

James Hanley *Drift*, Ch. 2

46 This life at best is but an inn,
And we the passengers.

James Howell *Familiar Letters*, Bk 1, 73

47 Life is just one damned thing after another.

Elbert Hubbard *One Thousand and One Epigrams*; also attrib. to F. W. O'Malley

See also Millay

48 Do not take life too seriously – you will never get out of it alive.

Elbert Hubbard *The Philosophy of Elbert Hubbard*: 'Epigrams'

49 Life is an abnormal business.

Eugene Ionesco *Rhinoceros*, Act 1

50 Such is life
Falling over seven times
And getting up eight.

Japanese folk poem quoted by Roland Barthes, *A Lover's Discourse: Fragments*: 'This can't go on'

51 It matters not how a man dies, but how he lives. The act of dying is not of importance, it lasts so short a time.

Dr Samuel Johnson in James Boswell, *Life of Johnson*, 26 October 1769

52 From the middle of life onward, only he remains vitally alive who is ready *to die with life*. For in the secret hour of life's midday the parabola is reversed, death is born . . . The negation of life's fulfilment is synonymous with the refusal to accept its ending. Both mean not wanting to live; not wanting to live is identical with not wanting to die. Waxing and waning make one curve.

C. G. Jung *The Meaning of Death*, first essay

53 Life is a cheap *table d'hôte* in a rather dirty restaurant, with time changing the plates before you've had enough of anything.

Thomas Kettle from his wife's memoir; in *A Book of Irish Quotations*, ed. Sean McMahon

54 It is perfectly true, as philosophers say, that life must be understood backwards. But they forget the other proposition, that it must be lived forwards.

Søren Kierkegaard *The Journals*, 1843

55 Life is an effort that deserves a better cause.

Karl Kraus *Half-Truths and One-and-a-Half Truths*: 'Lord, forgive the . . .'

56 There are only three events in a man's life; birth, life, and death; he is unaware of being born, he dies in pain, and he forgets to live.

Jean de La Bruyère *Characters*: 'Of Man', 48

57 Life makes no absolute statement. It is all Call and Answer.

D. H. Lawrence *Kangaroo*, Ch. 4

58 Life is what happens to us while we're making other plans.

John Lennon song: *Beautiful Boy*

59 Life would be tolerable, but for its amusements.

Sir George Cornewall Lewis in *The Times*, 18 September 1872; also attrib. to Edward Bulwer-Lytton

60 Who would venture on the journey of life if compelled to begin it at the end?

Mme de Maintenon quoted in Sagittarius and Daniel George, *The Perpetual Pessimist*, 19 March

61 live so that you
can stick out your tongue
at the insurance
doctor

Don Marquis *archy and mehitabel*, XII: 'certain maxims of archy'

62 It is not true that life is one damn thing after another – it is one damn thing over and over.

Edna St Vincent Millay letter to A. D. Fiske, 24 October 1930, *Letters of Edna St Vincent Millay*

See also Hubbard

63 A suicide kills two people, Maggie, that's what it's for!

Arthur Miller *After the Fall*, Act 2

64 One only dies once – but one is dead so long!

Molière *The Amorous Quarrel*, Act 5, Sc. 3

65 The continuous labour of your life is to build the house of death.

Michel de Montaigne *Essays*, Bk 1, Ch. 20

66 Suicide is despise of life.

Ethel Watts Mumford, Oliver Herford, Addison Mizner *The Entirely New Cynic's Calendar of Revised Wisdom for 1905*, December

67 Life is not having been told that the man has just waxed the floor.

Ogden Nash *You and Me and P. B. Shelley*

68 The thought of suicide is a great consolation; in that way one gets through many a bad night.

Friedrich Nietzsche *Beyond Good and Evil*, Ch. 4, Aphorism 157

69 Guns aren't lawful;
Nooses give;
Gas smells awful;
You might as well live.

Dorothy Parker *Résumé*

70 Man is born to live, not to prepare for life.
Boris Pasternak *Doctor Zhivago*, Pt 2, Ch. 9, Sect. 14

71 The great task of life is to justify oneself, and to justify oneself is to celebrate a rite. Always.
Cesare Pavese *This Business of Living: Diary 1935–1950*, 27 August 1944

72 When a man is dying, he does not die solely from his disease. He dies from his whole life. **Charles Péguy** *Basic Verities*: 'The Search for Truth'

73 I began my comedy as its only actor; and I come to the end of it as its only spectator. **Antonio Porchia** *Voices*

74 How many people have wanted to commit suicide, and have had to be satisfied with tearing up their photographs.
Jules Renard *Journal 1887–1910*, 29 December 1888

75 There is no wealth but Life. **John Ruskin** *Unto This Last*, Sect. 77

76 There is no cure for birth and death save to enjoy the interval.
George Santayana *Soliloquies in England*: 'War Shrines'

77 Life is not a spectacle or a feast; it is a predicament.
George Santayana from *various articles and essays*

78 Life is nothing until it is lived; but it is yours to make sense of, and the value of it is nothing other than the sense you choose.
Jean-Paul Sartre *Existentialism is a Humanism*

79 There must be more to life than having everything!
Maurice Sendak *Higglety Pigglety Pop!*, Ch. 1

80 Anyone can stop a man's life, but no one his death; a thousand doors open on to it. **Seneca** *Letters* 1, 152

81 Life would not be accepted if it were offered unto such as knew it.
Seneca quoted in Sir Thomas Browne, *Christian Morals*, Pt 3, 25

See also Stoppard

82 Death is the veil which those who live call life:
They sleep, and it is lifted. **P. B. Shelley** *Prometheus Unbound*, Act 3, Sc. 3, 113

83 The unexamined life is not worth living.
Socrates quoted in Plato, *Apology*, 38

84 Life is a gamble, at terrible odds – if it was a bet, you wouldn't take it.
Tom Stoppard *Rosencrantz and Guildenstern are Dead*, Act 3

See also Seneca

85 Let us endeavour so to live that when we come to die even the undertaker will be sorry. **Mark Twain** *Pudd'nhead Wilson*, Ch. 6: epigraph

86 All say, 'How hard it is to die' – a strange complaint to come from the mouths of people who have had to live.

Mark Twain *Pudd'nhead Wilson*, Ch. 10: epigraph

87 Mem. – to think more of the living and less of the dead; for the dead have a world of their own. **Tom Tyers** *Resolutions*

88 In the Parliament of life reality is always in the opposition.

Paul Valéry *Bad Thoughts and Not So Bad*, M

89 Religion may promise life everlasting, but we should grow up and accept that life has an end as well as a beginning . . . Mortality is inevitable, but morbidity is not.

Nicholas Walter quoted in his obituary in the *Guardian*, 13 March 2000

90 It is not good to live in Jest; since we must die in Earnest.

Benjamin Whichcote *Moral and Religious Aphorisms*, 1186

91 Who was it who said the living are the dead on holiday?

Dr Who: Destiny of the Daleks BBC TV, 1980; quoted in *The Oxford Book of Death*, ed. D. J. Enright

92 One's real life is so often the life that one does not lead.

Oscar Wilde *L'Envoi to Rose-Leaf and Apple-Leaf*

93 LORD ILLINGWORTH: The Book of Life begins with a man and a woman in a garden.
MRS ALLONBY: It ends with Revelations.

Oscar Wilde *A Woman of No Importance*, Act 1

94 Death is not an event in life; we do not live to experience death.

Ludwig Wittgenstein *Tractatus Logico-Philosophicus*; quoted in Michael Frayn, *Constructions*, 116

95 It's not catastrophes, murders, deaths, diseases, that age and kill us; it's the way people look and laugh, and run up the steps of omnibuses.

Virginia Woolf *Jacob's Room*, Ch. 6

96 Nothing is stronger than the position of the dead among the living.

Virginia Woolf quoted by Penelope Lively in the *Sunday Times*, 2 April 1989

97 Death and life were not
Till man made up the whole,
Made lock, stock and barrel
Out of his bitter soul. **W. B. Yeats** *The Tower*, 3

See also ***Birth and Death; Existence***

Literature

1 I like men who take sides more than literatures that do.

Albert Camus *Notebooks 5*

2 Literature as a profession is destructive; one should *fear* words more.

Elias Canetti quoted in D. J. Enright, *Interplay*, p. 42

3 When all is said and done, no literature can outdo the cynicism of real life; as you won't intoxicate with one glass someone who has already drunk a whole barrel. **Anton Chekhov** letter to Maria Kiselyova, 14 January 1887

4 With writers who have nothing to say, who have no world of their own, what can you talk about but literature?

E. M. Cioran *Anathemas and Admirations, 7*

5 Half of literature was about it: young women struggling to escape from under the weight of old men, for the sake of the species.

J. M. Coetzee *Disgrace*, 21

6 Nothing can permanently please, which does not contain in itself the reason why it is so, and not otherwise.

Samuel Taylor Coleridge *Biographia Literaria*, Ch. 14

7 Literature is the art of writing something that will be read twice; journalism what will be grasped at once. **Cyril Connolly** *Enemies of Promise*, Ch. 3

See also Pound, Wilde

8 Literature flourishes best when it is half a trade and half an art.

W. R. Inge *The Victorian Age*, p. 49

9 It takes a great deal of history to produce a little literature.

Henry James *Hawthorne*, Ch. 1

10 Biography is merely nosiness dressed up as literature.

Nigel Jones in the *Guardian*, 8 November 1997

11 Literature is mostly about having sex and not much about having children; life is the other way round.

David Lodge *The British Museum is Falling Down*, Ch. 4

12 A novelist is, like all mortals, more fully at home on the surface of the present than in the ooze of the past.

Vladimir Nabokov *Strong Opinions*, Ch. 20

13 Literature is news that *stays* news. **Ezra Pound** *ABC of Reading*, Ch. 2

See also Connolly, Wilde

14 Great Literature is simply language charged with meaning to the utmost possible degree. **Ezra Pound** *How to Read*, Pt 2

15 If evil does not exist, what is going to happen to literature? **V. S. Pritchett** *Mr Beluncle*, 23

16 Literature in many of its branches is no other than the shadow of good talk. **Robert Louis Stevenson** *Memories and Portraits*, p. 145

17 Literature happens to be the only occupation in which wages are not given in proportion to the goodness of the work done.
Anthony Trollope speech on 10 April 1869, St George's Hall, Liverpool, for Dickens's farewell tour

18 The art of literature, vocal or written, is to adjust the language so that it embodies what it indicates.
Alfred North Whitehead in *The Faber Book of Aphorisms*, ed. W. H. Auden and Louis Kronenberger

19 What is the difference between literature and journalism? Oh! Journalism is unreadable and literature is not read. **Oscar Wilde** *The Critic as Artist*, 1

See also Connolly, Pound

See also ***Books; Fiction and Fact; Poetry and Poets; Reading; Writing***

Love

1 Love is the power to see similarity in the dissimilar.
Theodor Adorno *Minima Memoralia*, Pt 3, 122

2 If you do not let love reside in the body it is homeless.
Martin Allwood *Something Like Aphorisms*: 'I Myself'

3 Love is, above all, the gift of oneself. **Jean Anouilh** *Ardèle*, Act 2

4 The love stories of women are written in indelible ink. The love stories of men are – not written. **Minna Antrim** *Phases, Mazes and Crazes of Love*

5 Love is subject to many a weakness, but it usually dies of indigestion.
Minna Antrim *Phases, Mazes and Crazes of Love*

6 Love, after all, is but the antithesis of hatred; and hatred is egotism turned inside out. **Minna Antrim** *The Wisdom of the Foolish*, p. 8

7 Love, and do what you will. **St Augustine** *In Epist. Ioann. Tractatus* 7, Sect. 8

8 Nuptial love maketh mankind; friendly love perfecteth it; but wanton love corrupteth and embaseth it. Love slays what we have been that we may be what we were not. **Francis Bacon** *Essays*: 'Of Love'

9 In love too much of it is not enough.
Pierre Augustin de Beaumarchais in J. de Finod, *A Thousand Flashes of French Wit*, p. 83

10 In expressing love we belong among the undeveloped countries.
Saul Bellow in *The Lover's Quotation Book*, ed. Helen Handley

11 Better is a dinner of herbs where love is, than a stalled ox and hatred therewith. **Bible, OT** Proverbs 15:17

12 There are those made for living love and those who are made for loving. **Albert Camus** *Notebooks 2*, 3 August 1939

13 Love, in present-day society, is just the exchange of two momentary desires, and the contact of two skins.
Nicholas-Sébastien Chamfort *Maxims and Considerations*, Ch. 6

14 Love is more attractive than marriage, for the same reason as novels are more entertaining than history.
Nicholas-Sébastien Chamfort *Maxims and Considerations*, Pt 4, iv

15 The heart has no alarm signal. **Malcolm de Chazal** *Sens plastique*, p. 50

16 Love's great (and sole) originality is to make happiness indistinct from misery. **E. M. Cioran** *Anathemas and Admirations*, 9

17 Love – is anterior to Life –
Posterior – to Death –
Initial of Creation, and
The Exponent of Death. **Emily Dickinson** *Complete Poems*, 917

18 The first sense of mutual love excludes other feelings; it will have the soul all to itself. **George Eliot** *Adam Bede*, Ch. 52

19 All mankind love a lover. **Ralph Waldo Emerson** *Essays*: 'Love'

20 Love is the bright foreigner, the foreign self.
Ralph Waldo Emerson *Journal*, 29 August 1849

21 Anyone who is loved by everybody doesn't deserve anybody's love.
Xavier Forneret *Sans titre, par un homme noir, blanc de visage*: 'August'

22 If an individual is able to love productively, he loves himself too; if he can love *only* others, he cannot love at all.
Erich Fromm *The Art of Loving*, Ch. 2, Sect. 3d

23 Lovers are always concentrating more on love than on the beloved.
Jean Giraudoux *Amphitryon*, Act 1

24 Few of us love others for what they really are. Most of us love what they imagine in others; they love their own idea in someone else.

Johann Wolfgang von Goethe *Goethe's Opinions*, p. 58

25 The pleasure love gives is not really worth the happiness it destroys.

Reynaldo Hahn *Notes: Journal d'un musicien*

26 It is better to desire than to enjoy – to love than to be loved.

William Hazlitt *Characteristics*, 205

27 I shall show you a love philtre compounded without drug or herb or witches' spell. It is this: if you wish to be loved, love.

Hecato quoted in Seneca, *Letters from a Stoic*, 9

28 Love is a fan club with only two fans. **Adrian Henri** *Love is . . .*

29 It is the same with love as with art: the man who can love great things just a little is poorer than the man who can love the little things passionately. **Hermann Hesse** *Reflections*, 613: 'Love'

30 Love's like the measles – all the worse when it comes late in life.

Douglas Jerrold *Wit and Opinions*: 'A Comic Author'

31 Men hate more steadily than they love.

Dr Samuel Johnson in James Boswell, *Life of Johnson*, Vol. 3, p. 150

32 Lovers. Whoever does not have their weaknesses cannot have their strengths. **Joseph Joubert** *Notebooks*, 1797

33 One is always a woman's first lover.

Pierre Choderlos de Laclos in J. de Finod, *A Thousand Flashes of French Wit*, p. 44

34 Thousands are hated, whilst none are ever loved, without a real cause.

Johann Kaspar Lavater *Aphorisms on Man*, 80; William Blake underlined the last part in approval

35 Love sees what no eye sees; love hears what no ear hears; and what never rose in the heart of man love prepares for its object.

Johann Kaspar Lavater *Aphorisms on Man*, 424

36 We can love more than once but not the same person.

Duc de Lévis *Réflexions: sur l'amour*

37 How alike are the groans of love to those of the dying.

Malcolm Lowry *Under the Volcano*, Ch. 12

38 Who ever loved, that loved not at first sight?

Christopher Marlowe *Hero and Leander*, I, 176

39 In the business of love, which is principally a matter of sight and sound, one can do something without the charms of the mind, nothing without the charms of the body. **Michel de Montaigne** *Essays*, Bk 3, Ch. 3

40 It is a misfortune not to be loved; but an insult to be no longer loved.
Charles de Montesquieu *Persian Letters*, 3

41 Pride does much and ill, Love does little and well.
Coventry Patmore *The Rod, the Root and the Flower*: 'Aurea Dicta', 154

42 Love is the cheapest of religions.
Cesare Pavese *This Business of Living: Diary 1935–1950*, 21 December 1939

43 In love it is easier to relinquish a feeling than to give up a habit.
Marcel Proust *Remembrance of Things Past: The Captive*, p. 406

44 The most exclusive love for a person is always a love for something else. **Marcel Proust** *Remembrance of Things Past: Within a Budding Grove*: 'Place-names'

45 Presence of mind in love is a sure sign of absence of heart; no man begins to be serious until he begins to be foolish.
Helen Rowland *A Guide to Men*: 'Finale'

46 Every love affair passes through three stages that flow imperceptibly into one another: the first in which the lovers are happy together even when silent; the second in which they silently grow bored with one another; and the third in which the silence, as if personified, stands between the lovers like a malicious enemy.
Arthur Schnitzler *Aphorismen und Betrachtungen*, 66

47 For a man, being beloved – means seven parts pain to one of joy.
Arthur Schnitzler *Aphorismen und Betrachtungen*, 292

48 Love means never having to say you're sorry.
Erich Segal last line of film *Love Story*; and in novel, Ch. 13

49 Love looks not with the eyes, but with the mind,
And therefore is winged Cupid painted blind.
William Shakespeare *A Midsummer Night's Dream*, Act 1, Sc. 1, 234

50 Love is not love
Which alters when it alteration finds,
Or bends with the remover to remove:
O, no! it is an ever-fixèd mark. **William Shakespeare** *Sonnets*, 116

51 Love sought is good, but giv'n unsought is better.
William Shakespeare *Twelfth Night*, Act 3, Sc. 1, (170)

52 We would never love anybody if we could see past our invention.
Tom Stoppard *The Invention of Love*, Act 1

53 Gallons of ink and miles of typewriter ribbon expended on the misery of the unrequited lover; not a word about the utter tedium of the unrequiting. **Tom Stoppard** *The Real Thing*, Act 1, Sc. 4

54 Love is an endless mystery, for it has nothing else to explain it.
Rabindranath Tagore *Fireflies*, p. 140

55 'Tis better to have loved and lost
Than never to have loved at all. **Alfred, Lord Tennyson** *In Memoriam*, Stanza 27

56 Love is a disease that kills nobody, but one whose time has come.
Marguerite de Valois in J. de Finod, *A Thousand Flashes of French Wit*, p. 238

57 *Omnia vincit Amor: et nos cedamus Amori.* –
Love carries all before him: we too must yield to Love.
Virgil *Eclogues*, X, 69

58 Nothing which exists is absolutely worthy of love.
We must therefore love that which does not exist.
Simone Weil *Gravity and Grace*: 'He Whom We Must Love'

59 To love purely is to consent to distance, it is to adore the distance between ourselves and that which we love.
Simone Weil *Gravity and Grace*: 'Love'

60 Those who are faithful know only the trivial side of love; it is the faithless who know love's tragedies. **Oscar Wilde** *The Picture of Dorian Gray*, Ch. 1

61 It is not enough to speak well of those you love, you must speak ill of those you hate. **Émile Zola** letter to Théodore Duret, 30 May 1870

*See also **Friends and Enemies***

Loyalties

1 Constancy is a moral virtue, fidelity a physical one. Men call themselves constant, women faithful. **Comtesse Diane** *Maxims of Life*, p. 75

2 If I had to choose between betraying my *country* and betraying my *friend*, I hope I should have the guts to betray my *country*.
E. M. Forster *Two Cheers for Democracy*: 'What I Believe'

3 Patriotism subordinates the individual to something bigger. But it is not really prized as a virtue until the shooting starts.
Hermann Hesse *Reflections*, 8

4 It is easier to die for a cause than to live for it.
Hermann Hesse *Reflections*, 204

5 Fidelity is a matter of perception; nobody is unfaithful to the sea or to mountains or to death: once recognized they fill the heart.
Russell Hoban *The Medusa Frequency*, 6

6 Patriotism is the last refuge of a scoundrel.

Dr Samuel Johnson in James Boswell, *Life of Johnson*, 7 April 1775

7 When a nation is filled with strife, then do patriots flourish.

Lao Tzu *Tao Te Ching*, Ch. 18

8 Constancy in love is perpetual inconstancy, inasmuch as the heart is drawn to one quality after another in the beloved, now preferring this, now that. Constancy is therefore inconstancy held in check and confined to the same object. **Due de La Rochefoucauld** *Maxims*, 175

9 Anyone who is disloyal to truth is disloyal to falsehood also.

Michel de Montaigne *Essays*, Bk 2, Ch. 7

10 Do you know the difference between involvement and commitment? Think of ham and eggs. The chicken is involved. The pig is committed.

Martina Navratilova in *Newsweek Magazine*, quoted in *International Herald Tribune*, 3 September 1982

11 The old Lie: *Dulce et decorum est*
Pro patria mori. **Wilfred Owen** *Dulce et Decorum Est*

12 One is only ever really faithful to fidelity itself, never merely to one's partner. **Adam Phillips** *Monogamy*, 33

13 Histories are more full of examples of the fidelity of dogs than of friends. **Alexander Pope** letter to Henry Cromwell, 9 October 1709

14 Patriots always talk of dying for their country, and never of killing for their country. **Bertrand Russell (attrib.)**

15 Men were deceivers ever;
One foot in sea, and one on shore,
To one thing constant never.

William Shakespeare *Much Ado About Nothing*, Act 2, Sc. 3, 65

16 The mark of the immature man is that he wants to die nobly for a cause, while the mark of the mature man is that he wants to live humbly for one. **Wilhelm Stekel** quoted in J. D. Salinger, *The Catcher in the Rye*, Ch. 24

17 It is easier for a man to be loyal to his club than to his planet; the by-laws are shorter, and he is personally acquainted with the other members. **E. B. White** *One Man's Meat*

18 Faithfulness is to the emotional life what consistency is to the life of the intellect – simply a confession of failure.

Oscar Wilde *The Picture of Dorian Gray*, Ch. 4

See also ***Trust and Mistrust***

Madness and Sanity

1 Blessed are the cracked, for they shall let in the light.

Anon. quoted in David Weeks with Kate Ward, *Eccentrics: The Scientific Investigation*, Ch. 3

2 We are all born mad. Some remain so.

Samuel Beckett *Waiting for Godot*, Act 2

3 The men who really believe in themselves are all in lunatic asylums.

G. K. Chesterton *Orthodoxy*, Ch. 2

4 The madman is not the man who has lost his reason. The madman is the man who has lost everything except his reason.

G. K. Chesterton *Orthodoxy*, Ch. 2

5 Whom God wishes to destroy, he first makes mad.

Euripides *Fragments*; exists in many forms: the Latin version '*Quos deus vult perdere, prius dementat*', for example, in James Boswell, *Life of Johnson*

6 Insanity is a kind of innocence.

Graham Greene *The Quiet American*, Pt 3, Ch. 2

7 When dealing with the insane, the best method is to pretend to be sane.

Hermann Hesse *Reflections*, 405: 'Reality and Imagination'

8 Insanity is often the logic of an accurate mind overtasked.

Oliver Wendell Holmes *The Autocrat at the Breakfast Table*, Ch. 2

9 Madness is an illness of the brain, not of the mind.

Joseph Joubert *Notebooks*, 1818

10 Madness need not be all breakdown. It may also be break-through. It is potential liberation and renewal as well as enslavement and existential death.

R. D. Laing *The Politics of Experience*, Ch. 6

11 Madness is something rare in individuals – but in groups, parties, peoples, ages it is the rule.

Friedrich Nietzsche *Beyond Good and Evil*: 'Maxims and Interludes', 156

12 Madness and magic have many similarities. A magician is an artist of madnesses. **Novalis** *Pollen*, 292

13 The worst of madmen is a saint run mad.

Alexander Pope *Imitations of Horace*, Bk 1, Epistle 6

14 Sanity is a madness put to good uses; waking life is a dream controlled. **George Santayana** *Little Essays*, 58

15 Psychiatrists classify a person as neurotic if he suffers from his problems in living, and as psychotic if he makes others suffer.

Thomas S. Szasz *The Second Sin*: 'Psychiatry'

See also ***Health and Illness***

Manners

1 A gentleman is any man who wouldn't hit a woman with his hat on.

Fred Allen in Laurence J. Peter, *Peter's Quotations*

2 The English are polite by telling lies. The Americans are polite by telling the truth. **Malcolm Bradbury** *Stepping Westward*, II, 5

3 That bad manners are so prevalent in the world is the fault of good manners. **Maria von Ebner-Eschenbach** *Aphorisms*, p. 72

4 There are bad manners everywhere but an aristocracy is bad manners organized.

Henry James in *The Faber Book of Aphorisms*, ed. W. H. Auden and Louis Kronenberger

5 To Americans English manners are far more frightening than none at all. **Randall Jarrell** *Pictures from an Institution*, Pt 2, Ch. 5

6 My father used to say,
'Superior people never make long visits.' **Marianne Moore** *Silence*

7 The Japanese have perfected good manners and made them indistinguishable from rudeness. **Paul Theroux** *The Great Railway Bazaar*, Ch. 28

8 Our manners have been corrupted by communication with the saints. **H. D. Thoreau** *Walden*: 'Economy'

Marriage and Divorce

1 Bigamy is having one husband too many. Monogamy is the same.

Anon. woman epigraph to Erica Jong, *Fear of Flying*, Ch. 1

2 I married beneath me. All women do.

Nancy Astor speech at Oldham, Lancashire, 1951

3 It is a truth universally acknowledged, that a single man in possession of a good fortune, must be in want of a wife.

Jane Austen *Pride and Prejudice*, Ch. 1

4 A lady's imagination is very rapid; it jumps from admiration to love, from love to matrimony in a moment.

Jane Austen *Pride and Prejudice*, Ch. 6

5 Thales being asked when a man should marry, said, young men not yet, old men not at all. **Francis Bacon** *Apothegms*, 73

6 Wives are young men's mistresses; companions for middle age; and old men's nurses. **Francis Bacon** *Essays*: 'Of Marriage and Single Life'

7 Alimony is like buying oats for a dead horse.

Arthur 'Bugs' Baer from *New York American*; in Jonathon Green, *Cassell Dictionary of Cynical Quotations*, p. 66

8 Being unable to abolish love, the Church sought at least to disinfect it, and thus created marriage.

Charles Baudelaire *Intimate Journals*: 'My Heart Laid Bare', 18

9 Of all serious things, marriage is the most ludicrous.

Pierre Augustin de Beaumarchais *The Marriage of Figaro*, Act 1, Sc. 9

10 There is much to be said for exotic marriages. If your husband is a bore, it takes years longer to discover it. **Saul Bellow** *Mr Sammler's Planet*, Ch. 6

11 Being a husband is a whole-time job. That is why so many husbands fail. They cannot give their entire attention to it.

Arnold Bennett *The Title*, Act 1

12 All weddings are similar but every marriage is different. Death comes to everyone but one mourns alone.

John Berger *The White Bird*: 'The Storyteller'

13 It is better to dwell in a corner of the house-top, than with a brawling woman in a wide house. **Bible, OT** Proverbs 21:9

14 It is better to marry than to burn. **Bible, NT** 1 Corinthians 7:9

15 **Marriage, n.** The state or condition of a community consisting of a master, a mistress and two slaves, making in all two.

Ambrose Bierce *The Devil's Dictionary*

16 **Fortune-hunter, n.** A man without wealth whom a rich woman catches and marries within an inch of his life.

Ambrose Bierce *The Enlarged Devil's Dictionary*

17 When a man has married a wife, he finds out whether
Her knees and elbows are only glued together.

William Blake *Miscellaneous Epigrams*

18 In a happy marriage it is the wife who provides the climate, the husband the landscape. **Gerald Brenan** *Thoughts in a Dry Season*: 'Marriage'

19 What is marriage but prostitution to one man instead of many?

Angela Carter *Nights at the Circus*: 'London 2'

20 Marriage and celibacy are both evils: it is better to choose the one which is not incurable. **Nicholas-Sébastien Chamfort** *Maxims and Considerations*, 389

21 A man and a woman marry because both of them don't know what to do with themselves. **Anton Chekhov** *Notebooks 1894–1902*, p. 15

22 If you are afraid of loneliness do not marry.

Anton Chekhov *Notebooks 1894–1902*, p. 49

See also Schnitzler

23 There are but two objects in marriage, love or money. If you marry for love, you will certainly have some very happy days, and probably many very uneasy ones; if for money, you will have no happy days and probably no uneasy ones.

Earl of Chesterfield letter to his godson and heir, to be delivered after his death

24 A man's friend likes him but leaves him as he is: his wife loves him and is always trying to turn him into somebody else.

G. K. Chesterton *Orthodoxy*, Ch. 5

25 There can be only one end to marriage without love, and that is love without marriage.

John Churton Collins aphorisms in the *English Review*, April 1914

See also Franklin

26 Marriage is a feast where the grace is often better than the *dinner*.

Charles Caleb Colton *Lacon*: 'Marriages'

27 Courtship to marriage, as a very witty prologue to a very dull play.

William Congreve *The Old Bachelor*, Act 5, Sc. 10

28 The true index of a man's character is the health of his wife.
Cyril Connolly *The Unquiet Grave*, Pt 1

29 Marriage is not all bed and breakfast. **R. Coulson** *Reflections*

30 She is always married too soon who gets a bad husband and she is never married too late who gets a good one. **Daniel Defoe** *Moll Flanders*

31 Divorce is a system whereby two people make a mistake and one of them goes on paying for it. **Len Deighton** quoted in A. Alvarez, *Life after Marriage*

32 Marriage is to courtship as humming is to singing.
Peter De Vries *Consenting Adults*, Ch. 6

33 The value of marriage is not that adults produce children but that children produce adults. **Peter De Vries** *The Tunnel of Love*, Ch. 8

34 I pray thee, good Lord, that I may not be married. But if I am to be married, that I may not be a cuckold. But if I am to be a cuckold, that I may not know. But if I am to know, that I may not mind.
Isak Dinesen *Seven Gothic Tales*: 'The Poet'; a saying described as 'The bachelor's prayer'

35 The chains of marriage are so heavy that it takes two to bear them, and sometimes three.
Alexandre Dumas, the younger quoted in L. Treich, *L'Esprit d'Alexandre Dumas*

36 That's what a man wants in a wife, mostly; he wants to make sure o' one fool as' ul tell him he's wise. **George Eliot** *Adam Bede*, Bk 6, Ch. 53

37 If you're looking for monogamy, you'd better marry a swan.
Nora Ephron screenplay of film *Heartburn*

38 When the blind lead the blind, no wonder they both fall into – matrimony. **George Farquhar** *Love and a Bottle*, Act 5, Sc. 1

39 Where there's marriage without love, there will be love without marriage. **Benjamin Franklin** *Poor Richard's Almanack*, 1734

See also Collins

40 Keep your eyes wide open before marriage, half shut afterwards.
Benjamin Franklin *Poor Richard's Almanack*, 1738

41 Next to no wife a good wife is best. **Dr Thomas Fuller** *Gnomologia*, 3539

42 Be not hasty to marry; it's better to have one Plough going than two Cradles; and more Profit to have a Barn filled, than a Bed.
Dr Thomas Fuller *Introductio ad Prudentium*, 2225

43 A man in love is incomplete until he has married. Then he's finished.
Zsa Zsa Gabor in *Newsweek*, 28 March 1960

44 The problem with marriage is that it ends every night after making love, and it must be rebuilt every morning before breakfast.

Gabriel García Márquez *Love in the Time of Cholera*, p. 209

45 Unfaithful husbands often love their wives; the unfaithful ones are sometimes the most faithful of all. **Jean Giraudoux** *Ondine*, Act 3

See also Guitry

46 When you marry your mistress you create a job vacancy.

James Goldsmith in the *Independent Magazine*, 22 April 1989

47 People have been marrying and bringing up children for centuries now. Nothing has ever come of it. **Celia Green** *The Decline of Science*: 'Aphorisms'

48 There are women whose infidelities are the sole link they still have with their husbands. **Sacha Guitry** *Elles et Toi*

See also Giraudoux

49 If men knew how women pass the time when they are alone, they'd never marry. **O. Henry** *Memoirs of a Yellow Dog*

50 The critical period in matrimony is breakfast time.

A. P. Herbert *Uncommon Law*: 'Is Marriage Lawful?'

51 There is radicalism in all getting, and conservatism in all keeping. Lovemaking is radical, while marriage is conservative.

Eric Hoffer *Between the Devil and the Dragon*, Pt 3: Introduction

52 If a couple walks along like th' woman wuz arrested they're married.

'Kin' Hubbard *Abe Martin's Wisecracks*, p. 67

53 Marriage has many pains, but celibacy has no pleasures.

Dr Samuel Johnson *Rasselas*, Ch. 26

54 Two people did not get married, since then they have been living in mutual widowhood. **Karl Kraus** *These Great Times*: caption to photograph

55 Being happily married means that you don't have to perform marriage, you just live in it like a fish lives in the sea. **David Lodge** *Therapy*, 1, p. 128

56 It's not the seven deadly virtues that make a man a good husband, but the three hundred pleasing amiabilities.

W. Somerset Maugham *The Constant Wife*, Act 1

57 No man is genuinely happy, married, who has to drink worse gin than he used to drink when he was single.

H. L. Mencken *Prejudices, Fourth Series*: 'Reflections on Monogamy', 14

58 As for marriage, not only is it a bargain to which only the entrance is free, continuance in it being constrained and compulsory, and depending upon other things than our will, but it is a bargain commonly made for other ends. **Michel de Montaigne** *Essays*, Bk 1, Ch. 28

59 It is like a cage; one sees the birds outside desperate to get in, and those inside equally desperate to get out. **Michel de Montaigne** *Essays*, Bk 3, Ch. 5

60 Frenchmen hardly ever talk about their wives: they are afraid to do so in front of people who may know them better than they.
Charles de Montesquieu *Persian Letters*, 55

61 Nothing has made a greater contribution to mutual attachment than the possibility of divorce. **Charles de Montesquieu** *Persian Letters*, 116

62 One doesn't have to get anywhere in a marriage. It's not a public conveyance. **Iris Murdoch** *A Severed Head*, Ch. 3

63 The trouble
with being best man is, you don't get a chance to prove it.
Les A. Murray *The Boy Who Stole the Funeral*

64 Why have hamburger out when you've got steak at home? That doesn't always mean it's tender.
Paul Newman in the *Observer*, 'Sayings of the Week', 11 March 1984; but earlier variants on this defence of marriage

65 Marriage is a splendid lie; it affirms the eternity of passion which experience shows is the most ephemeral of passions.
Friedrich Nietzsche *Nietzsche in Outline and Aphorism*: 'Man and Woman'

66 Marriage, as our world sees it, is simply a convenience; a somewhat clumsy contrivance to tide over a social difficulty.
Ouida *Wisdom, Wit, and Pathos*: 'Moths'

67 Marriage may often be a stormy lake, but celibacy is almost always a muddy horse-pond. **Thomas Love Peacock** *Melincourt*, Ch. 7

68 Infidelity makes a life of absolute monogamy essential.
Adam Phillips *Monogamy*, 7

69 Two's company but three's a couple. **Adam Phillips** *Monogamy*, 94

See also Wilde

70 A 'disastrous' marriage may be the only poetical action in a man's life.
Marcel Proust *Remembrance of Things Past: The Fugitive*, p. 782

71 It doesn't much signify whom one marries, for one is sure to find next morning that it was someone else. **Samuel Rogers** *Table Talk*

72 Love is a matter of chance; matrimony is a matter of money, and divorce – a matter of course. **Helen Rowland** *A Guide to Men*: 'Blondes'

73 After marriage, a woman's sight becomes so keen that she can see right through her husband without looking at him, and a man's so dull that he can look right through his wife without seeing her.
Helen Rowland *A Guide to Men*: 'First Interlude'

74 About the only things in connection with his wife for which a man shows any respect after a few years of marriage are her reputation and her toothbrush. **Helen Rowland** *A Guide to Men*: 'True Love'

75 Love is a matter of give and take – marriage, a matter of misgive and mistake. **Helen Rowland** *A Guide to Men*: 'What Every Woman Wonders'

76 Men who have a pierced ear are better prepared for marriage – they've experienced pain and bought jewellery.
Rita Rudner on Channel 4 TV, 5 December 1989

77 Marriage is the school of loneliness. But one does not learn enough in it. **Arthur Schnitzler** *Aphorismen und Betrachtungen*, p. 292

See also Chekhov

78 The happiest marriages I have seen have been those which began under circumstances which required oeconomy.
Sir Walter Scott *Letters*, Vol. 6, p. 24

79 Marriage is nothing but a civil contract. **John Selden** *Table Talk*, 85

80 For a light wife doth make a heavy husband.
William Shakespeare *The Merchant of Venice*, Act 5, Sc. 1, 130

81 Many a good hanging prevents a bad marriage.
William Shakespeare *Twelfth Night*, Act 1, Sc. 5, (20)

82 'Tis safest in matrimony to begin with a little aversion.
Richard Brinsley Sheridan *The Rivals*, Act 1, Sc. 2

83 Twelve years doesn't mean you're a *happy* couple. It just means you're a *long* couple. **Neil Simon** *The Odd Couple*, Act 1

84 [Of marriage] A pair of shears, so joined that they cannot be separated; often moving in opposite directions, yet always punishing anyone who comes between them.
Revd Sydney Smith in his daughter, Lady Holland's, *Memoir*, Vol. 1, Ch. 11

85 To marry is to domesticate the Recording Angel. Once you are married, there is nothing left for you, not even suicide, but to be good.
Robert Louis Stevenson *Virginibus Puerisque*: title essay, I, 2

86 The reason why so few marriages are happy is because young ladies spend their time in making nets, not in making cages.

Jonathan Swift *Thoughts on Various Subjects*, p. 277

87 Marriage is a gift man gives to a woman for which she never forgives him. **Thomas S. Szasz** *The Second Sin*: 'Marriage'

88 A happy bridesmaid makes a happy bride.

Alfred, Lord Tennyson *The Bridesmaid*

89 Remember, it is as easy to marry a rich woman as a poor woman.

W. M. Thackeray *Pendennis*, Ch. 28

90 Every marriage tends to consist of an aristocrat and a peasant. Of a teacher and a learner. **John Updike** *Couples*, Ch. 1

91 May you have a wife who doesn't believe what she sees.

Paul Valéry *Bad Thoughts and Not So Bad*, O

92 Marriage isn't a word – it's a sentence.

King Vidor caption to silent film *The Crowd* (1928), written with John V. A. Weaver and Harry Behn

93 Probably divorce is nearly the same age as marriage. However, I believe that marriage is older – by a week or two.

Voltaire *Philosophical Dictionary*: 'Divorce'

94 For every marriage then is best in tune,
When that the wife is May, the husband June.

Rowland Watkyns 'To the Most Courteous and Fair Gentlewoman, Mrs Elinor Williams'

95 If we men married the women we deserved, we should have a very bad time of it. **Oscar Wilde** *An Ideal Husband*, Act 4

96 In married life three is company and two is none.

Oscar Wilde *The Importance of Being Earnest*, Act 1

See also Phillips

97 I am not in favour of long engagements. They give people the opportunity of finding out each other's character before marriage, which I think is never advisable. **Oscar Wilde** *The Importance of Being Earnest*, Act 3

98 Men marry because they are tired; women because they are curious; both are disappointed. **Oscar Wilde** *The Picture of Dorian Gray*, Ch. 4

99 When a woman marries again, it is because she detested her first husband. When a man marries again, it is because he adored his first wife. Women try their luck; men risk theirs.

Oscar Wilde *The Picture of Dorian Gray*, Ch. 15

100 Marriage is a bribe to make a housekeeper think she's a householder.
Thornton Wilder *The Matchmaker*, Act 1

101 Adultery is bad morals, but divorce is bad metaphysics.
Charles Williams *The Forgiveness of Sins*, quoted in G. K. Chesterton, *Brave New Family*, Pt 7

See also ***Love; Men and Women; Women***

The Media

1 A free nation never hears any side but its own.
Walter Bagehot *The English Constitution*, Ch. 5

2 The difference between directing yourself and being directed is the difference between masturbating and making love.
Warren Beatty in film *Première*, quoted in the *Independent on Sunday*, 5 January 1992

See also Penn

3 Theatre is like operating with a scalpel. Film is operating with a laser.
Michael Caine in BBC TV programme *Acting*, 28 August 1987

4 Newspapers, to help you forget the previous day.
Elias Canetti *The Secret Heart of the Clock*: '1977'

5 Journalism largely consists in saying 'Lord Jones Dead' to people who never knew Lord Jones was alive.
G. K. Chesterton *The Wisdom of Father Brown*: 'The Purple Wig'

6 Television: the key to all minds and hearts because it permits people to be entertained by their government without ever having to participate in it.
Richard Condon in the *Observer*, 'Sayings of the Week', 10 June 1990

7 When a dog bites a man that is not news, but when a man bites a dog that is news.
Charles A. Dana in *New York Sun*, 1882: 'What is News?'

8 An editor: a person who knows precisely what he wants – but isn't quite sure.
Walter Davenport quoted by Bennett Cerf in *Saturday Review Reader*, no. 2

9 It's the duty of a newspaper to comfort the afflicted and to flick the comfortable.
Nathan E. Douglas and Harold Jacob Smith screenplay for film *Inherit the Wind*; said by Gene Kelly

10 Television is an invention that permits you to be entertained in your living room by people you wouldn't have in your home.
David Frost in CBC TV programme *David Frost Revue*, 1971, quoted in Jonathon Green, *Says Who?*

11 I call journalism everything that will interest less tomorrow than it does today. **André Gide (attrib.)**

12 Photography is truth. And cinema is truth twenty-four times a second. **Jean-Luc Godard** in film *Le Petit soldat*

13 The camera is a between, between what goes in and what comes out; the camera is communication in a solid state.
Jean-Luc Godard in *Godard: Images, Sounds and Politics*, ed. Colin MacCabe, 3

14 Good films get smaller audiences, but more of the viewer.
Jean-Luc Godard in interview in the *Guardian*, 11 February 2000

15 Whoever says the first word to the world is right.
Josef Goebbels quoted in *The Media in British Politics*, ed. Ben Pimlott and Jean Seaton

16 As far as the film-making process is concerned, stars are essentially worthless and absolutely essential.
William Goldman *Adventures in the Screen Trade*, Pt 1, Ch. 1

17 You can't make a 'Hamlet' without breaking a few egos.
William Goldman in the *Observer*, 8 April 1984; of the screenwriter's problems over the star system

18 A wide screen just makes a bad film twice as bad.
Sam Goldwyn said on 9 September 1956

19 The propagandist's purpose is to make one set of people forget that certain other sets of people are human.
Aldous Huxley *The Olive Tree*: 'Writers and Readers'

20 Newspapers have roughly the same relationship to life as fortune-tellers to metaphysics. **Karl Kraus** *Half-Truths and One-and-a-Half Truths*: 'In hollow heads'

21 Journalists write because they have nothing to say, and have something to say because they write.
Karl Kraus *Half-Truths and One-and-a-Half Truths*: 'In hollow heads'

22 In front of the small screen, life becomes fiction, and fiction life.
John Lahr in the *Independent on Sunday*, 29 September 1991

23 Publishers can get their minds halfway round anything.
John Le Carré *The Russia House*, Ch. 5

24 Freedom of the press is guaranteed only to those who own one.
A. J. Liebling in the *New Yorker*, 14 May 1960

25 The horror of the Twentieth Century was the size of each new event, and the paucity of its reverberation.
Norman Mailer *A Fire on the Moon*, Pt 2, Ch. 2, 1

26 A good newspaper, I suppose, is a nation talking to itself.
Arthur Miller in the *Observer*, 'Sayings of the Week', 26 November 1961

27 A reporter is a man who has renounced everything in life but the world, the flesh, and the devil.
David Murray in the *Observer*, 'Sayings of the Week', 5 July 1931

28 The difference between being a director and being an actor is the difference between being the carpenter banging the nails into the wood, and being the piece of wood the nails are being banged into.
Sean Penn interview in the *Guardian*, 28 November 1991

See also Beatty

29 I like to have my news from different sources;
How else find out the truth? **Alexander Pushkin** *Boris Godunov*

30 In Hollywood, if you don't have happiness you send out for it.
Rex Reed quoted in J. R. Colombo, *Colombo's Hollywood*: 'Hollywood the Bad'

31 The longest-lived editor is the one least distinguishable from his average reader. **Robert Robinson** *Dog Chairman*: 'Our Betters'

32 In America, journalism is apt to be regarded as an extension of history: in Britain, as an extension of conversation.
Anthony Sampson *Anatomy of Britain Today*, Ch. 18

33 Freedom of the press must be regarded as a permit to sell poison.
Arthur Schopenhauer *Essays and Aphorisms*: 'On Law and Politics', 7

34 Comment is free but facts are sacred.
C. P. Scott in the *Manchester Guardian*, 5 May 1921

35 Though it be honest, it is never good
To bring bad news. **William Shakespeare** *Antony and Cleopatra*, Act 2, Sc. 5, 85

36 Some of the worst films of all time have been made by people who think too much.
Steven Soderbergh interview in the *Guardian*, 7 September 1989

37 The most powerful weapon of ignorance – the diffusion of printed material. **Leo Tolstoy** *War and Peace*: Epilogue, Pt 2, Ch. 8

38 That's what show business is for – to prove that it's not what you are that counts, it's what they *think* you are. **Andy Warhol** *POPism*: '1967'

39 The Lords Temporal say nothing, the Lords Spiritual have nothing to say, and the House of Commons has nothing to say and says it. We are dominated by Journalism. **Oscar Wilde** *The Soul of Man Under Socialism*

Memory

1 On days when you have, always recall the days when you didn't have – so that in times when you haven't you won't be recalling times when you had. **Anon.** *Chinese Couplets, Aphorisms and Apothegms*, ed. W. Dolby, 6

2 All of us are creatures of a day; the rememberer and the remembered alike. **Marcus Aurelius** *Meditations*, Bk 4, 35

3 Memory is not only a trip but also a structure. Recollections are not only stories retold but also aspects of present feeling.
John Berger *Nineteen Nineteen*, afterword to film script by Hugh Brody and Michael Ignatieff

4 Blessed are those who can give without remembering and take without forgetting. **Elizabeth Bibesco** *Haven*: 'Aphorisms'

5 Our Fathers find their graves in our short memories, and sadly tell us how we may be buried in our survivors.
Sir Thomas Browne *Urn Burial*, Ch. 5

6 The finest statue of a man would be a horse that has thrown him off.
Elias Canetti *The Human Province*: '1955'

7 Just *declare* something to be a memory and it will be taken seriously.
Elias Canetti *The Secret Heart of the Clock*: '1980'

8 An injury is much sooner forgotten than an insult.
Earl of Chesterfield *Letters to His Son*, 9 October 1746

9 In plucking the fruit of memory one runs the risk of spoiling its bloom. **Joseph Conrad** *Arrow of Gold*: author's note

10 A memory is what is left when something happens and does not completely unhappen. **Edward de Bono** *The Mechanism of Mind*

11 We only forget those we have not loved enough to hate.
Comtesse Diane *Maxims of Life*, p. 51

12 Perhaps a novelist has a greater ability to forget than other men – he has to forget or become sterile. What he forgets is the compost of the imagination. **Graham Greene** *A Sort of Life*, 10, 4

13 One forgets what is hard to bear, and what we don't forget was unbearable for us. **Georg Groddeck** *The Book of the It*, Letter 20

14 Men often *mistake* themselves, but they never *forget* themselves.
Marquis of Halifax *Moral Thoughts and Reflections*: 'Of Vanity'

15 The more a person can forget, the greater the number of metamorphoses which his life can go through, the more he can remember the more divine his life becomes. **Søren Kierkegaard** *The Journals*, 1842

16 All folly, all vice, all incredulity, arise from neglect of remembering what once you knew. **Johann Kaspar Lavater** *Aphorisms on Man*, 613

17 It is not what old men forget that shadows their senescence, but what they remember.
George Lyttelton letter, 27 October 1955, in *Lyttelton–Hart-Davis Letters*, Vol. 2

18 One man's remorse is another man's reminiscence.
Ogden Nash *A Clean Conscience Never Relaxes*

19 Good memory. – many a man fails to become a thinker only because his memory is good.
Friedrich Nietzsche *Human, All Too Human*: 'Assorted Opinions and Maxims', 122

20 A retentive memory is of great use to a man, no doubt; but the talent of oblivion is on the whole more useful.
Ouida *Wisdom, Wit, and Pathos*: 'A Village Commune'

21 Memories are the only possessions which no one can take from us.
Jean Paul (attrib.) in Theodor Adorno, *Minima Memoralia*, Pt 3, 106

22 The richness of life lies in the memories we have forgotten.
Cesare Pavese *This Business of Living, A Diary 1935–1950*, 13 February 1944

23 Memory is not what we remember, but that which remembers us. Memory is a present that never stops passing.
Octavio Paz *The Curse*; epigraph to David Suzuki and Peter Knudtson, *Genethics*, Ch. 1

24 People may be dead and be remembered; but they only disappear when they are completely forgotten, when no one ever uses their name.
Adam Phillips *Darwin's Bones*: Epilogue

25 It is only after a memory has lost all life that it can be classed in time, just as only desiccated flowers find their way into the herbarium of a botanist.
Henri Poincaré *On Measuring Time*, quoted in T. Dantzig, *Henri Poincaré*, Ch. 8, epigraph

26 The memory is always under orders from the heart.
Antoine de Rivarol *Notes, réflexions et maximes*: 'Philosophe'

27 Many are saved by the deficiency of their memory from being spoiled by their education. **Archbishop Whately** *Apophthegms*, 67B

See also ***Past and Present***

Men and Women

1 One plus one is not two, but two plus something.

Martin Allwood *Something Like Aphorisms*: 'Men with Women'

2 Men say about women whatever they fancy, women do with men whatever they like. **Anon.** quoted in J. Raymond Solly, *A Cynic's Breviary*

3 A woman's as bold as she looks; a man as bold as he feels.

Minna Antrim *The Wisdom of the Foolish*, p. 12

4 No sane woman ever loved a man before she knew him. Did any sane woman afterward? **Minna Antrim** *The Wisdom of the Foolish*, p. 20

5 If a woman has given a man her heart, she will give him her purse as well. **Honoré de Balzac** quoted in Abram Tertz, *A Voice from the Chorus*, Pt 2

6 How many a man would recognize a woman undressed of his emotions? **Elizabeth Bibesco** *Haven*: 'Aphorisms'

7 Mature woman is physically polygamous but emotionally monogamous, while mature man is emotionally polygamous but physically monogamous. **Alan Brien** in the *New Statesman*, 6 December 1968

8 It's women, rather than men, who have the art of doing two things at once. **Malcolm de Chazal** *Sens plastique*, p. 224

9 Women deprived of the company of men pine, men deprived of the company of women become stupid. **Anton Chekhov** *Notebooks 1894–1902*, p. 10

10 A man of sense only trifles with them [women], plays with them, humours and flatters them, as he does with a sprightly and forward child; but he neither consults them about, nor trusts them with, serious matters. **Earl of Chesterfield** *Letters to His Son*, 5 September 1748

11 If men were as unselfish as women, women would very soon become more selfish than men. **John Churton Collins** *Maxims and Reflections*, 90

12 Women distrust men too much in general, and not enough in particular. **Jean Commerson** in J. de Finod, *A Thousand Flashes of French Wit*, p. 96

13 There is more difference within the sexes than between them.

Ivy Compton-Burnett *Mother and Son*, Ch. 9

14 In the sex-war thoughtlessness is the weapon of the male, vindictiveness of the female. **Cyril Connolly** *The Unquiet Grave*, Pt 1: 'Women'

15 Most women set out to try to change a man, and when they have changed him they do not like him.

Marlene Dietrich in A. Andrews, *Quotations for Speakers and Writers*

16 Man and woman are two locked caskets, of which each contains the key to the other. **Isak Dinesen** *Winter's Tales*: 'A Consolatory Tale'

17 Where women love each other, men learn to smother their mutual dislike. **George Eliot** *Middlemarch*: 'Finale'

See also Schopenhauer

18 Charming women can true converts make,
We love the precepts for the teacher's sake.
George Farquhar *The Constant Couple*, Act 5, Sc. 3

19 Men get to be a mixture of the charming mannerisms of the women they have known. **F. Scott Fitzgerald** *Notebooks*, G

20 Women never look at, or at least never see, the men they love.
Edmond and Jules de Goncourt *Journal*, 25 October 1878

21 Most men who rail against women are only railing at one woman.
Rémy de Gourmont *Selected Writings*

22 The tragedy of machismo is that a man is never quite man enough.
Germaine Greer *The Madwoman's Underclothes*: 'My Mailer Problem'

23 For the female of the species is more deadly than the male.
Rudyard Kipling *The Female of the Species*

24 The silliest woman can manage a clever man; but it needs a very clever woman to manage a fool.
Rudyard Kipling *Plain Tales from the Hills*: 'Three and – an Extra'

25 Men who call women ladies generally treat them as maids.
Aidan Mathews *Lipstick on the Host*: title story

26 Men, some to business, some to pleasure take;
But every woman is at heart a rake. **Alexander Pope** *Moral Essays*, Epistle II, 215

27 A man leaves a woman for another woman, but a woman leaves a man for herself. **Stefanie Powers** in the *Observer*, 4 July 1999

28 There is only a slight difference between the chemical composition of men and women. Nature has divided the species at minimal expense.
Jean Rostand *Pensées d'un biologiste*, p. 60

29 Women always want to be our last love, and we their first.
Arthur Schnitzler *Aphorismen und Betrachtungen*, p. 286

See also Wilde

30 Men are by nature merely indifferent to one another; but women are by nature enemies. **Arthur Schopenhauer** *Essays and Aphorisms*: 'On Women', 7

See also Eliot

31 Generally about the age of forty, women get tired of being virtuous and men of being honest.

Revd Sydney Smith quoted by Mrs A. Jameson, *A Commonplace Book*

32 The one certain way for a woman to hold a man is to leave him for religion.

Muriel Spark *The Comforters*, Ch. 1

33 A woman without a man is like a fish without a bicycle.

Gloria Steinem (attrib.) in *Quotable Women*, compiled Elaine Partnow

34 Men come of age at sixty, women at fifteen.

James Stephens in the *Observer*, 'Sayings of the Week', 1 October 1944

35 For men at most differ as Heaven and Earth,
But women, worst and best, as Heaven and Hell.

Alfred, Lord Tennyson *Idylls of the King*: 'Merlin and Vivien', 812

36 'Tis strange what a man may do, and a woman yet think him an angel.

W. M. Thackeray *Henry Esmond*, Bk 1, Ch. 7

37 A man in the house is worth two in the street.

Mae West in film *Belle of the Nineties*, screenplay by West

38 There is, of course, no reason for the existence of the male sex except that one sometimes needs help with moving the piano.

Rebecca West in Victoria Glendinning, *Rebecca West*, Pt 6, Ch. 5

39 Women represent the triumph of matter over mind – just as men represent the triumph of mind over morals.

Oscar Wilde *The Picture of Dorian Gray*, Ch. 4

40 Men always want to be a woman's first love. That is their clumsy vanity. We women have a more subtle instinct about things. What we like is to be a man's last romance.

Oscar Wilde *A Woman of No Importance*, Act 2

See also Schnitzler

41 Oh, the Ideal Man should talk to us as if we were goddesses, and treat us as if we were children . . . He should always say much more than he means, and always mean much more than he says.

Oscar Wilde *A Woman of No Importance*, Act 2

42 Women have served all these centuries as looking-glasses possessing the magic and delicious power of reflecting the figure of man at twice its natural size.

Virginia Woolf *A Room of One's Own*, Ch. 2

See also ***Family; Relationships; Women***

The Mind

1 The English mind was one-sided, eccentric, systematically unsystematic, and logically illogical. **Henry Adams** *The Education of Henry Adams*, Ch. 12

2 Through not observing what is in the mind of another a man has seldom been seen to be unhappy; but those who do not observe the movements of their own minds must of necessity be unhappy.

Marcus Aurelius *Meditations*, Bk 2, 8

3 Fix your thought closely on what is being said, and let your mind enter fully into what is being done, and into what is doing it.

Marcus Aurelius *Meditations*, Bk 7, 30

4 What impresses men is not mind, but the result of mind.

Walter Bagehot *The English Constitution*, Ch. 8

5 The easiest place in which to carry technology is in the mind.

Hugh Brody *Living Arctic*, Ch. 6

6 Our minds want clothes as much as our bodies.

Samuel Butler 2 quoted in *The Faber Book of Aphorisms*, ed. W. H. Auden and Louis Kronenberger

7 In making up one's mind one closes one's mind.

John Jay Chapman *The Selected Writings*: 'The Negro Question'

8 The object of opening the mind, as of opening the mouth, is to shut it again on something solid.

G. K. Chesterton quoted by Katharine Whitehorn in the *Observer*, 28 December 1986

9 The empires of the future are the empires of the mind.

Winston S. Churchill speech at Harvard University, 16 September 1943

10 To keep the mind vigilant, there is only coffee, disease, insomnia, or the obsession of death. **E. M. Cioran** *A Short History of Decay*, 6: 'Poverty: Mental Stimulant'

11 Absence of occupation is not rest,
A mind quite vacant is a mind distressed. **William Cowper** *Retirement*, 623

12 We know the human brain is a device to keep the ears from grating on one another. **Peter De Vries** *Comfort Me with Apples*, Ch. 1

13 What we are today comes from our thoughts of yesterday, and our present thoughts build our life of tomorrow: our life is the creation of our mind. ***The Dhammapada*** 1

14 An enemy can hurt an enemy, and a man who hates can harm another man; but a man's own mind, if wrongly directed, can do him a far greater harm. ***The Dhammapada*** 42

15 A foolish consistency is the hobgoblin of little minds, adored by little statesmen and philosophers and divines.

Ralph Waldo Emerson *Essays, First Series*: 'Self-Reliance'

16 The brain is a wonderful organ; it starts working the moment you get up in the morning and doesn't stop until you get into the office.

Robert Frost in *The Executive's Quotation Book*, ed. James Charlton

17 It is slavery to live in the mind unless it has become part of the body.

Kahlil Gibran *Spiritual Sayings*

18 The remarkable thing about the human mind is its range of limitations. **Celia Green** *The Decline and Fall of Science*: 'Aphorisms'

19 There is an unseemly exposure of the mind, as well as of the body.

William Hazlitt *Sketches and Essays*: 'On Disagreeable People'

20 The human brain has a mind of its own. **Joseph Heller** *God Knows*, Ch. 12

21 Little minds are interested in the extraordinary; great minds in the commonplace. **Elbert Hubbard** *The Roycroft Dictionary*

22 Each new mind brings its own edition of the universe of space along with it, its own room to inhabit; and these spaces never crowd each other. **William James** *The Will to Believe and Other Essays*

23 Money never made any man rich, but his mind.

Ben Jonson *Timber or Discoveries Made Upon Men and Matter*, 101

24 Our mind must not be more difficult than our taste, nor our judgement more severe than our conscience. **Joseph Joubert** *Notebooks*, 1799

25 The pendulum of the mind oscillates between sense and nonsense, not between right and wrong. **C. G. Jung** *Memories, Dreams, Reflections*, Ch. 5

26 Strength and weakness of mind are misnomers; they are really nothing but the good or bad health of our bodily organs.

Duc de La Rochefoucauld *Maxims*, 44

27 Too much gravity argues a shallow mind.

Johann Kaspar Lavater *Aphorisms on Man*, 183

28 Two heads are better than one, not because either is infallible, but because they are unlikely to go wrong in the same direction.

C. S. Lewis introduction to St Athanasius, *The Incarnation of the Word of God*

29 Taking an overall view of a thing the mind sees every side of it obscurely, which is often of more value than a clear idea of only one side of it.

Georg Christoph Lichtenberg *Aphorisms*, Notebook D, 47

30 The sure conviction that we could if we wanted to is the reason so many good minds are idle. **Georg Christoph Lichtenberg** *Aphorisms*, Notebook K, 27

31 When he was expected to use his mind, he felt like a right-handed person who has to do something with his left.

Georg Christoph Lichtenberg *The Lichtenberg Reader*: Aphorisms 1768–71

32 A girl with brains ought to do something else with them besides think.
Anita Loos *Gentlemen Prefer Blondes*, Ch. 1

33 I wrote somewhere once that the third rate mind was only happy when it was thinking with the majority, the second rate mind was only happy when it was thinking with the minority, and the first rate mind was only happy when it was thinking.
A. A. Milne *War with Honour*

34 The mind that has no fixed aim loses itself, for, as they say, to be everywhere is to be nowhere.
Michel de Montaigne *Essays*, Bk 1, Ch. 8

35 For we must not misunderstand ourselves; we are as much machines as mind.
Blaise Pascal *Pensées*, 470

36 Some minds speak about things, and some minds speak the things themselves.

Friedrich von Schelling quoted in Ralph Waldo Emerson, *Journal*, September–October 1850

37 As for the brain, it is all mystery and memory and electricity.

Richard Selzer *Confessions of a Knife*: 'Liver'

38 A man's mind does not differ in colour from his soul.

Seneca *Letters*, 195

39 It is the mind that maketh good or ill,
That maketh wretch or happy, rich or poor.

Edmund Spenser *The Faerie Queene*, Bk 6, Canto 9, Stanza 30

40 There is no psychology; there is only biography and autobiography.

Thomas S. Szasz *The Second Sin*: 'Psychology'

41 A mind all logic is like a knife all blade. It makes the hand bleed that uses it.
Rabindranath Tagore *Stray Birds*, 193

42 Once we are destined to live out our lives in the prison of our mind, our one duty is to furnish it well.

Peter Ustinov quoting his own play *Photo Finish*, in *Dear Me*, Ch. 20

43 The mind can also be an erogenous zone.

Raquel Welch quoted in J. R. Colombo, *Colombo's Hollywood*

See also ***Conscience and Consciousness; Intellect and Intelligence; Thought; Wisdom***

Money

1 An actuary is someone who finds accountancy too exciting.
Anon. definition quoted by Richard Boston in the *Guardian*, 20 July 1987

2 We may see the value God has for riches, by the people he gives them to.
Dr Arbuthnot in Alexander Pope, *Thoughts on Various Subjects*, 72

See also Baring; La Bruyère

3 Money is like muck, not good except it be spread.
Francis Bacon *Essays*: 'Of Seditions and Troubles'

4 Among bankers, the heart is just an internal organ and nothing more.
Honoré de Balzac *César Birotteau*, Ch. 4

5 If you would know what the Lord God thinks of money, you have only to look at those to whom He gives it.
Maurice Baring quoted by Dorothy Parker in Malcolm Cowley (ed.), *Writers at Work, First Series*

See also Arbuthnot; La Bruyère

6 So long as there are beggars, there will be mythology.
Walter Benjamin *Selected Writing*, Vol. 1, 1913–1926

7 Money is the instrument of measuring the quantity of pain or pleasure. Those who are not satisfied with the accuracy of this instrument must find out some other that shall be more accurate, or bid adieu to politics and morals.
Jeremy Bentham 'The Philosophy of Economic Science', in *Economic Writings*, p. 117

8 Wine maketh merry: but money answereth all things.
Bible, OT Ecclesiastes 10:19

9 To tax and to please, no more than to love and be wise, is not given to men.
Edmund Burke first speech on conciliation with America, 19 April 1774

10 Though Wisdom cannot be gotten for gold, still less can it be gotten without it. Gold, or the value that is equivalent to gold, lies at the root of Wisdom, and enters so largely into the very essence of the Holy Ghost that 'No gold, no Holy Ghost' may pass as an axiom.
Samuel Butler 2 *Notebooks*, Ch. 11: 'Modern Simony'

11 To a shower of gold most things are penetrable.
Thomas Carlyle *The French Revolution*, Pt 1, iii, 7

12 To be clever enough to get all that money, one must be stupid enough to want it.
G. K. Chesterton *The Wisdom of Father Brown*: 'Paradise of Thieves'

13 Only spending on yourself is enough to make you a miser.

Comtesse Diane *Les Glanes de la vie*, p. 36

14 Annual income twenty pounds, annual expenditure nineteen nineteen six, result happiness. Annual income twenty pounds, annual expenditure twenty pounds ought and six, result misery.

Charles Dickens *David Copperfield*, Ch. 12

15 Money doesn't talk, it swears.

Bob Dylan song: *It's Alright, Ma (I'm Only Bleeding)*

16 Everybody is always in favour of general economy and particular expenditure. **Anthony Eden** in the *Observer*, 'Sayings of the Week', 17 June 1956

17 God makes; and apparel shapes: but it's Money that finishes the Man. **Dr Thomas Fuller** *Gnomologia*, 1680

18 As soon as it comes up against reality, anything that is abstract or symbolic swallows both it and itself. So credit swallows money as well as itself.

Johann Wolfgang von Goethe *Maxims and Reflections*: 'Life and Character', 203

19 They who are of the opinion that Money will do every thing, may very well be suspected to do every thing for Money.

Marquis of Halifax *Moral Thoughts and Reflections*: 'Of Money'

20 Much money makes a Country poor, for it sets a dearer price upon everything. **George Herbert** *Jacula Prudentum*

21 People are reluctant to pay with confidence and love; they prefer to pay with money and goods. **Hermann Hesse** *Reflections*, 628

22 Put not your trust in money, but put your money in trust.

Oliver Wendell Holmes *The Autocrat at the Breakfast Table*, Ch. 2

23 Economy is going without something you do want in case you should, some day, want something you probably won't want.

Anthony Hope *The Dolly Dialogues*, 12

24 A bank is a place that will lend you money if you can prove you don't need it.

Bob Hope quoted in Alan Harrington, *Life in the Crystal Palace*: 'The Tyranny of Forms'

25 The size of sums of money appears to vary in a remarkable way according as they are being paid in or paid out.

Julian Huxley *Essays of a Biologist*, Ch. 5

26 Money is a horrid thing to follow, but a charming thing to meet.

Henry James *The Portrait of a Lady*, Ch. 35

27 There are few ways in which a man can be more innocently employed than in getting money.

Dr Samuel Johnson in James Boswell, *Life of Johnson*: to William Strahan, 27 March 1775

28 The importance of money essentially flows from its being a link between the present and the future.

John Maynard Keynes *The General Theory of Employment*, Bk 5, Ch. 21

29 Nothing shows more clearly how little God values the wealth, money, position and other worldly goods that he distributes than how and to what sort of men he gives them most generously.

Jean de La Bruyère *Characters*: 'Of Worldly Goods', 24

See also Arbuthnot; Baring

30 Money is like a sixth sense, without which you cannot make a complete use of the other five. **W. Somerset Maugham** *Of Human Bondage*, Ch. 51

31 The chief value of money lies in the fact that one lives in a world in which it is over-estimated.

H. L. Mencken *Chrestomathy*, 30: 'The Mind of Man'

32 Money can't buy friends, but you can get a better class of enemy.

Spike Milligan *Puckoon*, Ch. 6

33 For one person who dreams of making fifty thousand pounds, a hundred people dream of being left fifty thousand pounds.

A. A. Milne *If I May*: 'The Future'

34 In the midst of life we are in debt.

Ethel Watts Mumford, Oliver Herford, Addison Mizner *The Altogether New Cynic's Calendar of Revised Wisdom for 1907*

35 People are usually much more moved by economics than by morals.

Norah Phillips in the *Independent*, 'Quote Unquote', 30 March 1991

36 Switzerland has given new meaning to the term *bank robbers*.

Joseph Prescott *Aphorisms and Other Observations, Third Series*: 'Miscellany'

37 What's fame? Think nothing of it –
A patch upon a poet's rags. We need profit, profit, profit,
Money in our money-bags!

Alexander Pushkin *Conversation between a Bookseller and a Poet*

38 Money is good for bribing yourself through the inconveniences of life. **Gottfried Reinhardt** in Lillian Ross, *Picture*: 'Looks Like We're Still in Business'

39 Never invest your money in anything that eats or needs repainting.

Billy Rose in the *New York Post*, 1957

40 Riches are a power like that of electricity, acting only through inequalities or negations of itself. The force of a guinea you have in your pocket depends wholly on the default of a guinea in your neighbour's pocket. **John Ruskin** *Unto This Last*, Sect. 27

41 All decent people live beyond their incomes nowadays, and those who aren't respectable live beyond other people's. A few gifted individuals manage to do both. **Saki** *The Match-Maker*

42 Finance is the art of passing currency from hand to hand until it finally disappears. **Robert W. Sarnoff** in *Executive's Quotation Book*, ed. James Charlton

43 Nothing comes amiss, so money comes withal.
William Shakespeare *The Taming of the Shrew*, Act 1, Sc. 2, (82)

44 Nothing links man to man like the frequent passage from hand to hand of cash. **Walter Sickert** in *New Age*, 28 July 1910

45 Solvency is entirely a matter of temperament and not of income.
Logan Pearsall Smith *Afterthoughts*, 1

46 The art of living easily is to pitch your scale of living one degree below your means. **Sir Henry Taylor** *Notes from Life*: 'Money'

47 Doänt thou marry for munny, but goä wheer munny is!
Alfred, Lord Tennyson *Northern Farmer. New Style*, 5

48 Almost any man knows how to earn money – but not one in a million knows how to spend it. If he had known how to spend it he would never have earned it. **H. D. Thoreau** *Journal*, Fall–Winter, 1845–6

49 Living in the lap of luxury isn't bad, except that you never know when luxury is going to stand up.
Tigers Don't Eat Grass: Oriental and Occidental Aphorisms 'Money'

50 Better a will in your favour than a will of your own.
Sydney Tremayne *Tatlings*, p. 52

51 A banker is a fellow who lends you his umbrella when the sun is shining and wants it back the minute it begins to rain.
Mark Twain (attrib.) in *Greatly Exaggerated*, ed. Alex Ayres

52 The man who leaves money to charity in his will is only giving away what no longer belongs to him. **Voltaire** letter, 1769

53 Nothing is as mean as the man who has a million, unless it be the man who has two. **Samuel Gray Ward** in Ralph Waldo Emerson, *Journal*, 25? December 1870

54 Algebra and money are essentially levellers; the first intellectually, the second effectively. **Simone Weil** *Grace and Gravity*: 'Algebra'

55 There is always more brass than brains in an aristocracy.
Oscar Wilde *Vera, or the Nihilists*, Act 3

56 You can be young without money but you can't be old without it.
Tennessee Williams *Cat on a Hot Tin Roof*, Act 1

57 Proportion your alms to your estate, lest God proportion your estate to your alms. **Bishop Thomas Wilson** *Sacra Privata*: 'Saturday'

58 A broker is a man who runs your fortune into a shoestring.
Alexander Woollcott in R. E. Drennan, *Wit's End*

*See also **Business; Rich and Poor***

Morals

1 I like the English. They have the most rigid code of immorality in the world. **Malcolm Bradbury** *Eating People is Wrong*, Ch. 5

2 The only absolute morality is absolute stagnation, but this is unpractical. **Samuel Butler 2** *Notebooks*, Ch. 11: 'Genius'

3 The only incorruptible thing is morals. All the religions soon go to ruin. They get encrusted with miracles, and divert attention from the rule.
Ralph Waldo Emerson *Journal*, May 1865

4 The human race has always been unable to distinguish clearly between metaphysics and morality. **Celia Green** *The Human Evasion*, Ch. 7

5 Morality is always the product of terror; its chains and strait-waist-coats are fashioned by those who dare not trust others, because they dare not trust themselves, to walk in liberty.
Aldous Huxley *Do What You Will*: 'Pascal', Sect. 23

6 The quality of moral behaviour varies in inverse ratio to the number of human beings involved. **Aldous Huxley** *Grey Eminence*, Ch. 10

7 The immorality of men triumphs over the amorality of women.
Karl Kraus *Half-Truths and One-and-a-Half Truths*: 'Not for women'

8 Morality which is based on ideas, or on an ideal, is an unmitigated evil. **D. H. Lawrence** *Fantasia of the Unconscious*, Ch. 7

9 The moral sensitivity of man is different at different times, stronger in the morning than in the evening.
Georg Christoph Lichtenberg *The Lichtenberg Reader*: Aphorisms 1764–70

10 I like a moral issue so much more than a real issue.

Elaine May quoted by Gore Vidal in the *New Statesman*, 4 May 1973

11 To some you must prove your morals useful, and to others useless.

Friedrich Nietzsche *Nietzsche in Outline and Aphorism*: 'Morality'

12 One becomes moral as soon as one is unhappy.

Marcel Proust *Remembrance of Things Past: Within a Budding Grove*: 'Madame Swann at Home'

13 Ethics is in origin the art of recommending to others the sacrifices required for co-operation with oneself.

Bertrand Russell *A Free Man's Worship and Other Essays*, Ch. 6

14 An Englishman thinks he is moral when he is only uncomfortable.

George Bernard Shaw *Man and Superman*, Act 3

15 The nations morals are like its teeth: the more decayed they are the more it hurts to touch them.

George Bernard Shaw *The Shewing Up of Blanco Posnet*: Preface, 'Star Chamber Sentimentality'

16 One should not destroy an insect, one should not quarrel with a dog, without a reason sufficient to vindicate one through all the courts of morality. **William Shenstone** *Essays on Men and Manners*: title essay

17 *Our whole life is* startlingly moral. There is never an instant's truce between virtue and vice. **H. D. Thoreau** *Walden*: 'Higher Laws'

18 The best laws cannot make a constitution work in spite of morals; morals can turn the worst laws to advantage.

Alexis de Tocqueville *Democracy in America*, Vol. 2, Appendix 5: 'Concerning the superiority of morals . . .'

19 To lower oneself is to rise in the domain of human gravity. Moral gravity makes us fall towards the heights. **Simone Weil** *Gravity and Grace*: title section

20 Morality is simply the attitude we adopt towards people whom we personally dislike. **Oscar Wilde** *An Ideal Husband*, Act 2

21 People are responsible for their *opinions*, but Providence is responsible for their morals. **W. B. Yeats** in Christopher Hassall, *Edward Marsh*, Ch. 6

See also ***Behaviour***

Music

1 Nothing is capable of being well set to music that is not nonsense.
Joseph Addison *The Spectator*, 18

2 If music in general is an imitation of history, opera in particular is an imitation of human wilfulness. **W. H. Auden** *The Dyer's Hand*, 8: 'Notes on Music'

3 Music is the best means we have of digesting time.
W. H. Auden in Robert Craft, *Stravinsky: Chronicle of a Friendship*

4 A musicologist is a man who can read music but can't hear it.
Sir Thomas Beecham in H. Proctor-Gregg, *Beecham Remembered*: 'Beecham's Obiter Dicta'

5 A tenor is not a man but a disease.
Hans von Bülow quoted in Harold C. Schonberg, *The Great Conductors*

6 Music says nothing to the reason: it is a kind of closely structured nonsense. **Anthony Burgess** in the *Observer*, 23 July 1989

7 Doubt creeps in everywhere, with, however, a signal exception: there is no *sceptical* music. **E. M. Cioran** *Anathemas and Admirations*, 9

8 Only since Beethoven has music addressed itself to men: before him, it was concerned only with god.
E. M. Cioran *A Short History of Decay*, 6: 'Secularization of Tears'

9 Music hath charms to soothe a savage breast,
To soften rocks, or bend a knotted oak.
William Congreve *The Mourning Bride*, Act 1, Sc. 1

10 Music is the arithmetic of sounds as optics is the geometry of light.
Claude Debussy in Nat Shapiro, *Encyclopedia of Quotations about Music*

11 Music does not change our frame of mind; it makes us feel what we think. **Comtesse Diane** *Maxims of Life*, p. 37

12 A song is anything that can walk by itself.
Bob Dylan song: *Bringing It All Back Home*, sleeve notes

13 The hidden harmony is better than the obvious. **Heraclitus** *Fragments*, 116

14 Music helps not the tooth-ache. **George Herbert** Jacula Prudentium

15 Painting transforms space into time. Music time into space.
Hugo von Hofmannsthal *The Book of Friends*, 4

16 Music – being identical with heaven – isn't a thing of momentary thrills or even hourly ones. It's a condition of eternity.
Gustav Holst letter to W. G. Whittaker, 4 June 1917

17 The piano is the easiest instrument to play in the beginning, and the hardest to master in the end.

Vladimir Horowitz in David Dubal, *Evenings with Horowitz*, Ch. 7

18 Of all musicians, flautists are most obviously the ones who know something we don't know.

Paul Jennings *The Jenguin Pennings*: 'Flautists Flaunt Afflatus'

19 Light music is music whose seriousness remains unnoticed.

Hans Keller *Maxims and Reflections*, 18

20 Talking about music is like dancing about architecture.

Steve Martin in the *Independent*, undated

21 Music creates order out of chaos; for rhythm imposes unanimity upon the divergent, melody imposes continuity upon the disjointed, and harmony imposes compatibility upon the incongruous.

Yehudi Menuhin quoted by Anthony Storr in the *Sunday Times*, 10 October 1976

22 Without music life would be a mistake.

Friedrich Nietzsche *Twilight of the Idols*: 'Maxims and Arrows', 33

23 The author's conviction . . . is that music begins to atrophy when it departs too far from the dance; that poetry begins to atrophy when it gets too far from music. **Ezra Pound** *ABC of Reading*: 'Warning'

24 Composition is notation of distortion of what composers think they've heard before. Masterpieces are marvellous misquotations.

Ned Rorem *Paris Diary*

25 Not everything in music is audible.

Charles Rosen on BBC Radio 3, 14 May 1997

26 Is it not strange that sheep's guts should hale souls out of men's bodies? **William Shakespeare** *Much Ado About Nothing*, Act 2, Sc. 3, (62)

27 Hell is full of musical amateurs: music is the brandy of the damned.

George Bernard Shaw *Man and Superman*, Act 3

28 A composer is not only an architect but also an inventor, and he should not build houses in which he cannot live.

Igor Stravinsky in *Neues Wiener Journal*, 26 March 1926

29 Instruments are nothing in themselves; the literature they play creates them. **Igor Stravinsky and Robert Craft** *Conversations with Igor Stravinsky*, 4

30 Music is natural law as related to the sense of hearing.

Anton von Webern *The Path to the New Music*

31 A tune is a kind of tautology, it is complete in itself; it satisfies itself.

Ludwig Wittgenstein *Notebooks 1914–16*, 4 March 1915

N

Nations and Races

1 One is always being told that they [the Americans] are a young nation, but they remain young only because they are rediscovered annually by Europeans. **Peter Ackroyd** *The Last Testament of Oscar Wilde*, 29 August 1900

2 A German is someone who cannot tell a lie without believing it himself. **Theodor Adorno** *Minima Memoralia*, Pt 2, 72

3 Every third German is a motor-car.
Martin Allwood *Something Like Aphorisms*: 'Life, Existence, and Death'

4 If nationality is consent, the state is compulsion.
Henri-Frédéric Amiel *Amiel's Journal*, 17 December 1856

5 France has always believed that a thing said is a thing done.
Henri-Frédéric Amiel *Amiel's Journal*, 23 May 1873

6 Frenchmen don't know what they want and will never be satisfied till they get it.
Anon. in Edward Meryon, *Epitaphs, Personal Anecdotes and Epigrams*: 'Quotations'

7 If the national mental illness of the United States is megalomania, that of Canada is paranoid schizophrenia.
Margaret Atwood in *Barnes and Noble Book of Quotations*, ed. Robert I. Fitzhenry: 'Canada'

8 The French are wiser than they seem, and the Spaniards seem wiser than they are. **Francis Bacon** *Essays*: 'Of Seeming Wise'

9 Of all nations in the world the English are perhaps the least a nation of pure philosophers. **Walter Bagehot** *The English Constitution*, Ch. 2

10 Everybody's coloured or else you wouldn't be able to see them.
Captain Beefheart in *Dictionary of Outrageous Quotations*, compiled C. R. S. Marsden

11 Other people have a nationality. The Irish and the Jews have a psychosis. **Brendan Behan** *Richard's Cork Leg*, Act 1

12 History had created something new in the USA, namely crookedness with self-respect or duplicity with honour.

Saul Bellow *Humboldt's Gift*, p. 217

13 Canada is a country so square that even the female impersonators are women.

Richard Benner in film *Outrageous*, quoted in the *Guardian*, 21 September 1978

14 Nations, like men, have their infancy.

Lord Bolingbroke *On the Study of History*, Letter 4

15 Every Spaniard is like a man-of-war, armed cap-à-pie to defend himself. That is why so much restraint and good manners are necessary. One man-of-war must reassure the other man-of-war that its guns will not be wanted. **Gerald Brenan** *Thoughts in a Dry Season*: 'People and Places'

16 The fate of nations depends on the way they eat.

Jean-Anthelme Brillat-Savarin *The Physiology of Taste*: Aphorisms, III

17 A nation is not conquered which is perpetually to be conquered.

Edmund Burke speech on conciliation with America, 22 March 1775

18 One day the United States discovered it was an empire. But it didn't know what an empire was. It thought that an empire was merely the biggest of all corporations.

Roberto Calasso *The Ruin of Kasch*: 'The Organization Wouldn't Like It'

19 The Englishman likes to imagine himself at sea, the German in a forest. It is impossible to express the difference of their national identity more concisely. **Elias Canetti** *Crowds and Power*: 'The Crowd in History'

20 The unity of a nation consists mainly in its being able to act, when necessary, like a single paranoic. **Elias Canetti** *The Human Province*: '1945'

21 The Germans classify, but the French arrange.

Willa Cather *Death Comes to the Archbishop*: 'Prologue'

22 France is that place where it is always useful to expose your vices and always dangerous to expose your virtues.

Nicholas-Sébastien Chamfort *Maxims and Considerations*, 494

23 An Englishman respects the law and rejects or despises authority; a Frenchman respects authority and despises the law.

Nicholas-Sébastien Chamfort *Maxims and Considerations*, 517

24 Our self-esteem and conceit are European, but our culture and actions are Asiatic. **Anton Chekhov** *Notebooks 1894–1902*, p. 51; of Russians

25 The English never draw a line without blurring it.

Winston S. Churchill speech in House of Commons, 16 November 1948

26 All sanctity is more or less Spanish; if god were a cyclops, Spain would be his eye. **E. M. Cioran** *A Short History of Decay*, 4: 'Spain'

27 America is the only nation in history which miraculously has gone directly from barbarism to degeneration without the usual interval of civilization. **Georges Clemenceau (attrib.)** in *Saturday Review*, 1 December 1945

28 I did not understand that America was a creation of Europeans who did not like Europe. **Cyril Connolly** epigraph to Hilde Spiel, *The Darkened Room*

29 Since both its [Switzerland's] national products, snow and chocolate, melt, the cuckoo clock was invented solely in order to give tourists something solid to remember it by.

Alan Coren *The Sanity Inspector*: 'And Though They Do Their Best'

30 In England, the system is benign and the people are hostile. In America, the people are friendly – and the system is brutal!

Quentin Crisp interview in the *Guardian*, 23 October 1985

31 The French tipple all the time and kill their livers, and the Scots drink in bouts and kill their neighbours.

John Crofton at press conference, Edinburgh, 18 January 1985

32 The Arabs are only Jews upon horseback.

Benjamin Disraeli *Tancred*, Bk 4, Ch. 3

33 The English and the Irish are very much alike, except that the Irish are more so. **Revd Mgr James Dunne** in conversation, during the Irish Troubles

34 Nationalism is an infantile disease. It is the measles of mankind.

Albert Einstein *The World as I See It*

35 It is remarked of the Americans that they value dexterity too much, and honour too little; that they think they praise a man more by saying he is 'smart' than by saying that he is right.

Ralph Waldo Emerson *The Fugitive Slave Law*

36 The American lays himself out to please. The Englishman has himself to please. **Ralph Waldo Emerson** *Journal*, 1853

37 For the black man there is only one destiny. And it is white.

Frantz Fanon *Black Skin, White Masks*: Introduction

38 The Swiss who are not a people so much as a neat clean quite solvent business. **William Faulkner** *Intruder in the Dust*, 7

39 There are no second acts in American lives.

F. Scott Fitzgerald *The Last Tycoon*: 'Notes'

40 Like all self-controlled people, the French talk to themselves.
F. Scott Fitzgerald *Notebooks*, O

41 England is the paradise of women, the purgatory of men, and the hell of horses. **John Florio** *Second Fruits*

42 Nationalism is a cheap instinct and a dangerous tool. Take away from any country what it *owes to* other countries; and then be proud of it if you can. **John Fowles** *The Aristos*, Ch. 9, 21

43 The Jews have undergone a one-sided development and admire brains more than bodies.
Sigmund Freud quoted in Adam Phillips, *On Kissing, Tickling and Being Bored*, Ch. 11

44 A proud little nation [Switzerland] sees itself in danger: it has asked for workers, and has been given human beings.
Max Frisch *Sketchbooks 1966–1971*, 1966

45 What the United States does best is to understand itself. What it does worst is understand others. **Carlos Fuentes** in *Time* magazine, 16 June 1986

46 The Muscovite women esteem none loving husbands except they beat their wives. **Thomas Fuller** *The Holy State, and the Profane State*, Bk 3, Ch. 13

47 Nation states do not have friends, only interests.
Charles de Gaulle (attrib.) in *New Society*, 8 August 1986

48 All American males are failed athletes.
Pete Gent in the *Weekend Guardian*, 8–9 July 1989

49 Nations, like men, die by imperceptible disorders. We recognize a doomed people by the way they sneeze or pare their nails.
Jean Giraudoux *Tiger at the Gates*, Act 2

50 I am a true Englishman, formed to discover nothing but to improve anything. **William Godwin** quoted in Don Locke, *A Fantasy of Reason*

51 Of all peoples, the Greeks have dreamt the dream of life the best.
Johann Wolfgang von Goethe *Maxims and Reflections*: 'Life and Character', 189

52 The English are crooked as a nation and honest as individuals. The contrary is true of the French, who are honest as a nation and crooked as individuals. **Edmond and Jules de Goncourt** *Journal*, 2 November 1868

53 An Englishman is a man who lives on an island in the North Sea governed by Scotsmen.
Philip Guedalla *Supers and Supermen*: 'Some More Frenchmen'

See also Johnson

54 It took man 250,000 years to transcend the hunting pack. It will not take him so long to transcend the nation.

J. B. S. Haldane *Daedalus or Science and the Future*

55 The English attitude to their own institutions: defend them to strangers but laugh at them yourselves. The privilege of not seeming to take anything seriously. But still making sure that nothing is changed!

David Hare *Amy's View*, Act 2

56 The true difference between the vanity of a Frenchman and an Englishman seems to be this – the one thinks everything right that is French, the other thinks everything wrong that is not English.

William Hazlitt *Characteristics*, 334

57 The Italians are wise before the deed, the Germans in the deed, the French after the deed. **George Herbert** *Jacula Prudentum*

58 The German has enormous objectivity and a very poor relationship to facts. **Hugo von Hofmannsthal** *The Book of Friends*, 3

59 A nation is a society united by a delusion about its ancestry and by a common hatred of its neighbours.

W. R. Inge in Sagittarius and Daniel George, *The Perpetual Pessimist*

60 A people, (The Romans), who, while they were poor, robbed mankind; and as soon as they became rich, robbed one another.

Dr Samuel Johnson reviewing *Memoirs of the Court of Augustus*, quoted in James Boswell, *Life of Johnson*, 1756

61 The Irish are a fair people; they never speak well of one another.

Dr Samuel Johnson in James Boswell, *Life of Johnson*, 1775

62 Sir, it is not so much to be lamented that Old England is lost, as that the Scotch have found it.

Dr Samuel Johnson in James Boswell, *Life of Johnson*, 1776

See also Guedalla

63 If the French were German in their essence, then how the Germans would admire them! **Franz Kafka** *The Diaries of Franz Kafka*, 17 December 1910

64 The people of the world respect a nation that can see beyond its own image.

President John F. Kennedy in the *Saturday Review*: 'Ideas, Attitudes, Purposes from his Speeches and Writings', 7 December 1963

65 In Ireland there's a precedent for everything. Except common sense.

Benedict Kiely *Nothing Happens in Carmincross*: 'The Landing'

66 The great nations have always acted like gangsters, and the small nations like prostitutes. **Stanley Kubrick** in the *Guardian*, 5 June 1963

67 The Jew is neither a race nor a religion
but a complaint. **Irving Layton** *The Whole Bloody Bird*: 'aphs'

68 Nationalism: a snarl wrapped up in a flag.
Irving Layton *The Whole Bloody Bird*: 'aphs'

69 Canadians are a good people –
I can find nothing else
to say against them. **Irving Layton** *The Whole Bloody Bird*: 'aphs'

70 The problem with Ireland is that it's a country full of genius, but with absolutely no talent. **Hugh Leonard** interview in *The Times*, August 1977

71 To an Englishman something is what it is called: to a Scotsman something is what it is.
Hugh MacDiarmid epigraph to Lewis Grassic Gibbon and Hugh MacDiarmid, *Scottish Scene*

72 North Americans have a peculiar bias. They go outside to be alone and they go home to be social.
Marshall McLuhan in the *Sunday Times Magazine*, 26 March 1978

73 But then the country is our religion. The true religion of America has always been America.
Norman Mailer interview in *Time Out*, 27 September–3 October 1984

74 Instead of leading the world, America appears to have resolved to buy it. **Thomas Mann** letter to Mr Gray, 12 October 1947

75 England is the only country where food is more dangerous than sex.
Jackie Mason *The World According to Me*

76 The worth of the state, in the long run, is the worth of the individuals composing it. **John Stuart Mill** *On Liberty*, Ch. 3

77 It will not do to say that Negroes are men, lest it turn out that whites are not. **Comte de Mirabeau** quoted by Ralph Waldo Emerson, *The Fugitive Slave Law*

78 A little of everything and nothing thoroughly, after the French fashion. **Michel de Montaigne** *Essays*, Bk 1, Ch. 26

79 Austria is Switzerland, speaking pure German and with history added. **J. E. Morpurgo** *The Road to Athens*

80 The master illusion of Spain is the conviction that the Spaniards are a people different, when they are only a people separate.
Jan Morris *The Presence of Spain*

81 Nations die of softening of the brain, which, for a long time, passes for softening of the heart.
Coventry Patmore *The Rod, the Root and the Flower*: 'Aurea Dicta', 101

82 It may be that Britain just before the millennium is a Teflon society where no principles find a sticking point.

Tom Paulin in the *Observer*, 24 October 1999

83 *Ex Africa semper aliquid novi.* – There is always something new out of Africa. **Proverbial adaptation of Pliny the Elder** *Natural History*, Bk 8, 17

84 The most civilized peoples are as close to barbarism as polished metal is to rust. Peoples, like metals, have only a surface brilliance.

Antoine de Rivarol *Les Plus belles pages*, Le Livre Club edn, p. 30

85 In America everything goes and nothing matters, while in Europe nothing goes and everything matters.

Philip Roth interview in *Time* magazine, November 1983

86 Our nationality is like our relations to women: too implicated in our moral nature to be changed honourably and too accidental to be worth changing. **George Santayana** epigraph to Ernest Gellner, *Nations and Nationalism*

87 Your average Frenchman, seeing another Frenchman, assumes he's an enemy unless he proves a friend. In Britain, it's the other way round.

Walter Schwarz in the *Guardian Weekly*, 9 September 1984

88 There is no race so quick to welcome the new as the English, and so slow to master the essence of novelty.

George Bernard Shaw *Dramatic Opinions* in W. Burton Baldry, *Topical Epigrams*

89 I look upon Switzerland as an inferior sort of Scotland.

Revd Sydney Smith letter to Lord Holland, 1815

90 Nationalism is, in fact, the counterpart among nations of what individualism is within them. **R. H. Tawney** *The Acquisitive Society*, 4

91 Nationalism was an economic force before nationality was a political fact. **R. H. Tawney** *Religion and the Rise of Capitalism*, Ch. 2, i

92 It sometimes happens that he who would not hurt a fly will hurt a nation. **Sir Henry Taylor** *The Statesman*, Ch. 9

93 A Russian does nothing but tempt God with various rational proposals about the best way to run the world. Russians give God a lot of trouble. **Abram Tertz** *A Voice from the Chorus*, Pt 3

94 There are still parts of Wales where the only concession to gaiety is a striped shroud. **Gwyn Thomas** in *Punch*, 18 June 1958

95 Russia is an enormous lunatic asylum. There is a heavy padlock on the door, but there are no walls. **Tatyana Tolstaya** in the *Guardian*, 19 March 1992

96 America is a large, friendly dog in a very small room. Every time it wags its tail it knocks over a chair.

Arnold Toynbee broadcast news summary, 14 July 1954

97 France has neither winter nor summer nor morals – apart from these drawbacks it is a fine country. **Mark Twain** *Notebooks*, 18, 1879

98 People have forgotten the effects of Prohibition. We have become the United States of Amnesia. **Gore Vidal** interview in the *Observer*, 20 August 2000

99 The Irish long to please: it is the secret of their charm. The English have a far deadlier quality. They yearn to be liked.
A. N. Wilson in the *Observer*, 'Sayings of the Week', 12 July 1998

100 It is never difficult to distinguish between a Scotsman with a grievance and a ray of sunshine.
P. G. Wodehouse *Blandings Castle*: 'The Custody of the Pumpkin'

101 What is patriotism but the love of the good things we ate in our childhood?
Lin Yutang quoted by W. H. Auden in M. F. K. Fisher, *The Art of Eating*: Introduction

Nature and the Natural

1 Nature, Mr Allnutt, is what we are put in this world to rise above.
James Agee in screenplay, *The African Queen*, based on novel by C. S. Forester

2 Nature, to be commanded, must be obeyed.
Francis Bacon *Novum Organum*, Bk 1, Aphorism 129

3 It is upon the flaws of Nature, not the laws of Nature, that the possibility of our existence hinges. **John D. Barrow** *The Artful Universe*, Ch. 2

4 Natural beauty is overpowering – it is the business of art to mitigate it. **Bernard Berenson** letter to Mary Berenson, 3 August 1936

5 A good naturalist cannot be a bad man.
Thomas Bewick quoted in Ralph Waldo Emerson, *Journal*, 1832

6 Natur iz a kind mother. She couldn't well afford to make us perfekt, so she made us blind to our failings.
Josh Billings *Wit and Humor*: Affurisms, 'Lobstir Sallad'

7 The cistern contains: the fountain overflows.
William Blake *The Marriage of Heaven and Hell*: 'Proverbs of Hell'

8 All things are artificial; for nature is the art of God.
Sir Thomas Browne *Religio Medici*, Pt 1, 16

9 In the natural world a good definition can only be a precise definition. **George-Louis de Buffon** *Histoire naturelle*: 'Premier discours'

10 A hen is only an egg's way of making another egg.
Samuel Butler 2 *Life and Habit*, Ch. 8

11 It clearly matters very little to nature whether man has a mind or not. **Eugène Delacroix** *Journal*, May 1850

12 Nature, like us is sometimes caught
without her diadem. **Emily Dickinson** *Complete Poems*, 1075

13 At no time and in no place, will nature ever ask your permission.
Fyodor Dostoevsky *Notes from the Underground*, Pt 1, 8

14 There is nothing so unnatural as the commonplace.
Arthur Conan Doyle *The Adventures of Sherlock Holmes*: 'A Case of Identity'

15 What is a weed? A plant whose virtues have not yet been discovered.
Ralph Waldo Emerson *The Fortune of the Republic*

16 Nature has a soft spot for humans, she's prejudiced in our favour, you might say. **Jean Giraudoux** *Ondine*, Act 1

17 Man and nature have such different views about the good of the world. **George Gissing** *Our Friend the Charlatan*, Ch. 21

See also Lawrence

18 The drama she plays is always new because she is always introducing a new audience. Life is her fairest invention, and Death is her device for having life in abundance. **Johann Wolfgang von Goethe** *Maxims and Reflections*: 'Nature'

19 Every moment she [Nature] embarks on the longest journey, and every moment reaches her goal.
Johann Wolfgang von Goethe *Maxims and Reflections*: 'Nature'

20 In nature there are neither rewards nor punishments – there are consequences. **R. G. Ingersoll** *Lectures and Essays, Third Series*: 'Some Reasons Why'

21 Nature is but a name for excess. **William James** *A Pluralistic Universe*, Ch. 7

22 The modern pantheist not only sees the god in everything, he takes photographs of it. **D. H. Lawrence** *St Mawr*

See also Gissing

23 In nature we find, not words, but only the initial letters of words, and if we then attempt to read them we find that the new so-called words are again merely the initial letters of other words.
Georg Christoph Lichtenberg *Aphorisms*, Notebook J, 265

24 Men have an extraordinarily erroneous opinion of their position in nature; and the error is ineradicable. **W. Somerset Maugham** *A Writer's Notebook*, 1896

25 One usually understands the artistic better than the natural. There is more spirit in the simple than the complicated, but less talent.

Novalis *Pollen*, 55

26 Nature has given to man nothing of more value than shortness of life. **Pliny** *Natural History*, vii, 5

27 Few and signally blest are those whom Jupiter has destined to be cabbage-planters. For they've always one foot on the ground, and the other not far from it. **François Rabelais** *Pantagruel*, IV, 18

28 Plants do not wish to rule the world like us: they have higher concerns. **Ned Rorem** *Paris Diary*, Pt 11

29 A large, branching, aged oak, is perhaps the most venerable of all inanimate objects. **William Shenstone** *Essays on Men and Manners*: 'Gardening'

30 Nature abhors a vacuum. **Benedict Spinoza** *Ethics*, Pt 1, Prop. 15, note

31 A lover of nature is pre-eminently a lover of man. If I have no friend – what is nature to me? She ceases to be morally significant.

H. D. Thoreau *Journal*, 29 June 1852

32 There are two worlds – the post office and Nature – I know them both. **H. D. Thoreau** *Journal*, 3 January 1853

33 It is a false dichotomy to think of nature *and* man. Mankind is that factor *in* nature which exhibits in its most intense form the plasticity of nature.

A. N. Whitehead in *The Faber Book of Aphorisms*, ed. W. H. Auden and Louis Kronenberger

34 It is fortunate for us, however, that Nature is so imperfect, as otherwise we should have no art at all. Art is our spirited protest, our gallant attempt to teach Nature her proper place. **Oscar Wilde** *The Decay of Lying*

35 One touch of Nature may make the whole world kin, but two touches of Nature will destroy any work of Art. **Oscar Wilde** *The Decay of Lying*

See also **Environments**

Needs and Necessity

1 In natural history, God's freedom is shown in the law of necessity. In moral history, God's necessity is shown in man's freedom.

Samuel Taylor Coleridge *Table Talk*, 18 May 1893

2 Most people need more love than they deserve.

Maria von Ebner-Eschenbach *Aphorisms*, p. 22

3 Nothing is enough to the man for whom enough is too little.

Epicurus *A Guide to Happiness*, ed. John Gaskin, p. 44

See also Halifax

4 We are designed to want: with nothing to want, we are like windmills in a world without wind. **John Fowles** *The Aristos*, Ch. 1, 34

5 For want of a nail the shoe was lost; for want of a shoe the horse was lost; and for want of a horse the rider was lost.

Benjamin Franklin *Poor Richard's (Improved) Almanack*, 1758

6 Modern man lives under the illusion that he knows what he wants, while he actually wants what he is supposed to want.

Erich Fromm *The Fear of Freedom*, 8

7 One of the best ways of avoiding necessary and even urgent tasks is to seem to be busily employed on things that are already done.

J. K. Galbraith *The Affluent Society*, Ch. 1, Sect. 2

8 The graveyards are full of indispensable men. **Charles de Gaulle (attrib.)**

9 Just enough of a good thing is always too little.

Marquis of Halifax *Miscellaneous Thoughts and Reflections*: 'Youth'

See also Epicurus

10 From each according to his abilities, to each according to his needs.

Karl Marx *Criticism of the Gotha Programme*

11 A man travels the world over in search of what he needs and returns home to find it. **George Moore** *The Brook Kerith*, Ch. 11

12 Give us the luxuries of life, and we will dispense with its necessities.

J. L. Motley quoted in Oliver Wendell Holmes, *The Autocrat at the Breakfast Table*, Ch. 6

13 Only useless things are indispensable.

Francis Picabia *Yes No, Poems and Sayings*: 'Sayings'

14 When I throw away what I don't want, it will fall within reach.

Antonio Porchia *Voices*

15 The loss of a thing affects us until we have lost it altogether.

Antonio Porchia *Voices*

16 Necessity gives the law, without acknowledging one itself.

Publilius Syrus *Moral Sayings*, 444; becomes proverb: Necessity has no law!

17 Logic only gives man what he needs. Magic gives him what he wants.

Tom Robbins *Another Roadside Attraction*, Pt 1

18 Sometimes we need to get a little more than we deserve.

Jean Rostand *Pensées d'un biologiste*, p. 142

19 The human need to find a strand of significance that will hold together everything that isn't on TV. **Philip Roth** *Sabbath's Theater*

20 Remember that the most beautiful things in the world are the most useless; peacocks and lilies for instance.
John Ruskin *The Stones of Venice*, I, Ch. 2, Sect. 17

21 It is the unnecessary things we sweat for. **Seneca** *Letters from a Stoic*, 4

22 Necessity may be the mother of lucrative invention; but is the death of poetical. **William Shenstone** *Essays on Men and Manners*, p. 195

23 The perfection of man is the love of use.
Emanuel Swedenborg *The Delights of Wisdom Concerning Conjugal Love*, p. 245

24 Having what you want is not nearly so interesting as getting what you want. **Sydney Tremayne** *Tatlings*, p. 27

25 The want of a thing is perplexing enough, but the possession of it is intolerable. **Sir John Vanbrugh** *The Confederacy*, Act 1, Sc. 2

26 The superfluous, a very necessary thing. **Voltaire** *Le Mondain*, 22

27 No man can lose what he never had.
Izaak Walton *The Compleat Angler*, Pt 1, Ch. 5

28 In this world there are only two tragedies. One is not getting what one wants, and the other is getting it. **Oscar Wilde** *Lady Windermere's Fan*, Act 3

29 Moderation is a fatal thing. Enough is as bad as a meal. More than enough is as good as a feast. **Oscar Wilde** *The Picture of Dorian Gray*, Ch. 15

30 It's better to be wanted for murder than not to be wanted at all.
Marty Winch *Psychology in the Wry*

31 Man wants but little; nor that little long.
Edward Young *Night Thoughts*: 'Night 4', 118

Numbers and Mathematics

1 Mathematics is a science of things thought of.
John D. Barrow *Theories of Everything*, Ch. 9

2 Like dreams, statistics are a form of wish fulfilment.
Jean Baudrillard *Cool Memories*, Ch. 4

3 As far as the laws of mathematics refer to reality, they are not certain, and as far as they are certain, they do not refer to reality.
Albert Einstein quoted in F. Capra, *The Tao of Physics*, Ch. 2

4 All operations with numbers are in essence counting, and short cuts to save counting all over again: that's to say, bringing the world into comparison with your fingers. **Michael Frayn** *Constructions*, 222

5 Mathematics becomes very odd when you apply it to people. One plus one can add up to so many different sums. **Michael Frayn** *Copenhagen*, Act 1

6 Indeed *number* cannot create a *new kind*; so that many trespasses cannot make a riot, many riots one treason, no more than many frogs make one toad. **Thomas Fuller** *The Worthies of England*: 'London: Writers'

7 Mathematicians are like a certain type of Frenchman: when you talk to them they translate it into their own language, and then it soon turns into something completely different.

Johann Wolfgang von Goethe *Maxims and Reflections* (Penguin), 1279

8 Statistics is the first of the inexact sciences.

Edmond and Jules de Goncourt *Journal*, 14 January 1861

9 We recognize a nothing at first sight, a something at second.

Friedrich Hebbel *Diaries*, entry 1641, 1839

10 The most I kin say fer some figgers is they'd be justified in lyin'.

'Kin' Hubbard *Abe Martin's Broadcast*: 'Family Albums'

11 Statistics show that of those who contract the habit of eating, very few ever survive.

William Wallace Irwin *Cook's Quotation Book*, ed. Maria Polushkin Robbins

12 Round numbers are always false.

Dr Samuel Johnson in James Boswell, *Life of Johnson*, Vol. 3, 226

13 Mathematics always follows where elegance leads.

Robert Kaplan *The Nothing That Is*, Ch. 7

14 He uses statistics as a drunken man uses lamp-posts – for support rather than illumination.

Andrew Lang in *A Dictionary of Scientific Quotations*, ed. A. L. Mackay

15 One geometry cannot be more true than another; it can only be more *convenient*. Geometry is not true, it is advantageous.

Henri Poincaré *Science and Hypothesis*, Ch. 3

16 A circle is the longest distance to the same point.

Tom Stoppard *Every Good Boy Deserves Favour*

Obstacles and Opportunities

1 A wise man will make more opportunities than he finds.

Francis Bacon *Essays*: 'Of Ceremonies and Respects'

2 A problem is simply the difference between what one has and what one wants . . . If description is a matter of looking back to see what one has then problem solving is a matter of looking forward to see what one can get.

Edward de Bono *Lateral Thinking*

3 Nothing is often or so irrevocably missed as the opportunity which crops up daily.

Maria von Ebner-Eschenbach *Aphorisms*, p. 21

4 For every complex problem there's a simple solution, and it's wrong.

Umberto Eco *Foucault's Pendulum*, Ch. 53

5 It's them as takes advantage that get advantage i' this world, I think: folks have to wait long enough afore it's brought to 'em.

George Eliot *Adam Bede*, Ch. 32

6 The best way out is always through.

Robert Frost *A Servant to Servants*

7 You can't set yourself a riddle.

Friedrich Hebbel *Diaries*, entry 3060, 1844

8 In order to prove its phoniness beyond reasonable doubt, a profession has to create grave problems which it then fails to solve.

Hans Keller *Criticism*, Pt 1, Ch. 1

9 There's one thing to be said for inviting trouble: it generally accepts.

Mae Maloo in *Reader's Digest*, September 1976

10 The world is an oyster, but you don't crack it open on a mattress.

Arthur Miller *Death of a Salesman*, Act 1

11 I have never managed to put only water in my water.

Francis Picabia *Yes No, Poems and Sayings*: 'Sayings'

12 Most people would like their own ways and other people's means.

Sydney Tremayne *Tatlings*, p. 62

13 One should, after a fashion, welcome and esteem the difficulties one encounters. A difficulty is a lamp. An insuperable difficulty, a sun.

Paul Valéry *Bad Thoughts and Not So Bad*, A

Opinions

1 To change your mind and defer to correction is not to sacrifice your independence; for doing this is your own decision and leaves you no less free than you were before. **Marcus Aurelius** *Meditations*, Bk 8, 16

2 The man who never alters his opinion is like standing water, and breeds reptiles of the mind.

William Blake *The Marriage of Heaven and Hell*: 'A Memorable Fancy: An Angel Came'

3 There is no Damocles like unto self opinion, nor any Siren to our own fawning conceptions. **Sir Thomas Browne** *Christian Morals*, Pt 1, 23

4 Every man speaks of public opinion, and means by public opinion, public opinion minus his opinion. **G. K. Chesterton** *Heretics*, Ch. 8

5 There's allays two 'pinions; there's the 'pinion a man has of himsen, and there's the 'pinion other folks have on him. There'd be two 'pinions about a cracked bell, if the bell could hear itself.

George Eliot *Silas Marner*, Ch. 6

6 The measure of a master is his success in bringing all men round to his opinion twenty years later.

Ralph Waldo Emerson *The Conduct of Life*: 'Culture'

7 Men are disturbed not by things themselves, but by their opinions or thoughts concerning those things. **Epictetus** *Manual*, 5

8 The advantage of being right is that you don't have to change your mind. **J. K. Galbraith** in BBC TV interview, June 1995

9 Our opponents think they have refuted us when they repeat their own opinions without paying any attention to ours.

Johann Wolfgang von Goethe *Goethe's Opinions*, p. 114

10 Men who borrow their Opinions can never repay their Debts.

Marquis of Halifax *Miscellaneous Thoughts and Reflections*

11 Those who never change their mind, love themselves better than the truth. **Joseph Joubert** *Thoughts and Maxims*, 161

12 A woman should not even be of *my* opinion, let alone hers.
Karl Kraus *Half-Truths and One-and-a-Half Truths*: 'Not for Women'

13 Innumerable people have never held any opinion that was not taken from their newspaper. **Gustave Le Bon** *Les Opinions et les croyances*

14 The greatest deception men suffer is from their own opinions.
Leonardo da Vinci *Selections from the Notebooks*, 6, III

15 What fresh views would we acquire if we could for once eliminate from our capital of truisms all that is not intrinsic but has accrued through frequent repetition?
Georg Christoph Lichtenberg *The Lichtenberg Reader*: Aphorisms, 1768–71

16 A golden rule: one must judge men not by their opinions, but by what their opinions have made of them.
Georg Christoph Lichtenberg *The Lichtenberg Reader*: Aphorisms 1789

17 New opinions are always suspected, and usually opposed, without any other reason but because they are not already common.
John Locke *Essay on the Human Understanding*: dedication

18 He who knows only his own side of the case knows little of that.
John Stuart Mill *On Liberty*, Ch. 2

19 Opinion in good men is but knowledge in the making.
John Milton *Areopagitica*

20 The nurse and mother of the falsest opinions, both public and private, is the excessive opinion that man has of himself.
Michel de Montaigne *Essays*, Bk 2, Ch. 17

21 No two men ever judged alike of the same thing, and it is impossible to find two opinions exactly similar, not only in different men but in the same man at different times. **Michel de Montaigne** *Essays*, Bk 3, Ch. 13

22 It is not the mind that forms opinions, but the heart.
Charles de Montesquieu *Essay on the Causes That Can Affect Minds and Characters*, Pt 2

23 A given opinion, as held by several individuals, even when of the most *congenial views, is as distinct as are their faces.*
Cardinal Newman *Oxford University Sermons*, 1843

24 Holding an opinion means preferring to be wrong in a particular way. **Jean Rostand** *Pensées d'un biologiste*, p. 144

25 The average man's opinions are much less foolish than they would be if he thought for himself. **Bertrand Russell (attrib.)**

26 A church can be so broadened that the roof falls in.

Michael Schmidt in *PN Review*, no. 61, 1988, editorial

27 My opinion is right but may be wrong and your opinion is wrong but may be right. **Imam al-Shafi'I (attrib.)**

28 As many opinions as there are men; each a law to himself.

Terence *Phormio*, 454

29 It is difference of opinion that makes horse races.

Mark Twain *Pudd'nhead Wilson*, Ch. 9: epigraph

30 It is only about things that do not interest one that one can give a really unbiased opinion, which is no doubt the reason why an unbiased opinion is always absolutely valueless. The man who sees both sides of a question is a man who sees absolutely nothing at all.

Oscar Wilde *The Critic as Artist*, 2

See also ***Agreement; Ideas; Prejudices; Thought***

Optimists and Pessimists

1 He is a real pessimist – he could look at a doughnut and only see the hole in it. **Anon.** in P. and J. Holton, *Quote and Unquote*

2 A pessimist is just a well-informed optimist.

Anon. quoted by Robert Mackenzie in the BBC TV programme *24 Hours*, 18 March 1968, as current Czech aphorism on Alexander Dubček's government

3 She not only expects the worst, but makes the worst of it when it happens. **Michael Arlen** in A. Andrews, *Quotations for Speakers and Writers*

4 Being a blind faith [optimism], it is inaccessible to the light of disproof – an intellectual disorder, yielding to no treatment but death. It is hereditary, but fortunately not contagious. **Ambrose Bierce** *The Devil's Dictionary*

5 The world is the best of all possible worlds, and *everything* in it is a necessary evil. **F. H. Bradley** *Appearance and Reality*: Preface

6 The pessimist is the man who believes things couldn't possibly be worse, to which the optimist replies: 'Oh yes they could!'

Vladimir Bukovsky in the *Guardian Weekly*, 10 July 1977

See also Cabell

7 The optimist proclaims that we live in the best of all possible worlds; and the pessimist fears this is so. **James Branch Cabell** *The Silver Stallion*, Bk 4, Ch. 26

See also Bukovsky

8 The best you can expect is to avoid the worst.

Italo Calvino *If on a Winter's Night a Traveller*, Ch. 1

9 Humanity never produces optimists till it has ceased to produce happy men.

G. K. Chesterton in *The Faber Book of Aphorisms*, ed. W. H. Auden and Louis Kronenberger

10 In arguments it is always the optimist who wins.

Hermann Hesse *Reflections*, 366

11 A pessimist is a man who has been compelled to live with an optimist. **Elbert Hubbard** *The Note Book of Elbert Hubbard*, p. 51

12 Never count on anything turnin' up but your toes.

'Kin' Hubbard *Abe Martin's Wisecracks*, p. 52

13 A man may be a pessimistic determinist before lunch and an optimistic believer in the will's freedom after it.

Aldous Huxley *Do What You Will*: 'Pascal', Sect. 23

14 The people who live in a Golden Age usually go around complaining how yellow everything looks. **Randall Jarrell** *A Sad Heart at the Supermarket*

15 Only a great cynic would be an optimist these days.

Milan Kundera interview with Philip Roth in the *Sunday Times Magazine*, 20 May 1984

16 If we see light at the end of the tunnel,
It's the light of the oncoming train. **Robert Lowell** *Day by Day*

17 Pessimism is a luxury that a Jew never can allow himself.

Golda Meir in the *Observer*, 'Sayings of the Year', 29 December 1974

18 A pessimist is a man who looks both ways before crossing a one-way street. **Laurence J. Peter** *Peter's Quotations*: 'Optimism – Pessimism'

19 I am an idealist. I don't know where I'm going but I'm on my way.

Carl Sandburg 'Incidentals'

20 The worst is not;
So long as we can say, 'This is the worst.'

William Shakespeare *King Lear*, Act 4, Sc. 1, 27

21 If you pretend to be good, the world takes you very seriously. If you pretend to be bad, it doesn't. Such is the astounding stupidity of optimism. **Oscar Wilde** *Lady Windermere's Fan*, Act 1

See also ***Hope and Despair; Ideals***

Others

1 Enter into the ruling principle of your neighbour's mind, and suffer him to enter into yours. **Marcus Aurelius** *Meditations*, Bk 8, 61

2 A crowd is not company, and faces are but a gallery of pictures.
Francis Bacon *Essays*: 'Of Friendship'

3 The life of him that dependeth on another man's table is not to be counted for a life; for he polluteth himself with other men's meat: but a wise man well nurtured will beware thereof.
Bible, Apocrypha Ecclesiasticus 40:29

4 Learn to shrink yourself to the size of the company you are in.
Earl of Chesterfield *Letters to His Son*, 18 December 1765

5 It is not the failure of others to appreciate your abilities which should trouble you, but rather their failure to appreciate theirs.
Confucius *The Analects*, Bk 1, 16

6 We put more effort into deceiving our neighbours than deceiving ourselves. **Comtesse Diane** *Les Glanes de la vie*, p. 199

7 One advantage of company, not the only one but considerable . . . It's pleasanter to agree with other people and exchange harmless little lies than to quarrel with oneself and exchange large hurtful truths.
D. J. Enright *Interplay*, p. 197

8 It is always possible to bind together a considerable number of people in love, so long as there are other people left over to receive the manifestations of their aggression. **Sigmund Freud** *Civilization and Its Discontents*, Ch. 5

9 The reality of the other person is not in what he reveals to you, but in what he cannot reveal to you. Therefore, if you would understand him, listen not to what he says, but to what he does not say.
Kahlil Gibran *Sand and Foam*, 14

10 We grow tired of everything but turning others into ridicule, and congratulating ourselves on their defects.
William Hazlitt *The Plain Speaker*: 'On the Pleasure of Hating'

11 Whenever two people meet there are really six people present. There is each man as he sees himself, each man as the other person sees him, and each man as he really is.
William James in Laurence J. Peter, *Peter's Quotations*

12 People are much more eccentric than they are supposed to be.
Randall Jarrell *Pictures from an Institution*, Ch. 3, 4

13 No two men can be half an hour together, but one shall acquire an evident superiority over the other.

Dr Samuel Johnson in James Boswell, *Life of Johnson*, 15 February 1766

14 A man's life – what is that worth? Another man exists only to the degree that he stands in your way. **Ryszard Kapuściński** *The Emperor*: 'The Throne'

15 The majority of men are subjective towards themselves and objective towards all others, terribly objective sometimes – but the real task is in fact to be objective towards oneself and subjective towards all others.

Søren Kierkegaard *The Journals*, 1847

16 All the people like us are We,
And every one else is They. **Rudyard Kipling** *We and They*

17 We all have strength enough to endure the troubles of others.

Duc de La Rochefoucauld *Maxims*, 19

See also Pope

18 I am convinced we do not only love ourselves in others but hate ourselves in others too.

Georg Christoph Lichtenberg *Aphorisms*, Notebook F, 54

19 I never knew any man in my life who could not bear another's misfortunes perfectly like a Christian.

Alexander Pope *Thoughts on Various Subjects*

See also Duc de La Rochefoucauld

20 Biology denies the individual any essential attribute that is not common to all beings. Whether he likes it or not, he drags them round with him like a huge army of beggars. And he has to share with them everything he calls his own. **Jean Rostand** *Pensées d'un biologiste*, p. 88

21 Hell is other people. **Jean-Paul Sartre** *Huis clos* (*In Camera*), Sc. 5

22 Quite a common observation is: 'It takes all sorts to make a world.' This may well be true: but if it is – where are they all?

Idries Shah *Reflections*: 'The Difference between Saying and Doing'

23 One touch of nature makes the whole world kin.

William Shakespeare *Troilus and Cressida*, Act 3, Sc. 3, 175

24 Do not do unto others as you would they should do unto you. Their tastes may not be the same.

George Bernard Shaw *Man and Superman*, 'Maxims for Revolutionists': 'The Golden Rule'

25 The world can be divided into people that read, people that write, people that think, and fox-hunters.

William Shenstone *Essays on Men and Manners*: 'On Writing and Books'

26 No one can be perfectly free till all are free; no one can be perfectly moral till all are moral; no one can be perfectly happy till all are happy.
Herbert Spencer *Social Statics*, Pt 4, Ch. 30, 16

27 We must all learn to be guests of each other.
George Steiner interview in the *Guardian*, 19 May 1981

28 If you cannot mould yourself as you would wish, how can you expect other people to be entirely to your liking?
Thomas à Kempis *Imitation of Christ*, 16

29 Humankind must at last grow up. We must recognize that the Other is ourselves.
E. P. Thompson *Beyond the Cold War*

30 We only die when we fail to take root in others.
Leon Trotsky quoted in Trevor Griffiths, *The Party*, Act 2

31 We find in ourselves what others hide from us; and recognize in others what we hide from ourselves.
Marquis de Vauvenargues *Reflections and Maxims*, 106

32 Other people are quite dreadful. The only possible society is oneself.
Oscar Wilde *An Ideal Husband*, Act 3

Pain and Suffering

1 From suffering, knowledge. **Aeschylus** *Agamemnon*, 177

2 Life is unbearable without suffering.
Margaret Mary Alacoque quoted in E. M. Cioran, *Tears and Saints*

3 It is characteristic of pain not to be ashamed of repeating itself. It is not by genius, it is by suffering, by suffering only, that one ceases to be a marionette. **E. M. Cioran** *Anathemas and Admirations*, 7

4 Cleanliness is sometimes a painful good, as anyone can vouch who has had his face washed the wrong way, by a pitiless hand with a gold ring on the third finger.
George Eliot *Scenes of Clerical Life*: 'Mr Gilfil's Love-Story', Ch. 3

5 Trouble has no necessary connection with discouragement – discouragement has a germ of its own, as different from trouble as arthritis is different from a stiff joint. **F. Scott Fitzgerald** *The Crack-up*: 'Handle with Care'

6 Eighteen is a good time for suffering. One has all the necessary strength, and no defences. **William Golding** *The Pyramid*, p. 12

7 The least pain in our little finger gives us more concern and uneasiness than the destruction of millions of our fellow-beings.
William Hazlitt 'American Literature – Dr Channing', in *Edinburgh Review*, October 1829

8 *The Two Ways*: One is to suffer; the other is to become a professor of the fact that another suffered. **Søren Kierkegaard** *The Journals*, p. 528

9 Rather suffer than die is man's motto.
Jean de La Fontaine *Fables*, I, 16: 'Death and the Woodcutter'

10 Most troubles only run at us, because we go to meet them half way.
Duc de Lévis *Maximes et réflexions*, 6

11 We feel public misfortune only in so far as it affects our private interests.
Livy *History of Rome*, Bk 30, 44

12 Nothing is necessary except God, and nothing is more unnecessary than pain.
Joseph de Maistre *St Petersburg Nights*: Fifth Conversation

13 A man who fears suffering is already suffering from what he fears.
Michel de Montaigne *Essays*, Bk 3, Ch. 13

14 The supreme greatness of man lies in his knowledge that he is miserable. A tree does not know that it is miserable.
Blaise Pascal *Pensées*, 255

15 One nail drives out another. But four nails make a cross.
Cesare Pavese *This Business of Living, A Diary 1935–1950*, 16 August 1950

16 If you could escape your sufferings, and did so, where would you go outside them?
Antonio Porchia *Voices*

17 Illness is the most heeded of doctors: to kindness and wisdom we make promises only; pain we obey.
Marcel Proust *Remembrance of Things Past: Cities of the Plain*, Pt 2, Ch. 1

18 Claude Bernard said in dying: I don't complain of suffering, but of suffering for nothing. The same could be said by humanity.
Jean Rostand *Pensées d'un biologiste*, p. 117

19 He that sleeps feels not the toothache.
William Shakespeare *Cymbeline*, Act 5, Sc. 4, (176)

20 Pain is needed for the complete, liberating feeling of happiness, which it leaves behind when it goes.
Abram Tertz *A Voice from the Chorus*, Pt 2

21 Pain is what we feel at once most intimately ours, and most foreign to ourselves.
Paul Valéry *Bad Thoughts and Not So Bad*, O

22 It is necessary to uproot oneself. To cut down the tree and make of it a cross, and then to carry it every day.
Simone Weil *Gravity and Grace*: 'Decreation'

23 Ulcers and the dung-heap were necessary before Job could receive the revelations of the world's beauty. For there is no detachment where there is no pain.
Simone Weil *Gravity and Grace*: 'Illusions'

See also ***Health and Illness; Sorrow***

Past and Present

1 For one thing is denied even to God,
To make what has been done undone again.
Agathon quoted in Aristotle, *Ethics*, Bk 6, ii

2 The past was never just the past, it was what made the present able to live with itself. **Julian Barnes** *England, England*, 1

3 There's no comeback for a has-been.
Busby Berkeley quoted in Robert Calasso, *The Ruin of Kasch*: 'Bien-Aimé'

4 People will not look forward to posterity, who never look backward to their ancestors. **Edmund Burke** *Reflections on the Revolution in France*, p. 119

5 Tradition may be defined as an extension of the franchise. Tradition means giving votes to the most obscure of all classes, our ancestors. It is the democracy of the dead. **G. K. Chesterton** *Orthodoxy*, Ch. 4

6 To remain ignorant of what happened before you were born is to remain always a child. **Cicero** quoted in the *Guardian*, 12 January 2000

7 No man can cause more grief than that one clinging blindly to the vices of his ancestors. **William Faulkner** *Intruder in the Dust*, Ch. 3

8 Today is Yesterday's Pupil.
Benjamin Franklin *Poor Richard's (Improved) Almanack*, 1751

9 Ah, *now*! That odd time – the oddest time of all times; the time it always is . . . by the time we've reached the 'w' of 'now' the 'n' is ancient history. **Michael Frayn** *Constructions*, 126

10 The preoccupation of the humanities with the past is sometimes made a reproach against them by those who forget that we face the past: it may be shadowy, but it is all that there is.
Northrop Frye quoted in Randall Jarrell, *A Sad Heart at the Supermarket*: title essay

11 Writing is a way of getting rid of the past.
Johann Wolfgang von Goethe *Maxims and Reflections*: 'Life and Character', 80

12 He who cannot draw on three thousand years is living from hand to mouth. **Johann Wolfgang von Goethe** epigraph to Jostein Gaarder, *Sophie's World*

13 The reason for the sadness of this modern age and the men who live in it is that it looks for the truth in everything and finds it.
Edmond and Jules de Goncourt *Journal*, 23 October 1864

14 Today has length, breadth, thickness, colour, smell, voice. As soon as it becomes *yesterday* it is a thin layer among many layers, without substance, colour, or articulate sound.

Thomas Hardy in notebook, 27 January 1907; quoted in Florence Emily Hardy, *The Life of Thomas Hardy*, Ch. 23

15 The most obscure period of time was that which was too old to be news and too young to be history – the day before yesterday as it were.

Rupert Hart-Davis letter, 8 April 1956, *Lyttelton–Hart-Davis Letters*, Vol. 3

16 The past is a foreign country: they do things differently there.

L. P. Hartley *The Go-between*: opening words

17 *Carpe diem, quam minimum credula postero.* – Seize today, and put as little trust as you can in the morrow. **Horace** *Odes*, xi, 8

18 Events in the past may roughly be divided into those which probably never happened and those which do not matter.

W. R. Inge *Assessments and Anticipations*: 'Prognostications'

19 I do not know which makes a man more conservative – to know nothing but the present, or nothing but the past.

John Maynard Keynes *The End of Laissez-faire*, Pt 1

20 As the present character of a man, so his past, so his future. Who knows intuitively the history of the past, knows his destiny to come.

Johann Kaspar Lavater *Aphorisms on Man*, 43; William Blake underlined the last part in approval

21 procrastination is the
art of keeping
up with yesterday **Don Marquis** *archy and mehitabel*, XII: 'certain maxims of archy'

22 The snows of yesterday can't be refreezed.

Denis Norden in BBC radio programme, *My Word*, 5 October 1977

23 If anyone examines his thoughts, he will find them entirely taken up with the past or the future. We hardly think of the present at all, and if we do give it a thought, it is only to borrow a light from it to direct the future. **Blaise Pascal** *Pensées*, 168

24 Homer is new this morning and perhaps nothing is as old as today's paper. **Charles Péguy** *Basic Verities*: 'The Future'

25 All I have ever made was made for the present, and with the hope that it will always remain in the present.

Pablo Picasso in John Berger, *The Success and Failure of Picasso*, 1

26 I think we should always look back on our own past with a sort of tender contempt.

Dennis Potter *Seeing the Blossom*, an interview with Melvyn Bragg, Channel 4 TV, April 1994

27 Every epoch is immediate to God.

Leopold von Ranke quoted in Peter Gay, *Style in History*, Ch. 2

28 Man spends his life in reasoning on the past, in complaining of the present, in fearing for the future.

Antoine de Rivarol in J. R. Solly, *Selected Thoughts from the French*: 'Life and Death'

29 Those who do not remember the past are condemned to repeat it.

George Santayana *The Life of Reason*, Vol. 1, Ch. 12

30 What's gone and what's past help
Should be past grief. **William Shakespeare** *The Winter's Tale*, Act 3, Sc. 2, 223

31 They don't sell tickets to the past.

Alexander Solzhenitsyn *The First Circle*, Ch. 37

32 The obscurest epoch is today. **Robert Louis Stevenson** *Ethical Studies*, p. 113

33 Life is one tenth Here and Now, nine-tenths a history lesson. For most of the time the Here and Now is neither now nor here.

Graham Swift *Waterland*, 8

34 For he to whom the present is the only thing that is present, knows nothing of the age in which he lives. **Oscar Wilde** *The Critic as Artist*, 2

35 What other people call one's past has, no doubt, everything to do with them, but has absolutely nothing to do with oneself. The man who regards his past is a man who deserves to have no future to look forward to. **Oscar Wilde** *The Critic as Artist*, 2

36 To be really medieval one should have no body. To be really modern one should have no soul. To be really Greek one should have no clothes. **Oscar Wilde** *For the Instruction of the Over-educated*

37 Even you are not rich enough, Sir Robert, to buy back the past.

Oscar Wilde *An Ideal Husband*, Act 1

38 Hindsight is always twenty-twenty.

Billy Wilder quoted in J. R. Colombo, *Colombo's Hollywood*

See also ***The Future; History; Time***

Patience

1 A fool uttereth all his mind: but a wise man keepeth it in till afterwards. **Bible, OT** Proverbs 29:11

2 **Patience, n.** A minor form of despair, disguised as a virtue.
Ambrose Bierce *The Devil's Dictionary*

3 We have but a bad bargain, God knows, of this life, and patience is the only way not to make bad worse.
Earl of Chesterfield *Letters to His Son*, 28 November 1765

4 Patience is passive, resignation is active. **Penelope Fitzgerald** *Innocence*, 32

5 Perhaps there is only one cardinal sin: impatience. Because of impatience they were expelled, because of impatience they do not return. **Franz Kafka** *Collected Aphorisms*, 3

6 Everything comes to a man who won't wait. Absurdly improbable things are quite as liable to happen in real life as in weak literature.
Ada Leverson *The Twelfth Hour*, Ch. 13

7 Men must endure
Their going hence, even as their coming hither:
Ripeness is all. **William Shakespeare** *King Lear*, Act 5, Sc. 2, 9

8 You just keep throwing your bread upon the water, and if you're lucky it will come back as ham sandwiches.
Judith Todd interview in the *Sunday Times Magazine*, 21 January 1990

9 Expect nothing. Live frugally
on surprise. **Alice Walker** *Expect Nothing*

The People

1 You cannot make a man by standing a sheep on its hind legs. But by standing a flock of sheep in that position you can make a crowd of men. **Max Beerbohm** *Zuleika Dobson*, Ch. 9

2 Where there is no vision, the people perish. **Bible, OT** Proverbs 29:18

3 The tyranny of a multitude is a multiplied tyranny.
Edmund Burke letter, 26 February 1790

4 The public only takes up yesterday as a stick to beat today.
Jean Cocteau *Cock and Harlequin*, p. 28

5 Nor is the people's judgement always true;
The most may err as grossly as the few.

John Dryden *Absalom and Achitophel*, Pt 1, 781

6 It is a great joy to get away from persons, and live under the dominion of the Multiplication Table. **Ralph Waldo Emerson** *Journal*, March–April 1843

7 The proletariat are far more skilled at discovering what they want than what they need; so giving them power constituted giving them power to say what they want, not giving them objectivity to see what they need. **John Fowles** *The Aristos*, Ch. 7, 54

8 The body of the people are generally either so dead that they cannot move, or so mad that they cannot be reclaimed: to be either all in a flame, nor quite cold, requireth more reason than great numbers can ever attain. **Marquis of Halifax** *Political Thoughts and Reflections*: 'Of the People'

9 The people are deceived by names, but not by things.

James Harrington *Aphorisms Political*, 4

10 The people cannot see, but they can feel.

James Harrington *Aphorisms Political*, 5

11 The people are that part of the state that does not know what it wants.

Georg Hegel *The Philosophy of History*; in *The Faber Book of Aphorisms*, ed. W. H. Auden and Louis Kronenberger

12 Is an institution always a man's shadow shortened in the sun, the lowest common denominator of everybody in it?

Randall Jarrell *Pictures from an Institution*, Pt 5, Ch. 9

13 About things on which the public thinks long it commonly attains to think right. **Dr Samuel Johnson** *The Lives of the English Poets*: 'Addison'

14 The people. They know how to know, but not how to choose.

Joseph Joubert *Notebooks*, 1796

15 Minorities are individuals or groups of individuals especially qualified. The masses are the collection of people not especially qualified.

José Ortega y Gasset *The Revolt of the Masses*, Ch. 1

16 The people's voice is odd,
It is, and it is not, the voice of God.

Alexander Pope *Satires and Epistles of Horace Imitated*, Epistle 1, 89

17 Living power is hateful to the mob,
Their love is given only to the dead. **Alexander Pushkin** *Boris Godunov*

18 The people grants its favour, but never its confidence.

Antoine de Rivarol *Les Plus belles pages*: 'Politics'

19 The multitude is always in the wrong.

Earl of Roscommon *Essay on Translated Verse*, 183

20 The mobs are people who are harmful when together and useful when dispersed.

Ali Ibn Abu Talib (attrib.)

See also ***Human Nature; Others; Society***

Perceptions

1 Each particular perception gives rise to a perceptive state, the permanence of which is memory.

Aristotle quoted in Coventry Patmore, *The Rod, the Root and the Flower*: 'Aurea Dicta', 87

2 Perception may be regarded as primarily the modification of an anticipation.

J. R. Beloff 'Perception and Extrapolation', in *Bulletin of the British Psychological Society*, no. 32, 1957

3 It is as important to see others as they see themselves as to see ourselves as others see us.

Elizabeth Bibesco *Haven*: 'Aphorisms'

4 The days on which we can see are days when the wise think twice before looking.

Elizabeth Bibesco *Haven*: 'Aphorisms'

5 Neither do men light a candle, and put it under a bushel.

Bible, NT Matthew 5:15

6 If the doors of perception were cleansed, everything would appear to man as it is, infinite.

William Blake *The Marriage of Heaven and Hell*: 'The ancient tradition . . .'

7 Reality is what I see, not what you see.

Anthony Burgess in the *Sunday Times Magazine*, 18 December 1983

8 When we apply it, you call it anarchy; and when you apply it, I call it exploitation.

G. K. Chesterton *The Scandal of Father Brown*: 'The Crime of the Communist'

9 What we see, we see from the very first *as* something. This is how we enable it to present itself to us. What we cannot see *as* something we do not see at all.

Michael Frayn *Constructions*, 172

10 We would know much more about things if we weren't intent on discerning them too precisely. For, surely, an object can only be comprehensible when viewed at an angle of forty-five degrees.

Johann Wolfgang von Goethe *Maxims and Reflections* (Penguin), from *Wilhelm Meister's Journeyman Years*, 501

11 There is no reality without interpretation, just as there is no innocent eye, there is no innocent ear. **E. H. Gombrich** *Art and Illusion*, Ch. 11

12 We live by information, not by sight. We exist by faith in others. The ear is the area-gate of truth but the front-door of lies.

Baltasar Gracián *The Art of Worldly Wisdom*, 80

13 The human being is a blind man who dreams he can see.

Friedrich Hebbel *Diaries*, entry 1421, 1839

14 Man has an irresistible instinct to believe he is not seen when he himself sees nothing. Like children who shut their eyes so as not to be seen.

Georg Christoph Lichtenberg *Aphorisms*, Notebook F, 62

15 When we believe we are seeing objects we are seeing only ourselves. We can really perceive nothing in the world except ourselves and the changes that take place in us.

Georg Christoph Lichtenberg *Aphorisms*, Notebook H, 35

16 The metaphor is far more intelligent than its author, and this is the case with many things. Everything has its depths. He who has eyes sees something in everything.

Georg Christoph Lichtenberg *The Lichtenberg Reader*: Aphorisms 1775–9

17 The most ingenious insight is discerning the proper employment of insight. **Novalis** *Pollen*, 81

18 Where observation is concerned, chance favours only the prepared mind.

Louis Pasteur address on the inauguration of the Faculty of Science at the University of Lille, 7 December 1854

19 One must always tell what one sees. Above all, which is more difficult, one must always see what one sees.

Charles Péguy *Basic Verities*: 'The Honest People'

20 It is our noticing them that puts things in a room, our growing used to them, that takes them away again and clears a space for us.

Marcel Proust *Remembrance of Things Past: Within a Budding Grove*, 'Place Names'

21 An absent-minded man is really a concentrated man. But not on the immediate or desired, but on something else and on his own.

V. V. Rozanov *Fallen Leaves*, p. 24

22 An observer under the stress of emotion observes badly; he fails to give chance her due. **Stendhal** *Love*, Bk 1, Ch. 34

23 What you are you do not see. What you see is your shadow.

Rabindranath Tagore *Stray Birds*, 18

24 We shall see but little way [*sic*] if we require to understand what we see – How few things can a man measure with the tape of his understanding – how many great things might he be seeing in the meanwhile.

H. D. Thoreau *Journal*, 14 February 1851

25 Absolutely unmixed attention is prayer.

Simone Weil *Gravity and Grace*: 'Attention and Will'

See also ***Eyes; The Senses***

Philosophy

1 Philosophy, which once seemed obsolete, lives on because the moment to realize it was missed.

Theodor Adorno quoted in *the London Review of Books*, 4 February 1999

2 Logic is the art of going wrong with confidence.

Anon. quoted in W. H. Auden, *A Certain World*

3 I dreamt a line that would make a motto for a sober philosophy: *Neither a be-all nor an end-all be.* **J. L. Austin** *Philosophical Papers*: 'Pretending'

4 The pursuit of the incorrigible is one of the most vulnerable bugbears in the history of philosophy. **J. L. Austin** *Philosophical Papers*, 10

5 All good moral philosophy is but an handmaid to religion.

Francis Bacon *The Advancement of Learning*, Bk 2, Ch. 22, Sect. 14

6 A little philosophy inclineth man's mind to atheism; but depth in philosophy bringeth men's minds about to religion.

Francis Bacon *Essays*: 'Of Atheism'

7 **Philosophy, n.** A route of many roads leading from nowhere to nothing. **Ambrose Bierce** *The Devil's Dictionary*

8 Az a general thing, the philosophers ov this world hav spent mutch ov their time eating stewed terrapins, and then telling other pholks – how unhelthy they am. **Josh Billings** *Life and Adventures of Josh Billings*, p. 72

9 *On a metaphysician*: A blind man in a dark room, looking for a black hat which is not there. **Lord Bowen (attrib.)** in *Notes and Queries*, 182, 123

10 Metaphysics is the finding of bad reasons for what we believe upon instinct; but to find these reasons is no less an instinct.

F. H. Bradley *Appearance and Reality*: Preface

11 The profoundest thoughts of the philosophers have something trick-like about them. A lot disappears in order for something to suddenly appear in the palm of the hand. **Elias Canetti** *The Secret Heart of the Clock*: '1973'

12 A philosophy that is free of power, yet presumes the existence of God, is impossible. **Elias Canetti** *The Secret Heart of the Clock*: '1985'

13 'Contrariwise,' continued Tweedledee, 'if it was so, it might be; and if it were so, it would be: but as it isn't, it ain't. That's logic.'
Lewis Carroll *Through the Looking Glass*, Ch. 4

14 For a lady considering a lodger, it is important to know his income, but still more important to know his philosophy.
G. K. Chesterton *Heretics*, Ch. 1

15 Nothing so absurd can be said, that some philosopher has not said it. **Cicero** *De Divinatione*, ii, 58

16 Philosophy may thus be called thought of the second degree, thought about thought. **R. G. Collingwood** *The Idea of History*: Introduction, 1

17 The beginning of philosophy is to know the condition of one's own mind. **Epictetus** *The Golden Sayings*, 46

18 To win true freedom you must be a slave to philosophy.
Epicurus quoted in Seneca, *Letters from a Stoic*, 8

19 All philosophy springs from two things: our inquiring minds and our bad eyes.
Bernard Le Bovier de Fontenelle *Entretien sur la pluralité des mondes*: 'Premier soir'

20 Every stage of life corresponds to a certain philosophy. A child appears as a realist; for it is as certain of the existence of pears and apples as it is of its own being. A young man, caught up in the storm of his inner passions, has to pay attention to himself, look and feel ahead; he is transformed into an idealist. A grown man, on the other hand, has every reason to be a sceptic; he is well advised to doubt whether the means he has chosen to achieve his purpose can really be right . . . An old man, however, will always vow mysticism. He sees that so much seems to depend on chance: unreason succeeds, reason fails.
Johann Wolfgang von Goethe *Maxims and Reflections* (Penguin), from *Wilhelm Meister's Journeyman Years*, 806

21 This same philosophy is a good horse in the stable, but an arrant jade on a journey. **Oliver Goldsmith** *The Good-Natured Man*, 1

22 He is no mean philosopher who can give a reason for one half of what he thinks. **William Hazlitt** *Characteristics*, 339

23 Leisure is the mother of philosophy. **Thomas Hobbes** *Leviathan*, Pt 4, Ch. 46

24 A new philosophy is not like a new religion, a thing to be merely thankful for, and accepted mutely by the faithful. It is more of the nature of food thrown to the lions; the pleasure lies in the fact that it can be devoured. **T. E. Hulme** *Speculations*, 1936: Preface

25 Every philosopher says the world is other than it seems to be; in the last chapter he tells you what he thinks it is.
T. E. Hulme *Speculations*: 'Modern Art'

26 You can only tell a Stoic from a Cynic because he wears a shirt.
Juvenal *Satires*, XIII, 121

27 Philosophy is concerned with two matters: soluble questions that are trivial and critical questions that are insoluble.
Stefan Kanfer in *Time* magazine, 19 April 1982

28 It is good to be a philosopher, it is scarcely desirable to pass for one.
Jean de La Bruyère *Characters*: 'Of opinions', 68

29 There's no greater sign of being a poor philosopher and wise man than wanting all of life to be wise and philosophical.
Giacomo Leopardi *Pensieri*, 27

30 If an angel were ever to tell us anything of his philosophy I believe many propositions would sound like 2 times 2 equals 13.
Georg Christoph Lichtenberg *Aphorisms*, Notebook B, 44

31 Philosophy can only exist by ignoring objections.
Joseph de Maistre *St Petersburg Nights*: Fifth Conversation

32 Philosophy! Empty thinking by ignorant conceited men who think they can digest without eating.
Iris Murdoch *The Book and the Brotherhood*, Pt 1: 'Midsummer'

33 It has gradually become clear to me what every great philosophy has hitherto been: a confession on the part of its author and a kind of involuntary and unconscious memoir.
Friedrich Nietzsche *Beyond Good and Evil*: 'On the Prejudices of Philosophers', 6

34 Philosophy is properly homesickness; the wish to be everywhere at home. **Novalis** *Pollen*, 161

35 To make light of philosophy is to be a true philosopher.
Blaise Pascal *Pensées*, 4

36 The real secrets of life lie too far within, not too far beyond, our mental focus to be seen. Philosophy consists in limiting the focus, not in extending it. **Coventry Patmore** *The Rod, the Root and the Flower*: 'Aurea Dicta', 110

37 Those races who possess a rich mythological background are those who thereafter become the most dogged philosophers: the Indians, the Greeks and the Germans.

Cesare Pavese *The Business of Living: Diary 1935–1950*, 24 April 1944

38 Philosophers are anatomists rather than doctors; they dissect but do not heal. **Antoine de Rivarol** *Notes, réflexions et maximes*: 'Philosophe'

39 The believer credits other people's visions; the philosopher only his own. **Antoine de Rivarol** *Notes, réflexions et maximes*: 'Philosophe'

40 Philosophy is the replacement of category-habits by category-disciplines. **Gilbert Ryle** *The Concept of Mind*: Introduction

41 Philosophy is a battle against the bewitchment of our intelligence by means of language. **Antoine de Saint-Exupéry (attrib.)**

42 It is a great advantage for a system of philosophy to be substantially true. **George Santayana** *The Unknowable*

43 Philosophy is good advice, and no one gives advice at the top of his voice. **Seneca** *Letters from a Stoic*, 36

44 For there was never yet philosopher
That could endure the toothache patiently.

William Shakespeare *Much Ado About Nothing*, Act 5, Sc. 1, 35

45 Mankind has, at least, this superiority over its philosophers, that great movements spring from the heart and embody faith, not the nice adjustments of the hedonistic calculus.

R. H. Tawney *The Acquisitive Society*, 2

46 Philosophy working inwards from the circumference, and theology working outwards from the centre have not yet met.

William Temple *Mens Creatrix*: Prologue

47 Philosophy contemplates reason, whence comes knowledge of the true; philology observes the authority of human choice, whence comes consciousness of the certain. **Giambattista Vico** *The New Science*, 138

48 In philosophy you need to distrust what you think you understand too easily just as much as what you can't understand.

Voltaire *Philosophical Letters*, Letter 13

49 Philosophy is the product of wonder.

A. N. Whitehead *Nature and Life*, Ch. 1

50 To the extent that philosophical positions both confuse and close doors to further inquiry, they are likely to be wrong.

Edward O. Wilson *Consilience*, Ch. 3

51 Philosophy, as we use the word, is a fight against the fascination which forms of expression exert upon us. **Ludwig Wittgenstein** *The Blue Book*, p. 27

52 The results of philosophy are the uncovering of one or another piece of plain nonsense and of bumps that the understanding has got by running its head up against the limits of language. These bumps make us see the value of the discovery.
Ludwig Wittgenstein *Philosophical Investigations*, Pt 1, Sect. 119

53 What is your aim in philosophy? To show the fly out of the fly-bottle.
Ludwig Wittgenstein *Philosophical Investigations*, Pt 1, Sect. 309

See also ***The Mind; Thought; Wisdom***

Places

1 London is a place unique – exactly half-way between everywhere in the world and nowhere in particular. **William Allingham** *By the Way*: Notes, 142

2 A man cannot be in two places at once unless he is a bird. **Anon.**

3 The moment we are rooted in a place, the place vanishes.
G. K. Chesterton *Heretics*, Ch. 3

4 One is always nearer by not keeping still. **Thom Gunn** *On the Move*

5 You had better be a round peg in a square hole than a square peg in a square hole. The latter is in for life, while the first is only an indeterminate sentence.
Elbert Hubbard in *The Faber Book of Aphorisms*, ed. W. H. Auden and L. Kronenberger

6 If you have been put in your place long enough, you begin to act like the place. **Randall Jarrell** *A Sad Heart at the Supermarket*

7 A man who has not been in Italy, is always conscious of an inferiority. **Dr Samuel Johnson** in James Boswell, *Life of Johnson*, 11 April 1776

8 When a man is tired of London he is tired of life; for there is in London all that life can afford.
Dr Samuel Johnson in James Boswell, *Life of Johnson*, 20 September 1777

9 The map is not the territory.
Alfred Korzybski slogan quoted in Fritjof Capra, *The Tao of Physics*, Ch. 2

10 The countries which we long for occupy, at any given moment, a far larger place in our actual life than the country in which we happen to be. **Marcel Proust** *Remembrance of Things Past: Swann's Way*: 'Swann in Love'

See also ***Environments; Nations and Races; Town and Country; Travel***

Pleasures

1 One half of the world cannot understand the pleasures of the other.
Jane Austen *Emma*, Ch. 9

2 For all knowledge and wonder [which is the seed of knowledge] is an impression of pleasure in itself. **Francis Bacon** *The Advancement of Learning*, Bk 1, 1, 3

3 God Almighty first planted a garden; and, indeed, it is the purest of human pleasures. **Francis Bacon** *Essays*: 'Of Gardens'

4 **Debauchee, n.** One who has so earnestly pursued pleasure that he has had the misfortune to overtake it. **Ambrose Bierce** *The Devil's Dictionary*

5 The race of delight is short, and pleasures have mutable faces.
Sir Thomas Browne *Christian Morals*, Pt 2, 1

6 Pleasure after all is a safer guide than either right or duty.
Samuel Butler 2 *The Way of All Flesh*, Ch. 19

7 To be fond of something is better than merely to know it, and to find joy in it is better than merely to be fond of it.
Confucius *The Analects*, Bk 6, 19

8 Anxiety is one of our pleasures.
Xavier Forneret *Sans titre, par un homme noir, blanc de visage*: 'January'

9 Pleasure is a product of death; not an escape from it.
John Fowles *The Aristos*, Ch. 2, 16

10 Transience value is scarcity value in time. Limitation in the possibility of an enjoyment raises the value of the enjoyment.
Sigmund Freud *On Transience*

11 The art of pleasing is to seem pleased. **William Hazlitt** *Characteristics*, 39

12 Our intercourse with the dead is better than our intercourse with the living. There are only three pleasures in life pure and lasting, and all derived from inanimate things – books, pictures, and the face of nature. **William Hazlitt** *Criticisms of Art*, Vol. 1, p. 40

13 Nothing characterizes an individual more clearly than what he finds pleasurable – and nothing is better suited to show up his lack of character. **Hans Keller** *Maxims and Reflections*, 27

14 One must have desired a thing in all seriousness, if one wishes to take serious pleasure in it. **Michel de Montaigne** *Essays*, Bk 3, Ch. 3

15 There is a strong disposition in youth, from which some individuals never escape, to suppose that everyone else is having a more enjoyable time than we are ourselves. **Anthony Powell** *A Buyer's Market*, Ch. 4

16 To strip our pleasures of imagination is to reduce them to their own dimensions, that is to say to nothing.
Marcel Proust *Remembrance of Things Past: Within a Budding Grove*: 'Place-names'

17 Pleasure is nothing else but the intermission of pain, the enjoying of something I am in great trouble for till I have it.
John Selden *Table Talk*, 104

18 Why, all delights are vain; but that most vain
Which, with pain purchased, doth inherit pain.
William Shakespeare *Love's Labour's Lost*, Act 1, Sc. 1, 72

19 There are two things to aim at in life: first, to get what you want; and, after that, to enjoy it. Only the wisest of mankind achieve the second. **Logan Pearsall Smith** *Afterthoughts*, 1

20 Man is not free to avoid doing what gives him greater pleasure than any other action. **Stendhal** *Love*, Bk 1, Ch. 5

21 I adore simple pleasures . . . They are the last refuge of the complex.
Oscar Wilde *The Picture of Dorian Gray*, Ch. 2; also *A Woman of No Importance*, Act 1

22 Anything becomes a pleasure if one does it too often.
Oscar Wilde *The Picture of Dorian Gray*, Ch. 19

*See also **Happiness and Unhappiness***

Poetry and Poets

1 Poets are . . . the only people to whom love is not only a crucial, but also an indispensable experience, which entitles them to mistake it for a universal one. **Hannah Arendt** *The Human Condition*: footnote to Ch. 33

2 Poetry is at bottom a criticism of life.
Matthew Arnold *Essays in Criticism, 2nd Series*: 'Wordsworth'

3 A verbal art like poetry is reflective; it stops to think. Music is immediate; it goes on to become. **W. H. Auden** *The Dyer's Hand*, 8: 'Notes on Music'

4 Poetry is devil's wine. **St Augustine** *Contra Academicos*

5 No poem is ever written for its story line's sake only, just as no life is lived for the sake of an obituary. **Joseph Brodsky** *Less Than One*: 'Keening Muse'

6 A poet without love were a physical and metaphysical impossibility.
Thomas Carlyle *Critical and Miscellaneous Essays*: 'Burns'

7 The man who does not look at his change is no true poet.
G. K. Chesterton *The Apostle and the Wild Ducks*, ed. Dorothy E. Collins

8 The central idea of poetry is guessing right, like a child.
G. K. Chesterton *The Victorian Age in Literature*, Ch. 1

9 A true poet does not bother to be poetical. Nor does a nursery gardener scent his roses. **Jean Cocteau** *Professional Secrets*

10 No man can leap over his own shadow, but poets leap over death.
Samuel Taylor Coleridge *Anima Poetae*, Ch. 2

11 No man was ever yet a great poet, without being at the same time a profound philosopher. **Samuel Taylor Coleridge** *Biographia Literaria*, Ch. 15

12 Poetry is certainly something more than good sense, but it must be good sense at all events; just as a palace is more than a house, but it must be a house, at least. **Samuel Taylor Coleridge** *Table Talk*, 9, May 1830

13 We do not write in order to be understood; we write in order to understand. **C. Day Lewis** *The Poet's Task*

14 A poem is what happens when an anxiety meets a technique.
Lawrence Durrell (attrib.)

15 Philosophers arrive at conclusions, poets must allow theirs to develop. **Maria von Ebner-Eschenbach** *Aphorisms*, p. 41

16 Poetry is not a turning loose of emotion, but an escape from emotion; it is not the expression of personality, but an escape from personality.
T. S. Eliot *Selected Essays*: 'Tradition and the Individual Talent', II

17 All one's inventions are true, you can be sure of that. Poetry is as exact a science as geometry. **Gustave Flaubert** letter to Louise Colet, 14 August 1853

18 We all write poems; it is simply that poets are the ones who write in words. **John Fowles** *The French Lieutenant's Woman*, Ch. 19

19 Poetry is a way of taking life by the throat.
Robert Frost in Elizabeth S. Sergeant, *Robert Frost: The Trial by Existence*, Ch. 18

20 A poem begins as a lump in the throat, a sense of wrong, a homesickness, a lovesickness . . . It finds the thought and the thought finds the words. **Robert Frost** letter to Louis Untermeyer, 1 January 1916

21 Writing free verse is like playing tennis with the net down.
Robert Frost address at Milton Academy, Massachusetts, 17 May 1935

22 Poetry is a dangerous honey. I advise thee only to taste it with the Tip of thy finger and not to live upon it. If thou do'st, it will disorder thy Head, and give thee dangerous Vertigo's.

Dr Thomas Fuller *Introductio ad Prudentium*, 989

23 As soon as war is declared it will be impossible to hold the poets back. Rhyme is still the most effective drum. **Jean Giraudoux** *Tiger at the Gates*, Act 1

24 To be a poet is a condition rather than a profession.

Robert Graves response to *Horizon* questionnaire, 1946

25 Poetry is emotion put into measure. The emotion must come by nature, but the measure can be acquired by art.

Thomas Hardy in Florence Emily Hardy, *The Life of Thomas Hardy*, Ch. 25

26 A poet should express the emotion of all the ages and the thought of his own.

Thomas Hardy in notebook, May 1918, in Florence Emily Hardy, *The Life of Thomas Hardy*, Ch. 34

27 Science sees signs; poetry the thing signified.

Julius and Augustus Hare *Guesses at Truth*, 2

28 The true poet is the doctor, the false poet the surgeon of his time.

Friedrich Hebbel *Diaries*, entry 2086, 1840

29 The function of the poet is not to point out ways, but most of all to arouse longing. **Hermann Hesse** *Reflections*, 528

30 I know poetry is indispensable, but I don't know to what.

Victor Hugo quoted by Jean Cocteau on his election to the Académie Française

31 To a poet nothing can be useless. **Dr Samuel Johnson** *Rasselas*, Ch. 10

32 For a good poet's made as well as born.

Ben Jonson *To the Memory of Master William Shakespeare*

33 The poet must not step across a space when he can jump across it.

Joseph Joubert *Notebooks*, 1800

34 Poetry can only be found anywhere if we bring it with us.

Joseph Joubert *Thoughts and Maxims*, 297

35 Poetry should surprise by a fine excess, and not by singularity; it should strike the reader as a wording of his own highest thoughts, and appear almost a remembrance. **John Keats** letter to John Taylor, 27 February 1818

36 A poet is the most unpoetical of anything in existence, because he has no identity – he is continually informing and filling some other body. **John Keats** letter to R. Woodhouse, 27 October 1818

37 What is a poet? An unhappy man who hides deep anguish in his heart, but whose lips are so formed that when the sigh and cry pass through them, it sounds like lovely music. **Søren Kierkegaard** *Either/Or*, Pt 1, Ch. 1

38 A poet is someone who is startled out of his trance
by his dreams. **Irving Layton** *The Whole Bloody Bird*: 'aphs'

39 A great lyric is very like a long, utterly adequate adjective.
C. S. Lewis *Letters to Malcolm*, Ch. 16

40 Perhaps no person can be a poet, or can even enjoy poetry, without a certain unsoundness of mind.
Thomas Babington Macaulay *Literary Essays*: 'Milton'

41 It's in the margins we'll find the poems. **Osip Mandelstam (attrib.)**

42 Poetry is what Milton saw when he went blind.
Don Marquis in the *New York Sun*: 'The Sun Dial'

43 Really there is no one more confident than a bad poet.
Martial *Epigrams*, 12, 63

44 Poetry is a comforting piece of fiction set to more or less lascivious music. **H. L. Mencken** *Prejudices, Third Series*: 'The Poet and His Art'

45 Poetry is an extra hand. It can caress or tickle. It can clench and fight. The hand is hot. Take it or leave it.
Adrian Mitchell 'Poetry Lives', in the *Sunday Times*, 13 February 1972

46 One can play the fool everywhere else, but not in poetry.
Michel de Montaigne *Essays*, Bk 2, Ch. 17

47 Poetry is an act of peace. Peace goes into the making of a poet as flour goes into the making of bread. **Pablo Neruda** *Memoirs*, Ch. 6

48 The man who is a poet at twenty is not a poet, but a man; the poet of over twenty is a poet. **Charles Péguy** *Clio*

49 It is the role of the poet to look at what is happening in the world and to know that quite other things are happening.
V. S. Pritchett *The Myth Makers*

50 Mallarmé is untranslatable, even into French.
Jules Renard *Journal 1887–1910*, 1 March 1898

51 In most men there is a dead poet whom the man survives.
Charles-Augustin Sainte-Beuve in J. de Finod, *A Thousand Flashes of French Wit*, p. 15

52 Poetry, surely, is a crisis, perhaps the only actionable one we can call our own. **J. D. Salinger** *Seymour: An Introduction*

53 Poetry is the achievement of the synthesis of hyacinths and biscuits.
Carl Sandburg 'Poetry Considered', *Atlantic Monthly*, March 1923

54 Poetry is the record of the best and happiest moments of the happiest and best minds. **P. B. Shelley** *A Defence of Poetry*

55 Poetry and consumptions are the most flattering of diseases.
William Shenstone *Essays on Men and Manners*: 'On Writing and Books'

56 The poet makes silk dresses out of worms. **Wallace Stevens** *Adagia*, 1

57 The purpose of poetry is to make life complete in itself.
Wallace Stevens *Materia Poetica*, 28

58 Every poet has trembled on the verge of science.
H. D. Thoreau *Journal*, 20 July 1852

59 'Poetry is for women, I suppose?' she said. 'Created by men with women in mind? Like Crimplene.' **Barbara Trapido** *Noah's Ark*, Ch. 25

60 The poet is the most defenceless of all beings – for the good reason that he is always walking on his hands.
Paul Valéry *Bad Thoughts and Not So Bad*, B

61 A poem is never finished, only abandoned. **Paul Valéry** *Literature*

62 A poetic idea is one which, stated in prose, still calls for verse.
Paul Valéry *Odds and Ends*, IV

63 A poem: a long-drawn hesitation between sound and sense.
Paul Valéry *Rhumbs*: 'Literature'

64 Poetry is to prose as dancing is to walking.
John Wain talk on BBC radio, 13 January 1976

65 When a man acts he is a puppet. When he describes, he is a poet.
Oscar Wilde *The Critic as Artist*, 1

66 The poet gives us his essence, but prose takes the mould of the body and mind entire. **Virginia Woolf** *The Captain's Death Bed*: 'Reading'

67 Poetry is the spontaneous overflow of powerful feelings: it takes its origin from emotion recollected in tranquillity.
William Wordsworth *Lyrical Ballads*: Preface

68 We make out of the quarrel with others, rhetoric, but of the quarrel with ourselves, poetry. **W. B. Yeats** *Anima Hominis*, 5

69 Great prose may occur by accident: but not great poetry.
G. M. Young in *Geoffrey Madan's Notebooks*, ed. J. A. Gere and John Sparrow: 'Extracts and Summaries'

See also ***Literature; Reading; Writing***

Politics and Politicians

1 Politics, as a practice, whatever its professions, has always been the systematic organization of hatreds.

Henry Adams *The Education of Henry Adams*, Ch. 1

2 A politician is an animal who can sit on a fence and yet keep both ears to the ground. **Anon.** in H. L. Mencken, *New Dictionary of Quotations*

3 Parties are much like fish, 'tis said,
Their tail directs them, not their head.

Anon. in Edward Meryon, *Epitaphs, Personal Anecdotes and Epigrams*: 'Epigrams'

4 A liberal is a conservative who has been arrested.

Anon. in Tom Wolfe, *The Bonfire of the Vanities*, Ch. 24

5 A constitutional statesman is in general a man of common opinion and uncommon abilities.

Walter Bagehot *Biographical Studies*: 'The Character of Sir Robert Peel'

6 In every country the extreme party is most irritated against the party which comes nearest to itself, but does not go so far.

Walter Bagehot in the *Economist*, 22 April 1876

7 A cabinet is a combining committee – a *hyphen* which joins, a *buckle* which fastens, the legislative part of the state to the executive part of the state. **Walter Bagehot** in the *The English Constitution*: 'The Cabinet'

8 Making capitalism out of socialism is like making eggs out of an omelette. **Vadim Bakatin** said in May 1991; quoted in *Hutchinson Gallup Info '92*

9 The accursed power which stands on Privilege
(And goes with Women, and Champagne, and Bridge)
Broke – and Democracy resumed her reign:
(Which goes with Bridge, and Women, and Champagne).

Hilaire Belloc *On a General Election*

10 Politics is the art of the possible.

Otto von Bismarck in conversation with Meyer von Waldeck, 11 August 1867

See also Galbraith

11 Liberals think that goats are just sheep from broken homes.

Malcolm Bradbury and Christopher Bigsby TV play *After Dinner Game*

12 Magnanimity in politics is not seldom the truest wisdom; and a great empire and little minds go ill together.

Edmund Burke speech on conciliation with America, 22 March 1775

13 A disposition to preserve, and an ability to improve, taken together, would be my standard of a statesman.

Edmund Burke *Reflections on the Revolution in France*, p. 267

14 In politics, actions themselves are less decisive than the time at which they are performed. A politician is someone who has time on his side.

Roberto Calasso *The Ruin of Kasch*: 'Mundus Patet'

See also Talleyrand

15 An honest politician is one who, when he is bought, will stay bought.

Simon Cameron in conversation, *c.* 1860

16 Politicians neither love nor hate. Interest, not sentiment, governs them.

Earl of Chesterfield *Letters to His Son*, p. 900; the first sentence is from John Dryden, *Absalom and Achitophel*, Pt 1, 223

17 Every politician is emphatically a promising politician.

G. K. Chesterton *The Scandal of Father Brown*: 'The Red Moon of Meru'

18 Socialism will only be possible when we are all perfect, and then it will not be needed.

Bishop Mandell Creighton *Life and Letters*, edited by his wife, Vol. 2

19 A politician is an arse upon which everyone has sat except a man.

e. e. cummings *1 × 1*, 10

20 Politics is not the art of the possible. It consists in choosing between the disastrous and the unpalatable.

J. K. Galbraith letter to President Kennedy, 2 March 1962, in *Ambassador's Journal*

See also Bismarck

21 Politics are too serious a matter to be left to the politicians.

Charles de Gaulle quoted in Clement Attlee, *A Prime Minister Remembers*, Ch. 4

22 Politics is the food of sense exposed to the hunger of folly.

Fulke Greville *Maxims, Characters and Reflections*, p. 40

23 A politician is a fellow who will lay down your life for his country.

Texas Guinan in *Hammer and Tongues*, ed. Michèle Brown and Ann O'Connor: 'Politics'

24 In Parliaments, Men wrangle on behalf of liberty, that do as little care for it, as they deserve it.

Marquis of Halifax *Political Thoughts and Reflections*: 'Of Parliaments'

25 Ignorance maketh most Men go into a Party, and Shame keepeth them from getting out of it.

Marquis of Halifax *Political Thoughts and Reflections*: 'Of Parties'

26 Politics does not reflect majorities, it constructs them.

Stuart Hall in *Marxism Today*, July 1987

27 The art of politics is to win people's support for a good cause even when the pursuit of that cause may interfere with their own particular momentary interests. **Vaclev Havel** in the *Observer*, 22 November 1998

28 Politics is a choice of enemas. You're going to get it up the ass, no matter what you do. **George V. Higgins** *Victories*, Ch. 7

29 For a politician rises on the backs of his friends (that's probably all they're good for), but it's through his enemies he'll have to govern afterwards. **Richard Hughes** *The Fox in the Attic*, Bk 2, Ch. 20

30 In political institutions, almost everything we call an abuse was once a remedy. **Joseph Joubert** *Notebooks*, 1813

31 There is a holy mistaken zeal in politics as well as in religion. By persuading others, we convince ourselves. **'Junius'** *Letters*, 35

32 Politicians are the same all over. They promise to build a bridge even where there is no river.

Nikita S. Khrushchev impromptu remark on visit to the USA at Glen Cove, NY, October 1960, repeated in Yugoslavia, 21 August 1963

33 The welfare of many countries is decided by a majority of votes, even though everyone admits there are more wicked men than good ones.

Georg Christoph Lichtenberg *Aphorisms*, Notebook F, 10

34 At home you always have to be a politician. When you're abroad you almost feel yourself a statesman.

Harold Macmillan speech in Melbourne, Australia, 17 February 1958

See also Truman

35 Politics is war without bloodshed while war is politics with bloodshed. **Mao Zedong** *On Protracted War*, May 1938

36 Men enter local politics solely as a result of being unhappily married.

C. Northcote Parkinson *Parkinson's Law*, Ch. 10

37 The triumph of demagogues is fleeting. But the ruins are eternal.

Charles Péguy *Basic Verities*: 'Politics and Mysticism'

38 Every party lives on its mysticism and dies from its politics.

Charles Péguy *Notre jeunesse*, p. 37

39 He that espouses parties, can hardly divorce himself from their fate: and more fall with their party, than rise with it.

William Penn *Reflections and Maxims*, I, 429

40 One, on God's side, is a majority.

Wendell Phillips speech at Brooklyn, New York, 1 November 1859

41 Party is the madness of many for the gain of the few.

Alexander Pope *Thoughts on Various Subjects*, 1

42 All political lives, unless they are cut off in mid-stream at a happy juncture, end in failure, because that is the nature of politics and of human affairs. **Enoch Powell** *Joseph Chamberlain*, 1977: epilogue

43 Radical: A person whose left hand does not know what his other left hand is doing. **Bernard Rosenberg** in Laurence J. Peter, *Peter's Quotations*

44 He knows nothing; and he thinks he knows everything. That points clearly to a political career. **George Bernard Shaw** *Major Barbara*, Act 3

45 *Politics* in the middle of things that concern the *imagination* are like a pistol shot in the middle of a concert. **Stendhal** *Scarlet and Black*, Ch. 22

46 A politician is a statesman who approaches every question with an open mouth.

Adlai Stevenson in Leon A. Harris, *The Fine Art of Political Wit*, Ch. 10; also attrib. to Arthur Goldberg describing diplomats

47 Politics is perhaps the only profession for which no preparation is thought necessary.

Robert Louis Stevenson *Familiar Studies of Men and Books*: 'Yoshida-Torajiro'

48 The quarrel between capitalism and communism is whether to sit upstairs or downstairs in a bus going the wrong way.

quoted by Revd John Stewart letter to the *Listener*, 18 December 1986

49 There are few political transactions whose nature will not admit of some postponement.

Charles-Maurice de Talleyrand instructions to General Andréossy in 1792, in *Correspondance diplomatique de Talleyrand*, ed. G. Pallain, p. 151

See also Calasso

50 It is of far greater importance to a statesman to make one friend who will hold out with him for twenty years, than to find twenty followers in each year, losing as many or even a tenth part as many.

Sir Henry Taylor *The Statesman*, Ch. 4

51 A politician is a man who understands government, and it takes a politician to run a government. A statesman is a politician who's been dead ten or fifteen years.

Harry S. Truman impromptu speech to Reciprocity Club, Washington, 11 April 1958

See also Macmillan

52 Whiskey is carried into committee rooms in demijohns and carried out in demagogues. **Mark Twain** *Notebook*, 1868

53 Politics is the art of preventing people from minding their own business. **Paul Valéry** *Rhumbs*: 'Moralities'

54 A candidate should not mean but be. **Gore Vidal** *The Best Man*

55 Socialism consists in imputing good to the conquered, and racialism in imputing good to the conquerors.
Simone Weil *Gravity and Grace*, 'Social Harmony'

56 In England a man who can't talk morality twice a week to a large, popular, immoral audience is quite over as a serious politician. There would be nothing left for him as a profession except Botany or the Church. **Oscar Wilde** *An Ideal Husband*, Act 2

See also ***Diplomacy; Governments***

Possible and Impossible

1 The only way of discovering the limits of the possible is to venture a little way past them into the impossible.
Arthur C. Clarke *Profiles of the Future*, Ch. 2: 'Clarke's Second Law'

2 To live in the realm of ideas means treating the impossible as though it were possible. The same goes for character: if the two coincide, events follow from which the world's astonishment takes centuries to recover.
Johann Wolfgang von Goethe *Maxims and Reflections* (Penguin), from *Art and Antiquity*, 262

3 It is very dangerous to go into eternity with possibilities which one has oneself prevented from becoming realities. A possibility is a hint from God. **Søren Kierkegaard** *The Journals*, 1848

4 Absurdly improbable things are quite as liable to happen in real life as in weak literature. **Ada Leverson** *The Twelfth Hour*, Ch. 2

5 The difficult is what takes a little time; the impossible is what takes a little longer.
Fridtjof Nansen also attrib. to others; variant form was motto placarded at South-East Asia HQ in Second World War

6 The becoming of man is the history of the exhaustion of his possibilities. **Susan Sontag** *Styles of Radical Will*: 'Thinking Against Oneself'

7 By means of man, the impossible brings pressure to bear on the real.
Paul Valéry *Suite*: 'Life and Death'

Power

1 Power tends to corrupt, and absolute power corrupts absolutely. Great men are almost always bad men.

Lord Acton letter to Bishop Mandell Creighton, 3 April 1887

2 Men in great place are thrice servants: servants of the sovereign or state; servants of fame; and servants of business. **Francis Bacon** *Essays*: 'Of Great Place'

3 You carry forever the fingerprint that comes from being under someone's thumb. **Nancy Banks-Smith** in the *Guardian*, 30 January 1991

4 Strength lies in improvisation. All the decisive blows are struck left-handed. **Walter Benjamin** *One-way Street*: 'Chinese Curios'

5 The most potent weapon in the hands of the oppressor is the mind of the oppressed. **Steve Biko** address to Cape Town Conference, 1971

6 The strongest poison ever known
Came from Caesar's laurel crown. **William Blake** *Auguries of Innocence*

7 The greater the power, the more dangerous the abuse.

Edmund Burke speech on the Middlesex Election, 1771

8 You can shear a wolf; but will he comply?

Edmund Burke on the colonies; quoted by Marianne Moore in *Writers at Work, Second Series*, ed. George Plimpton

9 To know the pains of power, we must go to those who have it; to know its pleasures, we must go to those who are seeking it: the pains of power are real, its pleasures imaginary.

Charles Caleb Colton *Lacon*: 'Power'

10 The more you are talked about, the less powerful you are.

Benjamin Disraeli in *The Faber Book of Aphorisms*, ed. W. H. Auden and Louis Kronenberger

11 All empire is no more than power in trust.

John Dryden *Absalom and Achitophel*, Pt 1, 411

12 The reason why men do not obey us is because they see the mud at the bottom of our eye. **Ralph Waldo Emerson** *The Conduct of Life*: 'Behaviour'

13 No man can rob us of our Will. **Epictetus** *The Golden Sayings*, 83

14 Their finest hair throws a shadow.

Erasmus quoted by Johann Wolfgang von Goethe, *Maxims and Reflections*: 'Life and Character', 63

15 A great empire, like a great cake, is most easily diminished at the edges. **Benjamin Franklin** quoted by Emerson in his *Journal*, 1823

16 Of all our passions and appetites, the love of power is of the imperious nature, since the pride of one man requires the submission of the multitude. **Edward Gibbon** *The Decline and Fall of the Roman Empire*, Ch. 4

17 Power and liberty are like Heat and Moisture; where they are well mixt, everything prospers; where they are single, they are destructive.
Marquis of Halifax *Maxims of State*

18 Life only demands from you the strength you possess. Only one feat is possible – not to have run away. **Dag Hammarskjöld** *Markings*: 'Thus It Was'

19 Unlimited power is helpless, as arbitrary power is capricious. Our energy is in proportion to the resistance it meets.
William Hazlitt *Characteristics*, 156

20 Man is a toad-eating animal. The admiration of power in others is as common to man as the love of it in himself; the one makes him a tyrant, the other a slave.
William Hazlitt *Political Essays*: 'On *The Times* Newspaper: On the Connection Between Toad-Eaters and Tyrants', 12 January 1817

21 Riches, knowledge and honour are but several sorts of power.
Thomas Hobbes *Leviathan*, Ch. 10

22 Brute force without wisdom falls by its own weight. **Horace** *Odes*, iv, 65

23 Atlas had a great reputation, but I'd like to have seen him carry a mattress upstairs. **'Kin' Hubbard** *Abe Martin's Wisecracks*, p. 35

24 Even a despot cannot govern for any length of time without the consent of his subjects. **Aldous Huxley** *The Olive Tree*: 'Writers and Readers'

25 A man may build himself a throne of bayonets, but he cannot sit on it.
W. R. Inge *The Philosophy of Plotinus*, Lecture 22; quoted by Boris Yeltsin of Russia at the time of the abortive military coup in 1991

26 *Quis custodiet ipsos*
Custodes? – Who is to guard the guards themselves? **Juvenal** *Satires*, VI, 347

27 Our scientific power has outrun our spiritual power. We have guided missiles and misguided men. **Martin Luther King Jr** *Strength to Love*, Ch. 7

28 Power is the ultimate aphrodisiac.
Henry Kissinger in the *New York Times*, 19 January 1971

29 The stronger man's argument is always the best.
Jean de La Fontaine *Fables*, I, 10: 'The Fox and the Lamb'

30 Competence without authority is as powerless as authority without competence. **Gustave Le Bon** *Aphorismes du temps présent*

31 There has never been a man who could straighten others by bending himself. **Mencius** Bk 3, Pt B, 1

32 Ten men acting together can make a hundred thousand tremble apart. **Comte de Mirabeau** quoted in Hannah Arendt, *On Revolution*, Ch. 6, 2

33 We have power over nothing except our will. **Michel de Montaigne** *Essays*, Bk 1, Ch. 7

34 All empires die of indigestion. **Napoleon Bonaparte** quoted in *Wit and Wisdom of Dean Inge*: Preface

35 God must have loved the People in Power, for he made them so very like their own image of him. **Kenneth Patchen** quoted by Adrian Mitchell in the *Guardian*, 1 February 1972

36 No one is a light unto himself, not even the sun. **Antonio Porchia** *Voices*

37 There thou mightst behold the great image of authority; a dog's obeyed in office. **William Shakespeare** *King Lear*, Act 4, Sc. 6, (163)

38 Power corrupts, but lack of power corrupts absolutely. **Adlai Stevenson** in the *Observer*, January 1963

See also Acton

39 The right to possess boasts foolishly
of its right to enjoy. **Rabindranath Tagore** *Fireflies*, p. 191

40 The man who forces a way to power is commonly more fit for it in some respects than the man who finds a way. **Sir Henry Taylor** *The Statesman*, Ch. 14

41 Tradition teaches us as touching the gods and experience shows us as regards men that, by a necessity of nature, every human being invariably exercises all the power of which it is capable. **Thucydides** quoted by Simone Weil, *Gravity and Grace*: 'To Accept the Void'

42 If you wish to be powerful, pretend to be powerful. **Horne Tooke** in S. T. Coleridge, *Table Talk*, 1 May 1832

43 A cyclone can raze a city, yet not even open a letter or untie the knot in this piece of string. **Paul Valéry** *Odds and Ends*: 'Notebook B'

44 *Non omnia possumus omnes.* – We are not all capable of everything. **Virgil** *Eclogues*, VIII, 63

45 There is no other force on this earth except force. **Simone Weil** *The Need for Roots*: 'The Growing of Roots'

46 There are two kinds of imperialists – imperialists and bloody imperialists. **Rebecca West** review in first issue of the *Freewoman*, 23 November 1911

47 All authority is quite degrading. It degrades those who exercise it, and it degrades those over whom it is exercised.

Oscar Wilde *The Soul of Man Under Socialism*

See also ***Strength and Weakness***

Praise and Blame

1 How strange are the ways of men! They will spare no word of praise for their contemporaries, who live in their very midst, and yet they covet greatly for themselves the praise of future generations, whom they have never seen and never will see. Almost like grumbling at absence of praise from one's ancestors!

Marcus Aurelius *Meditations*, Bk 6, 18

2 **Eulogy, n.** Praise of a person who has either the advantages of wealth and power, or the consideration to be dead.

Ambrose Bierce *The Enlarged Devil's Dictionary*

3 Praises of the unworthy are felt by ardent minds as robberies of the deserving. **Samuel Taylor Coleridge** *Biographia Literaria*, Ch. 3

4 When men abuse us, we should suspect ourselves; and when they praise us, *them*. **Charles Caleb Colton** *Lacon*: 'Praise and Censure'

5 Praise does not console us for criticism; it strikes us as less sincere.

Comtesse Diane *Les Glanes de la vie*, p. 12

6 No compliment can be eloquent except as an expression of indifference. **George Eliot** *The Mill on the Floss*, Bk 6, Ch. 2

7 It is often harder to praise a friend than an enemy. By the last we may acquire a reputation for candour; by the first we only seem to discharge a debt, and are liable to a suspicion of partiality.

William Hazlitt *Characteristics*, 2

8 No man ever praised two persons *equally* – and pleased them both.

Sir Arthur Helps *Thoughts in the Cloister and the Crowd*

9 To approve is more difficult than to admire.

Hugo von Hofmannsthal *The Book of Friends*, 1

10 Several excuses are always less convincing than one.

Aldous Huxley *Point Counter Point*, Ch. 1

11 Unmerited abuse wounds, while unmerited praise has not the power to heal. **Thomas Jefferson** letter to Edward Rutledge, 27 December 1796

12 All censure of a man's self is oblique praise. It is in order to show how much he can spare.

Dr Samuel Johnson in James Boswell, *Life of Johnson*, 25 April 1778

13 The applause of a single human being is of great consequence.

Dr Samuel Johnson in James Boswell, *Life of Johnson*, 1780

14 There is as great a vice in praising, and as frequent, as in detracting.

Ben Jonson *Timber or Discoveries Made Upon Men and Matter*, 113

15 Censure acquits the raven, but pursues the dove. **Juvenal** *Satires*, II, 63

16 Never praise a sister to a sister, in the hope of your compliments reaching the proper ears . . . sisters are women first, and sisters afterwards.

Rudyard Kipling *Plain Tales from the Hills*: 'False Dawn'

17 People ask you for criticism, but they only want praise.

W. Somerset Maugham *Of Human Bondage*, Ch. 50

18 So long as you are praised think only that you are not yet on your own path but on someone else's.

Friedrich Nietzsche *Assorted Opinions and Maxims*, 340

19 In applause there is always a kind of noise – even when we applaud ourselves. **Friedrich Nietzsche** *The Gay Science*, Bk 3, 201

20 To express admiration one says that a thing is like something else: a confirmation of the fact that we never see a thing the first time but only the second – when it has changed into something else.

Cesare Pavese *This Business of Living: A Diary 1935–1950*, 25 March 1945

21 Praise undeserved is scandal in disguise.

Alexander Pope *Imitations of Horace*, Bk 2, Epistle 1, 413

22 *Qui s'accuse s'excuse.* [Self-blame makes a good excuse – inversion of French proverb]

Christopher Ricks *Dickens and the Twentieth Century*: 'Great Expectations'

23 We give others praise which we ourselves don't believe, as long as they respond with praise we can believe. **Jean Rostand** *De la Vanité*

24 There is nothing more universally commended than a fine day; the reason is, that people can commend it without envy.

William Shenstone *Essays on Men and Manners*: title essay

25 All panegyrics are mingled with an infusion of poppy.

Jonathan Swift *Thoughts on Various Subjects*, p. 286

26 A man who desires to soften another man's heart, should always abuse himself. In softening a woman's heart, he should blame her.

Anthony Trollope *The Last Chronicle of Barset*, Ch. 44

27 It is difficult to esteem a man as he would like to be esteemed.

Marquis de Vauvenargues *Reflections and Maxims*, 67

28 There is a luxury in self-reproach. When we blame ourselves we feel that no one else has a right to blame us.

Oscar Wilde *The Picture of Dorian Gray*, Ch. 8

29 It is a good rule in life never to apologize. The right sort of people do not want apologies, and the wrong sort take a mean advantage of them. **P. G. Wodehouse** *The Man Upstairs*: title story

Prejudice

1 **Prejudice, n.** A vagrant opinion without visible means of support.

Ambrose Bierce *The Devil's Dictionary*

2 No wise man can have a contempt for the prejudices of others; and he should stand in certain awe of his own, as if they were aged instructors. They may in the end prove wiser than he.

Edmund Burke *Reflections on the Revolution in France*

See also Hazlitt

3 Our prejudices are our mistresses; reason is at best our wife, very often heard indeed but seldom minded.

Earl of Chesterfield *Letters to His Son*, 13 April 1752

4 Bigotry may be roughly defined as the anger of men who have no opinions. **G. K. Chesterton** *Heretics*, Ch. 18

5 Judgement can be refuted, but never a prejudice.

Maria von Ebner-Eschenbach *Aphorisms*, p. 19

6 He flattered himself on being a man without any prejudices; and this pretension itself is a very great prejudice.

Anatole France *The Crime of Sylvestre Bonnard*, Ch. 3: 'Same Day'

7 A bigot is a stone-deaf orator. **Kahlil Gibran** *Sand and Foam*

8 When someone says his conclusions are objective, he means that they are based on prejudices which many other people share.

Celia Green *The Decline and Fall of Science*: 'Aphorisms'

9 To divest oneself of some prejudices would be like taking off the skin to feel better. **Fulke Greville** *Maxims, Characters and Reflections*, p. 181

10 Any stigma, as the old saying is, will serve to beat a dogma.

Philip Guedalla *Masters and Men*: 'Ministers of State'

11 No wise man can have a contempt for the prejudices of others; and he should even stand in a certain awe of his own, as if they were aged parents and monitors. They may in the end prove wiser than he.
William Hazlitt *Characteristics*, 132; he was repeating Burke

12 Without the aid of prejudice and custom, I should not be able to find my way across the room. **William Hazlitt** *Sketches and Essays*: 'On Prejudice'

13 Prejudice in short is egotism: we see a part, and substitute it for the whole. **William Hazlitt** *Sketches and Essays*: 'On Prejudice'

14 Prejudice is never easy unless it can pass itself off for reason.
William Hazlitt *Sketches and Essays*: 'On Prejudice'

15 The anthropocentric is also a form of chauvinism.
Hugo von Hofmannsthal *The Book of Friends*, 3

16 Prejudices are so to speak the mechanical interests of men: through their prejudices they do without any effort many things they would find too difficult to think through to the point of resolving to do them. **Georg Christoph Lichtenberg** *Aphorisms*, Notebook A, 17

17 One should always cultivate one's prejudices.
W. Somerset Maugham *A Writer's Notebook*, 1900

18 It is with narrow-souled people as with narrow-necked bottles: the less they have in them, the more noise they make in pouring it out.
Alexander Pope *Thoughts on Various Subjects*, 54

19 Man has a prejudice against himself: anything which is a product of his mind seems to him to be unreal or comparatively insignificant.
George Santayana *Little Essays*, 1

20 Prejudice is the reason of fools.
Voltaire in J. de Finod, *A Thousand Flashes of French Wit*, p. 18

See also ***Judgement; Opinions***

Pride and Modesty

1 Other sins find their vent in the accomplishment of evil deeds, whereas pride lies in wait for good deeds to destroy them. **St Augustine (attrib.)**

2 One cannot touch a fig-leaf without it turning into a price tag.
Saul Bellow (attrib.)

3 All modesty is false, otherwise it's not modesty.
Alan Bennett *Kafka's Dick*, Act 1

4 Pride goeth before destruction, and an haughty spirit before a fall.

Bible, OT Proverbs 16:18

5 Pride was not made for men, nor furious anger for them that are born of a woman. **Bible, Apocrypha** Ecclesiasticus 10:18

6 False modesty is the most decent of all lies.

Nicholas-Sébastien Chamfort *Maxims and Considerations*, Pt 1

7 Modesty is as little approved in Spain as vanity in France.

Jean Cocteau *Diaries*, Vol. 2, 25 July 1953

8 It's surely better to be arrogant than to look it. The arrogant character insults you only now and then; the arrogant look insults you continually. **Denis Diderot** *Rameau's Nephew*

9 Pride is faith in the idea that God had, when he made us. A proud man is conscious of the idea, and aspires to realize it.

Isak Dinesen *Out of Africa*: 'On Pride'

10 The meek shall inherit the earth, but not the mineral rights.

Paul Getty (attrib.)

See also Hubbard

11 There is a way of getting over French pride, for it is related to vanity. But English pride is invulnerable, for it is founded on the power of money. **Johann Wolfgang von Goethe** *Goethe's Opinions*, p. 45

12 Vanity is other people's pride. **Sacha Guitry** *Jusqu'à nouvel ordre*

13 Men often *mistake* themselves, but they never *forget* themselves.

Marquis of Halifax *Moral Thoughts and Reflections*: 'Of Vanity'

14 Vanity does not refer to the opinion a man entertains of himself, but to that which he wishes others to entertain of him.

William Hazlitt *Characteristics*, 107

15 It's goin' t' be fun t' watch an' see how long th' meek kin keep the earth after they inherit it. **'Kin' Hubbard** *Abe Martin's Wisecracks*, p. 77

See also Getty

16 Try not to despise yourself too much – it's only conceit.

P. J. Kavanagh *A Song and Dance*, Ch. 6

17 Shyness is just egoism out of its depth.

Penelope Keith in the *Observer*, 'Sayings of the Week', 3 July 1988

18 Vanity: The more often we are given to contemplating ourselves in the mirror, the less likely we are to recognize ourselves in the street.

David Kipp *Aphorisms*, p. 6

19 She had so much modesty that she blushed when caught not sinning. **Karl Kraus** *Half-Truths and One-and-a-Half Truths*: 'Not for women'

20 Sensitive people wish to be loved; vain people wish only to be preferred. **Duc de Lévis** in J. de Finod, *A Thousand Flashes of French Wit*, p. 107

21 Whenever someone makes badly what we expected to be well made, we say: *I could do as well as that myself*. There are few expressions that betray so much modesty. **Georg Christoph Lichtenberg** *Aphorisms*, Notebook K, 91

22 One may be humble out of pride. **Michel de Montaigne** *Essays*, Bk 2, Ch. 17

23 He who despises himself nonetheless still respects himself for his contempt. **Friedrich Nietzsche** *Beyond Good and Evil*: 'Maxims and Interludes', 78

24 Of all the causes which conspire to blind
Man's erring judgement, and misguide the mind,
What the weak head with strongest bias rules,
Is pride, the never-failing vice of fools. **Alexander Pope** *Essay on Criticism*, 201

25 Nor walk on the earth with insolence:
for thou canst not rend the earth asunder nor reach the mountains in height. ***Holy Qur'an*** Ch. 17

26 Although modesty is natural to man, it is not natural to children. Modesty only starts with the knowledge of evil. **Jean-Jacques Rousseau** *Émile*, Bk 4

27 A confessional passage has probably never been written that didn't stink a little bit of the writer's pride in having given up his pride.
J. D. Salinger *Seymour: An Introduction*

28 Humility is a virtue all preach, none practise, and yet everybody is content to hear. The master thinks it a good doctrine for his servant, the laity for the clergy, and the clergy for the laity.
John Selden *Table Talk*, 54

29 The more things a man is ashamed of, the more respectable he is.
George Bernard Shaw *Man and Superman*: Preface

30 A man never looks down on those below him except as he humbles himself towards those above him. **Abu Hayyan al-Tawhidi (attrib.)**

31 Pleasing oneself is pride; pleasing others, vanity.
Paul Valéry *At Moments*: 'Glimpses'

32 The modest man is one in whom the feelings of being one man among others is stronger than the feeling of being himself.
Paul Valéry *Odds and Ends*: 'Moralities'

33 We are rarely proud when we are alone. **Voltaire** *Philosophical Dictionary*

34 We do not have to acquire humility. There is humility in us – only we humiliate ourselves before false gods.

Simone Weil *Gravity and Grace*: 'Idolatry'

35 None so Empty as those who are Full of themselves.

Benjamin Whichcote *Moral and Religious Aphorisms*, 987

See also ***Vices and Virtues***

Progress

1 Progress would not have been the rarity it is if the early food had not been the late poison. **Walter Bagehot** *Physics and Politics*, Ch. 2, Sect. 3

2 Belief in progress is a lazy man's creed, a creed for Belgians. It is the individual counting on his neighbour to perform his task for him.

Charles Baudelaire *Intimate Journals*: 'My Heart Laid Bare', 9

3 Society moves by some degree of parricide, by which the children, on the whole, kill, if not their fathers, at least the beliefs of their fathers, and arrive at new beliefs. This is what progress is.

Isaiah Berlin in BBC TV programme *Men of Ideas*, 19 January 1978

4 The march of the human mind is slow.

Edmund Burke speech on conciliation with America, 22 March 1775

5 All progress is based upon a universal innate desire on the part of every organism to live beyond its income. **Samuel Butler 2** *Notebooks*, Ch. 1: 'Life', 16

6 As enunciated today, 'progress' is simply a comparative of which we have not settled the superlative. **G. K. Chesterton** *Heretics*, Ch. 2

7 What we call progress is the exchange of one nuisance for another nuisance. **Henry Havelock Ellis** *Impressions and Comments*, 31 July 1912

8 All that is human must be retrograde if it does not advance.

Edward Gibbon *The Decline and Fall of the Roman Empire*, Ch. 71

9 It is because nations tend towards stupidity and baseness that mankind moves so slowly; it is because individuals have a capacity for better things that it moves at all.

George Gissing *The Private Papers of Henry Ryecroft*: 'Spring', XVI

10 All eras in a state of decline and dissolution are subjective; whereas all progressive eras tend to be objective.

Johann Wolfgang von Goethe *Conversations with Eckermann*, 29 January 1826

11 Progress can be good or bad, like Jews or Germans or films!

Eugene Ionesco *Maid to Marry*

12 The decisive moment in the development of mankind is everlasting. That is why the revolutionary spiritual movements that declare all former things to be of no account are in the right, for nothing has yet occurred. **Franz Kafka** *Collected Aphorisms*, 6

13 To believe in progress does not mean believing that any progress has yet been made. That would not amount to belief.

Franz Kafka *Collected Aphorisms*, 48

14 Progress makes purses out of human skin.

Karl Kraus *Half-Truths and One-and-a-Half Truths*: 'Lord, forgive the . . .'

15 People fascinated by the idea of progress never suspect that every step forward is also a step on the way to the end.

Milan Kundera *The Book of Laughter and Forgetting*, 6, 17

16 Is it progress if a cannibal uses a knife and fork?

Stanislaw Lec *Unkempt Thoughts*, p. 78

17 A converted cannibal is one who, on Friday, eats only fishermen.

Emily Lotney in Laurence J. Peter, *Peter's Quotations*: 'Religion'

18 Real progress is progress in charity, all other advances being secondary thereto. **Dr R. R. Marett** quoted in Aldous Huxley, *Ends and Means*, Ch. 1

19 Progress would be wonderful – if only it would stop.

Robert Musil (attrib.)

20 If you don't know where you are going, you will probably end up somewhere else. **Laurence J. Peter and Raymond Hull** *The Peter Principle*, Ch. 15

21 Progress is lame.

Charles-Augustin Sainte-Beuve in J. de Finod, *A Thousand Flashes of French Wit*, p. 19

22 Progress, far from consisting in change, depends on retentiveness . . . Those who do not remember the past are condemned to repeat it.

George Santayana *The Life of Reason*, Vol. 1, Ch. 12

23 The reasonable man adapts himself to the world; the unreasonable one persists in trying to adapt the world to himself. Therefore all progress depends on the unreasonable man.

George Bernard Shaw *Man and Superman*, 'Maxims for Revolutionists': 'Reason'

24 Progress in any aspect is a movement through changes of terminology. **Wallace Stevens** *Adagia*, 1

25 It's dogged as does it. It ain't thinking about it.

Anthony Trollope *The Last Chronicle of Barset*, Ch. 61

26 This was the order of human things: first the forests, after that the huts, thence the villages, next the cities and finally the academies.
Giambattista Vico *The New Sciences*, Bk 1, Para. 239

27 Sin is an essential element of progress. Without it the world would stagnate. **Oscar Wilde** *The Critic as Artist*, 1

See also ***The Future***

Prophecy

1 A prophet is not without honour, save in his own country.
Bible, NT Matthew 13:57

2 It's a habit with prophets to be unhealthy.
Most seers are cripples. **Joseph Brodsky** *Adieu, Mademoiselle Véronique*, V

3 Study Prophecies when they are become histories, and past hovering in their causes. Eye well things past and present, and let conjectural sagacity suffice for things to come.
Sir Thomas Browne *Christian Morals*, Pt 3, 13

4 A hopeful disposition is not the sole qualification to be a prophet.
Winston S. Churchill speech in House of Commons, 30 April 1927

5 In every man sleeps a prophet, and when he wakes there is a little more evil in the world. **E. M. Cioran** *A Short History of Decay*, 1: 'The Anti-prophet'

6 Among all forms of mistake, prophecy is the most gratuitous.
George Eliot *Middlemarch*, Bk 1, Ch. 10

7 The best qualification of a prophet is to have a good memory.
Marquis of Halifax *Miscellaneous Thoughts and Reflections*

8 Some people would take comfort from the end of the world, if only they had prophesied it. **Friedrich Hebbel** *Diaries*, entry 3292, 1845

9 There is no God and Man is his prophet.
Jens Peter Jacobsen *Niels Lyhne*, Ch. 8

10 The 'second sight' possessed by the Highlanders in Scotland is actually a foreknowledge of future events. I believe they possess this gift because they don't wear trousers. That is also why in all countries women are more prone to utter prophecies.
Georg Christoph Lichtenberg *Aphorisms*, Notebook L, 26

See also ***The Future***

Q

Questions and Answers

1 History is, strictly speaking, the study of questions; the study of answers belongs to anthropology and sociology.
W. H. Auden *The Dyer's Hand*, 3: 'Hic et Ille', Sect. B

2 To ask the hard question is simple. **W. H. Auden** *The Question*

3 Women were brought up to believe that men were the answer. They weren't. They weren't even one of the questions.
Julian Barnes *Staring at the Sun*, Pt 2

4 The Socratic manner is not a game at which two can play.
Max Beerbohm *Zuleika Dobson*, Ch. 15

5 Answer a fool according to his folly, lest he be wise in his own conceit. **Bible, OT** Proverbs 26:5

6 You know what charm is: a way of getting the answer yes without having asked any clear question. **Albert Camus** *The Fall*

7 Examinations are formidable even to the best prepared, for the greatest fool may ask more than the wisest man can answer.
Charles Caleb Colton *Lacon*, 1, 322

8 Curiosity being one of the forms of self-revelation, a systematically incurious person remains always partly mysterious.
Joseph Conrad *The Secret Agent*, Ch. 11

9 Commonplace people have an answer for everything and nothing ever surprises them. **Eugène Delacroix** *Journal*, 25 February 1852

10 No one thing can explain everything; though everything can illuminate something. **Lawrence Durrell** *Justine*, Pt 2, p. 140

11 Everything should be made as simple as possible, but not simpler.

Albert Einstein quoted in *Reader's Digest*, October 1977

12 I admire answers to which no answers can be made.

Ralph Waldo Emerson *Journal*, June–July 1853

13 Curiosity is one of the lowest of the human faculties. You will have noticed that in daily life when people are inquisitive they nearly always have bad memories and are usually stupid at bottom.

E. M. Forster *Aspects of the Novel*, Ch. 5

14 Questions of why are dangerous in history.

E. H. Gombrich *Art and Illusion*, Ch. 10

15 Questioning is not the mode of conversation among gentlemen.

Dr Samuel Johnson in James Boswell, *Life of Johnson*, 25 March 1776

16 It is better to debate a question without settling it, than to settle it without debate. **Joseph Joubert** *Thoughts and Maxims*, 115

17 As long as the answer is right, who cares if the question is wrong?

Norton Juster *The Phantom Tollbooth*, Ch. 14

18 Only he is an artist who can make a riddle out of a solution.

Karl Kraus *Half-Truths and One-and-a-Half Truths*: 'Riddles'

19 Fly him who, from mere curiosity, asks three questions running about a thing that cannot interest him.

Johann Kaspar Lavater *Aphorisms on Man*, 368

20 The world is but a school of inquiry. **Michel de Montaigne** *Essays*, Bk 3, Ch. 8

21 A radical – one who not only knows all the answers but keeps on thinking up new questions. ***New Statesman*** undated

22 Don't ask *what are* questions, ask *what do* questions, don't ask *why* questions, ask *how* questions.

Karl Popper quoted by Bernard Levin in the *Sunday Times, Books*, 16 April 1989

23 Curious minds ask arbitrarily any question without ever questioning their own right to ask or their own power to understand and to enact the answer.

Eugen Rosenstock-Huessy *The Christian Future or the Modern Mind Outrun*, Ch. 5

24 It's the little questions from women about tappets that finally push men over the edge. **Philip Roth** *Letting Go*, Pt 1, Ch. 1

25 To be and not to be, that is the answer. **Michael Rubinstein** in conversation

26 I never met with a question yet, of any importance, which did not need, for the right solution of it, at least one positive and one negative answer.

John Ruskin said in 1858, quoted in 'Ruskin, Turner and the Pre-Raphaelites' exhibition, London, 2000

27 There are no solutions in life. There are active forces: first create these and the solutions will follow. **Antoine de Saint-Exupéry** *Night Flight*, Ch. 19

28 We Yankees are not so far from right, who answer one question by asking another. Yes and No are lies – a true answer will not aim to establish anything, but rather to set all well afloat.

H. D. Thoreau *Journal*, 22 June 1840

29 If love is the answer, could you rephrase the question?

Lily Tomlin quoted in David Housham and John Frank-Keyes, *Funny Business*

30 He was all answer with no question. **John Updike** *Gertrude and Claudius*

31 The outcome of any serious research can only be to make two questions grow where only one grew before.

Thorstein Veblen *The Place of Science in Modern Civilization*

32 Anything that can be explained in a variety of ways does not deserve any explanation at all. **Voltaire** *The Century of Louis XIV*, Ch. 19

33 Questions are never indiscreet. Answers sometimes are.

Oscar Wilde *An Ideal Husband*, Act 1

Reading

1 Read not to contradict and confute, nor to believe and take for granted, nor to find talk and discourse, but to weigh and consider.

Francis Bacon *Essays*: 'Of Studies'

2 Classics – and in particular modern classics – are the books one thinks one ought to read, thinks one has read.

Alan Bennett *Kafka's Dick*: Introduction

See also Twain

3 A book chooses its readers as a play chooses its audience.

Alan Bennett in *With Great Pleasure*, ed. Alec Reid

4 A good reader is rarer than a good writer.

Jorge Luis Borges quoted in Robert Robinson, *Dog Chairman*: 'Arm in Arm with Borges'

See also Emerson

5 Reading is getting more difficult; *more* gets stirred up.

Elias Canetti *The Secret Heart of the Clock*: '1980'

6 To read until one no longer understands a single sentence, that alone is reading.

Elias Canetti *The Secret Heart of the Clock*: '1984'

7 To read is to let someone else do the work for you – the most delicate form of exploitation.

E. M. Cioran *Anathemas and Admirations*, 9

8 We read often with as much talent as we write.

Ralph Waldo Emerson *Journal*, Vol. 10, p. 140

See also Borges

9 Men of power have no time to read; yet the men who do not read are unfit for power.

Michael Foot *Debts of Honour*, Ch. 4

10 By our inmost animal nature we are readers. We read the world around us continuously, obsessively, necessarily. Reading our notations is a late specialization of a general skill. **Michael Frayn** *Constructions*, 4

11 No tears in the writer, no tears in the reader. No surprise for the writer, no surprise for the reader.
Robert Frost in *Writers at Work, Second Series*, ed. George Plimpton

12 Reading is sometimes an ingenious device for avoiding thought.
Sir Arthur Helps *Friends in Council*, Bk 2, Ch. 1

13 We read to train the mind, to fill the mind, to rest the mind, to recreate the mind, or to escape the mind.
Holbrook Jackson *Maxims of Books and Reading*, 2

14 In reading you discover yourself under the impression that you are discovering your author. **Holbrook Jackson** *Maxims of Books and Reading*, 5

15 Reading to pass the time is sleeping without the advantages of sleep.
Holbrook Jackson *Maxims of Books and Reading*, 15

16 Notes are often necessary, but they are necessary evils.
Dr Samuel Johnson *Preface to Shakespeare*

17 A man ought to read just as inclination leads him; for what he reads as a task will do him little good.
Dr Samuel Johnson in James Boswell, *Life of Johnson*, 14 July 1763

18 One must read all writers twice – the good as well as the bad. The one will be recognized; the other, unmasked.
Karl Kraus *Half-Truths and One-and-a-Half Truths*: 'Riddles'

19 That everyone is allowed to learn to read will in the long run ruin not only writing but thinking, too.
Friedrich Nietzsche *Thus Spake Zarathustra*, Pt 1: 'Of Reading and Writing'

20 There are no foreign books; there are only foreign readers.
Joseph Prescott *Aphorisms and Other Observations*: 'Literature'

21 In reality, people read because they want to write. Anyway, reading is a sort of rewriting.
Jean-Paul Sartre *Between Existentialism and Marxism*: 'The Purposes of Writing'

22 People say that life is the thing, but I prefer reading.
Logan Pearsall Smith *Afterthoughts*, 5

23 Reading is to the mind what exercise is to the body.
Sir Richard Steele *The Tatler*, 147

24 You should only read what is truly good or what is frankly bad.
Gertrude Stein quoted in Ernest Hemingway, *A Moveable Feast*, 3

25 Whatever sentence will bear to be read twice, we may be sure was thought twice. **H. D. Thoreau** *Journals*, 1842

26 A classic is something that everybody wants to have read and nobody wants to read.

Mark Twain speech, 20 November 1900, Nineteenth Century Club, New York, quoting Professor Caleb Winchester, 'The Disappearance of Literature'

See also Bennett

27 If one cannot enjoy reading a book over and over again, there is no use in reading it at all. **Oscar Wilde** *The Decay of Lying*

28 No two people read the same book.

Edmund Wilson quoted by John Russell in the *Sunday Times*, 25 July 1971

See also ***Books; Literature; Poetry and Poets; Writing***

Reason

1 Reason is itself a matter of faith. It is an act of faith to assert that our thoughts have any relation to reality at all. **G. K. Chesterton** *Orthodoxy*, Ch. 3

2 Common sense is the most widely distributed commodity in the world, for everyone thinks himself so well endowed with it that those who are hardest to please in every other respect generally have no desire to possess more of it than they have. **René Descartes** *Discourse on Method*, 1

3 Common sense is the collection of prejudices acquired by age eighteen. **Albert Einstein** in *Scientific American*, February 1976

4 The conservative has but little to fear from the man whose reason is the servant of his passions, but let him beware of him in whom reason has become the greatest and most terrible of passions.

J. B. S. Haldane *Daedalus or Science and the Future*

5 Reason may be extinguished by oppressing it with the weight of too many strange things; especially if we are forbidden to chew what we are commanded to swallow. **Marquis of Halifax** *Advice to a Daughter*: 'Religion'

6 A Man that doth not use his Reason, is a tame Beast; a Man that abuses it, is a wild one. **Marquis of Halifax** *Miscellaneous Thoughts and Reflections*

7 Sense must be very good indeed, to be as good as nonsense.

Julius and Augustus Hare *Guesses at Truth*, 2

8 Irrationality is the square root of all evil.

Douglas Hofstadter epigraph to John D. Barrow, *Theories of Everything*

9 Reason is like truth, it is indivisible; you reach it by a single path and you may stray from it by a thousand.

Jean de La Bruyère *Characters*: 'Of Man', 156

10 Reason is incapable of transforming men's convictions.

Gustave Le Bon *The Psychology of Peoples*: 'Introduction'

11 A man who does not lose his reason over certain things has none to lose. **Gotthold Ephraim Lessing** *Emilia Galotti*, Act 4, Sc. 7

12 Pure reason avoids extremes, and requires one to be wise in moderation. **Molière** *The Misanthrope*, Act 1, Sc. 1

13 Reason and imagination are religion – reason and understanding are science. **Novalis** *Pollen*, 320

14 Reason commands us much more imperiously than a master. If we disobey a master we are unhappy but if we defy reason we are fools.

Blaise Pascal *Pensées*, 266

15 The heart has its reasons of which the reason knows nothing.

Blaise Pascal *Pensées*, 477

16 Reason consists of truths which must be spoken and truths which must remain unspoken. **Antoine de Rivarol** *Notes, réflexions et maximes*: 'Philosophe'

17 Reason, an *ignis fatuus* of the mind,
Which leaves the light of nature, sense, behind.

John Wilmot, Earl of Rochester *A Satire against Mankind*, 12

18 If rationality were the criterion of things being allowed to exist, the world would be a gigantic field of soya beans! **Tom Stoppard** *Jumpers*, Act 1

See also ***The Mind; Thought***

Relationships

1 We are made for co-operation, like feet, like hands, like eye-lids, like the rows of the upper and lower teeth. To act against one another is contrary to nature. **Marcus Aurelius** *Meditations*, Bk 2, 1

2 Every *tête à tête* is *à quatre*. **Elizabeth Bibesco** *Haven*: 'Aphorisms'

3 Those who stand in a confessional relationship to ourselves can never love us, never truly love us. **Lawrence Durrell** *Justine*, Pt 4, p. 243

4 Men love women, women love children, children love hamsters, hamsters don't love anybody.

Alice Thomas Ellis in BBC TV programme, *Bookmark*, 16 December 1987

5 Every deed and every relationship is surrounded by an atmosphere of silence. Friendship needs no words – it is solitude delivered from the anguish of loneliness. **Dag Hammarskjöld** *Markings*: 'Thus It Was'

6 Some folks should live in non-shatter glass-houses.
'Kin' Hubbard *Abe Martin's Broadcast*: 'Drunkenness'

7 The best friend of a boy is his mother, of a man his horse; only it's not clear when the transition takes place.
Joseph L. Mankiewicz in A. Andrews, *Quotations for Speakers and Writers*

8 Everybody, one might say, is left out of being someone else. But that is no comfort. Coupledom is as close as you can get.
Adam Phillips *Monogamy*, 116

9 Relationships are often constituted by what one dare not say to the other person. **Adam Phillips** *Terrors and Experts*, Ch. 4

10 We keep passing unseen through little moments of other people's lives. **Robert M. Pirsig** *Zen and the Art of Motorcycle Maintenance*, Pt 3, Ch. 24

11 If a man makes me keep my distance, the comfort is he keeps his at the same time. **Jonathan Swift** *Thoughts on Various Subjects*, p. 281

12 Romance should never begin with sentiment. It should begin with science and end with a settlement. **Oscar Wilde** *An Ideal Husband*, Act 3

13 The most dangerous word in any human tongue is the word for brother. It's inflammatory. **Tennessee Williams** *Camino Real*, Block 2

See also ***Family; Others; People***

Religion

1 Catholicism – that's die now and pay later.
Woody Allen in film *Hannah and Her Sisters*

2 The nearer the Church the further from God.
Lancelot Andrewes *Sermon on the Nativity*, 1622

3 Half of Christendom worships a Jew, and the other half a Jewess.
Anon. in H. L. Mencken, *New Dictionary of Quotations*

4 Every man thinks God is on his side. The rich and powerful know he is. **Jean Anouilh** *The Lark*, Pt. 1

5 No man, who knows nothing else, knows even his Bible.
Matthew Arnold *Culture and Anarchy*, 5

6 The true meaning of religion is thus not simply morality, but morality touched by emotion. **Matthew Arnold** *Literature and Dogma*, Ch. 1, Sect. 2

7 The white man discovered the Cross by way of the Bible, but the black man discovered the Bible by way of the Cross.
James Baldwin *Evidence of Things Not Seen*

8 The wish to pray is a prayer in itself.
Georges Bernanos *The Diary of a Country Priest*, Ch. 4

9 Argument, generally speaking, in religion, can do no more than clear the track; it cannot make the engine move. **Edwyn Bevan** *Hellenism and Christianity*

10 In religion we believe only what we do not understand, except in the instance of an intelligible doctrine that contradicts an incomprehensible one. In that case we believe the former as part of the latter.
Ambrose Bierce *The Devil's Dictionary*

11 As the caterpillar chooses the fairest leaves to lay her eggs on, so the priest lays his curse on the fairest joys.
William Blake *The Marriage of Heaven and Hell*: 'Proverbs of Hell'

12 Religions are kept alive by heresies, which are really sudden explosions of faith. Dead religions do not produce them.
Gerald Brenan *Thoughts in a Dry Season*: 'Religion'

13 The Religion of one seems madness unto another.
Sir Thomas Browne *Urn Burial*, Ch. 4

14 Nothing is so fatal to religion as indifference, which is, at least, half infidelity. **Edmund Burke** letter to William Smith, 29 January 1795

15 Men will never utterly give over the other world for this, nor this world for the other. **Samuel Butler 1** in *Wit and Wisdom of Dean Inge*: Preface

16 To be at all is to be religious more or less.
Samuel Butler 2 *Notebooks*, Ch. 22: 'Religion'

17 The only thing that stops God from sending a second Flood is that the first one was useless. **Nicholas-Sébastien Chamfort** *Characters and Anecdotes*

18 *The Bible*: a book which either reads us or is worthless.
Malcolm de Chazal *Sens plastique*

19 Religion is by no means a proper subject of conversation in a mixed company. **Earl of Chesterfield** letter to his godson, no. 112 (undated)

20 Everything suffers by *translation* except a bishop.
Earl of Chesterfield letter to the Bishop of Waterford, 12 September 1761, in editor's footnote

21 Religion is exactly the thing which cannot be left out – because it includes everything. **G. K. Chesterton** *Heretics*, Ch. 20

22 Whenever men really believe that they can get to the spiritual, they always employ the material. When the purpose is good, it is bread and wine; when the purpose is evil, it is eye of newt and toe of frog.

G. K. Chesterton in *Illustrated London News*, 22 September 1906

23 A religion is not the church a man goes to but the cosmos he lives in.

G. K. Chesterton *Irish Impressions*

24 He who begins by loving Christianity better than Truth will proceed by loving his own sect or church better than Christianity, and end by loving himself better than all.

Samuel Taylor Coleridge *Aids to Reflection, Moral and Religious Aphorisms*, 25

25 Men will wrangle for religion; write for it; fight for it; anything but – live for it. **Charles Caleb Colton** *Lacon*, 1, 25

26 The parson knows enough who knows a duke. **William Cowper** *Tirocinium*, 403

27 You need to be very religious to change religions.

Comtesse Diane *Les Glanes de la vie*, p. 89

28 Christians are only an anaemic variety of Jews.

Norman Douglas *An Almanac 1945*

29 Science without religion is lame, religion without science is blind.

Albert Einstein *Out of My Later Years*, Ch. 7

30 We know too much and are convinced of too little. Our literature is a substitute for religion, and so is our religion.

T. S. Eliot *Selected Essays*: 'A Dialogue on Dramatic Poetry'

31 The religions we call false were once true.

Ralph Waldo Emerson *Essays*: 'Character'

32 It's the generally accepted privilege of theologians to stretch the heavens, that is the scriptures, like tanners with a hide.

Desiderius Erasmus *Praise of Folly*, Ch. 64

33 The average curate at home was something between a eunuch and a snigger. **Ronald Firbank** *The Flower Beneath the Foot*, Ch. 4

34 Miracles are the swaddling-clothes of infant churches.

Thomas Fuller *The Church History of Britain*, Vol. 2, p. 239

35 To a philosophic eye, the vices of the clergy are far less dangerous than their virtues. **Edward Gibbon** *The Decline and Fall of the Roman Empire*, Ch. 49

36 There are only two true religions: one of them recognizes and worships the Holy that without form or shape dwells in and around us; the other recognizes and worships it in its fairest form. Everything that lies between these two is idolatry.

Johann Wolfgang von Goethe *Maxims and Reflections*: 'Life and Character', 312

37 Mysticism is the scholastic of the heart, the dialectic of the feelings.
Johann Wolfgang von Goethe *Maxims and Reflections*: 'Literature and Art', 430

38 If there is a God, atheism must strike Him as less of an insult than religion. **Edmond and Jules de Goncourt** *Journal*, 24 January 1868

39 We only really respond to religion as children – throughout our lives.
Edmond and Jules de Goncourt *Journal*, 17 April 1868

40 It is not he who adorns but he who adores the idol that makes it divine. **Baltasar Gracián** *The Oracle*, 5

41 Religion is exalted reason, refined and sifted from the grosser parts of it. **Marquis of Halifax** *Advice to a Daughter*: 'Religion'

42 Every man, either unto his terror or consolation, hath some sense of religion. **James Harrington** *Aphorisms Political*, 26

43 Some people only worship what they can destroy.
Friedrich Hebbel *Diaries*, entry 1082, 1838

44 Religion can be a great danger as well as a great health-giver: religion is what some people do with their madness.
Revd Richard Holloway launching book, *Churches and How to Survive Them*; quoted in the *Observer*, 4 September 1994

45 A priest's life is not supposed to be well-rounded; it is supposed to be one-pointed – a compass, not a weathercock.
Aldous Huxley *The Devils of Loudun*, Ch. 1

46 Christianity promises to make men free; it never promises to make them independent. **W. R. Inge** *The Philosophy of Plotinus*

47 Religion is a way of walking, not a way of talking. **W. R. Inge (attrib.)**

48 I have always considered a clergyman as the father of a larger family than he is able to maintain.
Dr Samuel Johnson in James Boswell, *Life of Johnson*, Vol. 3, 304

49 Nowhere probably is there more true feeling, and nowhere worse taste, than in a churchyard. **Benjamin Jowett** *Letters*, p. 244

50 Religion is the frozen thought of men out of which they build temples. **J. Krishnamurti** in the *Observer*, 'Sayings of the Week', 22 April 1928

51 If atheism spread, it would become a religion as intolerable as the ancient ones. **Gustave Le Bon** *Aphorismes du temps présent*

52 In science we have been reading only the notes to a poem; in Christianity we find the poem itself. **C. S. Lewis** *Miracles*, Ch. 14

53 Such are the heights of wickedness to which men are driven by religion. **Lucretius** *On the Nature of Things*, I, 101

54 Bishops tend to live long lives – apparently the Lord is not all that keen for them to join him.

Jonathan Lynn and Antony Jay *Yes, Prime Minister*: 'The Bishop's Gambit'

55 All true teaching [i.e. religion], so mingling fear with consolatory ideas, warns the free being not to advance to the limit beyond which there is no limit.

Joseph de Maistre *The Saint Petersburg Dialogues*, 5

56 Religion . . . is the opium of the people.

Karl Marx *Criticism of Hegel's Philosophy of Right*: Introduction

57 All religions are useless to the philosopher and useful to the magistrate.

Iqbal Masood quoted in M. Tully, *No Full Stops in India*, Ch. 4

58 No kingdom has ever had as many civil wars as that of Christ.

Charles de Montesquieu *Persian Letters*, 29

59 Where religion is concerned, those most closely related are the greatest enemies.

Charles de Montesquieu *Persian Letters*, 60

60 The Churches grow old but do not grow up.

Doris Langley Moore *The Vulgar Heart*, Ch. 2

61 Basically, the secret of life is to act as though we possessed the thing we most painfully lack. In that lies the whole doctrine of Christianity.

Cesare Pavese *This Business of Living, Diary 1935–1950*, 3 February 1941

62 Religion is the meeting of truth and justice. Every crisis can be reduced to a lack of balance between these vital necessities.

Cesare Pavese *This Business of Living, Diary 1935–1950*, 1 September 1944

63 Religion to me has always been the wound, not the bandage.

Dennis Potter *Seeing the Blossom*; an interview with Melvyn Bragg, Channel 4 TV, April 1994

64 Pagans proceed on precedent, but Christians remain unpredictable: they *pre*cede.

Eugen Rosenstock-Huessy *The Christian Future or the Modern Mind Outrun*, Ch. 5

65 There is only one necessary axiom in religion: the source of my life lies outside myself.

Colin Ross *Adecarcinoma and Other Poems*, Aphorism 23

66 No article of a man's religion can be spoken.

Mark Rutherford *Last Pages from a Journal*: Notes, p. 307

67 People may say what they like about the decay of Christianity; the religious system that produced green Chartreuse can never really die.

Saki *Reginald on Christmas Presents*

68 The Bible is literature, not dogma.

George Santayana *Introduction to the Ethics of Spinoza*

69 The Old and the New Testaments are for this reason diametrically opposed, and their union forms a very strange centaur; for the Old Testament is optimistic, the New Testament pessimistic. The former is a tune in the major, the latter a tune in the minor.

Arthur Schopenhauer *Essays and Aphorisms*: 'On Religion', 7

70 There is only one religion though there are a hundred versions of it.

George Bernard Shaw *Plays Pleasant*: Preface

71 Don't you know, as the French say, there are three sexes – men, women, and clergymen?

Revd Sydney Smith in his daughter, Lady Holland's, *Memoir*, Vol. 1, Ch. 9

72 I never saw, heard, nor read, that the clergy were beloved in any nation where Christianity was the religion of the country. Nothing can render them popular but some degree of persecution.

Jonathan Swift *Thoughts on Religion*

73 We have just enough religion to make us hate, but not enough to make us love one another. **Jonathan Swift** *Thoughts on Various Subjects*, p. 273

74 Query, whether churches are not dormitories of the living as well as of the dead? **Jonathan Swift** *Thoughts on Various Subjects*, p. 283

75 The power of religion in the individual soul is nicely proportioned to its powerlessness in society. **R. H. Tawney** *The Acquisitive Society*, 11

76 The blood of the martyrs is the seed of the Church.

Tertullian *Apologeticus*, 50

77 The entertaining a single thought of a certain elevation makes all men of one religion. **H. D. Thoreau** *Journal*, 8 August 1852

78 The Christian's Bible is a drug store. Its contents remain the same, but the medical practice changes.

Mark Twain *Bible Teaching and Religious Practice*

79 Christianity is an allegory reflecting a true idea; but the allegory itself is not what is true. **Mark Twain** *Bible Teaching and Religious Practice*

80 The extreme greatness of Christianity lies in the fact that it does not seek a supernatural remedy for suffering but a supernatural use for it.

Simone Weil *Gravity and Grace*: 'Affliction'

81 The progress of religion is defined by the denunciation of gods. The keynote of idolatry is contentment with the prevalent gods.

A. N. Whitehead *Adventures of Ideas*, Ch. 2, 1

82 Prayer must never be answered: if it is, it ceases to be prayer and becomes correspondence.

Oscar Wilde in conversation; in *Epigrams of Oscar Wilde*, ed. Alvin Redman: 'Religion'

83 Scratch the Christian and you find the pagan – spoiled.
Israel Zangwill *Children of the Ghetto*, Bk 2, Ch. 6

See also ***Belief; Faith; Gods***

Rich and Poor

1 Riches are a good handmaiden, but the worst mistress.
Francis Bacon *De dignitate et augmentis scientiarum*, Bk 6, Ch. 3, Pt 3

2 As the baggage is to an army, so is riches to virtue. It cannot be spared, nor left behind, but it hindereth the march.
Francis Bacon *Essays*: 'Of Riches'

3 Poverty is an anomaly to rich people. It is very difficult to make out why people who want dinner do not ring the bell.
Walter Bagehot *Literary Studies*: 'The Waverley Novels'

4 Greed begins where poverty ends.
Honoré de Balzac *Illusions Perdues*: 'Les deux poètes'

5 So long as there are beggars, there will be mythology.
Walter Benjamin *Selected Writings* Vol. 1, 1913–1926

6 The rich man's wealth is his strong city: the destruction of the poor is their poverty.
Bible, OT Proverbs 10:15

7 As the wild ass is the lion's prey in the wilderness: so the rich eat up the poor.
Bible, Apocrypha Ecclesiasticus 13:19

8 Be not made a beggar by banqueting upon borrowing, when thou hast nothing in thy purse; for thou shalt lie in wait for thine own life, and be talked on.
Bible, Apocrypha Ecclesiasticus 18:33

9 It is easier for a camel to go through the eye of a needle, than for a rich man to enter into the kingdom of God.
Bible, NT Matthew 19:24

10 **Distance, n.** The only thing that the rich are willing for the poor to call theirs, and keep.
Ambrose Bierce *The Devil's Dictionary*

11 **Improvidence, n.** Provision for the needs of today from the revenues of tomorrow.
Ambrose Bierce *The Devil's Dictionary*

12 The best condishun in life iz not to be so ritch az tew be envyed, nor so poor az to be damned.
Josh Billings *Wit and Humor*, Affurisms: 'Chips'

13 Unto some 'tis Wealth enough not to be Poor, and others are well content, if they be but Rich enough to be Honest, and to give every Man his due.
Sir Thomas Browne *Christian Morals*, Pt 1, 26

14 If we command our wealth, we shall be rich and free; if our wealth commands us, we are poor indeed. **Edmund Burke** *Letters on a Regicide Peace*, 1

15 There are only two families in the world, my old grandmother used to say, the *Haves* and the *Have-nots*. **Miguel Cervantes** *Don Quixote*, Pt 2, 20

16 It is easier to ask of the poor than of the rich.
Anton Chekhov *Notebooks 1894–1902*, p. 14

17 People don't resent having nothing nearly as much as too little.
Ivy Compton-Burnett *A Family and a Fortune*, Ch. 2

18 It is more difficult not to complain of injustice when poor than not to behave with arrogance when rich. **Confucius** *The Analects*, Bk 14, 10

19 Mankind is fed up with poverty,
but poverty is hungry for mankind.
Hasan Dewran *A Thousand Winds May Make a Storm*: 'Foreign Aid'

20 Poverty and oysters always seem to go together.
Charles Dickens *Pickwick Papers*, Ch. 22

21 Poverty destroys pride. It is difficult for an empty bag to stand upright.
Alexandre Dumas, the younger in J. de Finod, *A Thousand Flashes of French Wit*, p. 117

22 Poverty is a great cutter-off and riches a great shutter-off.
Lawrence Durrell *Justine*, Pt 3, p. 167

23 It is only the poor who are forbidden to beg. **Anatole France** *Crainquebille*

24 In every state wealth is a sacred thing; in democracies it is the only sacred thing. **Anatole France** *Penguin Island*, Bk 6, Ch. 2

25 Poverty wants some things, Luxury many things, Avarice all things.
Benjamin Franklin *Poor Richard's Almanack*, 1735

26 Widows are always rich. **Dr Thomas Fuller** *Gnomologia*, 5740

27 Wealth has never been a sufficient source of honour in itself. It must be advertised and the normal medium is obtrusively expensive goods.
J. K. Galbraith *The Affluent Society*, Ch. 7, Sect. 5

See also Smith

28 If a man wishes to become rich, he must appear rich.
Oliver Goldsmith (attrib.)

29 In both rich and poor nations consumption is polarized while expectation is equalized. **Ivan D. Illich** *Celebration of Awareness*, Ch. 12

30 Man must choose whether to be rich in things or in the freedom to use them. **Ivan D. Illich** *Deschooling Society*, Ch. 4

31 Few rich men own their own property. The property owns them.

R. G. Ingersoll address to the McKinley League, New York, 29 October 1896

32 The rich are only defeated when running for their lives.

C. L. R. James *Black Jacobins*, Ch. 3

33 It is better to *live* rich than to *die* rich.

Dr Samuel Johnson in James Boswell, *Life of Johnson*, 17 April 1778

34 If you are poor, distinguish yourself by your virtues; if rich, by your good deeds. **Joseph Joubert** *Thoughts and Maxims*, 74

35 Poverty is bitter, but it has no harder pang than that it makes men ridiculous. **Juvenal** *Satires*, III, 152

36 Great wealth is the immediate cause of poverty.

Jean de La Bruyère *Characters*: 'Of Worldly Goods', 49

37 Wealth enables people to discover
their mediocrity much sooner
than is good for them. **Irving Layton** *The Whole Bloody Bird*: 'aphs'

38 If one's aim is wealth one cannot be beneficent; if one's aim is benevolence one cannot be worthy. **Mencius** Bk 3, Pt A, 3

39 In this world beggars are the only people who can be choosers. Everyone else has his side chosen for him.

V. S. Naipaul *A Bend in the River*, Ch. 9

40 If those who owe us nothing gave us nothing, how poor we would be. **Antonio Porchia** *Voices*

41 The poor lack much, the greedy everything.

Publilius Syrus play fragment quoted in Seneca, *Letters from a Stoic*, 108

42 It is not the man who has too little who is poor, but the one who hankers after more. **Seneca** *Letters from a Stoic*, 3

43 With the greater part of rich people, the chief enjoyment of riches consists in the parade of riches.

Adam Smith *The Wealth of Nations*, Bk 1, Ch. 11

See also Galbraith

44 It is the wretchedness of being rich that you have to live with rich people. **Logan Pearsall Smith** *Afterthoughts*, 4

45 Poverty is no disgrace to a man, but it is confoundedly inconvenient.

Revd Sydney Smith *His Wit and Wisdom*

46 If all the rich men in the world divided up their money amongst themselves, there wouldn't be enough to go round.

Christina Stead *House of All Nations*: 'Credo'

47 Sometimes the poor are praised for being thrifty. But to recommend thrift to the poor is both grotesque and insulting. It is like advising a man who is starving to eat less. **Oscar Wilde** *The Soul of Man under Socialism*

See also ***Money***

Right and Wrong

1 Where life is possible at all, a right life is possible; life in a palace is possible; therefore in a palace a right life is possible.
Marcus Aurelius *Meditations*, Bk 5, 16

2 It is easier to say you were wrong when you were right than when you were wrong. **Elizabeth Bibesco** *Haven*: 'Aphorisms'

3 The man was proud of being orthodox, was proud of being right. If he stood alone in a howling wilderness he was more than a man; he was a church. **G. K. Chesterton** *Heretics*, Ch. 1

4 Perhaps it is better to be irresponsible and right than to be responsible and wrong. **Winston S. Churchill** party political broadcast, London, 26 August 1950

5 The absent are always in the wrong.
Philippe Destouches *L'Obstacle Imprévu*, Act 1, Sc. 6

6 There are some things that are sure to go wrong as soon as they stop going right. **Celia Green** *The Decline and Fall of Science*: 'Aphorisms'

7 A Man cannot be more in the Wrong than to own without distinction the being in the Right.
Marquis of Halifax *Miscellaneous Thoughts and Reflections*

8 If mankind had wished for what is right, they might have had it long ago. **William Hazlitt** *The Plain Speaker*, 1826, Vol. 1, p. 325

9 We humans are so often right about things because we are so seldom *completely* right. **Friedrich Hebbel** *Diaries*, entry 701, 1837

10 The minority is always right. **Henrik Ibsen** *An Enemy of the People*, Act 4

11 Woe to those who are never wrong: they are never right.
Prince de Ligne in J. Raymond Solly, *A Cynic's Breviary*

12 It is the necessities of life which generate ideas of right and wrong.
W. Somerset Maugham *A Writer's Notebook*, 1896

13 Being right is less important to us than the freedom to be wrong.
Jean Rostand *Pensées d'un biologiste*, p. 144

14 Two wrongs don't make a right, but they make a good excuse.
Thomas S. Szasz *The Second Sin*: 'Social Relations'

15 Wrong cannot afford defeat but right can.
Rabindranath Tagore *Stray Birds*, 68

16 It is dangerous to be right in matters on which the established authorities are wrong. **Voltaire** in J. Raymond Solly, *A Cynic's Breviary*

See also ***Good and Evil***

Rules

1 The letter killeth, but the spirit giveth life. **Bible NT** 2 Corinthians 3:6

2 An exception disproves the rule. **Arthur Conan Doyle** *The Sign of Four*, Ch. 2

3 Every truth has two faces, every rule two surfaces, every precept two applications. **Joseph Joubert** *Thoughts and Maxims*, 153

4 If anything can go wrong it will.
Captain Ed Murphy Murphy's Law, 1949, attrib. Arthur Bloch, *Murphy's Law*, 1979, but other claimants

5 There are two Newman's Laws. First, it's useless to put on your brakes when you're upside down. Second, just when things look darkest, they go black. **Paul Newman** in *Playboy*, April 1983

6 'The exception proves the rule,' runs the proverb; but why, I wonder, is it that you always only believe in the rule, and are always utterly sceptical of the exception? **Ouida** *Wisdom, Wit, and Pathos*: 'Puck'

7 If you want to achieve something in business, in writing, in painting, you must *follow the rules without knowing them*.
Arthur Schopenhauer *Essays and Aphorisms*: 'On Psychology', 20

8 Academism results when the reasons for the rule change, but not the rule.
Igor Stravinsky and Robert Craft *Conversations with Stravinsky*: 'Some Musical Questions'

See also ***Laws***

S

Scandal

1 He that repeateth a matter separateth very friends. **Bible, OT** Proverbs 17:9

2 In scandal, as in robbery, the receiver is always thought as bad as the thief. **Earl of Chesterfield** advice to his son: 'Rules for Conversation'

3 Love and scandal are the best sweeteners of tea.
Henry Fielding *Love in Several Masques*, Act 4, Sc. 11

4 If a man spreads my failings abroad, he is my master, even if he is my servant.
Johann Wolfgang von Goethe *Maxims and Reflections*: 'Life and Character', 148

5 A cruel story runs on wheels, and every hand oils the wheels as they run. **Ouida** *Wisdom, Wit, and Pathos*: 'Moths'

6 So live that you wouldn't be ashamed to sell the family parrot to the town gossip. **Will Rogers** in *The Dictionary of Humorous Quotations*, ed. Evan Esar

7 No one gossips about other people's secret virtues.
Bertrand Russell *On Education*

8 I love scandals about other people, but scandals about myself don't interest me. They have not got the charm of novelty.
Oscar Wilde *The Picture of Dorian Gray*, Ch. 12

9 The basis for every scandal is an immoral certainty.
Oscar Wilde *The Picture of Dorian Gray*, Ch. 18

10 It is perfectly monstrous the way people go about nowadays, saying things against one behind one's back that are absolutely and entirely true. **Oscar Wilde** *A Woman of No Importance*, Act 1

See also ***Lies and Deceit; Secrets; The Spoken Word***

Science and Technology

1 Technology is not the mastery of nature but of the relation between nature and man. **Walter Benjamin** *One-way Street*: 'To the Planetarium'

2 That is the essence of science: ask an impertinent question, and you are on the way to the pertinent answer.

J. Bronowski *The Ascent of Man*, Ch. 4

3 If it [science] tends to thicken the crust of ice on which, as it were, we are skating, it is all right. If it tries to find, or professes to have found, the solid ground at the bottom of the water, it is all wrong.

Samuel Butler 2 *Notebooks*, 20: 'Science'

4 Technology takes the place not of magic but sacrifice. Like sacrifice, it is chiefly a way to control danger, which not only means violent conflict within society but also the destructive and self-destructive power within life itself. **Roberto Calasso** *The Ruin of Kasch*: 'Sacrificial Crumbs'

5 There is no national science, just as there is no national multiplication table; what is national is no longer science.

Anton Chekhov *Notebooks 1894–1902*, p. 4

6 When one longs for a drink, it seems as though one could drink a whole ocean – that is faith; but when one begins to drink, one can only drink altogether two glasses – that is science.

Anton Chekhov *Notebooks 1894–1902*, p. 62

7 When a distinguished but elderly scientist states that something is possible he is almost certainly right. When he states that something is impossible, he is very probably wrong.

Arthur C. Clarke *Profiles of the Future*, Ch. 2: 'Clarke's First Law'

8 Any sufficiently advanced technology is indistinguishable from magic. **Arthur C. Clarke** *Profiles of the Future*, Ch. 2: 'Clarke's Third Law'

9 Poetry is not the proper antithesis to prose, but to science. Poetry is opposed to science, and prose to metre.

Samuel Taylor Coleridge *Lectures and Notes of 1818*, Sect. 1

10 Biology is the study of complicated things that give the appearance of having been designed for a purpose. Physics is the study of simple things that do not tempt us to invoke design.

Richard Dawkins *The Blind Watchmaker*, Ch. 1

11 Every abstract is simply juggling with symbols.

Denis Diderot *D'Alembert's Dream*, p. 221

12 Science without religion is lame, religion without science is blind.
Albert Einstein paper for conference on science, New York, 9/11 September 1940

13 The scientific method can teach us nothing else beyond how facts are related to, and conditioned by, each other.
Albert Einstein *Out of My Later Years*, Ch. 7, i

14 Science can only ascertain what *is*, but not what *should be*.
Albert Einstein *Out of My Later Years*, Ch. 7, ii

15 Science is the century-old endeavour to bring together by means of systematic thought the perceptible phenomena of this world into as thoroughgoing an association as possible. **Albert Einstein** *Out of My Later Years*, Ch. 7, ii

16 A tool is that which is used purely for my benefit without any regard for its own. **Ralph Waldo Emerson** *Journal*, 1847: 'Real Aristocracy'

17 Machinery is aggressive. The weaver becomes a web, the machinist a machine. If you do not use the tools, they use you.
Ralph Waldo Emerson *Society and Solitude*: 'Works and Days'

18 Science is what a machine can do; art is what it will never do.
John Fowles *The Aristos*, Ch. 9, 41

19 A science is any discipline in which the fool of this generation can go beyond the point reached by the genius of the last generation.
Max Gluckman *Politics, Law and Ritual in a Tribal Society*, Ch. 1

20 Scientific knowledge helps us mainly because it makes the wonder to which we are called by nature rather more intelligible.
Johann Wolfgang von Goethe *Maxims and Reflections* (Penguin), from *Periodical Issues*, 417

21 Science is all those things which are confirmed to such a degree that it would be unreasonable to withhold one's provisional consent.
Stephen J. Gould lecture on evolution, Cambridge, England 1984; in *Dictionary of Scientific Quotations*, ed. A. L. Mackay

22 The way to do research is to attack the facts at the point of greatest astonishment. **Celia Green** *The Decline and Fall of Science*: 'Aphorisms'

23 Natural science does not simply describe and explain nature; it is part of the interplay between nature and ourselves; it describes nature as exposed to our method of questioning.
Werner Heisenberg *Physics and Philosophy*, Ch. 6

24 Life is short, science is long.
Hippocrates *Aphorisms*, I, 1; often quoted in Latin: *Ars longa, vita brevis*

25 Science is the knowledge of consequences, and the dependence of one fact upon another. **Thomas Hobbes** *Leviathan*, Pt 1, Ch. 5

26 A generation that wearies of technology is bound to turn to magic. Those who refuse to use machines to move mountains will pray for a faith that moves mountains.

Eric Hoffer *Between the Devil and the Dragon*: Diaries, 25 January 1975

27 Science and literature are not two things, but sides of one thing.

T. H. Huxley *Aphorisms and Reflections*, 296

28 Science is nothing but trained and organized common sense.

T. H. Huxley *Collected Essays*, 4: 'The Method of Zadig'

29 A first-rate theory predicts; a second-rate theory forbids; and a third-rate theory explains after the event.

A. I. Kitaigorodskii lecture in Amsterdam, August 1975

30 Science is spectral analysis. Art is light synthesis.

Karl Kraus *Half-Truths and One-and-a-Half Truths*: 'Riddles'

31 Astronomy teaches the correct use of the sun and the planets.

Stephen Leacock *Literary Lapses*: 'A Manual of Education'

32 It is a good morning exercise for a research scientist to discard a pet hypothesis every day before breakfast. It keeps him young.

Konrad Lorenz *On Aggression*, Ch. 2

33 No scientist is admired for failing in the attempt to solve problems that lie beyond his competence. The most he can hope for is the kindly contempt earned by the Utopian politician. If politics is the art of the possible, research is surely the art of the soluble. Both are immensely practical-minded affairs. **Peter Medawar** *The Art of the Soluble*: Introduction

34 There is no spiritual copyright in scientific discoveries, unless they should happen to be quite mistaken. Only in making a blunder does a scientist do something which, conceivably, no one might ever do again. **Peter Medawar** *Pluto's Republic*

35 If you fall in love with a machine there is something wrong with your love life. If you worship a machine there is something wrong with your religion. **Lewis Mumford** *Art and Technics*

36 It is not true that the scientist goes after truth. It goes after him.

Robert Musil *The Man without Qualities*; in *Dictionary of Scientific Quotations*, ed. A. L. Mackay

37 *Laboratorium est oratorium.* The place where we do our scientific work is a place of prayer.

Joseph Needham in *Dictionary of Scientific Quotations*, ed. A. L. Mackay

38 Man shall not join what God has torn asunder.

Wolfgang Pauli epigraph to John D. Barrow, *Theories of Everything*

39 Traditional scientific method has always been at the very *best*, 20-20 hindsight. It's good for seeing where you've been.

Robert M. Pirsig *Zen and the Art of Motorcycle Maintenance*, Pt 3, Ch. 24

40 Science must begin with myths, and with the criticism of myths.

Karl Popper 'Philosophy of Science: A Personal Report', in *British Philosophy in the Mid-century*, ed. C. A. Mace

41 Information is the mortal enemy of science when information is sought by curiosity.

Eugen Rosenstock-Huessy *The Christian Future or the Modern Mind Outrun*, Pt 1, Ch. 2

42 Scientific research: the only form of poetry that may be rewarded by the state. **Jean Rostand** *Carnets d'un biologiste*

43 Science should not set minds free until it has tamed the instincts.

Jean Rostand *Pensées d'un biologiste*, p. 29

44 It is sometimes important for science to know how to forget the things she is surest of. **Jean Rostand** *Pensées d'un biologiste*, p. 124

45 Nothing leads the scientist so astray as a truth before its time.

Jean Rostand *Pensées d'un biologiste*, p. 127

46 All science is either physics or stamp-collecting.

Ernest Rutherford quoted by P. M. S. Blackett in *Rutherford at Manchester*, ed. J. B. Birks, p. 108

47 Science is the great antidote to the poison of enthusiasm and superstition. **Adam Smith** *The Wealth of Nations*, Bk 1, Ch. 3, Sect. 3

48 Science is organized knowledge. **Herbert Spencer** *Education*, Ch. 2

49 There is no evil in the atom; only in men's souls.

Adlai Stevenson speech in Hartford, Connecticut, 18 September 1952

50 Science knows that the isolated mountains on the horizon are but portions of an unseen range. **H. D. Thoreau** *Journal*, 1842

51 We are accustomed properly to call that only a scientific discovery which knows the relative value of the thing discovered – uncovers a fact to mankind. **H. D. Thoreau** *Journal*, 20 November 1850

52 Science is a differential equation. Religion is a boundary condition.

Alan Turing epigraph to John D. Barrow, *Theories of Everything*

53 Nothing holds up the progress of science so much as the right idea at the wrong time. **Vincent de Vignaud** in R. V. Jones, *Most Secret War*, Ch. 9

54 It would be a poor thing to be an atom in a universe without physicists. And physicists are made of atoms. A physicist is an atom's way of knowing about atoms. **George Wald** Foreword to L. J. Henderson, *The Fitness of the Environment*

55 Nothing is *less* instructive than a machine.

Simone Weil *Factory Journal*: 'The Mystery of the Factory 1934–35'

56 A science which hesitates to forget its founders is lost.

A. N. Whitehead (attrib.)

57 Religions die when they are proved to be true. Science is the record of dead religions. **Oscar Wilde** *Phrases and Philosophies for the Use of the Young*

58 Complexity is what interests scientists in the end, not simplicity. Reductionism is the way to understand it. The love of complexity without reductionism makes art; the love of complexity with reductionism, makes science. **Edward O. Wilson** *Consilience*, Ch. 4

59 The ideal scientist thinks like a poet and works like a book-keeper.

Edward O. Wilson *Consilience*, Ch. 4

60 Scientists, when told something is impossible, as a habit set out to do it. **Edward O. Wilson** *Consilience*, Ch. 6

61 Man has to awake to wonder – and so perhaps do peoples. Science is a way of sending him to sleep again.

Ludwig Wittgenstein *Culture and Value*, 1930 entry

62 Science appears but what in truth she is,
Not as our glory and our absolute boast,
But as a succedaneum, and a prop
To our infirmity. **William Wordsworth** *The Prelude*, Bk 2, 212

See also ***Numbers and Mathematics***

The Sea

1 It is the drawback of all sea-side places that half the landscape is unavailable for purposes of human locomotion, being covered by useless water. **Norman Douglas** *Alone*: 'Mentone'

2 I hate to be near the sea, and to hear it roaring and raging like a wild animal in its den. It puts me in mind of the everlasting efforts of the human mind, struggling to be free, and ending just where it began.

William Hazlitt *Commonplaces*, 60

3 He complains wrongly on the sea, that twice suffers ship-wreck.

George Herbert *Jacula Prudentum*

4 Even a luxury liner is really just a bad play surrounded by water.

Clive James *Unreliable Memoirs*, Ch. 7

5 No man will be a sailor who has contrivance enough to get himself into a jail; for being in a ship is being in a jail, with the chance of being drowned . . . A man in a jail has more room, better food and commonly better company.

Dr Samuel Johnson in James Boswell, *Life of Johnson*, March 1759

6 Is it not more attractive to be a sailor than a farmer – ? The farmer's son is restive and wants to go to sea – Is it not better to plough the ocean than the land – [no?] In the former case the plough runs further in its furrow before it turns. You may go round the world before the mast but not behind the plough. **H. D. Thoreau** *Journal*, 15 July 1852

Secrets

1 There's always an ear on the other side of the wall, and there's bound to be someone outside the window.

Anon. *Chinese Couplets, Aphorisms and Apothegms*, ed. W. Dolby, 35

2 You know there are no secrets in America. It's quite different in England, where people think of a secret as a shared relationship between two people. **W. H. Auden** in *The Table Talk of W. H. Auden* by Alan Anson, 6 March 1948

3 All secret services share a mission that is far more important than all the conflicts; the annihilation of secrecy.

Roberto Calasso *The Ruin of Kasch*: 'History Experiments'

4 A man who tells nothing, or who tells all, will equally have nothing told him. **Earl of Chesterfield** *Letters to his Son*: Maxims, in 1810 edn

5 Privacy is like property in this: that while a few people ought to have less of it, most people ought to have more of it.

G. K. Chesterton in *New Witness*, 7 October 1921

6 Most people are furtive but very few are ashamed.

Edward Dahlberg *Sorrows of Priapus*: 'But to the Girdle', 1

7 You should only confide your secrets to someone who has not tried to guess them. **Comtesse Diane** *Maxims of Life*, p. 33

8 Probably one of the most private things in the world is an egg until it is broken. **M. F. K. Fisher** *How to Cook a Wolf*

9 Three may keep a Secret, if two of them are dead.

Benjamin Franklin *Poor Richard's Almanack*, 1733

10 He knows little, who will tell his wife all he knows.

Thomas Fuller *The Holy State, and the Profane State*, Bk 1, Ch. 3

11 Whatever thou wouldst hide from thine enemy, do not disclose to thy friend. **Solomon Ibn Gabirol** *Choice of Pearls*, 315

12 Once the toothpaste is out of the tube, it is awfully hard to get it back in. **H. R. Haldeman** comment to John Dean on Watergate affair, 8 April 1973

13 A man has no excuse for betraying the secrets of his friends, unless he also divulges his own. **William Hazlitt** *Characteristics*, 122

14 Trust not him with your secrets, who, when left alone in your room, turns over your papers.
Johann Kaspar Lavater *Aphorisms on Man*, 449; William Blake commented: 'Uneasy, yet I hope I should not do it'

15 The Official Secrets Act is not to protect secrets but to protect officials.
Jonathan Lynn and Antony Jay *Yes, Minister*, Ch. 7

16 A man that does not confide in himself, will never confide sincerely in anybody. **Cardinal de Retz** *Memoirs*, Bk 3, 1649–51

17 A real secret is something which only one person knows.
Idries Shah *Reflections*: 'Secrets'

18 A secret may be sometimes best kept by keeping the secret of its being a secret. **Sir Henry Taylor** *The Statesman*, Ch. 18

See also ***Scandal; The Spoken Word***

The Self

1 The gods help them that help themselves.
Aesop *Fables*: 'Hercules and the Wagoner'

2 Everyone fears they are a joke which other people will one day get.
Martin Amis interview in the *Guardian*, 3 October 1998

3 A little flesh, a little breath, and a Reason to rule all – that is myself.
Marcus Aurelius *Meditations*, Bk 2, 2

4 I have often wondered why everyone loves himself more than everything else, but values his own opinion of himself less than that of others. **Marcus Aurelius** *Meditations*, Bk 12, 4

5 Certainly it is the nature of extreme self-lovers, as they will set an house on fire, and it were but to roast their eggs.
Francis Bacon *Essays*: 'Of Wisdom for a Man's Self'

6 To be a law unto oneself one must know oneself.
George Bedborough *Narcotics and Stimulants*

7 We are continually being discarded by others, and every day we have to find ourselves again, piece ourselves together, reconstitute ourselves.

Thomas Berhard *Gathering Evidence*: 'The Cellar'

8 We know better the needs of ourselves than of others. To serve oneself is economy of administration. **Ambrose Bierce** *The Enlarged Devil's Dictionary*

9 The only effort worth making is the one it takes to learn the geography of one's own nature. **Paul Bowles** in the *Sunday Times, Books*, 23 July 1989

10 There are two ways of losing oneself: by insulation in the particular or by dilution in the 'universal'. **Aimé Césaire** *Letter to Maurice Thorez*, 1956

11 A man does not seek to see himself in running water, but in still water. For only what is itself still can instil stillness into others.

Chuang Tzŭ *Musings of a Chinese Mystic*

12 We are all serving a life-sentence in the dungeon of self.

Cyril Connolly *The Unquiet Grave*, Ch. 1

13 Each person has a deity in him which is ravaged by a frump.

Edward Dahlberg *Sorrows of Priapus*: 'But to the Girdle', Prologue

14 The greatest of victories is the victory over oneself.

The Dhammapada 105

15 Egoism exacts from everybody what love only asks of one person.

Comtesse Diane *Les Glanes de la vie*, p. 150

16 What we love and what we hate most in other people, is always and only ourselves. **Comtesse Diane** *Maxims of Life*, p. 31

17 A man never gets acquainted with himself, but is always a surprise. We get news daily of the world within, as well as the world outside, and not less of the central than of the surface facts. A new thought is awaiting him every morning.

Ralph Waldo Emerson *Journal*, Summer–Fall 1868

18 Selfishness and unselfishness battle in man's heart. Almost always selfishness kills unselfishness; and on the few occasions the latter wins, it is still selfishness.

Xavier Forneret *Sans titre, par un homme noir, blanc de visage*: 'March'

19 Each man in his time plays many parts. And not just for long runs as Shakespeare seems to suggest, but in repertory – one part on Monday night, another on Tuesday, and a third at the Wednesday matinée.

Michael Frayn *Constructions*, 160

20 The ego is not master in its own house.

Sigmund Freud *A Difficulty in the Path of Psychoanalysis*, in *Complete Works*, Vol. 17

21 Man's main task in life is to give *birth* to himself.

Erich Fromm *Man for Himself*, Ch. 4

22 Few are fit to be entrusted with themselves.

Dr Thomas Fuller *Gnomologia*, 1523

23 Who hath sailed about the world of his own heart, sounded each creek, surveyed each corner, but that still there remains therein much *terra incognita* to himself?

Thomas Fuller *The Holy State, and the Profane State*, Bk 1, Ch. 12

24 You cannot master yourself unless you know yourself. There are mirrors for the face but none for the mind. **Baltasar Gracián** *The Art of Worldly Wisdom*, 89

25 We cannot love others, so the theologians teach, unless in some degree, we love ourselves, and curiosity too begins at home.

Graham Greene *A Sort of Life*: Introduction

26 No man was ever so much deceived by another as by himself.

Fulke Greville *Maxims, Characters and Reflections*, p. 1

27 Whatever you blame, that you have done yourself.

Georg Groddeck *The Book of the It*, Letter 20

28 Men mean so very well to themselves, that they forget to mean well to any body else. **Marquis of Halifax** *Miscellaneous Thoughts and Reflections*

29 None is offended but by himself. **George Herbert** *Jacula Prudentum*

30 Without self-love it is impossible to love our fellow men. Self-hatred is exactly the same thing as blatant egoism; it leads in the end to the same cruel isolation and despair. **Hermann Hesse** *Reflections*, 618

31 Me, what's that after all? An arbitrary limitation of being bounded by the people before and after and on either side. Where they leave off I begin, and vice versa. **Russell Hoban** *Turtle Diary*, 11

32 There's only one corner of the universe you can be certain of improving, and that's your own self. **Aldous Huxley** *Time Must Have a Stop*, 7

33 It's all right letting yourself go, as long as you can let yourself back.

Mick Jagger in Jonathon Green, *Book of Rock Quotes*

34 Two tasks at the beginning of your life: to narrow your orbit increasingly, and constantly to check whether you are not hiding away somewhere outside your orbit. **Franz Kafka** *Collected Aphorisms*, 94

35 Himself he knows, the others he believes; everything is sawn apart for him by this antithesis. **Franz Kafka** *Collected Aphorisms*, 14 January 1920

36 What makes egotists offensive is not so much loving themselves as needing to be loved by those they hate. **David Kipp** *Aphorisms*, p. 4

37 Help yourself, and heaven will help you.

Jean de La Fontaine *Fables*, Bk 6, 18: 'The Wagoner in Trouble'

38 Our self-esteem is more inclined to resent criticism of our tastes than of our opinions. **Duc de La Rochefoucauld** *Maxims*, 13

39 At times we are as different from ourselves as we are from others.

Duc de La Rochefoucauld *Maxims*, 135

40 The terms we are on with other men are always a reflection of the terms we are on with ourselves. **Louis Lavelle** *L'Erreur de Narcisse*, p. 165

41 A woman means by Unselfishness chiefly taking trouble for others; a man means not giving trouble to others.

C. S. Lewis *The Screwtape Letters*, 26

42 He who is in love with himself has at least this advantage – he won't encounter many rivals in his love.

Georg Christoph Lichtenberg *The Lichtenberg Reader*, Aphorisms 1779–88

43 Everywhere turns elsewhere and to the future, since no one has discovered himself. **Michel de Montaigne** *Essays*, Bk 3, Ch. 12

44 Man is an indifferent egoist: even the cleverest regards his habits as more important than his advantage.

Friedrich Nietzsche *The Will to Power*, 363

45 Egoism is the identification of the Seer with the limitations of the eye. **Bhagwān Shree Patanjali** *Aphorisms of Yoga*, II, 6

46 In general, the man who is readily disposed to sacrifice himself is one who does not know how else to give meaning to his life.

Cesare Pavese *This Business of Living: A Diary 1935–1950*, 9 February 1940

47 Life is not a search for experience, but for ourselves.

Cesare Pavese *This Business of Living: A Diary 1935–1950*, 8 August 1940

48 I am there from where no news of myself reaches me.

Persian aphorism quoted in Adam Phillips, *On Kissing, Tickling and Being Bored*, Ch. 6

49 We can never be quite sure whether we are competing for something that doesn't exist, or winning a competition in which no one else is competing. **Adam Phillips** *Monogamy*, 47

50 I am always true to myself, that is the problem. Who else could I be true to? **Adam Phillips** *Monogamy*, 60

51 I am prejudiced in favour of myself
I know of no other way
to conduct relations with myself. **Francis Picabia** *Yes No, Poems and Sayings*

52 That true self-love and social are the same.

Alexander Pope *An Essay on Man*, Bk 3, 396

53 Almost always it is the fear of being ourselves that brings us to the mirror.

Antonio Porchia *Voices*

54 Self-love seems so often unrequited.

Anthony Powell *The Acceptance World*, Ch. 1

55 Few words have the power of *my* to divide people.

Joseph Prescott *Aphorisms and Other Observations, Third Series*: 'Ego'

56 Our social personality is a creation of the thoughts of other people.

Marcel Proust *Remembrance of Things Past: Swann's Way*, p. 20

57 Amnesia is not knowing who one is and wanting desperately to find out. Euphoria is not knowing who one is and not caring. Ecstasy is knowing exactly who one is – and still not caring.

Tom Robbins *Another Roadside Attraction*

58 A man never quite knows who he is, but who he says he thinks he is, gives a fair notion of who he thinks he is, if not in fact, who he is.

Ned Rorem *An Absolute Gift*, Ch. 5

59 Self-love is the opposite of love.

Antoine de Saint-Exupéry *The Wisdom of the Sands*, 25

60 To understand oneself is the classic form of consolation; to elude oneself is the romantic.

George Santayana *The Genteel Tradition in American Philosophy*

61 People often say that this or that person has not yet found himself. But the self is not something one finds; it is something one creates.

Thomas S. Szasz *The Second Sin*: 'Personal Conduct'

62 Man barricades against himself. **Rabindranath Tagore** *Stray Birds*, 79

63 Not only are selves conditional but they die. Each day, we wake slightly altered, and the person we were yesterday is dead.

John Updike *Self-Consciousness*, Ch. 6

64 Love is not as touchy as self-love.

Marquis de Vauvenargues *Reflections and Maxims*, 551

65 Self-love promotes the love of others; it is through our mutual dependence that we are useful to the human species.

Voltaire *Philosophical Letters*, Letter 13

66 It is not love that should be pictured as blind, but self-love.

Voltaire letter to M. Damilaville, 11 May 1764

67 Selfishness is caught from those who have least of it.
Archbishop Whately *Apophthegms*, 102B

68 We cannot be Undone, but by our Selves.
Benjamin Whichcote *Moral and Religious Aphorisms*, 926

69 Egotism itself, which is so necessary to a proper sense of human dignity, is entirely the result of indoor life. Out of doors one becomes abstract and impersonal. **Oscar Wilde** *The Decay of Lying*

70 To love oneself is the beginning of a lifelong romance.
Oscar Wilde *An Ideal Husband*, Act 3

71 Only the shallow know themselves.
Oscar Wilde *Phrases and Philosophies for the Use of the Young*

72 Selfishness is not living as one wishes to live, it is asking others to live as one wishes to live. **Oscar Wilde** *The Soul of Man under Socialism*

73 We're all of us sentenced to solitary confinement inside our own skins, for life! **Tennessee Williams** *Orpheus Descending*, Act 2, Sc. 1

See also ***Individuals; Others***

The Senses

1 Men are born with two eyes, but with *one* tongue, in order that they should see twice as much as they say; but, from their conduct, one would suppose that they were born with two tongues and one eye.
Charles Caleb Colton *Lacon*: 'Loquacity'

See also Disraeli, in ***The Spoken Word***

2 For surely everyone only hears what he understands.
Johann Wolfgang von Goethe *Maxims and Reflections* (Penguin), from *Wilhelm Meister's Journeyman Years*, 887

3 The ear says more
Than any tongue. **W. S. Graham** *The Hill of Intrusion*

4 Smells are far more evocative of the past than noises can ever be. Sounds are the clichés of memory. **Roy Hattersley** in the *Guardian*, 19 October 1985

5 Description only excites curiosity: seeing satisfies it.
Dr Samuel Johnson in James Boswell, *Life of Johnson*, 10 April 1773

6 You want to talk to someone; first open your ears.
Joseph Joubert *Notebooks*, 1818

7 All man's life among men is nothing more than a battle for the ears of others. **Milan Kundera** *The Book of Laughter and Forgetting*, 4, 1

8 There are many people who won't listen until their ears are cut off.
Georg Christoph Lichtenberg *The Lichtenberg Reader*, Aphorisms, 1789

9 Those who know God know that it is quite a mistake to suppose that there are only five senses.
Coventry Patmore *The Rod, the Root and the Flower*: 'Aurea Dicta', 142

10 The senses are less afflicted by physical suffering than by the thought of it. **Quintilian** *Inst. Orat*, 1, 12; slightly altered by Michel de Montaigne, *Essays*, Bk 3, Ch. 12

11 To sleep soon after taking food,
And exercise when frequently renewed,
With drunkenness – all these in turn appear
To dull, betimes, the sharpness of the ear.
Code of Health of the School of Salernum *Medical Maxims in Verse Form*: 'Of Dullness of Hearing'

12 Anything one is remembering is a repetition, but existing as a human being, that is being, listening and hearing is never repetition.
Gertrude Stein quoted in David Lodge, *Changing Places*, Ch. 5

13 One should never listen. To listen is a sign of indifference to one's hearers. **Oscar Wilde** *For the Instruction of the Over-educated*

14 We women, as someone says, love with our ears, just as you men love with your eyes, if you ever love at all. **Oscar Wilde** *The Picture of Dorian Gray*, Ch. 17

See also ***Body and Soul; Eyes; Perceptions***

Servants and Service

1 No man can serve two masters. **Bible, NT** Matthew 6:24

2 Slavery they can have anywhere. It is a weed that grows in every soil.
Edmund Burke speech on conciliation with America, 22 March 1775

3 One of the greatest advantages of princes over other men is that they are waited on by servants as good as themselves.
Miguel Cervantes *Don Quixote*, Pt 2, 31

4 It may be that no man would be a hero to his valet. But any man would be a valet to his hero. **G. K. Chesterton** *Heretics*, Ch. 12

See also de Cornuel, Montaigne

5 No man is a hero to his valet.

Anne Bigot de Cornuel *Lettres de Mlle Aïssé*, 13 August 1728

See also Chesterton, Montaigne

6 Pressed into service means pressed out of shape.

Robert Frost *The Self-seeker*

7 If Thou hast a loitering Servant, send him on thy errand just before dinner. **Dr Thomas Fuller** *Introductio ad Prudentium*, 423

8 A Man that will serve well must often rule the Master so hard that it will hurt him. **Marquis of Halifax** *Political Thoughts and Reflections*, 'Princes'

9 He can give little to his servant that licks his knife.

George Herbert *Jacula Prudentum*

10 American women expect to find in their husbands a perfection that English women only hope to find in their butlers.

W. Somerset Maugham *A Writer's Notebook*, 1896

11 Many a man has been a wonder to the world, whose wife and valet have seen nothing in him that was even remarkable. Few men have been admired by their servants. **Michel de Montaigne** *Essays*, Bk 3, Ch. 2

See also Chesterton, de Cornuel

12 Masters and servants are both tyrannical; but the masters are the more dependent of the two.

George Bernard Shaw *Man and Superman*: 'Maxims for Revolutionists', 'Servants'

13 He profits most who serves best.

A. F. Sheldon speech at first Rotary Convention, 1910

14 For slavery will work – as long as the slaves will let it; and freedom will work when men have learnt to be free.

R. H. Tawney *The Acquisitive Society*, 9

15 Live? Our servants will do that for us.

Philippe-Auguste Villiers de l'Isle Adam *Axel*, Pt 4, ii

16 Among men, a slave does not become like his master by obeying him. On the contrary, the more he obeys the greater is the distance between them. **Simone Weil** *Waiting on God*: 'The Love of God'

See also ***Work and Leisure***

Sex

1 He who enjoys a good neighbour, said the Greeks, has a precious possession. Same goes for the neighbour's wife.

Nicolas Bentley in *A Treasury of Humorous Quotations*, ed. Evan Esar and Nicolas Bentley

2 There are three sexes; men, women and girls.

Ambrose Bierce *The Enlarged Devil's Dictionary*

3 Sex. In America an obsession. In other parts of the world a fact.

Marlene Dietrich *Marlene Dietrich's ABC*: 'Sex'

4 If you're a sexual maniac, you don't want sex: you want the excitement of its theft, you want the victim's resistance and despair. If sex is handed to you on a platter, here it is, go to it, naturally you're not interested, otherwise what sort of sexual maniac would you be?

Umberto Eco *Foucault's Pendulum*, Ch. 118

5 Sex suppressed will go berserk,
But it keeps us all alive.
It's a wonderful change from wives and work
And it ends at half-past five.

Gavin Ewart *Office Friendships*

6 'Bed' as the Italian proverb succinctly puts it, 'is the poor man's opera'.

Aldous Huxley *Heaven and Hell*

7 Chastity always takes its toll. In some it produces pimples; in others, sex laws.

Karl Kraus *Half-Truths and One-and-a-Half Truths*: 'Not for Women'

8 Men are those creatures with two legs and eight hands.

Jayne Mansfield quoted in *The Woman's Hour Book of Humour*, ed. Sally Feldman

9 Continental people have sex life; the English have hot-water bottles.

George Mikes *How to be an Alien*, 'Sex'

10 Contraceptives should be used on every conceivable occasion.

Spike Milligan *The Last Goon Show of All*

11 The daughter-in-law of Pythagoras said that a woman who goes to bed with a man ought to lay aside her modesty with her skirt, and put it on again with her petticoat.

Michel de Montaigne *Essays*, Bk 1, Ch. 21

12 The orgasm has replaced the Cross as the focus of longing and the image of fulfilment.

Malcolm Muggeridge *The Most of Malcolm Muggeridge*: 'Down with Sex'

13 Men seldom make passes
At girls who wear glasses.

Dorothy Parker *News Item*

14 A couple is a conspiracy in search of a crime. Sex is often the closest they can get.
Adam Phillips *Monogamy*, 21

15 Love lasts. It's lust that moves out on us when we're not looking, it's lust which always skips town – and love without lust just isn't enough.
Tom Robbins *Still Life with Woodpecker*, p. 51

16 Natural freedoms are but just;
There's something generous in mere lust.
John Wilmot, Earl of Rochester *A Ramble in St James' Park*

17 The essence of sex is communication. All the rest is just plumbing.
Chuck Spezzano *Awaken the Gods*, p. 145

18 Sex is like money; only too much is enough.
John Updike *Couples*, Ch. 5

19 All this fuss about sleeping together. For physical pleasure I'd sooner go to my dentist any day.
Evelyn Waugh *Vile Bodies*, Ch. 6

20 In answer to: Inside every thin woman there's a fat woman trying to get out, I always think it's: Outside every thin woman there's a fat man trying to get in.
Katharine Whitehorn in BBC radio programme *Quote, Unquote*, 27 July 1985

See also Amis, Connolly, Orwell, Waugh, in **Body and Soul**

21 Debauchery is only an art against thinking.
Bishop Thomas Wilson *Maxims of Piety and Christianity*: 'Debauchery'

See also ***Love; Men and Women***

Silence

1 Silence iz one of the hardest arguments to refute.
Josh Billings *Wit And Humor*, Affurisms: 'Mollassis Kandy'

2 Think not silence the wisdom of fools, but, if rightly timed, the honour of wise Men, who have not the Infirmity, but the virtue of Taciturnity.
Sir Thomas Browne *Christian Morals*, Pt 3, 18

3 Silence is not always tact and it is tact that is golden, not silence.
Samuel Butler 2 *Notebooks*, Ch. 14: 'Silence and Tact'

4 How much one has to say in order to be heard when silent.
Elias Canetti *The Human Province*: '1943'

5 When you have nothing to say, say nothing.
Charles Caleb Colton *Lacon*, Vol. 1, 183

6 People who talk little always impress. It is hard to think that they have no other secret to hide than their insignificance.

Maria von Ebner-Eschenbach *Aphorisms*, p. 39

7 A great singer is he who sings our silences.

Kahlil Gibran *Sand and Foam*, 24

8 Silence is one great art of conversation. He is not a fool who knows when to hold his tongue; and a person may gain credit for sense, eloquence, wit, who merely says nothing to lessen the opinion which others have of these qualities in themselves.

William Hazlitt *Characteristics*, 59

9 The learning of the grammar of silence is an art much more difficult to learn than the grammar of sounds.

Ivan D. Illich *Celebration of Awareness*, Ch. 4

10 It is a great misfortune to have neither wit enough to talk well, nor sense enough to keep silence.

Jean de La Bruyère *Characters*: 'Of Society and Conversation', 18

11 The silence went straight from rapt to fraught without pausing at pregnant. **Bernard Levin** in *The Times*, 17 October 1974

12 Silence is the real crime against humanity.

Nadezhda Mandelstam *Hope against Hope*, 11

13 Speech is the small change of silence

George Meredith *The Ordeal of Richard Feverel*, Ch. 34

14 It's only the silent whose word counts. **Charles Péguy** *Notre jeunesse*, p. 48

15 Language can only deal meaningfully with a special, restricted segment of reality. The rest, and it is presumably the much larger part, is silence. **George Steiner** *Language and Silence*: 'The Retreat from the Word'

16 The cruellest lies are often told in silence.

Robert Louis Stevenson *Virginibus Puerisque*, 4: 'Truth of Intercourse'

17 I have been breaking silence these twenty-three years and have hardly made a rent in it. **H. D. Thoreau** *Journal*, 9 February 1841

18 Silence alone is worthy to be heard. Silence is of various depth and fertility like soil. **H. D. Thoreau** *Journal*, 21 January 1853

19 Whereof one cannot speak, thereof one must be silent.

Ludwig Wittgenstein *Tractatus Logico-philosophicus*, 7

See also ***The Spoken Word***

Sins and Temptations

1 All sin tends to be addictive, and the terminal point of addiction is what is called damnation. **W. H. Auden** *A Certain World*: 'Hell'

2 The best way to put a stop to temptation, is to succumb to it.
Tristan Bernard *Contes, répliques et bons mots*: 'Le morale'

3 He that toucheth pitch shall be defiled therewith.
Bible, Apocrypha Ecclesiasticus 13:1

4 Where no law is, there is no transgression. **Bible, NT** Romans 4:15

5 The wages of sin is death. **Bible, NT** Romans 6:23

6 It iz comparitively eazy tew repent ov the sins that we hav committed, but tew repent ov thoze which we intend to commit, is asking tew mutch ov enny man, now days.
Josh Billings *Wit and Humor*, Affurisms: 'Glass Dimonds'

7 *Sins* cut boldly up through every level in society, but mere misdemeanours show a certain level in life.
Elizabeth Bowen *The Death of the Heart*, Pt 1, Ch. 4

8 You won't become a saint through other people's sins.
Anton Chekhov *Notebooks 1894–1902*, p. 87

9 The devil tempts us not – 'tis we tempt him.
Beckoning his skill with opportunity. **George Eliot** *Felix Holt*, Ch. 47

10 Original sin, the ancient wrong committed by man, consists in the complaint which man makes and never ceases making; that a wrong has been done to him, that it was upon him that original sin was committed. **Franz Kafka** *Collected Aphorisms*, 15 February 1920

11 Who pursues means of enjoyment contradictory, irreconcilable, and self-destructive, is a fool, or what is called a sinner – sin and destruction of order are the same.
Johann Kaspar Lavater *Aphorisms on Man*, 8; William Blake underlined the last sentence and commented: 'A golden sentence'

12 Original thought is like original sin: both happened before you were born to people you could not possibly have met.
Fran Lebowitz *Social Studies*: 'People'

13 The most successful tempters and thus the most dangerous are the deluded deluders. **Georg Christoph Lichtenberg** *Aphorisms*, Notebook F, 120

14 To make a vow is a greater sin than to break one.
Georg Christoph Lichtenberg *Aphorisms*, Notebook K, 38

15 It is a public scandal that offends; to sin in secret is no sin at all.

Molière *Tartuffe*, Act 4, Sc. 5

16 Sin is God's private pasture; if you graze in its vicinity, you will run the risk of entering it.

Muhammad *The Sayings of Muhammad*: 'Work, Commerce and Industry'

17 The most dastardly sin on earth is the desertion of the fallen.

Ouida *Wisdom, Wit, and Pathos*: 'Chandos'

18 I prefer a saint with faults to a sinner with none.

Charles Péguy *The Mystery of Innocent Saints*

19 There is a great difference between a man who does not want to sin and one who does not know how to.

Seneca *Letters*, 90; quoted in Michel de Montaigne, *Essays*, Bk 1, Ch. 26

20 Some rise by sin, and some by virtue fall.

William Shakespeare *Measure for Measure*, Act 2, Sc. 1, 38

21 The worst sin towards our fellow creatures is not to hate them, but to be indifferent to them: that's the essence of inhumanity.

George Bernard Shaw *The Devil's Disciple*, Act 2

22 You can never forget a sin you have confessed.

Sydney Tremayne *Tatlings*, p. 28

23 Adam was the author of sin and I wish he had taken out an international copyright on it.

Mark Twain *Notebook*, 1877

24 All sins are attempts to fill voids.

Simone Weil *Gravity and Grace*: 'To Desire . . .'

25 I can resist everything except temptation.

Oscar Wilde *Lady Windermere's Fan*, Act 1

26 Nothing makes one so vain as being told that one is a sinner. Conscience makes egotists of us all.

Oscar Wilde *The Picture of Dorian Gray*, Ch. 8

27 Never support two weaknesses at the same time. It's your combination sinners – your lecherous liars and your miserly drunkards – who dishonour the vices and bring them into bad repute.

Thornton Wilder *The Matchmaker*, Act 3

28 The devil never tempts us with more success, than when he tempts us with a sight of our own good actions.

Bishop Thomas Wilson *Maxims of Piety and Christianity*: 'Pride'

29 One sin very naturally leans on another.

Bishop Thomas Wilson *Maxims of Piety and Christianity*: 'Sin'

See also ***Vices and Virtues***

Society and Class

1 If the professional classes put half the energy, imagination and tenacity into their businesses that the idle rich do into being bored to tears in exactly the right place on exactly the right date all over Europe, they would soon make their fortunes. **Jean Anouilh** *Time Remembered*, Act 3

2 He who is unable to live in society, or who has no need, because he is sufficient for himself, must be either a beast or a god.
Aristotle *Politics*, Bk 1, 1253a

3 Awareness that his actions are social is the mark of a social being.
Marcus Aurelius *Meditations*, Bk 5, 6

4 What is no good for the hive is no good for the bee.
Marcus Aurelius *Meditations*, Bk 6, 54

5 New nobility is but the act of power, but ancient nobility is the act of time. **Francis Bacon** *Essays*: 'Of Nobility'

6 There is only one way left to escape the alienation of present day society: *to retreat ahead of it.* **Roland Barthes** *The Pleasure of the Text*: 'Modern'

7 Man was formed for society.
Sir William Blackstone *Commentary on the Laws of England*: Introduction

8 In all societies, whether animal or human, violence breeds tyrants, and gentle authority monarchs.
George-Louis de Buffon *Histoire naturelle*: 'Les Oiseaux aquatiques, le cygne'

9 If we would please in society, we must be prepared to be taught many things we know already by people who do not know them.
Nicholas-Sébastien Chamfort *Maxims and Considerations*

10 The strength of the aristocracy is not in the aristocracy at all; it is in the slums. **G. K. Chesterton** *Heretics*, Ch. 15

11 An institution is the lengthened shadow of one man.
Ralph Waldo Emerson *Essays*: 'Self Reliance'

12 A man must be in sympathy with society about him, or else, not wish to be in sympathy with it. If neither of these two, he must be wretched. **Ralph Waldo Emerson** *Journal*, March–April 1848

13 Freedom of will can be increased only by exercise. But the only place where such exercise can be got is in society; and to opt out of that is to opt out of opting. **John Fowles** *The Aristos*, Ch. 7, 36

14 If society fits you comfortably enough, you call it freedom.
Robert Frost quoted in *Esquire* magazine, 1965

15 A quiet scholar came home one night,
From a social gathering, large and polite.
Asked how he'd liked it, the scholar said:
'If they were books, I'd leave them unread.'
Johann Wolfgang von Goethe *West-Eastern Divan*: 'Society'

16 The closer together people sit, the harder it is for them to get acquainted. **Hermann Hesse** *Reflections*, 93

17 Who takes social life as anything but symbolic errs.
Hugo von Hofmannsthal *The Book of Friends*, 1

18 There are few who would not rather be taken in adultery than in provincialism. **Aldous Huxley** *Antic Hay*, Ch. 10

19 The nice thing about social life, as opposed to real life, is that in social life you are what you seem. **Clive James** *Brilliant Creatures*, Ch. 5

20 The essence of a class system is not that the privileged are conscious of their privileges, but that the deprived are conscious of their deprivation. **Clive James** *Unreliable Memoirs*, Ch. 12

21 Society is based on the assumption that everyone is alike and no one is alive. **Hugh Kingsmill** *The Best of Hugh Kingsmill*, ed. Michael Holroyd: Introduction

22 How beastly the bourgeois is especially the male of the species.
D. H. Lawrence *How Beastly the Bourgeois Is*

23 *Noblesse oblige*. – Nobility carries its obligations.
Duc de Lévis *Maximes et réflexions*, 73

24 Our own society is the only one which we can transform and yet not destroy, since the changes which we should introduce would come from within. **Claude Lévi-Strauss** *A World on the Wane*, Ch. 35

25 Man loves company, even if only that of a small burning candle.
Georg Christoph Lichtenberg *Aphorisms*, Notebook K, 40

26 The relations between the individual and society are like a roulette table. Society is the banker. Individuals sometimes win and sometimes lose; but the banker wins always.
W. Somerset Maugham *A Writer's Notebook*, 1896

27 I only know three ways of surviving in society: you have to be either a beggar, a thief or an employee. **Comte de Mirabeau** *Pensées diverses*

28 When society is healthy, the artist reinforces its health; but when it is ailing, he likewise reinforces its ailments.
Lewis Mumford *Art and Technics*: 'Art and the Symbol'

29 The whole trouble with Western society today is the lack of anything worth concealing. **Joe Orton** *Diary*, 11 July 1966

30 A society which enslaves its women is a society doomed to decay.
Ibn Rushd, a.k.a. Averroës (attrib.)

31 Society is like the air, necessary to breathe, but insufficient to live on.
George Santayana *The Life of Reason*, Ch. 8

32 Titles distinguish the mediocre, embarrass the superior, and are disgraced by the inferior.
George Bernard Shaw *Man and Superman*, 'Maxims for Revolutionists': 'Titles'

33 Societies, I suppose then, are not divine, but human bundles.
William Shenstone *Essays on Men and Manners*: 'On Religion'

34 As long as men are men, a poor society cannot be too poor to find a right order of life, nor a rich society too rich to have need to seek it.
R. H. Tawney *The Acquisitive Society*

35 It is an interesting question how far men would retain their relative rank if they were divested of their clothes. **H. D. Thoreau** *Walden*: 'Economy'

36 Never speak disrespectfully of Society, Algernon. Only people who can't get into it do that. **Oscar Wilde** *The Importance of Being Earnest*, Act 3

See also ***The People***

Solitude

1 It had been hard for him that spake it to have put more truth and untruth together, in few words, than in that speech: 'Whosoever is delighted in solitude is either a wild beast, or a god.'
Francis Bacon *Essays*: 'Of Friendship'

2 Unthinking Heads, who have not learned to be alone, are in a Prison to themselves if they be not also with others: whereas on the contrary, they whose thoughts are in a fair, and hurry within, are sometimes fain to retire into Company, to be out of the crowd of themselves.
Sir Thomas Browne *Christian Morals*, Pt 3, 9

3 We live, as we dream – alone. **Joseph Conrad** *Heart of Darkness*, Ch. 1

4 We are only really alone when we have stopped expecting.
Comtesse Diane *Les Glanes de la vie*, p. 194

5 Comfort is like the wrong memory at the wrong place or time: if one is lonely one prefers discomfort. **Graham Greene** *The End of the Affair*, Pt 1, Ch. 1

6 Pray that your loneliness may spur you into finding something to live for, great enough to die for. **Dag Hammarskjöld** *Diaries*, 1951

7 The strongest man upon earth is the man who stands most alone.
Henrik Ibsen *An Enemy of the People*, Act 5

8 Solitude would be an ideal state if one were able to pick the people one avoids. **Karl Kraus** *Half-Truths and One-and-a-Half Truths*: 'Lord, forgive the . . .'

9 Solitude is not very likely, there is so little of it in life, so what can we expect after death! After all, the dead far outnumber the living!
Milan Kundera *Immortality*, Pt 1, 3

10 It is the pardonable vanity of lonely people everywhere to assume they have no counterparts. **John Le Carré** *The Honourable Schoolboy*, Ch. 13

11 How did you enjoy yourself with these people? Answer: very much, almost as much as I do when alone.
Georg Christoph Lichtenberg *Aphorisms*, Notebook B, 50

12 To be alone frequently and to think about ourselves and to create our world out of ourselves, may give us great joy; but in this way we work, without noticing it, towards a philosophy according to which suicide is only right and permissible. It is good, therefore, to hook oneself to the world by means of a girl or friend, in order not to fall off completely.
Georg Christoph Lichtenberg *The Lichtenberg Reader*, Aphorisms 1768–71

13 No one has ever been excluded from feeling left out.
Adam Phillips *Monogamy*, 1

14 I hold this to be the highest function of the bond between two people: that each protects the other's solitude.
Rainer Maria Rilke letter to Paula Modersohn-Becker, 12 February 1902

15 To be alone is the fate of all great minds – a fate deplored at times, but still always preferable as the less grievous of two evils.
Arthur Schopenhauer *Aphorisms on the Wisdom of Life*: 'Von dem was Einer ist'

16 The love of solitude increases by indulgence.
Sir Walter Scott *Journal*, p. 89

17 One can acquire everything in solitude except character.
Stendhal *Love*: 'Various Fragments', 1

18 Solitude is to the mind what diet is to the body, a necessity that proves fatal if suffered too long.
Marquis de Vauvenargues *Reflections and Maxims*, 598

19 When so many are lonely as seem to be lonely, it would be inexcusably selfish to be lonely alone. **Tennessee Williams** *Camino Real*: Prologue

Sorrow

1 In much wisdom is much grief: and he that increaseth knowledge increaseth sorrow. **Bible, OT** Ecclesiastes 1:8

2 A grain of sand can't resign itself to the desert; and perhaps what's ultimately good about melancholics is that they seldom get hysterical. **Joseph Brodsky** *On Grief and Reason*: 'Homage to Marcus Aurelius'

3 Afflictions induce callosities; miseries are slippery, or fall like snow upon us. **Sir Thomas Browne** *Urn Burial*, Ch. 5

4 Pessimism is a thing which is learnt from books, as sorrow is a thing learnt from life. Sorrow can never be pessimistic, for it is founded on the value of things. **G. K. Chesterton** in the *Daily News*, 13 June 1903

5 It is our incapacity to weep which sustains our taste for things, which makes them exist at all; it keeps us from exhausting their savour and from turning away.
E. M. Cioran *A Short History of Decay*, 1: 'In the Margin of Moments'

6 Stolidity is more dreadful than sorrow, for it is the stubble of the soil where sorrow grew. **Emily Dickinson** *Notebook*, c. 1880

7 It is a good thing to have a great sorrow. Or should human beings allow Christ to have died on the Cross for the sake of their toothaches?
Isak Dinesen *Last Tales*: 'Of Hidden Thoughts and Heaven'

8 Man only notices his sorrows; he takes his happiness for granted.
Fyodor Dostoevsky *Notes from the Underground*, Pt 2, 6

9 Now you can reach forty and get no nearer a real grief than the television news. **P. J. Kavanagh** *People and Weather*, 4

10 What we call mourning for our dead is perhaps not so much grief at not being able to call them back as it is grief at not being able to want to do so. **Thomas Mann** *The Magic Mountain*, Ch. 7

11 The cure for imaginary sorrow is real sorrow.
Friedrich Nietzsche *Nietzsche in Outline and Aphorism*: 'New Commandments'

12 Sorrow is tranquillity remembered in emotion.
Dorothy Parker *Sentiment*

13 Showing grief is more exacting than grief itself. How few of us are sad when alone! **Seneca** *Letters from a Stoic*, 99

14 There are some sorrows for which we should never be consoled.
Mme de Sévigné in J. de Finod, *A Thousand Flashes of French Wit*, p. 110

15 When sorrows come, they come not single spies,
But in battalions. **William Shakespeare** *Hamlet*, Act 4, Sc. 5, (78)

16 Well, every one can master a grief but he that has it.
William Shakespeare *Much Ado About Nothing*, Act 3, Sc. 2, (28)

17 To mourn a mischief that is past and gone,
Is the next way to draw new mischief on.
William Shakespeare *Othello*, Act 1, Sc. 3, (204)

18 'American girls do have regrets,' Amy said. 'That is what distinguishes them from French girls.' **Amanda Vail** *Love Me Little*, Ch. 10

See also ***Pain and Suffering; Sympathy***

The Spoken Word

1 It's not the party of life in the end that's important. It's the comment in the bedroom. **Enid Bagnold** *The Loved and the Envied*, Ch. 26

2 We do not see the power which is in speech because we forget that all speech is classification, and that all classifications are oppressive.
Roland Barthes inaugural lecture as Professor of Literary Semiology at the Collège de France, Paris, 7 January 1977

3 In the multitude of words there wanteth not sin: but he that refraineth his lips is wise. **Bible, OT** Proverbs 10:19

4 A word fitly spoken is like apples of gold in pictures of silver.
Bible, OT Proverbs 25:11

5 Honour and shame is in talk: and the tongue of man is his fall.
Bible, Apocrypha Ecclesiasticus 5:3

6 The stroke of the whip maketh marks in the flesh; but the stroke of the tongue breaketh bones. **Bible, Apocrypha** Ecclesiasticus 28:17

7 The tongue can no man tame; it is an unruly evil.
Bible, NT James 3:8; commonly misquoted as 'The tongue is an unruly member'

8 Not that which goeth into the mouth defileth a man; but that which cometh out of the mouth, this defileth a man. **Bible, NT** Matthew 15:11

9 Talking to yourself is an art; conversing with others is a pastime.
Roberto Calasso *The Ruin of Kasch*: 'The Moscow Gatekeeper'

10 The aim of the sculptor is to convince us that he is a sculptor; the aim of the orator is to convince us that he is not an orator.
G. K. Chesterton *Heretics*, Ch. 4

11 The origins of speech lie in song, and the origin of song in the need to fill out with sound the overlarge and rather empty human soul.

J. M. Coetzee *Disgrace*, 1

12 The best conversation between two people is a monologue.

Edward Dahlberg *Alms for Oblivion*: 'My Friends'

See also Ustinov

13 Men were made to listen as well as to talk . . . nature has given us two ears but only one mouth.

Benjamin Disraeli *Henrietta Temple*, Bk 6, Ch. 24

See also Colton, in ***The Senses***

14 There are two ways of speaking an audience will always like; one, is to tell them what they don't understand; and the other, is to tell them what they're used to. **George Eliot** *Felix Holt*, Ch. 17

15 In conversation, speak Reason, rather than authors, rather Sense than a Syllogism; rather thy own Thought than another's.

Dr Thomas Fuller *Introductio ad Prudentium*, 1503

16 I am better able to retract what I did than what I did say.

Solomon Ibn Gabirol *Choice of Pearls*, 339

17 People don't talk to themselves nearly enough these days. No doubt they are afraid of finding out what they really think.

Jean Giraudoux *Intermezzo*, Act 3

18 A spoken word demands itself in reply.

Johann Wolfgang von Goethe *Maxims and Reflections* (Penguin), 1000

19 The job of a citizen is to keep his mouth open.

Günter Grass in *Contradictory Quotations*, ed. M. Rogers

20 Most Men make little other use of their speech than to give evidence against their own Understanding.

Marquis of Halifax *Moral Thoughts and Reflections*: 'Of Folly and Fools'

21 A genius for repartee is a gift for saying what a wise man thinks only.

Thomas Hardy in *Notebook*, 13 April 1909; in Florence Emily Hardy, *The Life of Thomas Hardy*, Ch. 29

22 He who does not understand your silence will probably not understand your words. **Elbert Hubbard** *The Note Book of Elbert Hubbard*, p. 176

23 A sharp tongue is the only edged tool that grows keener with constant use. **Washington Irving** *The Sketch Book*: 'Rip Van Winkle'

24 Most English talk is a quadrille in a sentry-box.

Henry James *The Awkward Age*, V, 19

25 It was the speech a vain average would make to an audience of means. **Randall Jarrell** *Pictures from an Institution*, Pt 6, Ch. 4

26 That people should endeavour to excel in conversation, I do not wonder; because in conversation praise is instantly reverberated.
Dr Samuel Johnson in James Boswell, *Journal of a Tour to the Hebrides*, 19 August 1773

27 All things that are easy to say have already been perfectly said.
Joseph Joubert *Notebooks*, 1805

28 With people who are shrewd enough to listen to everything and to speak very little, you should speak even less; or if you speak a lot, say very little. **Jean de La Bruyère** *Characters*: 'Of the Court', 85

29 There are some people who speak a moment before they think.
Jean de La Bruyère *Characters*: 'Of Society and Conversation', 15

30 The opposite of talking isn't listening. The opposite of talking is waiting. **Fran Lebowitz** *Social Studies*: 'People'

31 Great people talk about ideas, average people talk about things, and small people talk about wine. **Fran Lebowitz** *Social Studies*: 'People'

32 Fatigue makes women talk more and men less.
C. S. Lewis *The Screwtape Letters*, 30

33 Whenever he spoke every mousetrap in the neighbourhood snapped shut. **Georg Christoph Lichtenberg** *Aphorisms*, Notebook F, 58

34 It is notorious that we speak no more than half-truths in our ordinary conversation, and even a soliloquy is likely to be affected by the apprehension that walls have ears. **Eric Linklater** *Juan in America*, Bk 2, 4

35 Conversation is like playing tennis with a ball made of Krazy Putty that keeps coming back over the net in a different shape.
David Lodge *Small World*, Pt 1, 1

36 The art of dialling has replaced the art of dialogue.
Gita Mehta *Karma Cola*, 8, 2

37 If a man's talk is commonplace and his writing distinguished, it means that his talent lies in the place from which he borrows and not in himself. **Michel de Montaigne** *Essays*, Bk 3, Ch. 2

38 Must not anyone who wants to move the crowd be an actor who impersonates himself?
Friedrich Nietzsche quoted in John Banville, *The Untouchable*

39 Continuous eloquence is wearisome. **Blaise Pascal** *Pensées*, 319

40 It happens that a conversation overheard makes us pause, interests and touches us more deeply than words addressed to us.

Cesare Pavese *This Business of Living: A Diary 1935–1950*, 17 August 1942

41 Whatever is well said by anyone belongs to me.

Seneca *Letters from a Stoic*, 16

42 Speech created thought,
Which is the measure of the universe.

P. B. Shelley *Prometheus Unbound*, Act 2, Sc. 4, 72

43 Speech was given to man to disguise his thoughts.

Charles-Maurice de Talleyrand also attrib. to others

44 Conversation is listening to yourself in the presence of others.

Sydney Tremayne *Tatlings*, p. 59

45 A dialogue is a good monologue spoiled by somebody else talking.

Peter Ustinov quoted in the *Observer*, 6 December 1998

See also Dahlberg

46 Conversation is imperative if gaps are to be filled, and old age, it is the last gap but one. **Patrick White** *The Tree of Man*, Ch. 22

47 A good listener is not someone who has nothing to say. A good listener is a good talker with a sore throat.

Katharine Whitehorn in Herbert V. Prochnow, *The Public Speaker's Treasure Chest*

48 It is far more difficult to talk about a thing than to do it.

Oscar Wilde *The Critic as Artist*, 1

49 Talks more and says less than anybody I ever met. She is made to be a public speaker. **Oscar Wilde** *An Ideal Husband*, Act 2

50 If one could only teach the English how to talk, and the Irish how to listen, society here would be quite civilized.

Oscar Wilde *An Ideal Husband*, Act 3

51 There is only one thing in the world worse than being talked about, and that is not being talked about.

Oscar Wilde *The Picture of Dorian Gray*, Ch. 1

52 Animals can be tamed, but not mouths.

D. W. Winnicott *Through Paediatrics to Psychoanalysis*, p. 41

53 Everything that can be said can be said clearly.

Ludwig Wittgenstein *Tractatus Logico-philosophicus*, 4, 116

See also ***Language; Silence; Words***

Strength and Weakness

1 The weakest man in the world can avail himself of the passion of the wisest. **Earl of Chesterfield** *Letters to His Son*, 15 January 1753

2 The weak are more likely to make the strong weak than the strong are likely to make the weak strong.
Marlene Dietrich *Marlene Dietrich's ABC*: 'Weakness'

3 A man can be destroyed but not defeated.
Ernest Hemingway *The Old Man and the Sea*

4 There are plenty of ruined buildings in the world but no ruined stones. **Hugh MacDiarmid** *On a Raised Beach*

5 Like all weak men he laid an exaggerated stress on not changing one's mind. **W. Somerset Maugham** *Of Human Bondage*, Ch. 37

6 Broken china lasts longer than unbroken.
Jules Renard *Journal 1887–1910*, 4 September 1890

7 Weak people never give way when they ought to.
Cardinal de Retz *Memoirs*, Pt 2

8 He has one of those terribly weak natures that is not susceptible to influence. **Oscar Wilde** *An Ideal Husband*, Act 4

See also ***Power***

Style and Fashion

1 Good taste is better than bad taste, but bad taste is better than no taste. **Arnold Bennett** in the *Observer*, 'Sayings of the Week', 24 August 1930

2 Makes of men date, like makes of cars.
Elizabeth Bowen *The Death of the Heart*, Pt 1, Ch. 7

3 Style is the man himself. **George-Louis de Buffon** *Discours sur le style*

4 Anyone who, in order to survive, succumbs to the moment and adopts its style will be killed by the moment that follows.
Roberto Calasso *The Ruin of Kasch*: 'Eulogius'

5 Surely in all the civilizations that the reactionaries dreamed of, taste did not exist. *Meaning* was enough to suppress it. And meaning must sway on its foundations before taste can appear.
Roberto Calasso *The Ruin of Kasch*: 'On Taste'

6 Change of fashion is the tax levied by the industry of the poor on the vanity of the rich. **Nicholas-Sébastien Chamfort** *Maxims and Considerations*, 163

7 Good taste is a choice; chic is a reflex.
Malcolm de Chazal *Sens plastique*, p. 94

8 Style is the imprint of what we are on what we do.
René Daumal *Les Pouvoirs et la parole*: 'Dialogue du style', p. 265

9 Fashion is the recourse of women who have no taste.
Comtesse Diane *Les Glanes de la vie*, p. 49

10 The style of an author should be the image of his mind, but the choice and command of language is the fruit of exercise.
Edward Gibbon *Miscellaneous Works*, Bk 1, p. 145

11 If you see a bandwagon, it's too late.
James Goldsmith in Jeffrey Robinson, *The Risk Takers 5 Years On*, Pt 2: Introduction

12 Fashion is gentility running away from vulgarity and afraid of being overtaken. **William Hazlitt** *The Conversations of James Northcote*

13 Never forget that only dead fish swim with the stream.
Malcolm Muggeridge in the *Radio Times*, 9 July 1964

14 Effectiveness of assertion is the alpha and omega of style.
George Bernard Shaw *Man and Superman*: Preface

15 Proper words in proper places, make the true definition of style.
Jonathan Swift *Letter to a Young Clergyman*, 9 January 1720

16 Taste is made of a host of distastes. **Paul Valéry** *Odds and Ends I*: 'Painting'

17 Fashion is what one wears oneself. What is unfashionable is what other people wear. **Oscar Wilde** *An Ideal Husband*, Act 3

18 In matters of grave importance, style, not sincerity, is the vital thing.
Oscar Wilde *The Importance of Being Earnest*, Act 3

19 The nineteenth century dislike of realism is the rage of Caliban seeing his own face in a glass. The nineteenth century dislike of romanticism is the rage of Caliban not seeing his own face in a glass.
Oscar Wilde *The Picture of Dorian Gray*: Preface

See also ***Dress***

Success and Failure

1 To be a success you need friends. To be very successful you need enemies.

Anon. embroidered motto in home of Glenn Ford, quoted in the *Guardian*, 15 August 1985

2 By their fruits ye shall know them. **Bible, NT** Matthew 7:20

3 Success don't konsist in never making blunders, but in never making the same one the seckond time. **Josh Billings** *Wit and Humor*, Affurisms: 'Mollassis Kandy'

4 The world is made of people who never quite get into the first team and who just miss the prizes at the flower show.

J. Bronowski *The Face of Violence*, Ch. 6

5 The only infallible criterion of wisdom to vulgar minds – success.

Edmund Burke *Letter to a Member of the National Assembly*

6 Every fulfilment is slavery. It drives us to a higher fulfilment.

Albert Camus *Notebooks*

7 Success is the space one occupies in the newspaper. Success is one day's insolence. **Elias Canetti** *The Secret Heart of the Clock*: '1974'

8 There is nothing that fails like success. **G. K. Chesterton** *Heretics*, Ch. 1

9 The secret of success in life is known only to those who have not succeeded. **John Churton Collins** *Life and Memoirs*, by his son: Appendix

10 Management is efficiency in climbing the ladder of success; leadership determines whether the ladder is standing against the right wall.

Stephen R. Covey *The 7 Habits of Highly Effective People*

11 No gains without pains. **Benjamin Franklin** *Poor Richard's Almanack*, 1745

12 The whole of life consists of
wanting and not-succeeding,
succeeding and not-wanting.

Johann Wolfgang von Goethe *Maxims and Reflections* (Penguin), from *Wilhelm Meister's Journeyman Years*, 915

13 Success is more dangerous than failure, the ripples break over a wider coastline. **Graham Greene** quoted in the *Independent*, 4 April 1991

14 The World is beholden to *generous Mistakes* for the greatest Part of the Good that is done to it. **Marquis of Halifax** *Moral Thoughts and Reflections*: 'Of the World'

15 The way to secure success is to be more anxious about obtaining than about deserving it.

William Hazlitt *The Plain Speaker*: 'On the Qualities Necessary to Success in Life'

16 He was a self-made man who owed his lack of success to nobody.

Joseph Heller *Catch-22*, Ch. 3

17 You can't make a sow's ear out of a silk purse.

Henry James letter to his brother William after failure of his play *Guy Domville*; quoted in D. J. Enright, *Interplay*, p. 230

18 When one door closes, a hundred others close.

Gray Joliffe in *Woman's Journal*, March 1998

19 If fortune wants to make a man admirable, she grants him virtues; if she wants him to be admired, she grants him success.

Joseph Joubert *Thoughts and Maxims*, 149

20 The race is not always to the swift, but that is where to look.

Hugh E. Keough quoted by F. P. Adams in the *Atlantic Monthly*, August 1942

21 In order to succeed in the world people do their utmost to appear successful. **Duc de La Rochefoucauld** *Maxims*, 56

See also Lasch

22 Nothing succeeds like the appearance of success.

Christopher Lasch *The Culture of Narcissism*, Ch. 3

See also La Rochefoucauld

23 The worst part of having success is to try finding someone who is happy for you.

Bette Midler (attrib.) in *The Penguin Dictionary of Modern Humorous Quotations*, compiled by Fred Metcalf

24 Be nice to people on your way up because you'll meet 'em on your way down.

Wilson Mizner in A. Johnston, *The Legendary Mizners*, Ch. 4; also attrib. to Jimmy Durante

25 Our very business in life is not to get ahead of others, but to get ahead of ourselves. **Thomas L. Monson (attrib.)**

26 It's better to be young in your failures than old in your successes.

Flannery O'Connor *The Habit of Being*, letter to 'A', 22 November 1958

27 In life . . . we end up doing whatever we do second best.

Marcel Proust *Remembrance of Things Past*; quoted in John Le Carré, *A Perfect Spy*, 15

28 The only place where success comes before work is in a dictionary.

Vidal Sassoon on BBC radio, quoting one of his teachers

29 Men shut their doors against a setting sun.

William Shakespeare *Timon of Athens*, Act 1, Sc. 2, (152)

30 A self-made man is one who believes in luck and sends his son to Oxford. **Christina Stead** *House of All Nations*: 'Credo'

31 Our business in this world is not to succeed, but to continue to fail, in good spirits. **Robert Louis Stevenson** *Ethical Studies*, p. 84

32 Success is the necessary misfortune of life, but it is only to the very unfortunate that it comes early. **Anthony Trollope** *Orley Farm*, Ch. 49

33 Whenever a friend succeeds, a little something inside me dies.
Gore Vidal in the *Sunday Times Magazine*, 16 September 1973

34 It's just as difficult to overcome success as it is to overcome failure.
William Walton on receiving the Order of Merit, 1967; quoted in Susanna Walton, *William Walton: Behind the Façade*, Ch. 16

35 To journey is better than to arrive – or so say those who have already arrived. **Fay Weldon** *The Heart of the Country*: 'Doing It All Wrong'

36 She's the kind of girl who climbed the ladder of success, wrong by wrong. **Mae West** in screenplay of film *I'm No Angel*

37 Success is paralysing only to those who have never wished for anything else. **Thornton Wilder** *Journals, 1939–61*, ed. Donald Gallup

See also ***Fame and Reputation; Victories and Defeats***

Superstition

1 There is a superstition in avoiding superstition.
Francis Bacon *Essays*: 'Of Superstition'

2 No man was ever truly superstitious who was not truly religious as far as he knew. **William Blake** marginalia to Johann Kaspar Lavater, *Aphorisms on Man*, 342

3 Superstition is the religion of feeble minds.
Edmund Burke *Reflections on the Revolution in France*, p. 269

4 One of the greatest superstitions of our time is the belief that it has none. **Celia Green** *The Decline and Fall of Science*: 'Aphorisms'

5 To become a popular religion, it is only necessary for a superstition to enslave a philosophy.
W. R. Inge *Outspoken Essays, Second Series*: 'The Idea of Progress'

6 As long as we believe in superstition we are not superstitious.
Cesare Pavese *This Business of Living: Diary 1935–1950*, 26 August 1944

7 Superstition sets the whole world alight, philosophy quenches the flames. **Voltaire** *Philosophical Dictionary*: 'Superstition'

See also ***Beliefs; Faith***

Sympathy

1 Human nature is so well disposed towards those who are in interesting situations, that a young person, who either marries or dies, is sure to be kindly spoken of. **Jane Austen** *Emma*, Ch. 22

2 No real English gentleman, in his secret soul, was ever sorry for the death of a political economist; he is much more likely to be sorry for his life. **Walter Bagehot** *Literary Studies*: 'The First Edinburgh Reviewers'

3 Then cherish pity, lest you drive an angel from your door. **William Blake** *Songs of Innocence*: 'Holy Thursday'

4 We forgive out of pity for others, we forget out of self-pity. **Comtesse Diane** *Les Glanes de la vie*, p. 132

5 Nothing dries sooner than a Tear. **Benjamin Franklin** *Poor Richard's (Improved) Almanack*, 1757

6 Our sympathy is cold to the relation of distant misery. **Edward Gibbon** *The Decline and Fall of the Roman Empire*, Ch. 49

7 Any one is to be pitied who has just sense enough to perceive his deficiencies. **William Hazlitt** *Characteristics*, 213

8 Personalize your sympathies, depersonalize your antipathies. **W. R. Inge** *More Lay Thoughts of a Dean*, Pt 4, Ch. 1

9 It is not through the head that men touch each other. **Joseph Joubert** *Notebooks*, 1807

10 All great minds sympathize. **Johann Kaspar Lavater** *Aphorisms on Man*, 610

11 Nature has joined men at the heart, and the professors would like them to be joined at the head. **Georg Christoph Lichtenberg** *Aphorisms*, Notebook E, 54

12 We feel pity only for those who have none for themselves. **Cesare Pavese** *The Business of Living: A Diary 1935–1950*, 12 November 1940

13 No beast so fierce but knows some touch of pity. **William Shakespeare** *Richard III*, Act 1, Sc. 2, 71

14 Compassion is the fellow-feeling of the unsound. **George Bernard Shaw** *Man and Superman*, 'Maxims for Revolutionists': 'Stray Sayings'

See also ***Charity; Sorrow***

Thought

1 True thoughts are those alone which do not understand themselves.

Theodor Adorno *Minima Memoralia*, Pt 3, 122

2 The universe is transformation; our life is what our thoughts make it.

Marcus Aurelius *Meditations*, Bk 4, 3

3 Your mind will be like its habitual thoughts; for the soul becomes dyed with the colour of its thoughts.

Marcus Aurelius *Meditations*, Bk 5, 16

4 It takes a nonentity to think of everything.

Honoré de Balzac *Pierre Grassou*

5 I have always found that the man whose second thoughts are good is worth watching.

J. M. Barrie *What Every Woman Knows*, Act 1

6 Which of you by taking thought can add one cubit unto his stature?

Bible, NT Matthew 6:27

7 **Brain, n.** An apparatus with which we think that we think.

Ambrose Bierce *The Devil's Dictionary*

8 One thought fills immensity.

William Blake *The Marriage of Heaven and Hell*: 'Proverbs of Hell'

9 There never was a thought to which a wish was not father. The only thing you can argue about: What wish? You may suspect that it is difficult to establish paternity, but that's no reason to suspect that a child had no father at all.

Bertolt Brecht *Tales from the Calendar*: 'Anecdotes of Mr Keuner'

10 It is not enough to think, one also has to breathe. Dangerous are the thinkers who have not breathed enough.

Elias Canetti *The Human Province*: '1960'

11 What one thinks daily may not always be important. But what one has not thought daily is tremendously important.

Elias Canetti *The Human Province*: '1972'

12 He who has nothing to think about finds it in the dictionary.

Elias Canetti *The Secret Heart of the Clock*: '1981'

13 Dogma does not mean the absence of thought, but the end of thought. **G. K. Chesterton** *The Victorian Age in Literature*, Ch. 1

14 Nothing so hampers continuity of thought as to feel the mind's insistent pressure. Perhaps this is why the mad think only in *flashes*.

E. M. Cioran *Anathemas and Admirations*, 9

15 The course of meditation; you begin by ignoring the object and end by ignoring the world. **E. M. Cioran** *Tears and Saints*

16 The highest possible stage in moral culture is when we recognize that we ought to control our thoughts. **Charles Darwin** *The Descent of Man*, Ch. 4

17 *Cogito, ergo sum*. – I think, therefore I am.

René Descartes *Discourse on Method*, 4

See also Kundera; Valéry

18 The thinker's job is to be suggestive: that of the saint to be silent about his discovery. **Lawrence Durrell** *Justine*, Pt 3, p. 156

19 A thought cannot awake without waking other thoughts.

Maria von Ebner-Eschenbach *Aphorisms*, p. 37

20 Think once before you give, twice before you accept, and a thousand times before you ask. **Maria von Ebner-Eschenbach** *Aphorisms*, p. 52

21 Our thoughts are often worse than we are, just as they are often better than we are. **George Eliot** *Scenes of Clerical Life*: 'Mr Gilfil's Love-Story', Ch. 19

22 All the thoughts of a turtle are turtle.

Ralph Waldo Emerson *Journal*, September–October 1854

23 We cannot think about our thinking without simplification, any more than we can about the world around us. **Michael Frayn** *Constructions*, 64

24 It is a far, far better thing to have a firm anchor in nonsense than to put out on the troubled seas of thought.

J. K. Galbraith *The Affluent Society*, Ch. 11, Sect. 4

25 There is nothing worth thinking that has not been thought before; we must just try to think it once more.

Johann Wolfgang von Goethe *Maxims and Reflections*: 'Life and Character', 1

See also Valéry

26 We're only really thinking when we can't think out fully what we are thinking about!

Johann Wolfgang von Goethe *Maxims and Reflections* (Penguin), from *Wilhelm Meister's Journeyman Years*, 939

27 A man may dwell so long upon a thought, that it may take him prisoner.

Marquis of Halifax *Miscellaneous Thoughts and Reflections*: 'Faculties of the Mind'

28 A thought must tell at once, or not at all. **William Hazlitt** *Characteristics*, 6

29 Only when we turn thoughtfully toward what has already been thought, will we be turned to use for what must still be thought.

Martin Heidegger *Identity and Difference*, p. 41

30 Those whose chief concern is thought can go far in it, but they mistake water for the dry land and one day they will drown in it.

Hermann Hesse *Reflections*, 331

31 Don't think too much youwl grow hair on the in side of your head.

Russell Hoban *Riddley Walker*, 10

32 Thought must be divided against itself before it can come to any knowledge of itself. **Aldous Huxley** *Do What You Will*: 'Wordsworth in the Tropics'

33 A great many people think they are thinking when they are merely rearranging their prejudices.

William James (attrib.) in Clifton Fadiman, *American Treasury*

34 He that thinks with more extent than another, will want words of larger meaning. **Dr Samuel Johnson** *The Idler*, 70

35 The thoughts that come to us are worth more than the ones we seek.

Joseph Joubert *Notebooks*, 1803

36 One always adds a little of one's soul to what one thinks.

Joseph Joubert *Notebooks*, 1806

37 A good thought is clear enough to be understood by all, and deep enough to baffle only a few. **David Kipp** *Aphorisms*, p. 10

38 The father of the arrow is the thought: how do I expand my reach?

Paul Klee *Pedagogical Sketchbook*, IV, 37

39 I think, therefore I am is the statement of an intellectual who underrates toothaches. **Milan Kundera** *Immortality*, Pt 4, Ch. 11

See also Descartes; Valéry

40 Sense seeks and finds the thought; the thought seeks and finds genius. **Johann Kaspar Lavater** *Aphorisms on Man*, 496

41 Thought is not a trick, or an exercise, or a set of dodges.
Thought is a man in his wholeness wholly attending.

D. H. Lawrence *Thought*

42 With many people the word precedes the thought. They only know what they think when they've heard what they say.

Gustave Le Bon *Aphorismes du temps présent*

43 He pondered things over so meticulously; he always saw a grain of sand before he saw a house.

Georg Christoph Lichtenberg *The Lichtenberg Reader*: Aphorisms 1773–75

44 *Gedanken sind zollfrei.* – Thoughts pay no duty.

Martin Luther motto of *Von weltlicher Obrigkeit*

45 Hindu thought is without dogma, and dogged by Dharma.

Gita Mehta *Karma Cola*, 40, 4

46 There is no exercise that is either feebler or more strenuous, according to the nature of the mind concerned, than that of conversing with one's own thoughts. **Michel de Montaigne** *Essays*, Bk 3, Ch. 3

47 He is a thinker; that means, he knows how to make things simpler than they are. **Friedrich Nietzsche** *The Gay Science*, Bk 3, 189

48 Profundity of thought belongs to youth, clarity of thought to old age.

Friedrich Nietzsche *Miscellaneous Maxims and Opinions*, 289

49 A second thought is never an odd thought.

Flann O'Brien *At Swim-Two-Birds*, Ch. 1

50 An Englishman thinks seated; a Frenchman, standing; an American, pacing; an Irishman afterward.

Austin O'Malley in A. Andrews, *Quotations for Speakers and Writers*

51 You can lead a whore to culture but you can't make her think.

Dorothy Parker speech to American Horticultural Society; in J. Keats, *You Might as Well Live*, Pt 1, Ch. 2

52 Man is but a reed, the weakest in nature; but he is a thinking reed.

Blaise Pascal *Pensées*, 264

53 Thought: just a flash in the middle of a long night. And this flash is all. **Henri Poincaré** *The Value of Science*, p. 142

54 The printworks is the artillery of thought.

Antoine de Rivarol *Les Plus belles pages*, Le Livre Club edn, p. 29

55 As well as thoughts which are unworthy of us, we have thoughts we are not worthy of. **Jean Rostand** *Journal d'un caractère*

56 There is a small number of men and women who think for all the others, and for whom all the rest talk and act.

Jean-Jacques Rousseau *Julie ou la nouvelle Héloise*, Pt 2, Letter 14

57 We love not in accordance with our mode of thinking, but we think in accordance with our mode of loving. **V. V. Rozanov** *Fallen Leaves*, p. 108

58 This seems to be the nature of thought that it leads to its own starting point, the timeless home of the mind.

Oliver Sacks *A Leg to Stand On*: final words

59 Most men will put off thinking definitely till they have to act, to write, or to speak. **Sir Henry Taylor** *The Statesman*, Ch. 8

60 Every thought that passes through the mind helps to wear and tear it and to deepen the ruts which as in the streets of Pompeii evince how much it has been used. **H. D. Thoreau** *Journal*, 7 July 1851

61 Man thinks of the going and seldom of the coming back.

Paul Valéry *At Moments*: 'A Free Man'

62 Cognition reigns but does not rule.

Paul Valéry *Bad Thoughts and Not So Bad*, D

63 A man is more complex, infinitely more so, than his thoughts.

Paul Valéry *Odds and Ends*, VII

64 *Variation on Descartes*: Sometimes I think; and sometimes I *am*.

Paul Valéry *Odds and Ends*, VIII

See also Kundera

65 'Thinkers' are people who re-think; who think that what was thought before was never thought *enough*. **Paul Valéry** *Suite*: 'Thinkers'

See also Goethe

66 None are as liable to make mistakes as those who act only upon reflection. **Marquis de Vauvenargues** *Reflections and Maxims*, 131

67 They [mankind] use thought only to justify their wrong-doings, and words only to conceal their thoughts.

Voltaire *Dialogue du chapon et de la poularde*

68 Method of investigation: as soon as we have thought something, try to see in what way the contrary is true.

Simone Weil *Gravity and Grace*: 'Contradiction'

69 We believe that thought does not commit us in any way, but it alone commits us and licence of thought includes all licence.

Simone Weil *Gravity and Grace*: 'Evil'

70 Thinking is the most unhealthy thing in the world, and people die of it just as they die of any other disease. Fortunately, in England at any rate, thought is not catching. **Oscar Wilde** *The Decay of Lying*

71 I can know what someone else is thinking, not what I am thinking.
Ludwig Wittgenstein *Philosophical Investigations*, Pt 2, Sect. 11

72 In order to draw a limit to thinking, we should have to be able to think both sides of this limit.
Ludwig Wittgenstein *Tractatus Logico-philosophicus*: Preface

See also ***Conscience and Consciousness; Intellect and Intelligence; The Mind***

Time

1 To choose time is to save time. **Francis Bacon** *Essays*: 'Of Dispatch'

2 He that will not apply new remedies must expect new evils; for time is the greatest innovator. **Francis Bacon** *Essays*: 'Of Innovations'

3 Time is a great teacher, they say. Unfortunately it kills all its pupils.
Hector Berlioz in *Almanac of French and Foreign Literature*

4 Winter draws what summer paints. **Elizabeth Bibesco** *Haven*: 'Aphorisms'

5 To every thing there is a season, and a time to every purpose under the heaven.
A time to be born, and a time to die; a time to plant, and a time to pluck up that which is planted. **Bible, OT** Ecclesiastes 3:1

6 Better late than before anybody has invited you.
Ambrose Bierce *The Devil's Dictionary*

7 In seed time learn, in harvest teach, in winter enjoy.
William Blake *The Marriage of Heaven and Hell*: 'Proverbs of Hell'

8 Eternity is in love with the productions of time.
William Blake *The Marriage of Heaven and Hell*: 'Proverbs of Hell'

9 The greatest part of time being already wrapt up in things behind us; it's now somewhat late to bait after things before us; for futurity still shortens, and time present sucks in time to come.
Sir Thomas Browne *Christian Morals*, Pt 3, 13

10 Take care of minutes: for hours will take care of themselves.
Earl of Chesterfield *Letters to His Son*, 6 November 1747

11 The less one has to do the less time one finds to do it in.

Earl of Chesterfield *Letters to His Son*

See also Lichtenberg

12 Man is the only animal to be troubled by time, and from that concern comes much of his finest art, a great deal of his religion, and almost all his science. **Arthur C. Clarke** *Profiles of the Future*, Ch. 11

13 God knows that time is precious for He never gives two moments in time side by side, but always in succession.

The Cloud of Unknowing, Ch. 4

14 When a work appears to be ahead of its time, it is only the time that is behind the work. **Jean Cocteau** *Cock and Harlequin*

15 Time is what prevents everything from happening at once.

Marvin Cohen in the *Guardian*, 21 April 1981

16 Six hours in sleep, in law's grave study six,
Four spend in prayer, the rest on Nature fix. **Sir Edward Coke** *Epigram*

17 Remember that time is money.

Benjamin Franklin *Advice to a Young Tradesman*

18 Make use of time if thou value Eternity.

Dr Thomas Fuller *Introductio ad Prudentium*, 1151

19 Time cures one of everything – even of living.

Edmond and Jules de Goncourt *Journal*, 14 October 1856

20 Man, whatever we may think, is a very limited being; the world is a narrow circle drawn about him; the horizon limits our immediate view; immortality means a century or two.

William Hazlitt *The Plain Speaker*: 'On Old English Writers and Speakers'

21 Everything hostile vanishes and is transcended the moment we succeed in excluding time from our thoughts. **Hermann Hesse** *Reflections*, 427

22 He that runs against Time has an antagonist not subject to casualties.

Dr Samuel Johnson in James Boswell, *Life of Johnson*, in footnote for 1756 in 1887 edn

23 We must use time as a tool not as a couch.

President John F. Kennedy in the *Observer*, 'Sayings of the Week', 10 December 1961

24 Time, which strengthens friendship, weakens love.

Jean de La Bruyère *Characters*: 'Of the Heart', 4

25 Those who never have time do least.

Georg Christoph Lichtenberg *Aphorisms*, Notebook K, 50

See also Chesterfield

26 Punctuality is the politeness of kings.
Louis XVIII (attrib.) in *Souvenirs de J. Lafitte*, Bk 1, Ch. 3

27 For tribal man space was the uncontrollable mystery. For technological man it is time that occupies the same role.
Marshall McLuhan *The Mechanical Bride*: 'Magic That Changes Mood'

28 One moment in this world is more precious than a thousand years in the next. **Nouri** quoted in Elias Canetti, *The Secret Heart of the Clock*: '1978'

29 But then life does not count by years. Some suffer a lifetime in a day, and grow old between the rising and the setting of the sun.
Ouida *Wisdom, Wit, and Pathos*: 'Signa'

30 The dropping of rain hollows out a stone; a ring is worn by use.
Ovid *Letters from the Black Sea*, Bk 4, X, 5

31 Time makes more converts than reason.
Thomas Paine *Common Sense*: Introduction

32 The time spent on any item on the agenda will be in inverse proportion to the sum involved. **C. Northcote Parkinson** *Parkinson's Law*, Ch. 3

33 It is only after a memory has lost all life that it can be classed in time, just as only desiccated flowers find their way into the herbarium of a botanist.
Henri Poincaré *On Measuring Time*, quoted in T. Dantzig, *Henri Poincaré*, Ch. 8, epigraph

34 The difference between a gun and a tree is a difference of tempo. The tree explodes every spring. **Ezra Pound** in *Criterion*, July 1937

35 Distances are only the relation of space to time and vary with it.
Marcel Proust *Remembrance of Things Past: Cities of the Plain*, Pt 2, Ch. 3

36 As there is a geometry of space so there is a psychology of time.
Marcel Proust *Remembrance of Things Past: The Fugitive*, p. 637

37 Since time sets its own tempo, like a heartbeat or an ebb tide, timepieces don't really keep time. They just keep up with it, if they're able.
Dava Sobel *Longitude*, Ch. 4

38 Time: That which man is always trying to kill, but which ends in killing him. **Herbert Spencer** *Definitions*

39 Time is the only critic without ambition.
John Steinbeck in *Writers at Work, Fourth Series*, ed. George Plimpton

40 The butterfly counts not months but moments, and has time enough. **Rabindranath Tagore** *Fireflies*, p. 15

41 Sometimes a day serves only to hold time together.
H. D. Thoreau *Journal*, 5 September 1841

42 One moment of life costs many hours. – Not of business but of preparation and invitation. **H. D. Thoreau** *Journal*, 28 September 1841

43 Time is an image of eternity, but it is also a substitute for eternity.
Simone Weil *Gravity and Grace*: 'Renunciation of Time'

44 An instant of time, without duration, is an imaginative logical construction. Also each duration of time mirrors in itself all temporal durations. **A. N. Whitehead** *Science and the Modern World*, Ch. 4

45 For time is the longest distance between two places.
Tennessee Williams *The Glass Menagerie*, Sc. 7

46 Hours which make the earth habitable
rely on the moon. **Wols** *Aphorisms and Pictures*, p. 47

See also ***History; Past and Present***

Town and Country

1 An industrial worker would sooner have a £5 note but a countryman must have praise. **Ronald Blythe** *Akenfield*, Ch. 5

2 No city should be too large for a man to walk out of in a morning.
Cyril Connolly *The Unquiet Grave*, Ch. 1

3 God made the country, and man made the town.
William Cowper *The Task*, Bk 1: 'The Sofa', 749

4 Cities give us a collision. 'Tis said, London and
New York take the nonsense out of a man.
Ralph Waldo Emerson *The Conduct of Life*: 'Culture'

5 The city is always recruited from the country. The men in cities who are the centres of energy, the driving wheels of trade, politics or practical arts, and the women of beauty and genius, are the children or grandchildren of farmers, and are spending the energies which their father's hardy, silent life accumulated in frosty furrows, in poverty, necessity and darkness.
Ralph Waldo Emerson *Society and Solitude*: 'Farming'

6 There is nothing good to be had in the country, or if there is, they will not let you have it.
William Hazlitt *Political Essays*: 'Observations on Mr Wordsworth's *Excursion*'

7 In the city, time becomes visible.
Lewis Mumford *The Culture of Cities*: Introduction

8 I have no relish for the country; it is a kind of healthy grave.

Revd Sydney Smith letter to Miss G. Harcourt, 1838

9 When one is in town one amuses oneself. When one is in the country one amuses other people.

Oscar Wilde *The Importance of Being Earnest*, Act 1

10 It is pure unadulterated country life. They get up early, because they have so much to do, and go to bed early because they have so little to think about.

Oscar Wilde *The Picture of Dorian Gray*, Ch. 15

See also ***Environments; Places***

Travel

1 The less a tourist knows, the fewer mistakes he need make, for he will not expect himself to explain ignorance.

Henry Adams *The Education of Henry Adams*, Ch. 27

2 Travel, in the younger sort, is a part of education; in the elder, a part of experience.

Francis Bacon *Essays*: 'Of Travel'

3 In America there are two classes of travel – first class, and with children.

Robert Benchley *Pluck and Luck*

4 The whole object of travel is not to set foot on foreign land; it is at last to set foot on one's own country as foreign land.

G. K. Chesterton in *The Faber Book of Aphorisms*, ed. W. H. Auden and Louis Kronenberger

5 Travelling is almost like talking with those of other centuries.

René Descartes *Discourse on Method*, I

6 There are two classes of pedestrians in these days of reckless motor traffic: the quick and the dead.

Lord Dewar quoted in George Robey, *Looking Back on Life*, Ch. 28

7 Like all great travellers I have seen more than I remember, and remember more than I have seen.

Benjamin Disraeli *Vivian Grey*, Bk 8, Ch. 4

8 The man who retains the same self-esteem while travelling that he had when he looked at himself in the mirror of his room at home is either a very great man or a very sturdy fool.

Gustave Flaubert letter to Louis Bouilhet from Constantinople, 14 November 1850

9 So it is in travelling; a man must carry knowledge with him if he would bring home knowledge.

Dr Samuel Johnson in James Boswell, *Life of Johnson*, 17 April 1778

10 He travels the fastest who travels alone. **Rudyard Kipling** *The Winners*

11 The British tourist is always happy abroad so long as the natives are waiters. **Robert Morley** in the *Observer*, 'Sayings of the Week', 20 April 1958

12 Writing about travels is nearly always tedious, travelling being, like war and fornication, exciting but not interesting.
Malcolm Muggeridge review of *Diaries of Evelyn Waugh* in the *Observer*, 5 September 1976

13 How can you wonder your travels do you no good, when you carry yourself around with you? **Socrates** quoted by Seneca, *Letters from a Stoic*, 28

14 A man should know something of his own country, too, before he goes abroad. **Laurence Sterne** *Tristram Shandy*, Vol. 7, Ch. 2

15 To travel hopefully is a better thing than to arrive, and the true success is to labour. **Robert Louis Stevenson** *Virginibus Puerisque*: 'El Dorado'

16 Extensive travelling induces a feeling of encapsulation, and travel, so broadening at first, contracts the mind.
Paul Theroux *The Great Railway Bazaar*, Ch. 21

17 Unanticipated invitations to travel are dancing lessons from God.
Kurt Vonnegut quoted by David Mamet in interview in the *Guardian*, 16 February 1989

18 I never travel without my diary. One should always have something sensational to read in the train.
Oscar Wilde *The Importance of Being Earnest*, Act 2

See also ***Places***

Trust and Mistrust

1 Men give their confidence at once, but never their money.
Tristan Bernard *Contes, répliques et bons mots*: 'Le Morale'

2 Distrust all those who love you extremely upon a very slight acquaintance, and without any visible reason. Be on your guard, too, against those who confess as their weaknesses all the cardinal virtues.
Earl of Chesterfield *Letters to His Son*, 15 January 1753

3 Men trust an ordinary man because they trust themselves. But men trust a great man because they do not trust themselves.
G. K. Chesterton *Heretics*, Ch. 19

4 Thrust ivrybody, but cut th' ca-ards.
Finley Peter Dunne *Mr Dooley's Opinions*: 'Casual Observations'

5 Never trust the man who hath reason to suspect that you know he hath injured you. **Henry Fielding** *Jonathan Wild*, Bk 3, Ch. 4

See also Lynn and Jay

6 Let me remind you of the old maxim: people under suspicion are better moving than at rest, since at rest they may be sitting in the balance without knowing it, being weighed together with their sins.

Franz Kafka *The Trial*, 8

7 You can fool all the people some of the time, and some of the people all the time, but you cannot fool all the people all the time.

Abraham Lincoln (attrib.) words in speech at Clinton, Illinois, 8 September 1858; also attrib. to P. T. Barnum

8 One never trusts anyone that one has deceived.

Jonathan Lynn and Antony Jay *Yes, Prime Minister*, Vol. 1: 'The Smokescreen'

See also Fielding

9 Everybody likes a kidder, but nobody lends him money.

Arthur Miller *Death of a Salesman*, Act 1

10 Mistrust deceives us more often than trust. **Cardinal de Retz** *Memoirs*, Pt 2

11 Suspicion of one's own motives is especially necessary for the philanthropist and the executive.

Bertrand Russell *The Conquest of Happiness*, Ch. 8

12 I wonder men dare trust themselves with men.

William Shakespeare *Timon of Athens*, Act 1, Sc. 2, (45)

13 Promises and pie-crust are made to be broken.

Jonathan Swift *Polite Conversation*, Dialogue 1

14 Mistrust first impulses; they are nearly always good.

Charles-Maurice de Talleyrand also attrib. to Count Montrond

15 Distrust a spider when it produces honey.

Tigers Don't Eat Grass: Oriental and Occidental Aphorisms: 'Rogues'

16 It's the suspicious who invite betrayal. **Voltaire** *Zaïre*, Act 1, Sc. 5

17 We have to distrust each other. It is our only defence against betrayal.

Tennessee Williams *Camino Real*, Block 10

18 One can mistrust one's own senses, but not one's own belief.

Ludwig Wittgenstein *Philosophical Investigations*, Pt 2, Sect. 10

See also ***Lies and Deceit; Loyalties***

Truth and Error

1 The truth that makes men free is for the most part the truth which men prefer not to hear. **Herbert Agar** *A Time for Greatness*, Ch. 7

See also Bible, NT

2 The more truth an error contains the more dangerous it is.
Henri-Frédéric Amiel *Amiel's Journal*, 12 November 1852

3 The scientific truth is demonstrable, whereas art and prudence are only concerned with the variable. **Aristotle** *Ethics*, Bk 6, vi

4 The truth of being and the truth of knowing are one, differing no more than the direct beam and the beam reflected.
Francis Bacon *The Advancement of Learning*, Bk 1, iv, 8

5 The truth is a lie that has not been found out.
Beryl Bainbridge on Channel 4 TV, Booker Prize presentation, 27 October 1998

6 It is unfortunate, considering that enthusiasm moves the world, that so few enthusiasts can be trusted to speak the truth.
A. J. Balfour letter to Mrs Drew, 19 May 1891

7 With the truth, you need to get rid of it as soon as possible and pass it on to someone else. As with illness, this is the only way to be cured of it. The person who keeps truth in his hands has lost.
Jean Baudrillard *Cool Memories*, Ch. 1

8 A man may say, 'From now on I'm going to speak the truth.' But the truth hears him and runs away and hides before he's even done speaking. **Saul Bellow** *Herzog*, p. 271

9 The truth shall make you free. **Bible, NT** John 8:32

See also Agar

10 If thare wa'n't nothing but truth in the world we could git along with one third ov the language we use now.
Josh Billings *Wit And Humor*: 'Billings' Proverbs'

11 A truth that's told with bad intent
Beats all the lies you can invent. **William Blake** *Auguries of Innocence*

12 Truth can never be told so as to be understood, and not be believed.
William Blake *The Marriage of Heaven and Hell*: 'Proverbs of Hell'

13 Two sorts of truth: trivialities, where opposites are obviously absurd, and profound truths, recognized by the fact that the opposite is also a profound truth. **Niels Bohr** in *Niels Bohr: His Life and Work*, ed. S. Rozental, p. 328

14 Truth lies within a little and certain compass, but error is immense.
Lord Bolingbroke *Reflections upon Exile*

15 Truth never penetrates an unwilling mind. **J. L. Borges** *The Aleph*

16 Truth exists; only lies are invented. **Georges Braque** *Pensées sur l'art*

17 A man may be in just possession of Truth as of a city, and yet be forced to surrender. **Sir Thomas Browne** *Religio Medici*, Pt 1, 9

18 A man may aspire to virtue, but he cannot reasonably aspire to truth.
Nicholas-Sébastien Chamfort *Maxims and Considerations*, 342

19 Every man seeks for truth; but God only knows who has found it.
Earl of Chesterfield *Letters to His Son*, 21 September 1747

20 Truth, of course, must of necessity be stranger than fiction; for we have made fiction to suit ourselves. **G. K. Chesterton** *Heretics*, Ch. 4

21 The essential often appears at the end of a long conversation. The great truths are spoken on the doorstep.
E. M. Cioran *Anathemas and Admirations*, 3

22 I have learned that whatever a man tells you about himself is true, even though it is a lie. **Edward Dahlberg** *Alms for Oblivion*: 'My Friends'

23 When you have excluded the impossible, whatever remains, however improbable, must be the truth.
Arthur Conan Doyle *The Adventures of Sherlock Holmes*: 'The Beryl Coronet'

24 Only the hand that erases can write the true thing.
Meister Eckhart epigraph to Dag Hammarskjöld, *Markings*

25 Truth has rough flavours if we bite it through. **George Eliot** *Armgart*, Sc. 2

26 The most intriguing concealed truths we can be offered are about what lies most plainly in our view. **Michael Frayn** *Constructions*, 23

27 The truth that needs proof is only half true.
Kahlil Gibran *Spiritual Settings*, 23

28 The difference between truth and cant often lies in the lips that give forth the words. **George Gissing** *Demos*, Ch. 31

29 Truth is a torch, but a huge one, and so we all of us try to get past it by blinking our eyes, for fear of being scorched.
Johann Wolfgang von Goethe *Maxims and Reflections*: 'Life and Character', 120

30 There are many truths, but there is no Truth.
Rémy de Gourmont *Selections*: 'The Velvet Path'

31 There are people who find somebody else's lie more soothing than their own truth. **Friedrich Hebbel** *Diaries*, entry 911, 1837

32 All truth is error in disguise. **Friedrich Hebbel** *Diaries*, entry 1020, 1838

33 The truth has a million faces, but there is only one truth.
Hermann Hesse *Reflections*, 422

34 Such truth as opposeth no man's profit, nor pleasure, is to all men welcome. **Thomas Hobbes** *Leviathan*: 'Review and Conclusion'

35 It's easy to make a man confess the lies he tells to himself; it's far harder to make him confess the truth. **Geoffrey Household** *Rogue Male*

36 Irrationally held truths may be more harmful than reasoned errors.
T. H. Huxley *Collected Essays*, xii: 'The Coming of Age of the Origin of Species'

37 It is the customary fate of new truths to begin as heresies and to end as superstitions.
T. H. Huxley *Collected Essays*, xii: 'The Coming of Age of the Origin of Species'

38 There is no worse lie than a truth misunderstood by those who hear it. **William James** *The Varieties of Religious Experience*, Lectures 14 and 15

39 The first casualty when war comes is truth.
Senator Hiram Johnson speech in US Senate, 1918; but can be traced back to Aeschylus

40 In lapidary inscriptions a man is not upon oath.
Dr Samuel Johnson in James Boswell, *Life of Johnson*, 1775

41 Every man has a right to utter what he thinks truth, and every other man has a right to knock him down for it. Martyrdom is the test.
Dr Samuel Johnson in James Boswell, *Life of Johnson*, 1780

42 All truths are double or doubled, or they all have a front and a back.
Joseph Joubert *Notebooks*, 1794

43 Truth consists of having the same idea about something that God has. **Joseph Joubert** *Notebooks*, 1800

44 Truth is indivisible, hence it cannot recognize itself; whoever wants to recognize it must be a lie. **Franz Kafka** *Collected Aphorisms*, 80

45 The truth is a snare: you cannot have it without being caught. You cannot have the truth in such a way that you catch it, but only in such a way that it catches you. **Søren Kierkegaard** *The Last Years: Journals, 1853–1855*

46 Truth does not do as much good in the world as the semblance of truth does evil. **Duc de La Rochefoucauld** *Maxims*, 64

47 The discovery of truth, by slow progressive meditation, is wisdom – Intuition of truth, not preceded by perceptible meditation, is genius.
Johann Kaspar Lavater *Aphorisms on Man*, 93; William Blake underlined the last part in approval

48 Truth and falsehood are opposed; but truth is the norm not of truth only but also of falsehood. **C. S. Lewis** *The Allegory of Love*, Ch. 7, Sect. 2

49 To ask in everything the question *Is it true?* By all means – but then to go on to seek grounds for believing it is not true.

Georg Christoph Lichtenberg *Aphorisms*, Notebook J, 247

50 All men are liable to error; and most men are, in many points, by passion or interest, under temptation to it.

John Locke *Essay Concerning Human Understanding*, Ch. 20, 17

51 There are no new truths, but only truths that have not been recognized by those who have perceived them without noticing. A truth is something that everyone can be shown to know and to have known, as people say, all along. **Mary McCarthy** *On the Contrary*: 'The *Vita Activa*'

52 In the long run a harmful truth is better than a useful lie.

Thomas Mann quoted by Arthur Koestler on leaving the Communist Party; in Koestler's obituary in the *Guardian*, 4 March 1983

53 Exactitude is not truth. **Henri Matisse** essay title in *Matisse on Art*, ed. J. D. Flam

54 Truth changes. Variety remains constant.

Pauline Melville *The Ventriloquist's Tale*: Prologue

55 What are man's truths ultimately? Merely his *irrefutable* errors.

Friedrich Nietzsche *The Gay Science*, Bk 3, 265

56 It is good to repeat oneself and thus bestow on a thing a right and a left foot. Truth may be able to stand on one leg; but with two it can walk and get around.

Friedrich Nietzsche *Human, All Too Human*: 'The Wanderer and His Shadow', 13

57 All truth is simple – is that not a compound lie?

Friedrich Nietzsche *Twilight of the Idols*: 'Maxims and Arrows', 4

58 For the greatest truths of our day, we are indebted to combinations of the long separated aspects of total knowledge. **Novalis** *Pollen*, 300

59 The source of all heresies is the failure to perceive the agreement between two opposite truths, and the belief that they are incompatible. The source of all heresies is the exclusion of some of these truths.

Blaise Pascal *Pensées*, 788

60 One fool will deny more truth in half an hour than a wise man can prove in seven years. **Coventry Patmore** *The Rod, the Root and the Flower*: 'Aurea Dicta', 99

61 The references you do not verify are the good ones.

Charles Péguy *Victor-Marie Comte Hugo*, p. 217

62 Truth is simply a compliment paid to sentences seen to be paying their way. **Richard Rorty** in the *New York Times Magazine*, 12 February 1990

63 Great minds are always in the service of truth, even when they are fighting it. **Jean Rostand** *Pensées d'un biologiste*, p. 121

64 Comforting truths need to be proven twice over.

Jean Rostand *Pensées d'un biologiste*, p. 131

65 The truth is too simple: one must always get there by way of the complicated. **George Sand** letter to Armand Barbès, May 1867

66 The truth, which is a standard for the naturalist, for the poet is only a stimulus. **George Santayana** *Soliloquies in England*: 'Ideas'

67 We often want one thing and pray for another, not telling even the gods the truth. **Seneca** *Letters from a Stoic*, 95

68 All great truths begin as blasphemies. **George Bernard Shaw** *Annajanska*

69 One's belief that one is sincere is not so dangerous, however, as one's conviction that one is right.

Igor Stravinsky and Robert Craft *Conversations with Igor Stravinsky*, Ch. 4

70 If you shut your door to all errors truth will be shut out.

Rabindranath Tagore *Stray Birds*, 130

71 Some circumstantial evidence is very strong, as when you find a trout in the milk. **H. D. Thoreau** *Journal*, 11 November 1850

72 Nothing is so sure to make itself known as the truth – for what else waits to be known? **H. D. Thoreau** *Journal*, 12 December 1851

73 It takes two to speak the truth – one to speak, and another to hear.

H. D. Thoreau *A Week on the Concord and Merrimack Rivers*: 'Wednesday'

74 Truth is the most valuable thing we have. Let us economize it.

Mark Twain *Following the Equator*, Ch. 7

75 Truth is naked; but under the skin lies the anatomy.

Paul Valéry *Bad Thoughts and Not So Bad*, M

76 A simple statement is bound to be untrue. One that is not simple cannot be utilized. **Paul Valéry** *Bad Thoughts and Not So Bad*, M

77 One owes respect to the living: but to the dead one owes nothing but the truth. **Voltaire** *Lettres sur Œdipe*, 1: note

78 Truth is one, but error is manifold.

Simone Weil *The Need for Roots*, Pt 2: 'Uprootedness in the Towns'

79 The trouble with man is twofold. He cannot learn truths which are too complicated; he forgets truths which are too simple.

Rebecca West quoted in L. and M. Cowan, *The Wit of Women*

80 There are no whole truths; all truths are half-truths. It is trying to treat them as whole truths that plays the devil.

A. N. Whitehead *Dialogues*: Prologue

81 Man is least himself when he talks in his own person. Give him a mask, and he will tell you the truth. **Oscar Wilde** *The Critic as Artist*, 2

82 Truth is rarely pure, and never simple. Modern life would be very tedious if it were either, and modern literature a complete impossibility. **Oscar Wilde** *The Importance of Being Earnest*, Act 1

83 If one tells the truth, one is sure, sooner or later, to be found out. **Oscar Wilde** *Phrases and Philosophies for the Use of the Young*

84 A truth ceases to be true when more than one person believes it. **Oscar Wilde** *Phrases and Philosophies for the Use of the Young*

85 No artist desires to prove anything. Even things that are true can be proved. **Oscar Wilde** *The Picture of Dorian Gray*: Preface

86 Truth provokes those whom it does not convert. **Bishop Thomas Wilson** *Maxims of Piety and Christianity*: 'Truth'

87 In order for a proposition to be capable of being true it must also be capable of being false. **Ludwig Wittgenstein** *Notebooks 1914–16*, 5 June 1915

88 When I try to put all into a phrase I say 'Man can embody truth, but he cannot know it.' **W. B. Yeats** letter, 4 January 1939, just before his death

See also ***Lies and Deceit***

Understanding

1 Understanding is the reward of faith. Therefore seek not to understand that you may believe, but believe that you may understand.

St Augustine *On St John's Gospel*

2 The man of ambition thinks to find his good in the operations of others; the man of pleasure, in his own sensations; but the man of understanding in his own actions. **Marcus Aurelius** *Meditations*, Bk 6, 51

3 It is the task of radical thought, since the world is given to us in unintelligibility, to make it more unintelligible, more enigmatic, more fabulous. **Jean Baudrillard** interview in the *Guardian*, 14 March 2000

4 Blessed are those whose understanding exceeds their capacity to understand. **Elizabeth Bibesco** *Haven*: 'Aphorisms'

5 Nothing is more fertile than understanding.

Roberto Calasso *The Ruin of Kasch*: 'History Experiments'

6 Reason is dependent on what is coming into being, understanding depends on what is already there; the former is unconcerned about 'what for?', the latter doesn't ask 'where from?' Reason rejoices in the process of development; understanding wants to keep hold of everything so as to put it to use.

Johann Wolfgang von Goethe *Maxims and Reflections* (Penguin), from *Wilhelm Meister's Journeyman Years*, 555

7 Some men methinks relish things more from not understanding them. **Fulke Greville** *Maxims, Characters and Reflections*, p. 136

8 Much learning does not teach understanding. **Heraclitus** *Fragments*, 6

9 Unless one is a genius, it is best to aim at being intelligible.

Anthony Hope *The Dolly Dialogues*, 15

10 Europeans and Americans are like men and women: they understand each other worse, and it matters less, than either of them suppose.

Randall Jarrell *Pictures from an Institution*, Pt 4, Ch. 10

11 Sir, that is the blundering economy of a narrow understanding. It is stopping one hole in a sieve.

Dr Samuel Johnson in James Boswell, *Life of Johnson*, 17 April 1778

12 It is the duty of the human understanding to understand that there are things which it cannot understand, and what those things are.

Søren Kierkegaard *The Journals*, 1854

13 Every profound thinker is more afraid of being understood than being misunderstood. **Friedrich Nietzsche** *Beyond Good and Evil*: 'What Is Noble?' 290

14 The highest is the most comprehensible, the nearest, the most indispensable. **Novalis** *Pollen*, 8

15 The most difficult task for every couple is to get the right amount of misunderstanding. Too little and you assume you know each other. Too much and you begin to believe there must be someone else, somewhere, who does understand you. **Adam Phillips** *Monogamy*, 84

16 Some people will never learn anything, for this reason, because they understand everything too soon.

Alexander Pope *Thoughts on Various Subjects*, 36

17 Our erected wit maketh us to know what perfection is.

Sir Philip Sidney *The Defence of Poesy*

18 The more we understand individual objects, the more we understand God. **Spinoza** *Ethics*, Pt 5, Proposition 25

19 *Tout comprendre c'est tout pardonner* – To understand all is to forgive all.

Mme de Staël *Corinne*, Bk 18, Ch. 5; common misquotation of her 'To understand everything makes one very indulgent'

20 Almost all our misfortunes in life come from the wrong notions we have about the things that happen to us. To know men thoroughly, to judge events sanely is, therefore, a great step towards happiness.

Stendhal *Journal*, 10 December 1801

21 If you would obtain insight, avoid anatomy.

H. D. Thoreau *Journal*, quoted in Ralph Waldo Emerson, *Journal*, 1862

22 There are, I have discovered, two kinds of people in this world, those who long to be understood and those who long to be misunderstood. It is the irony of life that neither is gratified.

Carl van Vechten *The Blind Bow-boy*, Ch. 8

23 Human beings do not understand each other. There are fewer fools than we think. **Marquis de Vauvenargues** *Reflections and Maxims*, 601

24 In my time, of course, we were taught not to understand anything. That was the old system, and wonderfully interesting it was. I assure you that the amount of things I and my poor sister were taught not to understand was quite extraordinary.

Oscar Wilde *An Ideal Husband*, Act 2

25 There is a danger in being persuaded before one understands.

Bishop Thomas Wilson *Maxims of Piety and Christianity*: 'Persuade'

See also ***Knowledge; Thought; Wisdom***

The Universe

1 The Mind of the universe is social. **Marcus Aurelius** *Meditations*, Bk 5, 30

2 Taken as a whole the universe is absurd. There seems an unalterable contradiction between the human mind and its employments.

Walter Bagehot *Literary Studies*: 'The First Edinburgh Reviewers'

3 The question is not whether the theory of the cosmos affects matters, but whether, in the long run, anything else affects them.

G. K. Chesterton *Heretics*, Ch. 1

4 For, the moment we have a view of the universe, we possess it.

G. K. Chesterton *Heretics*, Ch. 3

5 The cosmos is about the smallest hole that a man can hide his head in. **G. K. Chesterton** *Orthodoxy*, Ch. 2

6 Everything in the universe goes by indirection. There are no straight lines. **Ralph Waldo Emerson** *Society and Solitude*: 'Works and Days'

7 The solar system has no anxiety about its reputation.

Ralph Waldo Emerson *The Works*, Vol. 2, p. 297 of 5 vol. 1913 edn

8 The moon is nothing
But a circumambulatory aphrodisiac
Divinely subsidized to provoke the world
Into a rising birth-rate. **Christopher Fry** *The Lady's Not for Burning*, Act 3

9 The universe is not only queerer than we suppose, but queerer than we *can* suppose. **J. B. S. Haldane** *Possible Worlds*: title essay

10 There is speculation. Then there is wild speculation. Then there is cosmology.

Martyn Harris *Odd Man Out*: 'A Brief History of Hawking'; quoting anonymous physicist

11 Even sleepers are workers and collaborators in what goes on in the universe. **Heraclitus** *Fragments*, 124

12 Planet: A large body of matter entirely surrounded by a void, as distinguished from a clergyman, who is a large void entirely surrounded by matter. **Elbert Hubbard** *The Roycroft Dictionary*

13 The universe begins to look more like a great thought than a great machine. **Sir James Jeans** *The Mysterious Universe*, Ch. 1

14 My theology, briefly, is that the universe was dictated but not signed.

Christopher Morley in A. Andrews, *Quotations for Speakers and Writers*

15 When the universe created mankind, it acquired simultaneously a victim and a judge. **Jean Rostand** *Pensées d'un biologiste*, p. 109

16 Do not malign
a single thing
for God
not only is its maker
but also its design.

Angelus Silesius *The Book of Angelus Silesius*: 'Of the One and the Many'

17 This truth within thy mind rehearse,
That in a boundless universe
Is boundless better, boundless worse.

Alfred, Lord Tennyson *The Two Voices*, Stanza 9

18 The universe is wider than our views of it.

H. D. Thoreau *Walden*: 'Conclusion'

19 The children of God should not have any other country here below but the universe itself, with the totality of all the reasoning creatures it ever has contained, contains, or ever will contain. That is the native city to which we owe our love. **Simone Weil** *Waiting on God*, Letter 6

20 The more the universe seems comprehensible, the more it also seems pointless. **Steve Weinberg** *The First Three Minutes*, Ch. 8: Conclusion

See also ***The World***

Value

1 When they belong to us things change their value in our eyes; they become better or worse, according to our character.

Comtesse Diane *Les Glanes de la vie*, p. 98

2 It is man's greatest failing to strive passionately for things before finding out what they're worth. **Friedrich Hebbel** *Diaries*, entry 4069, 1847

3 Most people are good only so long as they believe other people to be so. He who can despise nothing can value nothing with propriety; and who can value nothing, has no right to despise anything.

Johann Kaspar Lavater *Aphorisms on Man*, 102

4 Those things are dearest to us that have cost us most; and it is harder to give than to receive. **Michel de Montaigne** *Essays*, Bk 2, Ch. 8

See also Pavese

5 No people could live that did not *value*.

Friedrich Nietzsche *Nietzsche in Outline and Aphorism*: 'On Will and Value'

6 What we obtain too cheap we esteem too lightly; it is dearness only that gives everything its value. **Thomas Paine** *The American Crisis*, No. 1

7 Things which cost nothing are those which cost the most. Why? Because they cost us the effort of understanding that they are free.

Cesare Pavese *This Business of Living: A Diary 1935–1950*, 21 January 1940

See also Montaigne

8 Charms strike the sight, but merit wins the soul.

Alexander Pope *The Rape of the Lock*, V, 34

9 What is a cynic? A man who knows the price of everything and the value of nothing. **Oscar Wilde** *Lady Windermere's Fan*, Act 3

See also ***Giving and Taking***

Vices and Virtues

1 Prosperity doth best discover vice, but adversity doth best discover virtue. **Francis Bacon** *Essays*: 'Of Adversity'

2 Virtue is like a rich stone, best plain set. **Francis Bacon** Essays: 'Of Beauty'

3 It is not for our faults that we are disliked and even hated, but for our qualities. **Bernard Berenson** diary, 31 March 1957

4 We are bound to those we love by their imperfections – their perfections help us to explain them to others. **Elizabeth Bibesco** *Haven*: 'Aphorisms'

5 Thare iz a grate del of what iz calld virtew in the world that iz nothing more than vice tired out. **Josh Billings** *Wit and Humor*: Affurisms

6 Prudence is a rich, ugly old maid courted by Incapacity.
William Blake *The Marriage of Heaven and Hell*: 'Proverbs of Hell'

7 There is no road or ready way to virtue.
Sir Thomas Browne *Religio Medici*, Pt 1, 55

8 Vice would not be altogether vice if it did not hate virtue.
Nicholas-Sébastien Chamfort *Maxims and Considerations*

9 If people had no vices but their own, few people would have so many as they have. For my own part, I would sooner wear other people's clothes than their vices; and they would sit upon me just as well.
Earl of Chesterfield *Letters to His Son*, 15 May 1749

10 Honour is a luxury for aristocrats, but it is a necessity for hall-porters.
G. K. Chesterton *Heretics*, Ch. 13

11 Virtue never stands alone. It is bound to have neighbours.
Confucius *The Analects*, Bk 4, 25

12 Puritanism in other people we admire is austerity in ourselves.
Cyril Connolly *Enemies of Promise*, Ch. 9

13 Cruelty, like every other vice, requires no motive outside itself – it only requires opportunity.
George Eliot *Scenes of Clerical Life*: 'Janet's Repentance', Ch. 13

14 The only reward of virtue is virtue.

Ralph Waldo Emerson *Essays*: 'Friendship'

15 Each vice you destroy has a corresponding virtue, which perishes along with it. **Anatole France** *The Garden of Epicurus*, p. 76

16 Virtue brings honour, and honour vanity.

Dr Thomas Fuller *Gnomologia*, 5367

17 It is a weakness of every good quality that its frequent exercise leads to its abuse. **Baltasar Gracián** *The Oracle*, 85

18 Our *Vices* and *Virtues* couple with one another, and get Children that resemble both their Parents.

Marquis of Halifax *Moral Thoughts and Reflections*: 'Of the World'

19 Many a man's vices have at first been nothing worse than good qualities run wild. **Julius and Augustus Hare** *Guesses at Truth*, 1

20 There is a division of labour, even in vice. Some people addict themselves to the speculation only, others to the practice.

William Hazlitt *Lectures Chiefly on the Dramatic Literature of the Age of Elizabeth*, p. 142

21 Many men mistake the love for the practice of virtue, and are not so much good men as the friends of goodness.

Dr Samuel Johnson *Lives of the Poets*: 'Savage'

22 Neither our virtues nor vices are all our own.

Dr Samuel Johnson *The Rambler*, 180, 7 December 1751

23 Wickedness is always easier than virtue; for it takes the short cut to everything.

Dr Samuel Johnson in James Boswell, *The Journal of a Tour to the Hebrides*, 17 September 1773

24 The limitation of awareness is a social requirement. All virtues are individual, all vices social; the things that pass for social virtues, such as love, disinterestedness, justice, self-sacrifice, are only 'astonishingly' enfeebled social vices. **Franz Kafka** *Collected Aphorisms*, 19 February 1920

25 When our vices give us up we flatter ourselves that it is we who are giving them up. **Duc de La Rochefoucauld** *Maxims*, 192

26 Most usually our virtues are only vices in disguise.

Duc de La Rochefoucauld *Maxims*, epigraph added to the fourth edn

27 Virtue is the triumph of generosity over self-interest.

Duc de Lévis *Maximes et réflexions*, 89

28 If mankind suddenly became virtuous, many thousands would die of hunger. **Georg Christoph Lichtenberg** *Aphorisms*, Notebook E, 48

29 For the word virtue, I think, presupposes difficulty and struggle, and something that cannot be practised without an adversary.

Michel de Montaigne *Essays*, Bk 2, Ch. 11

30 Prudence is like an oak: it is long agrowing and it is old before it dies.

Margaret, Duchess of Newcastle in *The Cavalier and His Lady*: Aphorisms, 6

31 One is punished most for one's virtues.

Friedrich Nietzsche *Beyond Good and Evil*: 'Maxims and Interludes', 132

32 Virtue is still the most expensive vice: *let* it remain so!

Friedrich Nietzsche *The Will to Power*, 325

33 Vice is a monster of so frightful mien,
As to be hated needs but to be seen;
Yet seen too oft, familiar with her face,
We first endure, then pity, then embrace.

Alexander Pope *An Essay on Man*, Bk 2, 217

34 Virtue only comes to a character which has been thoroughly schooled and trained and brought to a pitch of perfection by unremitting practice. We are born for it, but not with it. And even in the best of people, until you cultivate it there is only the material for virtue, not virtue itself. **Seneca** *Letters from a Stoic*, 90

35 Men's evil manners live in brass; their virtues
We write in water. **William Shakespeare** *Henry VIII*, Act 4, Sc. 2, 45

36 Virtue itself turns vice, being misapplied;
And vice sometime's by action dignified.

William Shakespeare *Romeo and Juliet*, Act 2, Sc. 3, 21

37 What is virtue but the Trade Unionism of the married?

George Bernard Shaw *Man and Superman*, Act 3

38 Virtue consists, not in abstaining from vice, but in not desiring it.

George Bernard Shaw *Man and Superman*, 'Maxims for Revolutionists': 'Virtues and Vices'

39 Virtues, like essences, lose their fragrance when exposed.

William Shenstone *Essays on Men and Manners*: 'On Reserve'

40 Woman's virtue is man's greatest invention. **Cornelia Otis Skinner (attrib.)**

41 More people are flattered into virtue than bullied out of vice.

R. S. Surtees *The Analysis of the Hunting Field*, Ch. 1

42 Vice and virtues are products like sulphuric acid and sugar.

Hippolyte Taine *The History of English Literature*: Introduction, 3

43 A dignity which has to be contended for is not worth a quarrel; for it is of the essence of real dignity to be self-sustained, and no man's dignity can be asserted without being impaired. **Sir Henry Taylor** *The Statesman*, Ch. 15

44 Contrary to what clergymen and policemen believe, gentleness is biological and aggression is cultural.

Stefan Themerson quoted in his obituary in the *Guardian*, 8 September 1988

45 Virtue knows to a farthing what it has lost by not being a vice.

Horace Walpole in L. Kronenberger, *The Extraordinary Mr Wilkes*, Pt 3, Ch. 2

46 Virtue is a goodness in a state of warfare.

Archbishop Whately *Apophthegms*, 7

See also ***Good and Evil***

Victories and Defeats

1 A people is great that takes defeat as an opportunity and victory as an ordeal.

Bernard Berenson notebooks, 7 May 1921

2 As always, victory finds a hundred fathers, but defeat is an orphan.

Count Galeazzo Ciano diary, 9 September 1942

3 'Tis better to have fought and lost,
Than never to have fought at all.

Arthur Hugh Clough *Peschiera*

4 Nice guys finish last.

Leo Durocher manager of Brooklyn Dodgers, baseball team, about New York Giants; according to P. F. Boller Jr and J. George, *They Never Said It*, he really said, 'Nice guys. Finish last', 6 July 1946

See also Johnson

5 There is a victory beyond defeat which the victorious know nothing of.

William Faulkner review of Erich Maria Remarque, *The Road Back*, in *New Republic*, 20 May 1931

6 All victories breed hate, and that over your superior is foolish or fatal.

Baltasar Gracián *The Art of Worldly Wisdom*, 7

7 The man of power is ruined by power, the man of money by money, the submissive man by subservience, the pleasure seeker by pleasure.

Hermann Hesse *Steppenwolf*: 'Treatise on the Steppenwolf'

8 Nice guys finish last, but last guys don't finish nice.

R. W. Johnson in the *London Review of Books*, 18 February 1999

See also Durocher

9 A man able to think isn't defeated – even when he is defeated.

Milan Kundera interview with Philip Roth in the *Sunday Times Magazine*, 20 May 1984

10 It's safer to be heartless than mindless. The history of the world is the triumph of the heartless over the mindless.

Jonathan Lynn and Antony Jay *Yes, Prime Minister*, 'A Victory for Democracy'

11 Who overcomes
By force hath overcome but half his foe. **John Milton** *Paradise Lost*, Bk 1, 648

12 The true victory lies in battle rather than in survival; the prize of valour in fighting, not in winning. **Michel de Montaigne** *Essays*, Bk 1, Ch. 31

13 The only victories, which leave no regret, are those over ignorance.

Napoleon Bonaparte *Maxims*

14 Victories and disasters establish an indissoluble link between an army and its commander. **Napoleon Bonaparte** *Maxims*

15 No victor believes in chance. **Friedrich Nietzsche** *The Gay Science*, Bk 3, 258

16 The soldier who never admits that he has been defeated is always right. **Charles Péguy** quoted in the *Independent*, 1 September 1995

17 Winning isn't everything, but losing isn't anything.

Charles M. Schulz 'Peanuts' strip cartoon

18 How much easier it can be to conquer a whole people than to conquer a single man. **Seneca** *Letters to a Stoic*, 9

19 The world is war, the victor in it is the man who lives at the expense of others.

Voltaire quoted in Sagittarius and Daniel George, *The Perpetual Pessimist*, 10 February

See also ***Games and Sports; Success and Failure; War and Peace***

War and Peace

1 Every man seeks peace by waging war, but no man seeks war by making peace. **St Augustine** *The City of God*, Bk 19, Ch. 12

2 Civil war is like the heat of fever; a foreign war is like the heat of exercise. **Francis Bacon** quoted by Marianne Moore in *Writers at Work, Second Series*, ed. George Plimpton

3 It is not the job of the general to be winning. It is his job to win. **Nancy Banks-Smith** in the *Guardian*, 9 May 1990

4 I have never understood this liking for war. It panders to instincts already catered for within the scope of any respectable domestic establishment. **Alan Bennett** *Forty Years On*, Act 1

5 **Peace, n.** In international affairs, a period of cheating between two periods of fighting. **Ambrose Bierce** *The Devil's Dictionary*

6 One knows what a war is about only when it is over. **H. N. Brailsford** *The Levellers and the English Revolution*, Ch. 1

7 When a soldier sees a clean face, there's one more whore in the world. **Bertolt Brecht** *Mother Courage*, Act 1

8 The army is a peasant's idea of order. **Joseph Brodsky** *Less Than One*: title essay

9 No one can guarantee success in war, but only deserve it. **Winston S. Churchill** *The Second World War*, Vol. 2, Ch. 27

10 An appeaser is one who feeds a crocodile – hoping that it will eat him last. **Winston S. Churchill** in *Reader's Digest*, December 1954

11 Laws are dumb in time of war. **Cicero** *Pro Milone*, Ch. 11

12 It is far easier to make war than to make peace.

Georges Clemenceau speech, 14 July 1919

13 Security is indivisible.

Albert Einstein *Out of My Later Years*, Ch. 2: 'Open Letter to the General Assembly of the UN'

14 Men were made for war. Without it they wandered greyly about, getting under the feet of the women, who were trying to organize the really important things of life. **Alice Thomas Ellis** *The Sin Eater*, p. 70

See also Ellman

15 Men like war: they do not hold much sway over birth, so they make up for it with death. Unlike women, men menstruate by shedding other people's blood. **Lucy Ellman** in the *Observer Magazine*, 4 October 1992

See also Ellis

16 That is the great distinction between the sexes. Men see objects, women see the relationship between objects. Whether the objects need each other, love each other, match each other. It is an extra dimension of feeling we men are without and one that makes war abhorrent to all real women – and absurd. **John Fowles** *The Magus*, revised edn, Ch. 52

17 There never was a good war or a bad peace.

Benjamin Franklin letter to Josiah Quincy, 11 September 1783

18 Security is the mother of danger and the grandmother of destruction.

Thomas Fuller *The Holy and the Profane State*, Bk 5, Ch. 18, 1

19 Fighting for peace is like fucking for chastity.

Graffito quoted in *Knave* magazine, March 1977

20 I'd like to see the government get out of war altogether and leave the whole field to private industry. **Joseph Heller** *Catch-22*, Ch. 24

21 Those who proclaim the brotherhood of men fight every war as if it were a civil war. **Eric Hoffer** *Between the Devil and the Dragon*, Pt 2: Introduction

22 I think with the Romans, that the general of today should be the soldier of tomorrow if necessary.

Dr Samuel Johnson in James Boswell, *Life of Johnson*, letter to Joseph Madison, 1 January 1779

23 The conventional army loses if it does not win. The guerrilla wins if he does not lose. **Henry Kissinger** *Foreign Affairs*, XIII: 'The Vietnam Negotiations', January 1969

24 The most persistent sound which reverberates through men's history is the beating of war drums. **Arthur Koestler** *Janus: A Summing Up*: Prologue

26 The opposite of peaceful coexistence is warlike non-existence.

Jonathan Lynn and Antony Jay *Yes, Prime Minister*: 'A Victory for Democracy'

27 Blunders are an inescapable feature of war, because choice in military affairs lies generally between the bad and the worse.

Alan Massie *A Question of Loyalties*, Pt 3, Ch. 11

28 War will never cease until babies begin to come into the world with larger cerebrums and smaller adrenal glands.

H. L. Mencken *Notebooks, Minority Report*, 164

29 Peace hath her victories
No less renowned than war. **John Milton** *Sonnet: To Cromwell*

30 One of the wisest maxims in the art of war is never to drive the enemy to despair. **Michel de Montaigne** *Essays*, Bk 1, Ch. 47

31 An empire founded by war has to maintain itself by war.

Charles de Montesquieu *Considerations of the Causes of Roman Greatness and Decadence*

32 In whatever country we do battle, it is always a civil war.

Napoleon Bonaparte *Maxims*

33 The strength of an army, like the power of mechanics, is estimated by multiplying the mass by the rapidity; a rapid march augments the morale of an army, and increases all the chances of victory.

Napoleon Bonaparte *The Military Maxims of Napoleon*, 9

34 It is an approved maxim of war, never to do what the enemy wishes you to do, for this reason alone, that he desires it.

Napoleon Bonaparte *The Military Maxims of Napoleon*, 16

35 Under conditions of peace the warlike man attacks himself.

Friedrich Nietzsche *Beyond Good and Evil*: 'Maxims and Interludes', 76

36 The quickest way of ending a war is to lose it.

George Orwell *Shooting an Elephant*: 'Second Thoughts on James Burnham'

37 What the wrong gods established
no army can ever save. **Tom Paulin** *A Partial State*

38 It is better to make war for justice than peace for injustice.

Charles Péguy *Basic Verities*: 'The Rights of Man'

39 One does not fight with men against material; it is with material served by men that one makes war.

Marshal Pétain in Alistair Horne, *The Price of Glory*, Ch. 27

40 War . . . does not escape the laws of our old Hegel. It is in a state of perpetual becoming.

Marcel Proust *Remembrance of Things Past: Time Regained*, Ch. 2, p. 943

41 The strength of a war waged without monetary reserves is as fleeting as a breath. Money is the sinews of battle.

François Rabelais *Gargantua*, Ch. 46; Francis Bacon disagreed and wrote: 'Neither is money the sinews of war (as it is trivially said).' *Essays*: 'Of the True Greatness of Kingdoms'

42 From the accountants' point of view, war was simply a speeded up kind of peace, with conspicuously increased consumption.

Frederic Raphael in *New Society*, 10 May 1984

43 War is not an adventure. It is a disease, like typhus.

Antoine de Saint-Exupéry *Flight to Arras*, Ch. 10

44 In a civil war the firing line is invisible; it passes through the hearts of men. **Antoine de Saint-Exupéry** *Wind, Sand and Stars*, 9, 1

45 In the arts of peace Man is a bungler.

George Bernard Shaw *Man and Superman*, Act 3

46 War is capitalism with the gloves off and many who go to war know it but they go to war because they don't want to be a hero.

Tom Stoppard *Travesties*, Act 1

47 War is much too serious a thing to be left to military men.

Charles-Maurice de Talleyrand attrib. also to Clemenceau; Aristide Briand quoted it to Lloyd George

48 Militarism is the characteristic, not of an army, but of a society.

R. H. Tawney *The Acquisitive Society*, 4

49 There are two things which will always be very difficult for a democratic nation: to start a war and to end it.

Alexis de Tocqueville *Democracy in America*, Vol. 2, Pt 3, Ch. 22

50 Dead battles, like dead generals, hold the military mind in their dead grip. **Barbara W. Tuchman** *The Guns of August*, Ch. 2

51 Since wars begin in the minds of men, it is in the minds of men that the defence of peace must be constructed.

UNESCO Constitution adopted 16 November 1945: Preamble; both Clement Attlee and Archibald Macleish, chairman of US delegation to 1945 conference, credited with authorship

52 Let him who desires peace prepare for war.

Vegetius *Epitoma Rei Militaris*, Bk 3: Prologue

53 An army is a nation within a nation; it is one of the vices of our age.

Alfred de Vigny *The Military Necessity*, 1, Ch. 2

54 The art of war is like that of medicine, murderous and conjectural.

Voltaire in J. Raymond Solly, *A Cynic's Breviary*

55 One of the main effects of war, after all, is that people are discouraged from being characters. **Kurt Vonnegut** *Slaughterhouse 5*, Ch. 7

56 Nothing except a battle lost can be half so melancholy as a battle won. **Duke of Wellington** dispatch from the battlefield of Waterloo

57 The deliberate aim at Peace very easily passes into its bastard substitute, Anaesthesia. **A. N. Whitehead** *Adventures of Ideas*, Ch. 20

See also ***Victories and Defeats***

Wisdom

1 Wisdom produces happiness, not as medical science produces health, but as healthiness is the cause of health. **Aristotle** *Ethics*, Bk 6, xii

2 Wise men learn more by fools than fools by wise men.
Francis Bacon *Apothegms*, 268; ascribed to Cato the Elder

3 Nothing doth more hurt in a state than that cunning men pass for wise. **Francis Bacon** *Essays*: 'Of Cunning'

4 The wise man thinks once before he speaks twice.
Robert Benchley *Maxims from the Chinese*

5 The wise shall inherit glory: but shame shall be the promotion of fools. **Bible, OT** Proverbs 3:35

6 Wisdom is better than rubies. **Bible, OT** Proverbs 8:11

7 The heart of fools is in their mouth: but the mouth of the wise is in their heart. **Bible, Apocrypha** Ecclesiasticus 21:26

8 Wisdom is justified of her children. **Bible, NT** Matthew 11:19

9 Wisdom is not the most severe corrector of folly.
Edmund Burke quoted in Conor Cruise O'Brien, memorial address to Seán O'Faoláin, Glasthule parish church, Ireland, 4 May 1991

10 In order to act wisely it is not enough to be wise.
Anton Chekhov *Notebooks 1894–1902*, p. 19; quoting Fyodor Dostoevsky, *Notes from the Underground*

11 Be wiser than other people if you can, but do not tell them so.
Earl of Chesterfield *Letters to His Son*, 19 November 1745

12 The extreme limit of wisdom is what the public call madness.
Jean Cocteau *Cock and Harlequin*, p. 29

13 You are wise. But the greatest wisdom, at that moment, is knowing that your wisdom is too late. You understand everything when there is no longer anything to understand. **Umberto Eco** *Foucault's Pendulum*, Ch. 120

14 No man can be wise on an empty stomach. **George Eliot** *Adam Bede*, Ch. 21

15 The wise through excess of wisdom is made a fool.
Ralph Waldo Emerson *Essays*: 'Experience'

16 The foolish man wonders at the unusual, but the wise man at the usual. **Ralph Waldo Emerson** *Journal*; quoted in Thomas Hardy, diary, July 1924

17 It is not to be believed, that wisdom speaks to her Disciples only in Latin, Greek, and Hebrew. **Dr Thomas Fuller** *Introductio ad Prudentium*, 2868

18 An intelligent man finds almost everything ridiculous, a wise man hardly anything.
Johann Wolfgang von Goethe *Maxims and Reflections*: 'Life and Character', 294

19 It wouldn't be worthwhile reaching the age of seventy if the sum total of the world's wisdom were folly before God.
Johann Wolfgang von Goethe *Maxims and Reflections* (Penguin), from *Wilhelm Meister's Journeyman Years*, 618

20 Nothing would more contribute to make a Man wise, than to have always an Enemy in his view.
Marquis of Halifax *Miscellaneous Thoughts and Reflections*

21 Such is the nature of men, that however they may acknowledge others to be more witty, or more eloquent, or more learned; yet they will hardly believe there be many so wise as themselves.
Thomas Hobbes *Leviathan*, Pt 1, Ch. 13

22 To flee vice is a virtue, and the beginning of wisdom is to be done with folly. **Horace** *Epistles*, I, i, 41

23 Wisdom denotes the pursuing of the best ends by the best means.
Francis Hutcheson *Inquiry into the Original of Our Ideas of Beauty and Virtue*, I, v

24 The art of being wise is the art of knowing what to overlook.
William James *The Principles of Psychology*, Ch. 22

25 It's bad taste to be wise all the time, like being at a perpetual funeral.
D. H. Lawrence *Pansies*: 'Peace and War'

26 He swallowed a lot of wisdom, but it seemed as if all of it had gone down the wrong way.
Georg Christoph Lichtenberg *The Lichtenberg Reader*: Aphorisms, 1779–88

27 Once and for all, there is a great deal I do *not* want to know. – Wisdom sets bounds even to knowledge.
Friedrich Nietzsche *Twilight of the Idols*: 'Maxims and Arrows', 5

28 Axiom: we can of ourselves know nothing. All true wisdom is given us. **Novalis** *Pollen*, 508

29 There is a great difference between being born wise and only looking it. **Publilius Syrus** *Moral Sayings*, 722

30 Be wisely worldly, but not worldly wise.
Francis Quarles *Emblems*, Bk 2, 2, 46

31 Some people take more care to hide their wisdom, than their folly.
Jonathan Swift *Thoughts on Various Subjects*, p. 278

32 Knowledge comes, but wisdom lingers.
Alfred, Lord Tennyson *Locksley Hall*, 143

33 All wisdom is the reward of a discipline conscious or unconscious.
H. D. Thoreau *Journal*, 5 September 1851

34 The well-bred contradict other people. The wise contradict themselves. **Oscar Wilde** *Phrases and Philosophies for the Use of the Young*

See also ***Fools and Folly; Intellect and Intelligence; Knowledge; Understanding***

Wit

1 Satire is the soured milk of human kindness.
Mr Agassiz quoted in *Dialogues of Alfred North Whitehead*, ed. Lucien Price: Dialogue 2, 22 April 1934

2 To be witty is to satisfy another's wits by the giving him two pleasures, that of understanding one thing and that of guessing another, and so achieving double satisfaction.
Henri-Frédéric Amiel *Amiel's Journal*, 20 September 1876

3 Wit is part of the machinery of the intellect.
Walter Bagehot *Literary Studies*: 'The First Edinburgh Reviewers'

4 Conquered people tend to be witty. **Saul Bellow** *Mr Sammler's Planet*, Ch. 2

5 Irony is the hygiene of the mind. **Elizabeth Bibesco** *Haven*: 'Aphorisms'

6 Humor iz wit with a roosters tail feathers stuck in its cap, and wit iz wisdom in tight harness.
Josh Billings *Wit and Humor*: 'Hints to Comik Lekturers'

7 Jolly men are most alwus good men.
It iz dredful eazy tew mistake spasmodik hilarity for good natur.
Josh Billings *Wit and Humor*: 'Hints to Comik Lekturers'

8 Wit in a man may save a marriage. Wit in a woman, destroy it.

Peter De Vries *Consenting Adults*, Ch. 14

9 A thing well said will be wit in all languages.

John Dryden *Essay of Dramatic Poesy*

10 Blows are sarcasms turned stupid: wit is a form of force that leaves the limbs at rest. **George Eliot** *Felix Holt*, Ch. 30

11 Of all wit's uses the main one
Is to live well with who have none.

Ralph Waldo Emerson *Poems*: 'Appendix', paraphrasing Voltaire

12 Wit is the only thing that Men are willing to think they can never have enough of. **Marquis of Halifax** *Miscellaneous Thoughts and Reflections*

13 Wit is the salt of conversation, not the food.

William Hazlitt *Lectures on the English Comic Writers*: 'On Wit and Humour'

14 Wit is the only thing that you are less likely to find it the more eagerly you search for it. **Friedrich Hebbel** *Diaries*, entry 456, 1836

15 It is better to be witty and wise than witty and otherwise.

Douglas Jerrold in Edward Meryon, *Epitaphs, Personal Anecdotes and Epigrams*: 'Personal Anecdotes'

16 Genuinely witty remarks surprise their speaker as well as their hearers. **Joseph Joubert** *Pensées*, 114

17 Satire must not be a kind of superfluous ill will, but ill will from a higher point of view. **Paul Klee** *Diaries 1898–1918*, Diary III, 420

18 Impropriety is the soul of wit.

Somerset Maugham *The Moon and Sixpence*, Ch. 4

See also Shakespeare

19 Irony is scissors, a divining rod, always pointing in two directions.

Anne Michaels *Fugitive Pieces*: 'Terra Nullius'

20 The English are very fond of humour, but they are afraid of wit. For wit is like a sword, but humour is like a jester's bladder.

J. B. Morton 'Beachcomber' from the *Spectator*, in the *Sunday Times*, 27 September 1987

21 Satire is a lesson, parody is a game. **Vladimir Nabokov** *Strong Opinions*, Ch. 6

22 Humour is primarily the study of human folly. It would be impossible to laugh at a place where the suffering was caused by an act of God – making fun of the results of a mud-slide would not be very funny.

P. J. O'Rourke interview in the *Observer*, 6 December 1998

23 He must have wit who understands he is a fool.

Publilius Syrus *Moral Sayings*, 451

24 Brevity is the soul of wit. **William Shakespeare** *Hamlet*, Act 2, Sc. 2, 90

See also Maugham

25 Satire is a sort of glass, wherein beholders do generally discover everybody's face but their own. **Jonathan Swift** *The Battle of the Books*: Preface

26 Sometimes we are inclined to class those who are one-and-a half witted with the half-witted, because we appreciate only a third part of their wit. **H. D. Thoreau** *Walden*: 'Conclusion'

27 Cynicism is humour in ill-health. **H. G. Wells** *Short Stories*: 'The Last Trump'

See also ***Comedy and Tragedy; Laughing Matters***

Women

1 Most women would rather be loved too well than too wisely.
Minna Antrim *The Wisdom of the Foolish*, p. 3

2 The distinction between the clever woman and the smart one is that at the approach of the smart woman all make way, whereas the clever woman makes her own way. **Minna Antrim** *The Wisdom of the Foolish*, p. 14

3 Women are really supposed to be much nicer than men. That's what they're here for.
W. H. Auden *The Table Talk of W. H. Auden* by Alan Anson, 10 May 1947

See also La Bruyère

4 Remember that woman never speaks more forcibly than when she is silent, nor acts with more energy than when in repose.
Honoré de Balzac quoted in Ralph Waldo Emerson, *Topical Notebooks of S. Salvage*, p. 213

5 One is not born, but rather becomes, a woman.
Simone de Beauvoir *The Second Sex*: opening words

6 Feminism is an insurrection, not a coffee morning.
Geraldine Bedell in the *Independent*, 14 November 1988

7 Most women are not so young as they are painted.
Max Beerbohm *A Defence of Cosmetics*

8 You will find that the woman who is really kind to dogs is always one who has failed to inspire sympathy in men.
Max Beerbohm *Zuleika Dobson*, Ch. 6

9 As a jewel of gold in a swine's snout, so is a fair woman which is without discretion. **Bible, OT** Proverbs 11:22

10 There is a tide in the affairs of women,
Which, taken at the flood, leads – God knows where.

Lord Byron *Don Juan*, VI, 12

11 There are girls who can sell, but cannot give themselves.

Nicholas-Sébastien Chamfort *Maxims and Considerations*, 367

12 But what is woman? – only one of Nature's agreeable blunders.

Hannah Cowley *Who's the Dupe?*, Act 2, Sc. 2

13 It is far more important for women to flatter our vanity than to touch our heart. **Claude-Prosper Crébillon** *Les Égarements du cœur et de l'esprit*, Pt 1

14 Women never have young minds. They are born three thousand years old. **Shelagh Delaney** *A Taste of Honey*, Act 1, Sc. 1

15 The weight of unexpended affection which is one of a woman's greatest inconveniences. **Penelope Fitzgerald** *The Means of Escape*: title story

16 Faithful women are the ones who expect from spring-time, from books or perfumes or earth tremors, the sort of revelation that others expect from their lovers. In fact, they are unfaithful to their husbands with their entire physical world, apart from men.

Jean Giraudoux *Amphitryon*, Act 1

17 When you speak well of a woman she is in the singular, when she has done you a wrong, she is in the plural.

Sacha Guitry *N'Écoutez pas, mesdames*, Act 1

18 A woman is never ambidextrous. **Hippocrates** *Aphorisms*, 7, 43

19 A woman's whole life is a history of the affections.

Washington Irving *The Sketch Book*: 'The Broken Heart'

20 Women run to extremes; they are either better than men or worse.

Jean de La Bruyère *Characters*: 'Of Women', 53

See also Auden

21 You don't know a woman until you've had a letter from her.

Ada Leverson *Tenterhooks*, Ch. 7

22 Women can be deceived; but they can never be surprised.

Louis-Sébastien Mercier *Tableau de Paris*, Vol. 3, Ch. 85

23 Women would rather be right than reasonable.

Ogden Nash *Frailty, Thy Name is a Misnomer*

24 Woman's at best a contradiction still.

Alexander Pope *Moral Essays*, Epistle Bk 2, 270

25 Women who are never surprised never entirely belong to any man.

Arthur Schnitzler *Little Novels*: 'Dead Gabriel'

26 The fundamental defect of the female character is a *lack of a sense of justice.* **Arthur Schopenhauer** *Essays and Aphorisms*: 'On Women', 5

27 Women are like teeth. Some tremble and never fall and some fall and never tremble. **Edith Templeton** *The Surprise of Cremona*: 'Urbino'

28 The woman is so hard
Upon the woman. **Alfred, Lord Tennyson** *The Princess*, Pt 6, 205

29 Womanist is to feminist as purple is to lavender.
Alice Walker *In Search of our Mothers' Gardens*: epigraph

30 There is only one real tragedy in a woman's life. The fact that her past is always her lover, and her future invariably her husband.
Oscar Wilde *An Ideal Husband*, Act 3

31 Women never know when the curtain has fallen. They always want a sixth act, and as soon as the interest of the play is entirely over they propose to continue it. If they were allowed their own way, every comedy would have a tragic ending, and every tragedy would culminate in a farce. **Oscar Wilde** *The Picture of Dorian Gray*, Ch. 8

32 A king is always a king – and a woman always a woman; his authority and her sex ever stand between them and rational converse.
Mary Wollstonecraft *A Vindication of the Rights of Woman*, Ch. 4

See also ***Family; Men and Women; Relationships***

Words

1 Words are not [except in their own little corner] facts or things: we need therefore to prise them off the world, to hold them apart from and against it, so that we can realize their inadequacies and arbitrariness, and can re-look at the world without blinkers.
J. L. Austin *Philosophical Papers*, 8

2 Words are but the images of matter; and except they have life of reason and invention, to fall in love with them is all one as to fall in love with a picture. **Francis Bacon** *The Advancement of Learning*, Bk 1, iii, 3

3 A definition is the enclosing a wilderness of idea within a wall of words. **Samuel Butler 2** *Notebooks*, Ch. 14: 'Definitions'

4 All conceptual systems live from refilling just a few words at whose expense others were emptied. **Elias Canetti** *The Human Province*: '1948'

5 The words contain the thoughts, they carry them lightly wrapped, wriggling slightly. **D. J. Enright** *Interplay*, p. 39

6 Words are the only thing which lasts for ever.

William Hazlitt *Table Talk*: 'On Thought and Action'

7 Words are wise men's counters, they do but reckon with them, but they are the money of fools. **Thomas Hobbes** *Leviathan*, Pt 1, Ch. 4

8 Once a word has been allowed to escape, it cannot be recalled.

Horace *Epistles*, I, xviii, 71

9 I am not yet so lost in lexicography as to forget that words are the daughters of earth, and things are the sons of heaven.

Dr Samuel Johnson *Dictionary of the English Language*: Preface

10 The word, in fact, is disembodied thought.

Joseph Joubert *Notebooks*, 1800

11 Words that open our eyes to the world are always the easiest to remember. **Ryszard Kapuściński** *Shah of Shahs*: 'Daguerreotypes'

12 Words are, of course, the most powerful drug used by mankind.

Rudyard Kipling speech, 14 February 1923

13 The agitator seizes the word. The artist is seized by it.

Karl Kraus quoted in Thomas S. Szasz, *Anti-Freud: Karl Kraus's Criticism of Psychoanalysis and Psychiatry*, Ch. 8

14 Words are like tofu: their tastes come from the emotions that drench them. **Deborah Moggach** *Close Relations*, Pt 3, 3

15 A word is not the same with one writer as with another. One tears it from his guts. Another pulls it out of his overcoat pocket.

Charles Péguy *Basic Verities*: 'The Honest People'

16 Words are the small change of thought. There are some blabber-mouths pay us in coppers. But there are others which are pure gold.

Jules Renard *Journal 1887–1910*, 15 November 1888

17 Names are priceless; words have their price. Words can be definite, *names must have an infinite appeal.*

Eugen Rosenstock-Huessy *The Christian Future or the Modern Mind Outrun*, Pt 1, Ch. 1

18 Syllables govern the world. **John Selden** *Table Talk*, 109

19 Nothing is worse than when the words advertise the subject matter. Words must not shout. Words must keep silent.

Abram Tertz *A Voice from the Chorus*, Pt 2

20 Of two possible words always choose the lesser.

Paul Valéry *Odds and Ends*: 'Advice to the Writer'

See also ***Language; The Spoken Word***

Work and Leisure

1 The pleasantness of an employment does not always evince its propriety. **Jane Austen** *Sense and Sensibility*, Ch. 13

2 One must work, if not from inclination, at least from despair – since it proves, on close examination, that work is less boring than amusing oneself. **Charles Baudelaire** *Intimate Journals*: 'My Heart Laid Bare', 10

3 In all labour there is profit: but the talk of the lips tendeth only to penury. **Bible, OT** Proverbs 14:23

4 Housework . . . expands to fill the time available plus half an hour. **Shirley Conran** *Superwoman*, 2

5 Politics and business can be settled by influence, cooks and doctors can only be promoted on their skill. **Penelope Fitzgerald** *Innocence*, 16

6 After all, work is still the best way of killing time. **Gustave Flaubert** in J. R. Solly, *Selected Thoughts from the French*: 'Work and Idleness'

7 Man is so made that he can only find relaxation from one kind of labour by taking up another. **Anatole France** *The Crime of Sylvestre Bonnard*, Ch. 4, 3 June

8 Work as if you were to live 100 Years, Pray as if you were to die Tomorrow. **Benjamin Franklin** *Poor Richard's (Improved) Almanack*, 1757

9 Hard work is undesirable for the underfed. **Hippocrates** *Aphorisms*, 2, 16

10 Our greatest weariness comes from work not done. **Eric Hoffer** 'Thoughts', in the *New York Times Magazine*, 25 April 1971

11 If you want work well done, select a busy man – the other kind has not time. **Elbert Hubbard** *The Note Book of Elbert Hubbard*, facing p. 48

See also Parkinson

12 Many a feller would be alive t'day if he hadn't saved enough t' retire. **'Kin' Hubbard** *Abe Martin's Wisecracks*, p. 36

13 Work is half of life –
And the other half too. **Erich Kästner** *Bürger, schont eure Anlagen*

14 It is said that man grows into his job. In reality, he shrinks into his job. **Hans Keller** *Maxims and Reflections*, 45

15 Oh, Adam was a gardener, and God who made him sees
That half a proper gardener's work is done upon his knees. **Rudyard Kipling** *The Glory of the Garden*, 8

16 It is easier to appear worthy of positions one does not occupy than of those one does. **Duc de La Rochefoucauld** *Maxims*, 164

17 Where there is no desire, there will be no industry.
John Locke *Some Thoughts Concerning Education*

18 Retirement is twice as much husband on half as much money.
Bette Midler (attrib.)

19 Work expands so as to fill the time available for its completion. General recognition of this fact is shown in the proverbial phrase. 'It is the busiest man who has time to spare.'
C. Northcote Parkinson *Parkinson's Law*, Ch. 1

See also Elbert Hubbard

20 Work is accomplished by those employees who have not yet reached their level of incompetence.
Laurence J. Peter and Raymond Hull *The Peter Principle*, Ch. 1

21 You must always work not just within but below your means. If you can handle three elements, handle only two. If you can handle ten, then handle only five. In that way the ones you do handle, you handle with more ease, more mastery, and you create a feeling of strength in reserve.
Pablo Picasso in Françoise Gilot and Carlton Lake, *Life with Picasso*, Pt 2

22 A good holiday is one spent among people whose notions of time are vaguer than yours.
J. B. Priestley in *The Penguin Dictionary of Modern Humorous Quotations*, comp. Fred Metcalf

23 Sunday was where God kept his woolly slippers. It was a day with a dull edge no amount of recreation could hone.
Tom Robbins *Still Life with Woodpecker*, 13

24 Leisure is work you volunteer for.
Robert Robinson *Dog Chairman*: 'Try a Grasshopper'

25 Exertion, like virtue, is its own reward. **Sir Walter Scott** *Waverley*, Ch. 43

26 The labour we delight in physics pain.
William Shakespeare *Macbeth*, Act 2, Sc. 3, (56)

27 All professions are conspiracies against the laity.
George Bernard Shaw *The Doctor's Dilemma*, Act 1; he was echoing Adam Smith in *The Wealth of Nations*, 1776

28 It's a recession when your neighbour loses his job; it's a depression when you lose your own.
Harry S. Truman in the *Observer*, 'Sayings of the Week', 6 April 1958

29 Work banishes those three great evils, boredom, vice, and poverty.

Voltaire *Candide*, Ch. 30

30 Filing is concerned with the past; anything you actually need to see again has to do with the future.

Katharine Whitehorn *Sunday Best*: 'Sorting Out'

31 It is always with the best intentions that the worst work is done.

Oscar Wilde *The Critic as Artist*, 2

See also ***Business***

The World

1 Take the people all out ov it, and this worlld would be a delitefull plase to liv.

Josh Billings *Wit and Humor*: 'Billings' Proverbs'

2 For the world, I count it not an inn, but an hospital; and a place not to live but to die in.

Sir Thomas Browne *Religio Medici*, Pt 2, 11

3 The Earth is one, but the world is not.

The Brundtland report, 1987 World Commission on Environment and Development, *Our Common Future*, opening words

See also Priestley

4 The world will, in the end, follow only those who have despised as well as served it.

Samuel Butler 2 *Notebooks*, Ch. 24: 'The World'

5 There is a vulgarity which makes us admit anything in this world, but which is not powerful enough to make us admit this world itself.

E. M. Cioran *A Short History of Decay*, Pt 1: 'Duality'

6 This world cannot explain its own difficulties without the assistance of another.

Charles Caleb Colton *Lacon*: 'Worldly Difficulties'

7 It's a funny old world – a man's lucky if he gets out of it alive.

W. C. Fields in film *You're Telling Me*, script Walter de Leon and Paul M. Jones

8 The world is disgracefully managed, one hardly knows to whom to complain.

Ronald Firbank *Vainglory*, 10

9 The world is a bell with a crack in it; it rattles, but does not ring.

Johann Wolfgang von Goethe *Maxims and Reflections*: 'Life and Character', 158

10 The world is one vast graveyard of defunct cities, all destroyed by the shifting of markets they could not control, and all compressed by literature into a handful of poems.

Alasdair Gray *The Emperor's Injustice*

11 The world is not black and white. More like black and grey.

Graham Greene in the *Observer*, 'Sayings of the Year', December 1982

12 A man that understandeth the world must be weary of it; and a man who doth not, for that reason ought not to be pleased with it.

Marquis of Halifax *Moral Thoughts and Reflections*: 'Of the World'

13 The World is nothing but Vanity cut out into several Shapes.

Marquis of Halifax *Moral Thoughts and Reflections*: 'Of Vanity'

14 Nothing is further than Earth from Heaven: nothing is nearer than Heaven to Earth. **Julius and Augustus Hare** *Guesses at Truth*, 2

15 If the world were good for nothing else, it is a fine subject for speculation. **William Hazlitt** *Characteristics*, 302

See also Montaigne

16 The world began without man, and it will end without him.

Claude Lévi-Strauss *Tristes tropiques*, Ch. 40

17 The only fence against the world is a thorough knowledge of it.

John Locke *Essay Concerning Human Understanding*, Sect. 88

18 The world is but a school of inquiry.

Michel de Montaigne *Essays*, Bk 3, Ch. 8

See also Hazlitt

19 The world is the sum-total of our vital possibilities.

José Ortega y Gasset *The Revolt of the Masses*, Ch. 4

20 The earth is nobler than the world we have put upon it.

J. B. Priestley *Johnson over Jordan*, Act 3

See also Brundtland

21 All the world's a stage,
And all the men and women merely players:
They have their exits and their entrances;
And one man in his time plays many parts.

William Shakespeare *As You Like It*, Act 2, Sc. 7, (139)

22 The world suffers most from the disinterested
tyranny
of its well-wisher. **Rabindranath Tagore** *Fireflies*, p. 84

23 The world is war, the victor in it is the man who lives at the expense of others.

Voltaire quoted in Sagittarius and Daniel George, *The Perpetual Pessimist*, 10 February

24 The world is the totality of facts not of things.

Ludwig Wittgenstein *Tractatus Logico-philosophicus*, 1, 1

25 The world is everything that is the case.
Ludwig Wittgenstein *Tractatus Logico-philosophicus*, 1, 1

See also ***The Universe***

Writing

1 A good writer has a calculated stupidity – first-rate intellectuals don't make good novelists. **Martin Amis** interview in the *Guardian*, 3 October 1998

2 Perhaps because of their addiction to form, writers always lag behind the contemporary formlessness. They write about an old reality, in a language that's even older. It's not the words: it's the rhythms of thought. In this sense all novels are historical novels.
Martin Amis *London Fields*, 13

3 Most writers need a wound, either physical or spiritual.
Martin Amis *Visiting Mrs Nabokov*: 'John Updike'

4 Everyone thinks writers must know about the inside of the human head, but that is wrong. They know less, that's why they write. Trying to find out what everyone else takes for granted.
Margaret Atwood *Dancing Girls*: 'Lives of the Poets'

5 The greatest writer cannot see through a brick wall but unlike the rest of us he does not build one. **W. H. Auden** *The Dyer's Hand*, 1: 'Writing'

6 Writers are usually in the unfortunate predicament of having to speak the truth without the authority to speak it.
W. H. Auden in Charles Osborne, *W. H. Auden: The Life of a Poet*, Ch. 13

7 So let great authors have their due, as time, which is the author of authors, be not deprived of his due, which is, further and further to discover truth. **Francis Bacon** *The Advancement of Learning*, Bk 1, iv, 12

8 Writers like teeth are divided into incisors and grinders.
Walter Bagehot *Literary Studies*: 'The First Edinburgh Reviewers'

9 The biggest obstacle to professional writing today is the necessity for changing a typewriter ribbon.
Robert Benchley *Chips off the Old Benchley*: 'Learn to Write'

10 Work on good prose has three steps: a musical stage when it is composed, an architectonic one when it is built, and a textile one when it is woven. **Walter Benjamin** *One-way Street*: 'Caution: Steps'

11 Autobiography begins with a sense of being alone. It is an orphan form. **John Berger** *Keeping a Rendezvous*: 'Mother'

12 No one who cannot limit himself has ever been able to write.
Nicolas Boileau *L'Art poétique*, I, 63

13 Writing is nothing more than a guided dream.
Jorge Luis Borges *Doctor Brodie's Report*: Preface

14 A diary, after all, is written to please oneself – therefore it's bound to be enormously written up. **Elizabeth Bowen** *The Death of the Heart*: 'The World', 1

15 When I write a page that reads badly I know that it is myself who has written it. When it reads well it has come through from somewhere else. **Gerald Brenan** *Thoughts in a Dry Season*: 'Writing'

16 In the business of writing what one accumulates is not expertise but uncertainties. **Joseph Brodsky** *Less Than One*: title essay

17 Those who write as they talk, will write ill, though they speak well.
George-Louis de Buffon *Discours sur le style*

18 Beneath the rule of men entirely great,
The pen is mightier than the sword.
Edward Bulwer-Lytton *Richelieu*, Act 2, Sc. 2

19 Because writing always means hiding something in such a way that it then is discovered. **Italo Calvino** *If on a Winter's Night a Traveller*, Ch. 8

20 Those who write clearly have readers; those who write obscurely have commentators. **Albert Camus** quoted in D. J. Enright, *Interplay*, p. 80

21 Every writer would like to push the next writer into the past and feel sorry for him there. **Elias Canetti** *The Human Province*: '1967'

22 In our rampantly secular world, biography is now the only certain form of life after death. **David Cannadine** in the *Observer*, 21 April 1991

23 What is more dull than a discreet diary? One might as well have a discreet soul. **Henry 'Chips' Channon** *Diary*, 26 July 1935

24 Every writer is a cutpurse. **Bruce Chatwin** quoted in the *Observer*, 4 April 1999

25 He loved to quote the axiom, 'Trust your editor, and you'll sleep on straw.' **John Cheever** quoted in Susan Cheever, *Home before Dark*, Ch. 11

26 Brevity – the sister of talent.
Anton Chekhov letter to Alexander Chekhov, 11 April 1889

27 With writers who have nothing to say, who have no world of their own, what can you talk about but literature?
E. M. Cioran *Anathemas and Admirations*, 7

28 The self-esteem of the quality writer depends on his belief that those readers who care about good stuff cannot afford to buy it.
Alan Coren *Seems Like Old Times*: 'January'

29 An autobiography is an obituary in serial form with the last instalment missing. **Quentin Crisp** *The Naked Civil Servant*, Ch. 29

30 Writing is conscience, scruple and the farming of our ancestors.
Edward Dahlberg *Alms for Oblivion*: 'For Sale'

31 A writer does not have to be a great reader, but what he does read should be good and honest and as wise as dust can be.
Edward Dahlberg *Alms for Oblivion*: 'No Love – No Thanks'

32 When a writer doesn't show his face he becomes a local symptom of God's famous reluctance to appear.
Don DeLillo *Mao II*; quoted in the *Independent on Sunday*, 26 March 2000

33 We are truer to ourselves when we write than when we talk, because we write alone. **Comtesse Diane** *Maxims of Life*, p. 33

34 Read no history, nothing but biography, for that is life without theory. **Benjamin Disraeli** *Contarini Fleming*, Pt 1, Ch. 23

35 Good writing is a kind of skating which carries off the performer where he would not go, and is only admirable when to all its beauty and speed a subserviency to the will, like that of walking, is added.
Ralph Waldo Emerson *Journal*, 1847: 'Real Aristocracy'

36 If a writer has to rob his mother, he will not hesitate; the 'Ode to a Grecian Urn' is worth any number of old ladies.
William Faulkner in *Writers at Work, First Series*, ed. Malcolm Cowley

37 Writers aren't people exactly. Or, if they're any good, they're a whole *lot* of people trying so hard to be one person.
F. Scott Fitzgerald *The Last Tycoon*, Ch. 1

38 You don't write because you want to say something; you write because you've got something to say. **F. Scott Fitzgerald** *Notebooks*, E

39 If a dictionary can catch up with an author, he is no good.
Johann Wolfgang von Goethe *Maxims and Reflections* (Penguin), 1059

40 My work is that of a composite being, which happens to be signed.
Johann Wolfgang von Goethe quoted in Robin Skelton, *Teach Yourself Poetry*, Ch. 2

41 A writer's knowledge of himself, realistic and unromantic, is like a store of energy on which he must draw for a lifetime: one volt of it properly directed will bring a character alive. **Graham Greene** *A Sort of Life*, 11, 2

42 Biography is a very definite region bounded on the north by history, on the south by fiction, on the east by obituary, and on the west by tedium. **Philip Guedalla** in the *Observer*, 'Sayings of the Week', 3 March 1929

43 The only impeccable writers are those that never wrote.
William Hazlitt *Table Talk*: 'On the Aristocracy of Letters'

44 Every writer is writing his autobiography, and most successfully when he is least aware of it. **Friedrich Hebbel** *Diaries*, entry 834, 1837

45 We really only learn from those books which we cannot criticize. The author of a book which we could criticize would have to learn from us. A writer should love not his public but mankind, the better part of which do not read his books, but need them nonetheless.
Hermann Hesse *Reflections*, 529

46 It is possible to be a writer, but not to become one.
Hermann Hesse *Reflections*, 552

47 There were two species: writers and people; and the writers were really people, and the people weren't. **Randall Jarrell** *Pictures from an Institution*, Pt 1, Ch. 9

48 What is written without effort is in general read without pleasure.
Dr Samuel Johnson *Johnsonian Miscellanies*, Vol. 2

49 Authors are like privateers, always fair game for one another.
Dr Samuel Johnson *Johnsonian Miscellanies*, Vol. 4

50 The only end of writing is to enable the readers better to enjoy life or better to endure it. **Dr Samuel Johnson** quoted in W. H. Auden, *A Certain World*: 'Writing'

51 In fact, the word is the sign of a thought and writing is the sign of the word. That is to say, it is only the sign of another sign.
Joseph Joubert *Notebooks*, 1803

52 Strength is not the same as energy; some writers have more muscle than talent. **Joseph Joubert** *Thoughts and Maxims*, 327

53 A writer's ambition should be to trade a hundred contemporary readers for ten readers in ten years' time and for one reader in a hundred years' time. **Arthur Koestler** interview in the *New York Times Book Review*, 1 April 1951

54 There are two kinds of writer, those who are and those who aren't. With the first, content and form belong together like soul and body; with the second, they match each other like body and clothes.
Karl Kraus quoted in W. H. Auden, *A Certain World*: 'Writing'

55 The glory or merit of certain men lies in writing well: that of certain others in not writing at all. **Jean de La Bruyère** *Characters*: 'Of Books', 59

56 Clear writers like clear fountains do not seem so deep as they are: the turbid look most profound.
Walter Savage Landor *Selections*, ed. Sidney Colvin: 'Literature and Language', 185

57 The true function of the writer in relation to mankind is continually to *say* what most men think or feel without realizing it. Mediocre writers say only what *everyone* would have said . . .
Georg Christoph Lichtenberg *Aphorisms*, Notebook J, 30

58 I don't know why critics expect writers always to do as well as they should have done. The writer seldom does what he wants to; he does the best he can. **W. Somerset Maugham** *A Writer's Notebook*, 1941

59 A writer is unfair to himself when he is unable to be hard on himself.
Marianne Moore in *Writers at Work: Second Series*, ed. George Plimpton

60 Any writer overwhelmingly honest about pleasing himself is almost sure to please others. **Marianne Moore** in *Writer's Quotation Book*, ed. James Charlton

61 Writing is like getting married. One should never commit oneself until one is amazed at one's luck.
Iris Murdoch *The Black Prince*: 'Bradley Pearson's Foreword'

62 In prose, the worst thing one can do with words is surrender to them.
George Orwell *Collected Essays*: 'Politics and the English Language'

63 Writing is a fine thing, because it combines the two pleasures of talking to yourself and talking to a crowd.
Cesare Pavese *This Business of Living: A Diary 1935–1950*, 4 May 1946

64 If a note is scholarly, a note on a note is scholarly squared.
Charles Péguy *Victor-Marie, Comte Hugo*, p. 275

65 A man writes a book, even as he stretches out his hand, so that he may find that he is not alone in the survival of mankind.
Eugen Rosenstock-Huessy *Out of Revolution*: final words

66 The acid test of a good piece of writing, even if it is of violence and cruelty, is that it must make one's ears water.
Bernice Rubens in the *Sunday Times*, 3 April 1988

67 Be sure that you go to the author to get at his meaning, not to find yours. **John Ruskin** *Sesame and Lilies*, 1, Sect. 13

68 There are above all two kinds of writer: those who write for the sake of what they have to say and those who write for the sake of writing.
Arthur Schopenhauer *Essays and Aphorisms*: 'On Books and Writing', 2

69 You write with ease, to show your breeding,
But easy writing's curst hard reading. **R. B. Sheridan** *Clio's Protest*

70 What I like in a good author is not what he says, but what he whispers. **Logan Pearsall Smith** *Afterthoughts*, 5

71 For a country to have a great writer is like having a second government. That is why no regime has ever loved great writers, only minor ones.
Alexander Solzhenitsyn *The First Circle*, Ch. 57

72 Writing, when properly managed, (as you may be sure I think mine is) is but a different name for conversation.
Laurence Sterne *Tristram Shandy*, Vol. 2, Ch. 11

73 Even dying is useful to a writer. **Abram Tertz** *A Voice from the Chorus*, Pt 2

74 All writing, even the clumsy kind, exposes in its loops and slants a yearning deeper than an intention, the soul of the writer flopping on the clothes-peg of his exclamation mark.

Paul Theroux *Saint Jack*, Ch. 1

75 How vain it is to sit down to write when you have not stood up to live! **H. D. Thoreau** *Journal*, 19 August 1851

76 'Prose' is a piece of writing whose aim could be as well expressed by another piece of writing.

Paul Valéry *Odds and Ends*: 'Literature', Theorem

77 It is wisest to write in 'I-natural'. But many write in 'I-sharp'.

Paul Valéry *Rhumbs*: 'Literature'

78 The best authors talk too much.

Marquis de Vauvenargues *Reflections and Maxims*, 115

79 American writers want to be not good but great; and so are neither.

Gore Vidal *Two Sisters*

80 Great writers are not those who tell us we shouldn't play with fire, but those who make our fingers burn.

Stephen Vizinczey *Truth and Lies in Literature*: 'The Genius whose Time Has Come'

81 Woe betide the writer whose sole aim is instruction.
He who tells all will bore to distraction. **Voltaire** *Discours en vers sur l'homme*, 6

82 You can never correct your work well until after you have forgotten it. **Voltaire** in J. R. Solly, *Selected Thoughts from the French*: 'Literature'

83 Only when one has lost all curiosity about the future has one reached the age to write an autobiography.

Evelyn Waugh *A Little Learning*: opening words

84 Biography is a form by which little people take revenge on big people. **Edmund White** quoted in the *Observer*, 25 June 2000

85 It is a test of good sane writing that we can read it out of doors.

William Hale White *More Pages from a Journal*

86 Every great man nowadays has his disciples, and it is always Judas who writes the biography. **Oscar Wilde** *The Critic as Artist*, 1

87 Only the great masters of style ever succeed in being obscure.

Oscar Wilde *Phrases and Philosophies for the Use of the Young*

88 Everyone should keep someone else's diary.

Oscar Wilde in conversation; in *Epigrams of Oscar Wilde*, ed. Alvin Redman: 'Conduct'

89 Every great and original writer, in proportion as he is great and original, must himself create the taste by which he is to be relished.

William Wordsworth *Lyrical Ballads*: Preface

See also ***Books; Fiction and Fact; Language; Literature; Poetry and Poets; Reading; Words***

Youth and Age

1 The old are trying to be young, as they always have, as we all do, youth being the model. But the young are not trying to be old.

Martin Amis *London Fields*, 14

2 Either is he a congenital fool who asks a woman her age, or he knows she is too young to lie. **Minna Antrim** *The Wisdom of the Foolish*, p. 26

3 Youth would be an ideal state if it came a little later in life.

Herbert Asquith in the *Observer*, 15 April 1923

4 Age will not be defied. **Francis Bacon** *Essays*: 'Of Regimen of Health'

5 Young men are fitter to invent than to judge; fitter for execution than for counsel; and fitter for new projects than for settled business.

Francis Bacon *Essays*: 'Of Youth and Age'

6 It is a failing of youth to imagine everyone is as strong as they are, a failing that is actually the reflection of a virtue.

Honoré de Balzac *César Birotteau*, Ch. 7

7 Whenever the older generation has lost its bearings, the younger generation is lost with it.

Bruno Bettelheim epigraph to Vance Packard, *The Sexual Wilderness*

8 The hoary head is a crown of glory, if it be found in the way of righteousness. **Bible, OT** Proverbs 16:31

9 Wisdom is the grey hair unto men, and an unspotted life is old age.

Bible, Apocrypha The Wisdom of Solomon 4:9

10 Any given generation gives the next generation advice that the given generation should have been given by the previous one but now it's too late. **Roy Blount Jr** *Don't Anybody Steal These*

11 One of the reasons why old people make so many journeys into the past is to satisfy themselves that it is still there.

Ronald Blythe *The View in Winter*: Introduction

12 Old age takes away from us what we have inherited and gives us what we have earned. **Gerald Brenan** *Thoughts in a Dry Season*: 'Life'

13 The arrogance of age must submit to be taught by youth.

Edmund Burke letter to Fanny Burney, 29 July 1782

14 In old age the senses get sticky.

Elias Canetti *The Secret Heart of the Clock*: '1973'

15 The old are always fond of new things. Young men read chronicles, but old men read newspapers. **G. K. Chesterton** *Heretics*, Ch. 18

16 Adolescence is an intermediary stage linking the paradise of childhood to the inferno of failure. **E. M. Cioran** *Tears and Saints*

17 Age and treachery will always overcome youth and skill.

John Cleese legend on T-shirt presented to veteran director Charles Crichton in making film *A Fish called Wanda*; quoted in obituary of Crichton in the *Guardian*, 25 September 1999

18 A man is as old as he's feeling,
A woman as old as she looks. **Mortimer Collins** *The Unknown Quantity*

19 It is better to waste one's youth than to do nothing with it at all.

Georges Courteline *La Philosophie de George Courteline*

20 It is better to wear out than to rust out.

Bishop Richard Cumberland quoted in G. Horne, *The Duty of Contending for the Faith*, 21

21 Young people are always more inclined to admire what is gigantic than what is reasonable. **Eugène Delacroix** *Journal*

22 A man is not old and venerable because grey hairs are on his head. If a man is old only in years then he is indeed old in vain.

The Dhammapada 260

23 The years a woman subtracts from her age are not lost: they are added to the age of other women. **Comtesse Diane** *Les Glanes de la vie*, p. 6

24 Youth is a blunder; Manhood a struggle; Old Age a regret.

Benjamin Disraeli *Coningsby*, Bk 3, Ch. 1

25 If youth knew, if age could. **Henri Estienne** *Les Prémices*, 191

26 I never dared be radical when young
For fear it would make me conservative when old. **Robert Frost** *Precaution*

27 God doesn't count on his hands, you know.

Lord Hailsham on reaching eighty; in BBC radio programme *Law in Action*, 9 October 1987

28 The task and yearning of youth is to become, whereas the mature man's task is to give himself away. **Hermann Hesse** *Reflections*, 660

29 The forties are the old age of youth and the fifties the youth of old age. **Edward Hoagland** in *Learning to Eat Soup*; in *Antaeus: Journals, Notebooks and Diaries*, ed. D. Halpern, p. 232

30 It would seem that for some of the mind's creations, the winter of the body is the autumn of the soul. **Joseph Joubert** *Thoughts and Maxims*, 88

31 The older people grow, the more they resemble themselves. **Hans Keller** *Maxims and Reflections*, 50

32 Nothing like turning fifty to make you feel a hundred years old. **Barbara Kingsolver** *The Poisonwood Bible*, Bk 6, p. 511

33 In ageing we become stupider and wiser. **Duc de La Rochefoucauld** *Maxims*: epigraph to N. C. Chaudhuri, *The Autobiography of an Unknown Indian*

34 Old age is woman's hell. **Duc de La Rochefoucauld** *Posthumous Maxims*, 562

35 Remember that as a teenager you are at the last stage in your life when you will be happy to hear that the phone is for you. **Fran Lebowitz** *Social Studies*: 'Tips for Teens'

36 From the earliest times the old have rubbed it into the young that they are wiser than they, and before the young had discovered what nonsense this was they were old too, and it profited them to carry on the imposture. **W. Somerset Maugham** *Cakes and Ale*, Ch. 9

37 He whom the gods love dies young. **Menander** *Fragments* from *The Double Dealer*

See also Mumford; Plautus; Wilde

38 It stamps more wrinkles on our minds than on our faces; seldom, or very rarely, does one find souls that do not acquire, as they age, a sour and musty smell. **Michel de Montaigne** *Essays*, Bk 3, Ch. 2

39 Only the young die good. **Ethel Watts Mumford, Oliver Herford, Addison Mizner** *The Entirely New Cynic's Calendar of Revised Wisdom for 1905*: 'July'

See also Menander; Plautus; Wilde

40 Senescence begins
and middle age ends,
the day your descendants
outnumber your friends. **Ogden Nash** *Crossing the Border*

41 No one renounces what he knows; we renounce only what we do not know. That is why the young are less egotistical than adults or old men. **Cesare Pavese** *This Business of Living: A Diary 1935–1950*, 14 October 1940

42 Forty can be forty years old or forty years long.

Charles Péguy *Victor-Marie, Comte Hugo*, p. 268

43 He whom the gods favour dies young **Plautus** *Bacchides*, Sc. 4, 816

See also Menander; Mumford; Wilde

44 When men grow virtuous in their old age, they only make a sacrifice to God of the devil's leavings. **Alexander Pope** *Thoughts on Various Subjects*

45 There is a strong disposition in youth, from which some individuals never escape, to suppose that everyone else is having a more enjoyable time than we are ourselves. **Anthony Powell** *A Buyer's Market*, Ch. 4

46 Growing old is like being increasingly penalized for a crime you haven't committed. **Anthony Powell** *Temporary Kings*, Ch. 1

47 Youth is the period of assumed personalities and disguises. It is the time of the sincerely insincere. **V. S. Pritchett** *Midnight Oil*, Ch. 8

48 In later life we look at things in a more practical way, in full conformity with the rest of society, but adolescence is the only period in which we learn anything.

Marcel Proust *Remembrance of Things Past: Within a Budding Grove*: 'Place-names'

49 The younger the person, the quicker they age. It's the old who age the slowest. **Jean Rostand** *Pensées d'un biologiste*, p. 67

50 But a bachelor who hath passed forty is a remnant; and there is no good material in him. His sentiments are moth-eaten and his tender speeches shop-worn. **Helen Rowland** *The Sayings of Mrs Solomon*: 'Book of Husbands', Ch. 3

51 Unfortunately there is too short an interval between the age when one is too young and that when one is too old.

Charles-Augustin Sainte-Beuve in J. R. Solly, *Selected Thoughts from the French*: 'Youth and Age'

52 The young have aspirations that never come to pass, the old have reminiscences of what never happened. **Saki** *Reginald at the Carlton*

53 The young man who has not wept is a savage, and the old man who will not laugh is a fool. **George Santayana** *Dialogues in Limbo*, Ch. 3

54 Don't laugh at a youth for his affectations; he is only trying on one face after another to find his own.

Logan Pearsall Smith *Afterthoughts*, 2: 'Age and Death'

55 Old and young, we are all on our last cruise.

Robert Louis Stevenson *Virginibus Puerisque*: 'Crabbed Age'

56 Every man desires to live long; no man would be old.

Jonathan Swift *Thoughts on Various Subjects*, p. 280

57 The greatest problem about old age is the fear that it may go on too long. **A. J. P. Taylor** in the *Listener*, 29 October 1981

58 We seem but to linger in manhood to tell the dreams of our childhood, and they vanish out of memory ere we learn the language.
H. D. Thoreau *Journal*, 19 February 1841

59 Old age is the most unexpected of all the things that happen to a man. **Leon Trotsky** *Diary in Exile*, 15 February 1935

60 Selfish old age is nothing more than childhood in which there is awareness of death. **Miguel de Unamuno** *Abel Sanchez*, Ch. 38

61 Youth is a way of making mistakes that changes all too rapidly into a way of not even being able to make mistakes.
Paul Valéry *Bad Thoughts and Not So Bad*, I

62 Every twenty years the middle-aged celebrate the decade of their youth. **Gore Vidal** in the *Observer Review*, 27 August 1989

63 Maturity is the assimilation of the features of every ancestor.
Derek Walcott 'The Muse of History', in *Is Massa Day Done?*, ed. Orde Coombs

64 Those whom the gods love grow young.
Oscar Wilde *For the Instruction of the Over-educated*

See also Menander; Mumford; Plautus

65 The old believe everything: the middle-aged suspect everything: the young know everything.
Oscar Wilde *Phrases and Philosophies for the Use of the Young*

66 Youth! There is nothing like it. It's absurd to talk of the ignorance of youth. The only people to whose opinions I listen with any respect are people much younger than myself. They seem in front of me.
Oscar Wilde *The Picture of Dorian Gray*, Ch. 19

See also ***Children and Adults; Time***

Index

A

C

D

E

I

J

K

T

U

V

W

Y

Z

News, reviews and previews of forthcoming books

read about your favourite authors

•

investigate over 12,000 titles

•

browse our online magazine

•

enter one of our literary quizzes

•

win some fantastic prizes in our competitions

•

e-mail us with your comments and book reviews

•

instantly order any Penguin book

'To be recommended without reservation ... a rich and rewarding online experience' *Internet Magazine*

www.penguin.com

PENGUIN CLASSICS

www.penguinclassics.com

- *Details about every Penguin Classic*
- *Advanced information about forthcoming titles*
- *Hundreds of author biographies*
- *FREE resources including critical essays on the books and their historical background, reader's and teacher's guides.*
- *Links to other web resources for the Classics*
- *Discussion area*
- *Online review copy ordering for academics*
- *Competitions with prizes, and challenging Classics trivia quizzes*

PENGUIN CLASSICS ONLINE

THE PENGUIN DICTIONARY OF MODERN HUMOROUS QUOTATIONS

If you've ever thought, 'I wish I'd said that', *The Penguin Dictionary of Modern Humorous Quotations* will ensure you're never again short of a joke, quip or put-down. Over 5,500 quotations from the funniest people of the past hundred years are here: from George Bernard Shaw ('I often quote myself. It adds spice to my conversation') to Woody Allen ('It's not that I'm afraid to die, I just don't want to be there when it happens') and, of course, to Homer Simpson ('To alcohol! The cause of – and solution to – all of life's problems!').

As well as such comedic luminaries, this book also contains witticisms from T-shirt slogans, internet sites and the ever-inventive Anon., and it ranges across themes from adultery and advertising to youth and even Yugoslavia, wealth, wine and work.

THE NEW PENGUIN DICTIONARY OF MODERN QUOTATIONS

Containing the witty one-liners of comedians, the pronouncements of politicians, references from films, literature, song lyrics, newspaper headlines and even the occasional piece of graffiti, *The New Penguin Dictionary of Modern Quotations* brings together 8,000 of the pithiest and most provocative quotations from 1914 to the present.

To complement the quotations, there are fascinating biographical sketches of everyone quoted, citing their views on themselves ('I play John Wayne in every picture regardless of the character') and the often caustic remarks of others ('The affair between Margot Asquith and Margot Asquith will live as one of the prettiest love stories in all literature'). In addition, there are illuminating insights into individual remarks and sayings, clarifying who said what (did James Cagney ever really say 'You dirty rat'?), why they said it and how they often wished they hadn't.

Both an essential companion to the modern age and an entertaining and useful reference tool, it offers constant food for thought.

ROGET'S THESAURUS OF ENGLISH WORDS AND PHRASES

Roget's Thesaurus is one of the greatest English language reference works. It is the authoritative desk companion for anyone wanting to write a letter, prepare a speech, solve a crossword, complete an imaginatively phrased CV or write any manner of prose or poetry. This new edition has been fully revised throughout to reflect contemporary vocabulary, but still retains Dr Roget's unique structure which enables the user to find words connected not only by meaning, but also by spirit and idea.

THE PENGUIN DICTIONARY OF PROVERBS

Whether you are looking for a few wise words of advice, like 'Least said soonest mended', some trenchant observation, such as 'You can lead a horse to water but you can't make it drink', or a common belief, such as 'A green Yule makes a fat churchyard', you will find them all in the newly revised and extended *Penguin Dictionary of Proverbs*. Entertaining and easy to use, it offers wit and wisdom to all.

READ MORE IN PENGUIN

In every corner of the world, on every subject under the sun, Penguin represents quality and variety – the very best in publishing today.

For complete information about books available from Penguin – including Puffins, Penguin Classics and Arkana – and how to order them, write to us at the appropriate address below. Please note that for copyright reasons the selection of books varies from country to country.

In the United Kingdom: Please write to *Dept. EP, Penguin Books Ltd, Bath Road, Harmondsworth, West Drayton, Middlesex UB7 0DA*

In the United States: Please write to *Consumer Services, Penguin Putnam Inc., 405 Murray Hill Parkway, East Rutherford, New Jersey 07073-2136.* VISA and MasterCard holders call 1-800-631-8571 to order Penguin titles

In Canada: Please write to *Penguin Books Canada Ltd, 10 Alcorn Avenue, Suite 300, Toronto, Ontario M4V 3B2*

In Australia: Please write to *Penguin Books Australia Ltd, 487 Maroondah Highway, Ringwood, Victoria 3134*

In New Zealand: Please write to *Penguin Books (NZ) Ltd, Private Bag 102902, North Shore Mail Centre, Auckland 10*

In India: Please write to *Penguin Books India Pvt Ltd, 11 Community Centre, Panchsheel Park, New Delhi 110017*

In the Netherlands: Please write to *Penguin Books Netherlands bv, Postbus 3507, NL-1001 AH Amsterdam*

In Germany: Please write to *Penguin Books Deutschland GmbH, Metzlerstrasse 26, 60594 Frankfurt am Main*

In Spain: Please write to *Penguin Books S. A., Bravo Murillo 19, 1°B, 28015 Madrid*

In Italy: Please write to *Penguin Italia s.r.l., Via Vittorio Emanuele 45/a, 20094 Corsico, Milano*

In France: Please write to *Penguin France, 12, Rue Prosper Ferradou, 31700 Blagnac*

In Japan: Please write to *Penguin Books Japan Ltd, Iidabashi KM-Bldg, 2-23-9 Koraku, Bunkyo-Ku, Tokyo 112-0004*

In South Africa: Please write to *Penguin Books South Africa (Pty) Ltd, P.O. Box 751093, Gardenview, 2047 Johannesburg*